犬夜叉

INUYASHA

ANI-MANGA

Vol. 4

D14 73709

CREATED BY
RUMIKO TAKAHASHI

Inuyasha Ani-Manga™
Vol. #4

Created by
Rumiko Takahashi

Translation based on the VIZ anime TV series
Translation Assistance/Katy Bridges
Lettering/John Clark
Cover Design & Graphics/Hidemi Sahara
Editor/Frances E. Wall

Managing Editor/Annette Roman
Editorial Director/Alvin Lu
Director of Production/Noboru Watanabe
Sr. Director of Licensing & Acquisitions/Rika Inouye
Vice President of Sales & Marketing/Liza Coppola
Executive Vice President/Hyoe Narita
Publisher/Seiji Horibuchi

Published by VIZ, LLC
P.O. Box 77010
San Francisco, CA 94107

10 9 8 7 6 5 4 3 2
First printing, July 2004
Second printing, October 2004

www.viz.com

store.viz.com

Story thus far

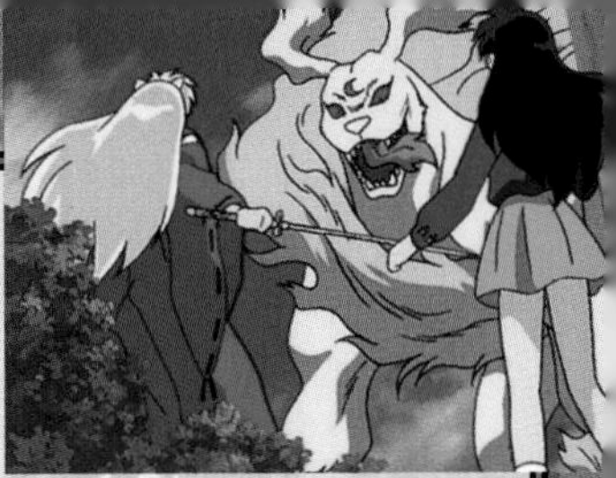

Kagome, a typical high school girl, has been transported into a mythical version of Japan's medieval past, a place filled with incredible magic and terrifying demons. Who would have guessed that the stories and legends Kagome's superstitious grandfather told her could really be true!?

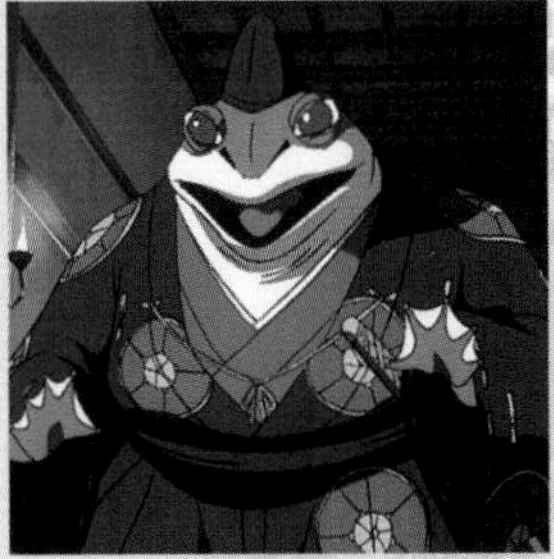

It turns out that Kagome is the reincarnation of Lady Kikyo, a great warrior and the defender of the Shikon Jewel, or the Jewel of Four Souls. In fact, the sacred jewel mysteriously emerges from Kagome's body during a battle with a horrible centipede-like monster. In her desperation to defeat the monster, Kagome frees Inuyasha, a dog-like half-demon who lusts for the power imparted by the jewel, and unwittingly releases him from the binding spell that was placed 50 years earlier by Lady Kikyo. To prevent Inuyasha from stealing the jewel, Kikyo's sister, Lady Kaede, puts a magical necklace around Inuyasha's neck that allows Kagome to make him "sit" on command.

In another skirmish for possession of the jewel, it accidentally shatters and is strewn across the land. Only Kagome has the power to find the jewel shards, and only Inuyasha has the strength to defeat the demons who now hold them, so the two unlikely partners are bound together in the quest to reclaim all the pieces of the Shikon Jewel.

Inuyasha has a new tool in the fight to recover the shards of the jewel: his father's sacred sword, the Tetsusaiga. The Tetsusaiga's power is only unleashed when it is being used to protect and defend humans... which is pretty frequently, considering the jams that Kagome gets herself into! Inuyasha also finds himself fighting alongside (and protecting) the orphaned fox-demon Shippo as they battle the despicable Thunder Brothers!

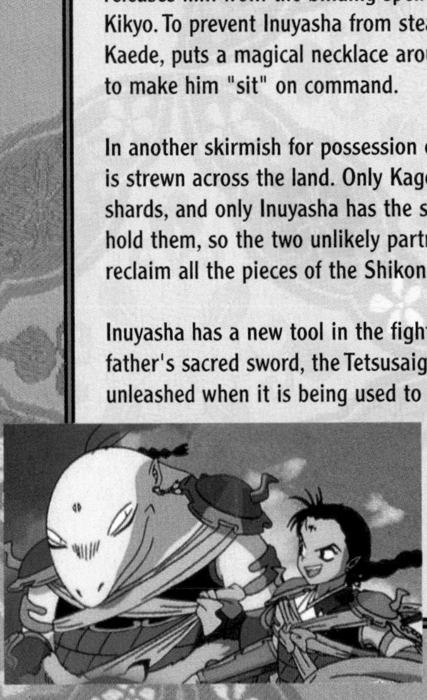

INUYASHA™
ANI-MANGA™ Vol. 4

Contents

10

Phantom Showdown–The Thunder Brothers vs. Tetsusaiga

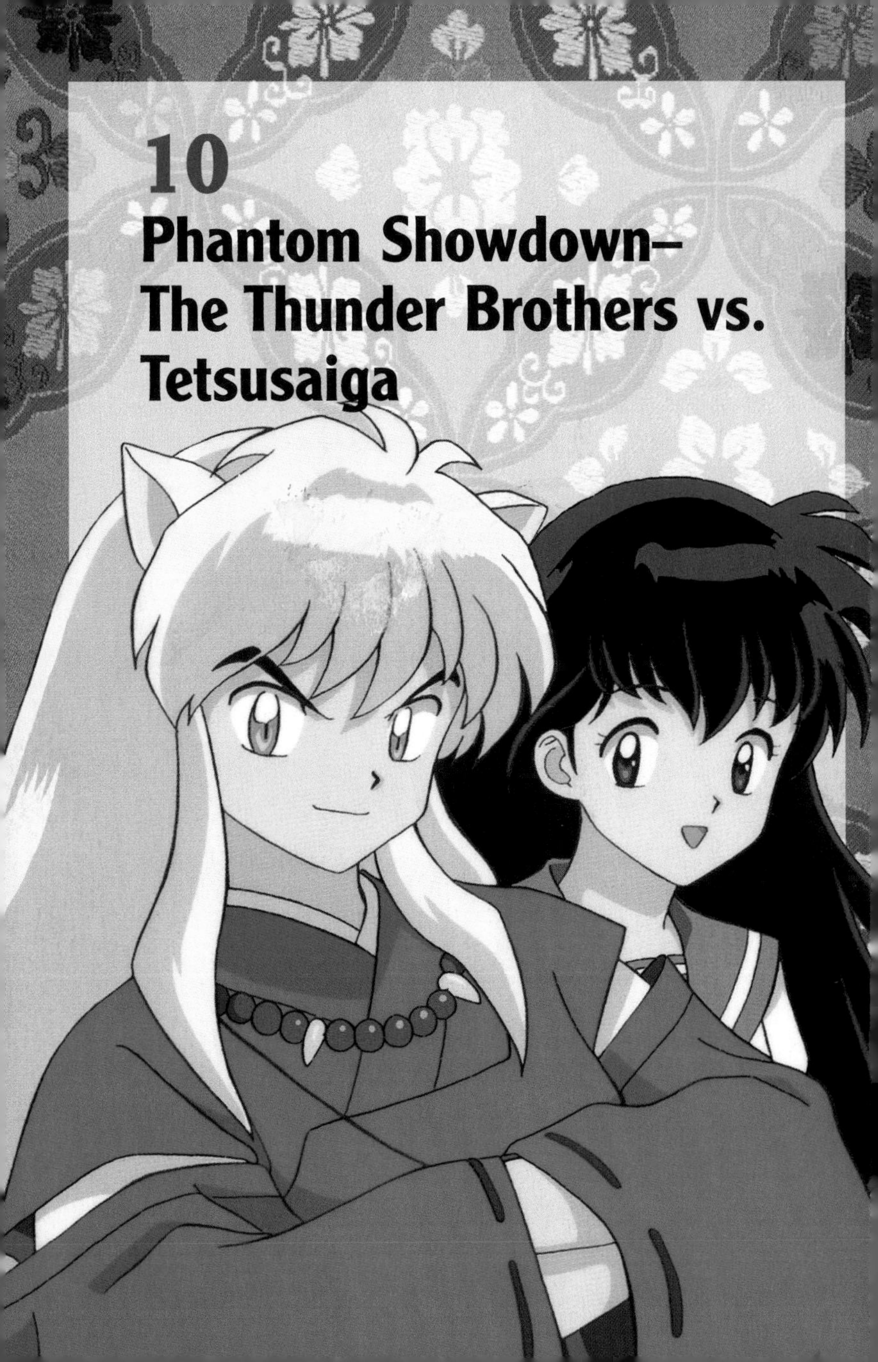

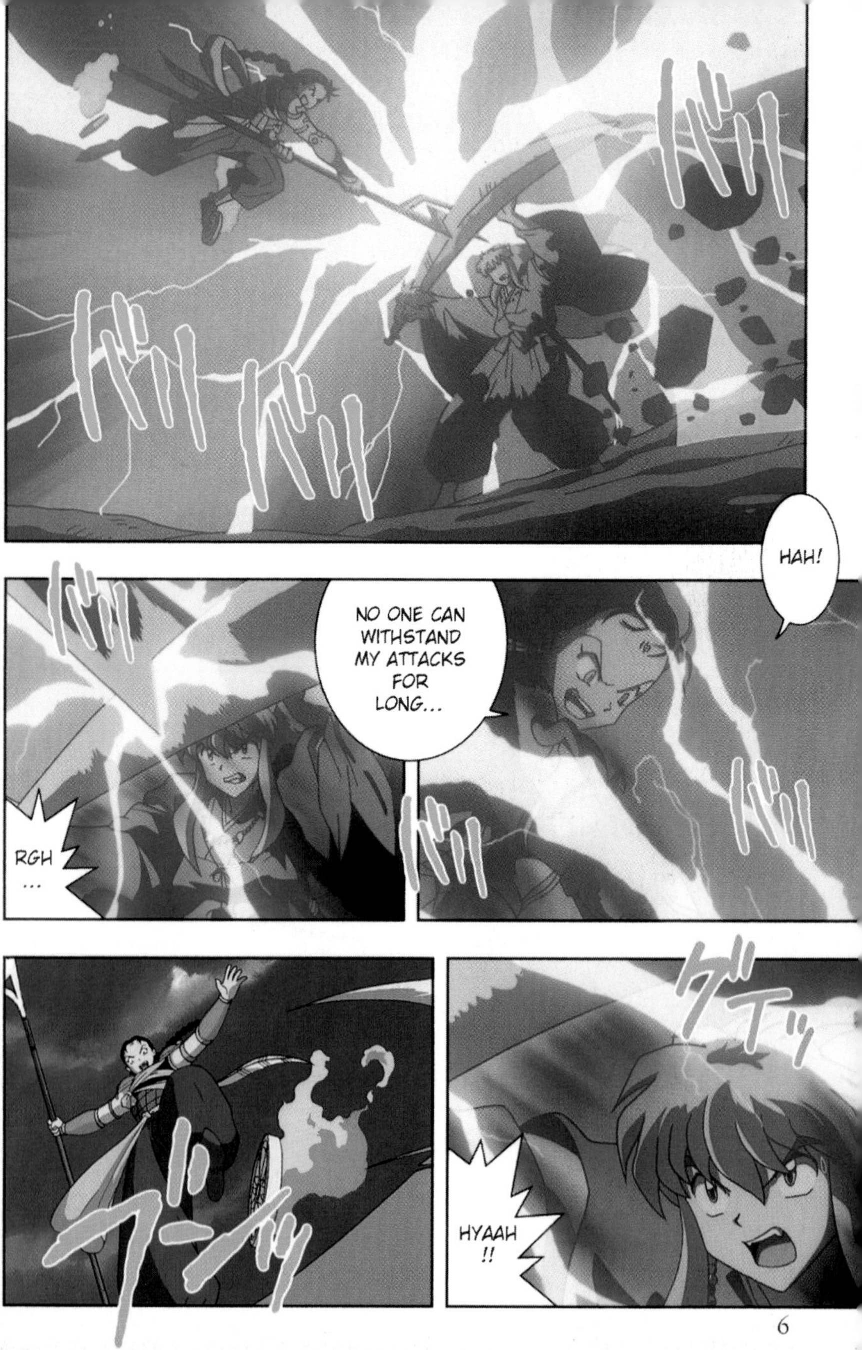
HAH!
NO ONE CAN WITHSTAND MY ATTACKS FOR LONG...
RGH ...
HYAAH !!

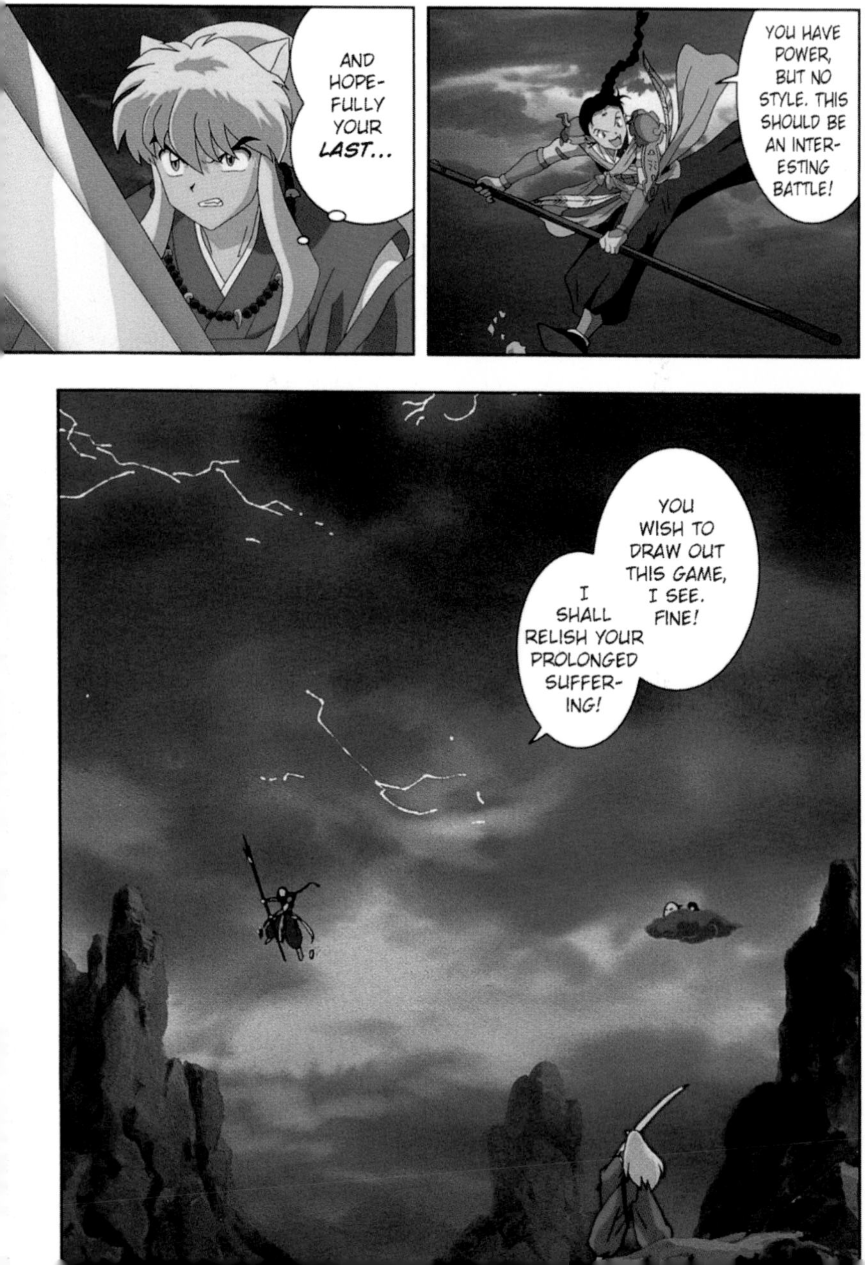
YOU HAVE POWER, BUT NO STYLE. THIS SHOULD BE AN INTERESTING BATTLE!
AND HOPEFULLY YOUR *LAST...*
YOU WISH TO DRAW OUT THIS GAME, I SEE. FINE!
I SHALL RELISH YOUR PROLONGED SUFFERING!

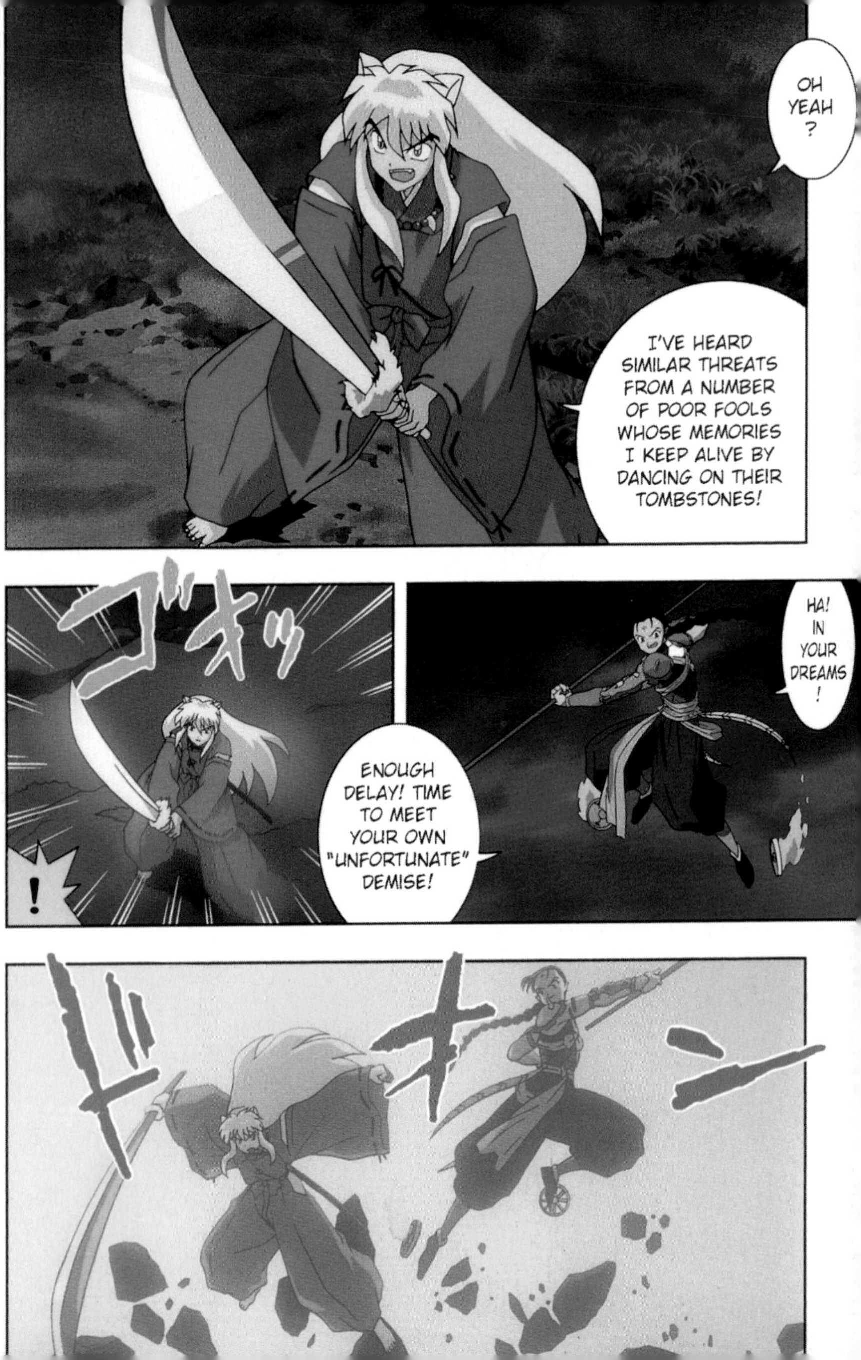
OH YEAH?
I'VE HEARD SIMILAR THREATS FROM A NUMBER OF POOR FOOLS WHOSE MEMORIES I KEEP ALIVE BY DANCING ON THEIR TOMBSTONES!
HA! IN YOUR DREAMS!
ENOUGH DELAY! TIME TO MEET YOUR OWN "UNFORTUNATE" DEMISE!
!

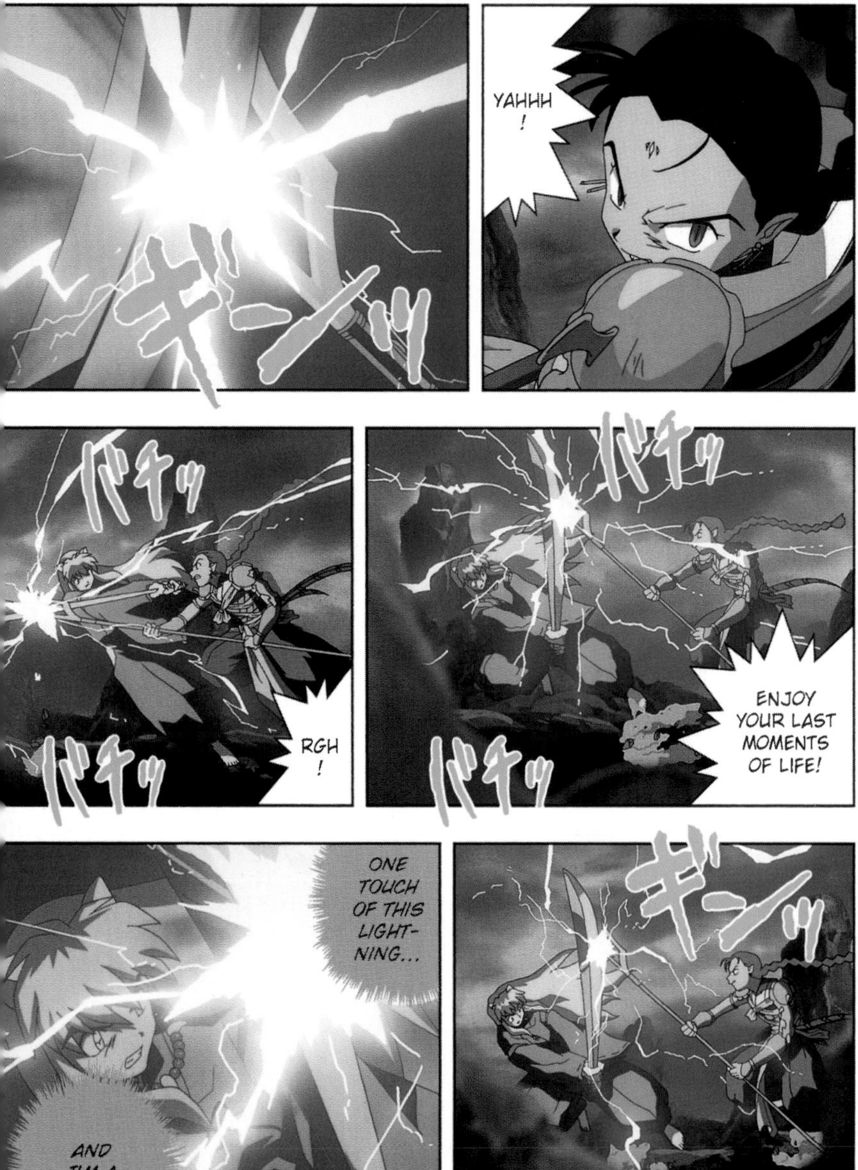
YAHHH!
ギーンッ
バチッ
ENJOY YOUR LAST MOMENTS OF LIFE!
バチッ
バチッ
RGH!
バチッ
ギンッ
ONE TOUCH OF THIS LIGHT-NING...
AND I'M A GONER!

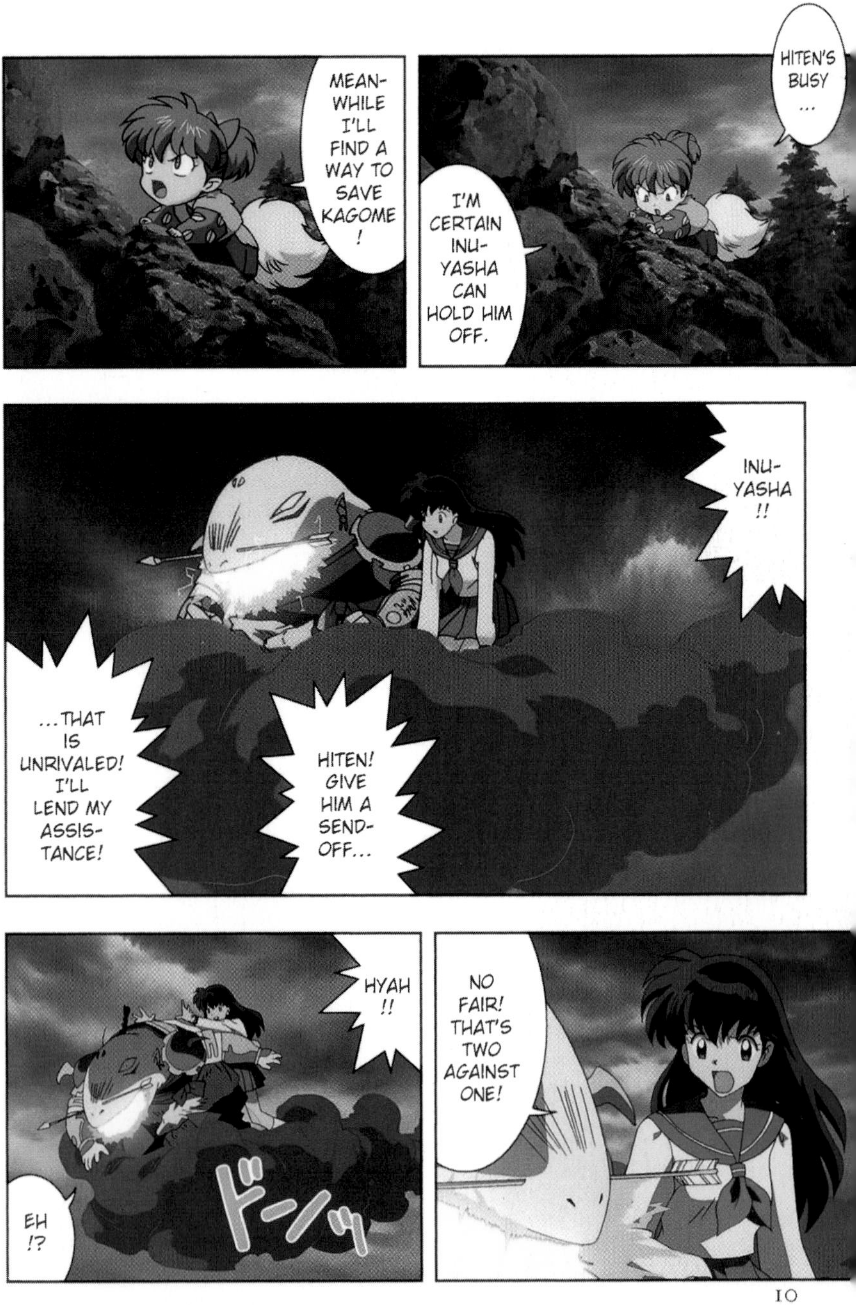
HITEN'S BUSY ...
I'M CERTAIN INU-YASHA CAN HOLD HIM OFF.
MEAN-WHILE I'LL FIND A WAY TO SAVE KAGOME!
INU-YASHA!!
HITEN! GIVE HIM A SEND-OFF...
...THAT IS UNRIVALED! I'LL LEND MY ASSISTANCE!
NO FAIR! THAT'S TWO AGAINST ONE!
HYAH!!
ドーンッ
EH!?

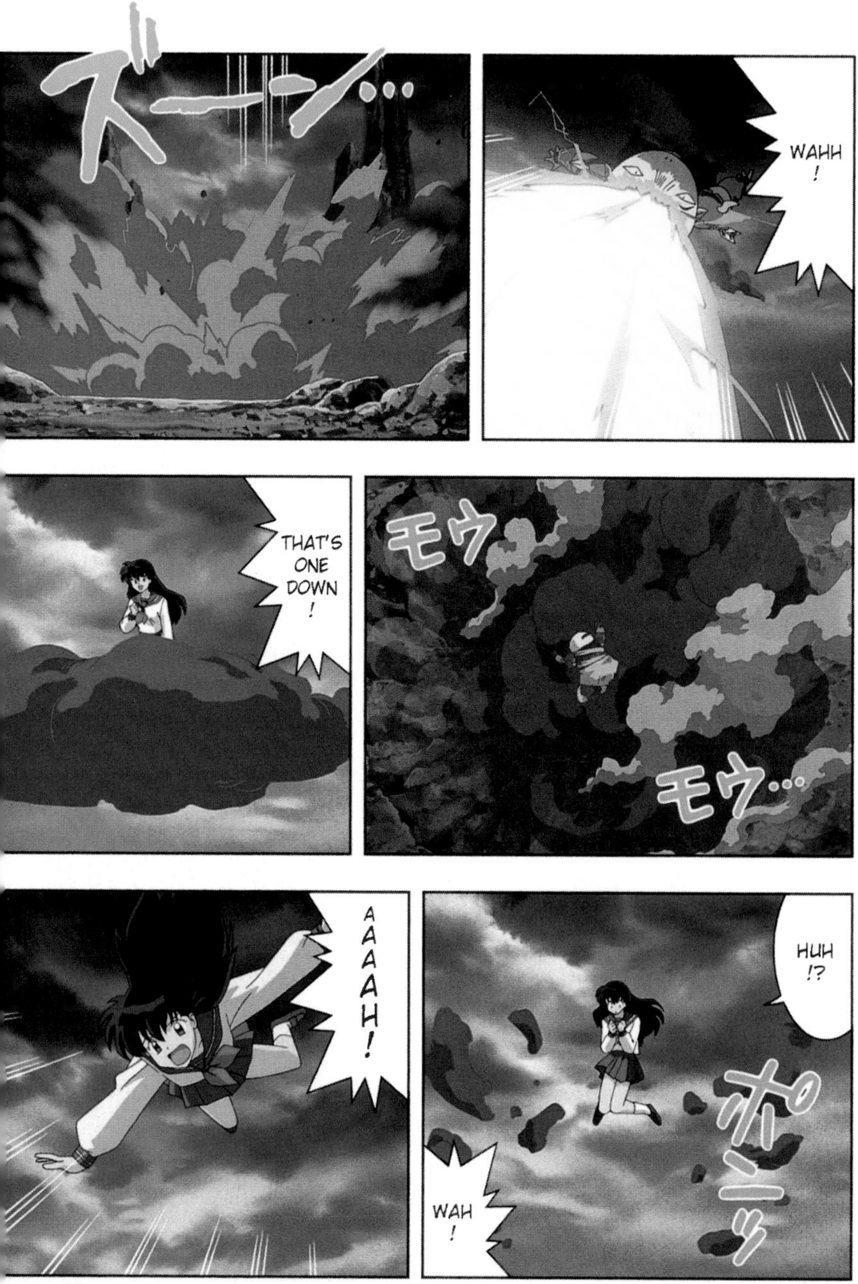
WAHH!
ズーン…
モウ
モウ…
THAT'S ONE DOWN!
HUH!?
ポニッ
WAH!
AAAAAH!

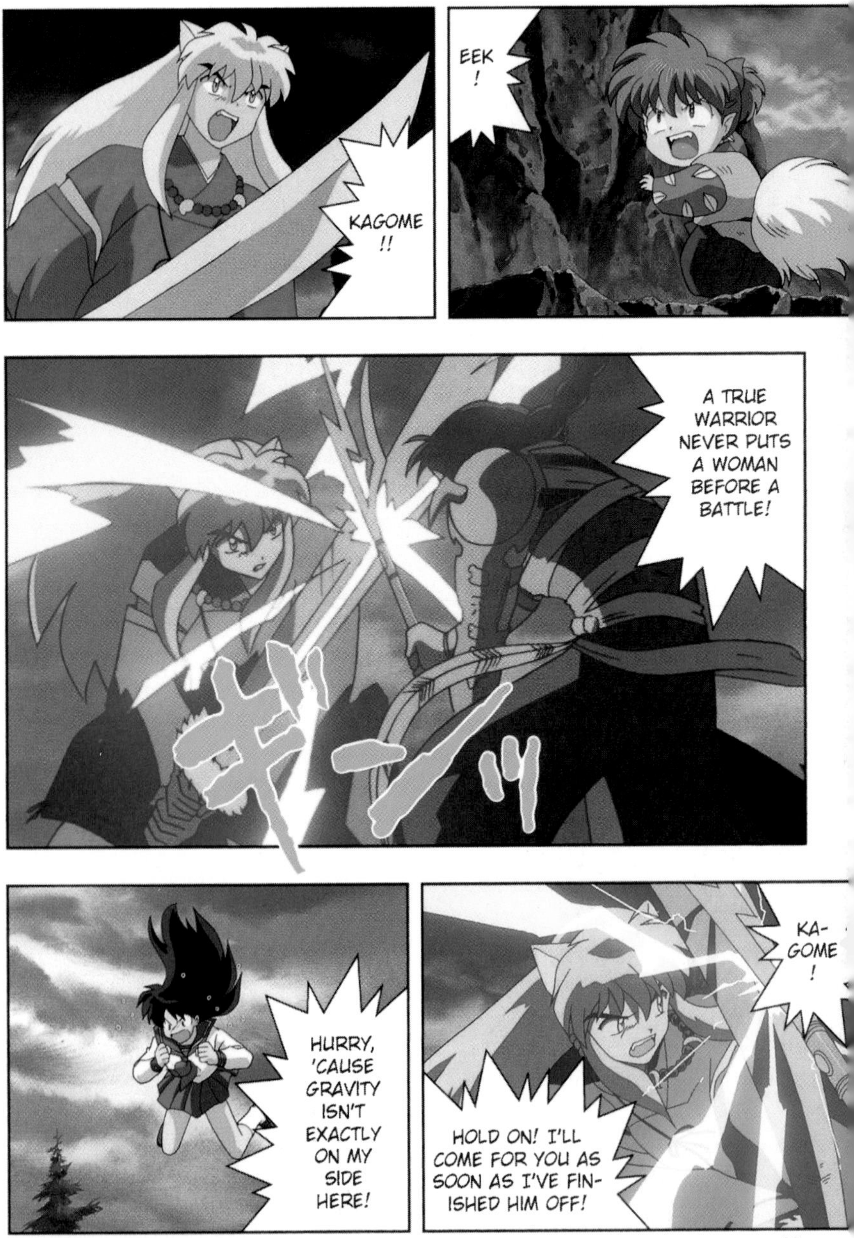
EEK!
KAGOME!!
A TRUE WARRIOR NEVER PUTS A WOMAN BEFORE A BATTLE!
ギーンッ
KA-GOME!
HOLD ON! I'LL COME FOR YOU AS SOON AS I'VE FIN-ISHED HIM OFF!
HURRY, 'CAUSE GRAVITY ISN'T EXACTLY ON MY SIDE HERE!

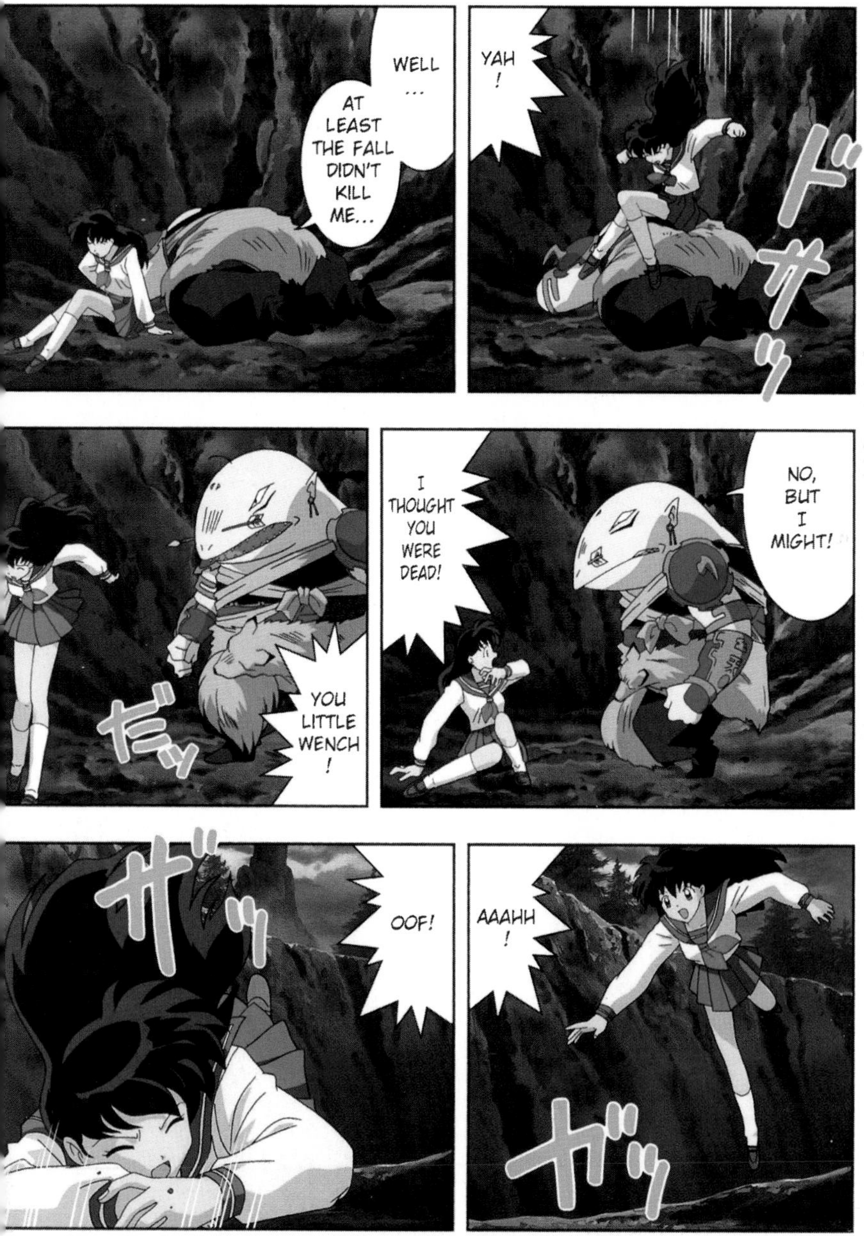
YAH!
ドサッ
WELL...
AT LEAST THE FALL DIDN'T KILL ME...
NO, BUT I MIGHT!
I THOUGHT YOU WERE DEAD!
YOU LITTLE WENCH!
だッ
AAAHH!
ガッ
OOF!
ザッ

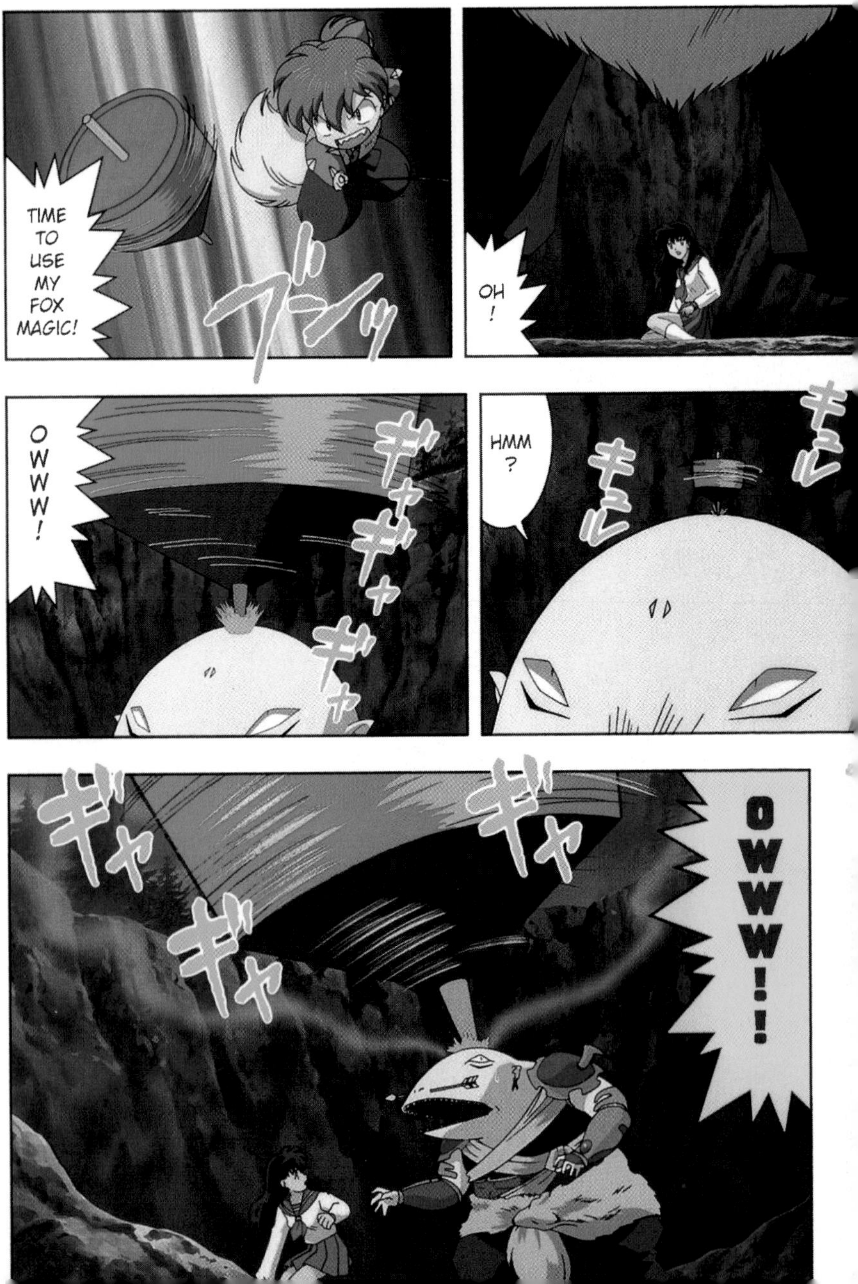
OH!
TIME TO USE MY FOX MAGIC!
ブンッ
HMM?
キュル
キュル
OWWW!
ギャギャギャ
OWWW!!!
ギャ
ギャ
ギャ

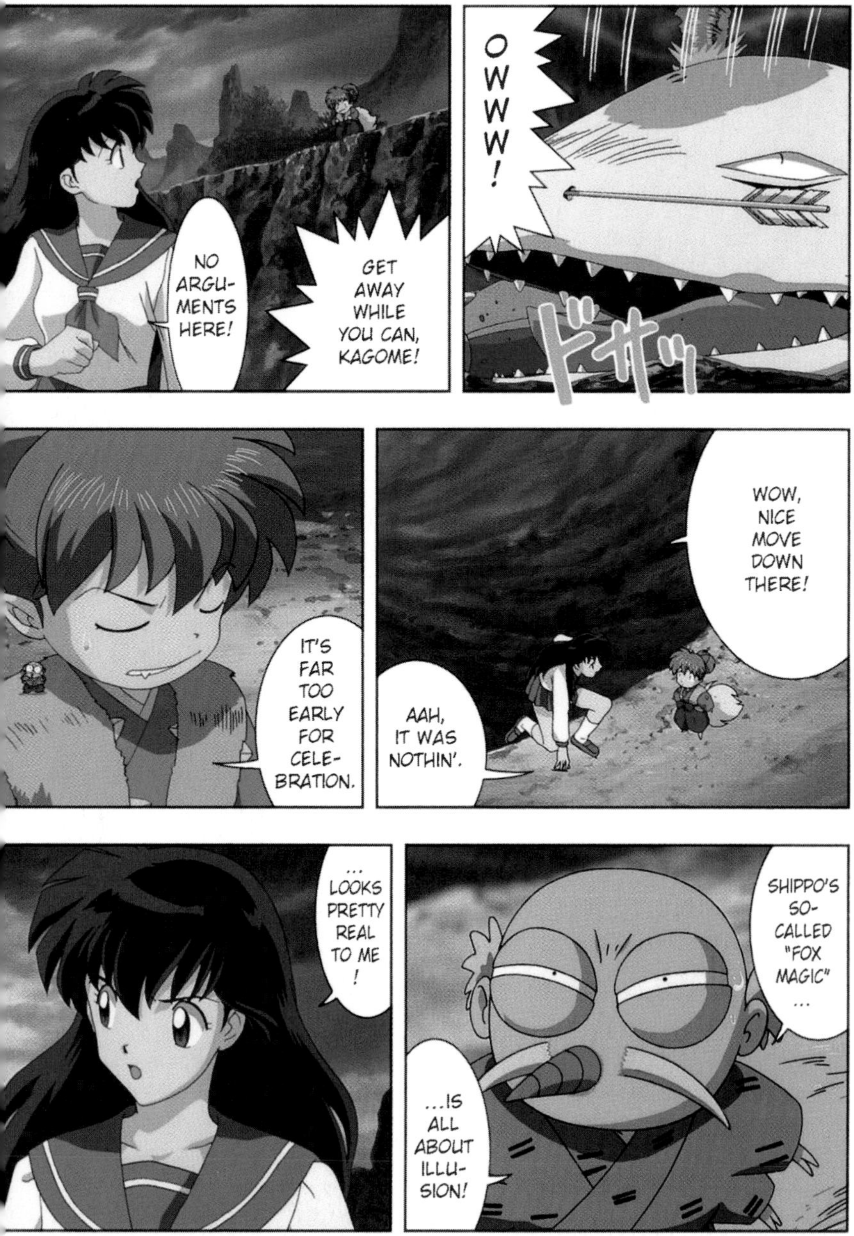
OWWW!
ドサッ
GET AWAY WHILE YOU CAN, KAGOME!
NO ARGU-MENTS HERE!
WOW, NICE MOVE DOWN THERE!
AAH, IT WAS NOTHIN'.
IT'S FAR TOO EARLY FOR CELE-BRATION.
SHIPPO'S SO-CALLED "FOX MAGIC" ...
...IS ALL ABOUT ILLU-SION!
... LOOKS PRETTY REAL TO ME !

OW
OW
OW!

NO
...!

THAT
FOX
TYKE
WILL PAY
FOR HIS
TRICKS!

CURSES
...

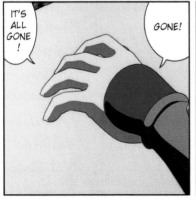

IT'S
ALL
GONE
!

GONE!

MY
BEAUTI-
FUL
HAIR!

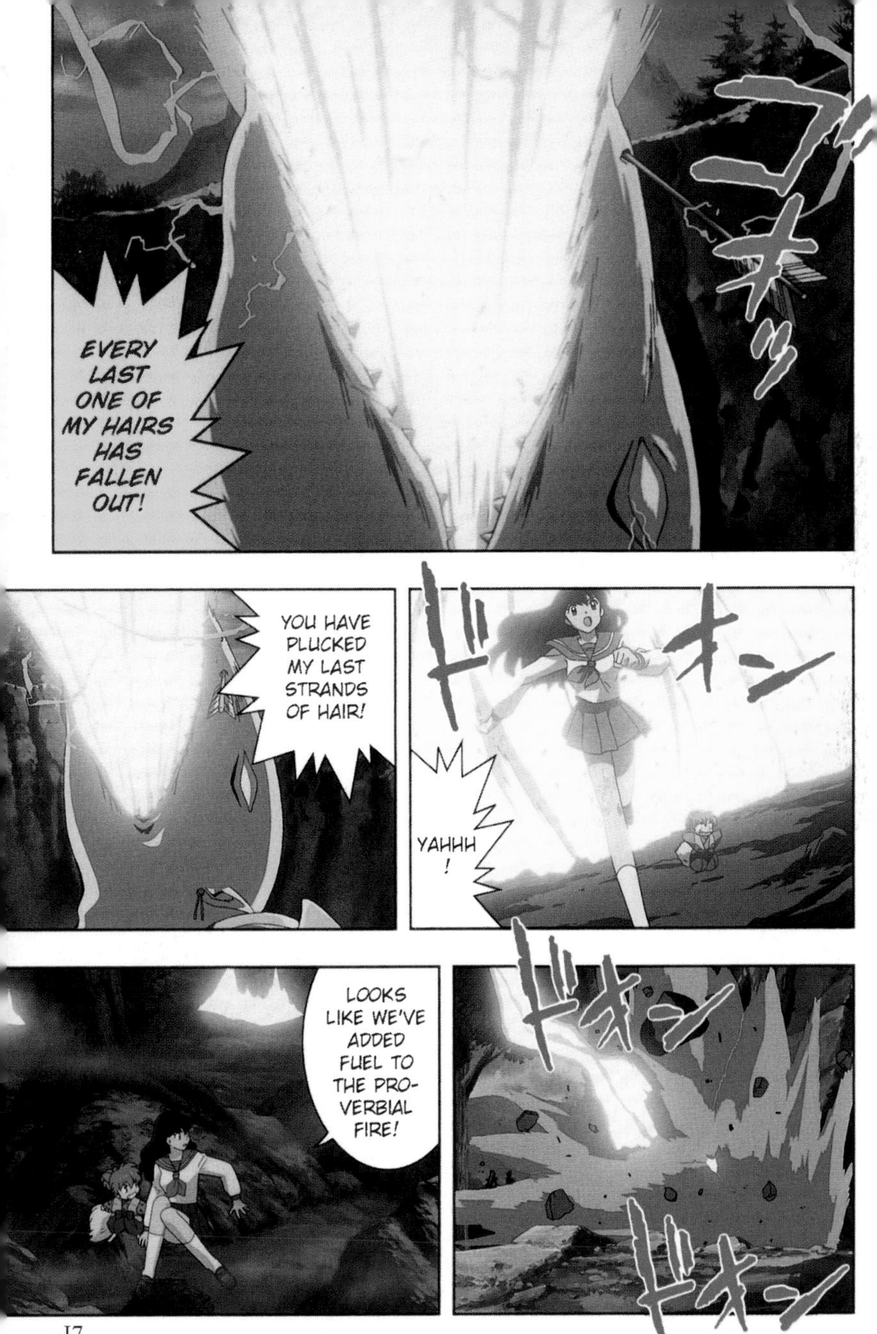
ゴオッ
EVERY LAST ONE OF MY HAIRS HAS FALLEN OUT!
ドオン
YAHHH!
YOU HAVE PLUCKED MY LAST STRANDS OF HAIR!
ドオン
ドオン
LOOKS LIKE WE'VE ADDED FUEL TO THE PRO-VERBIAL FIRE!

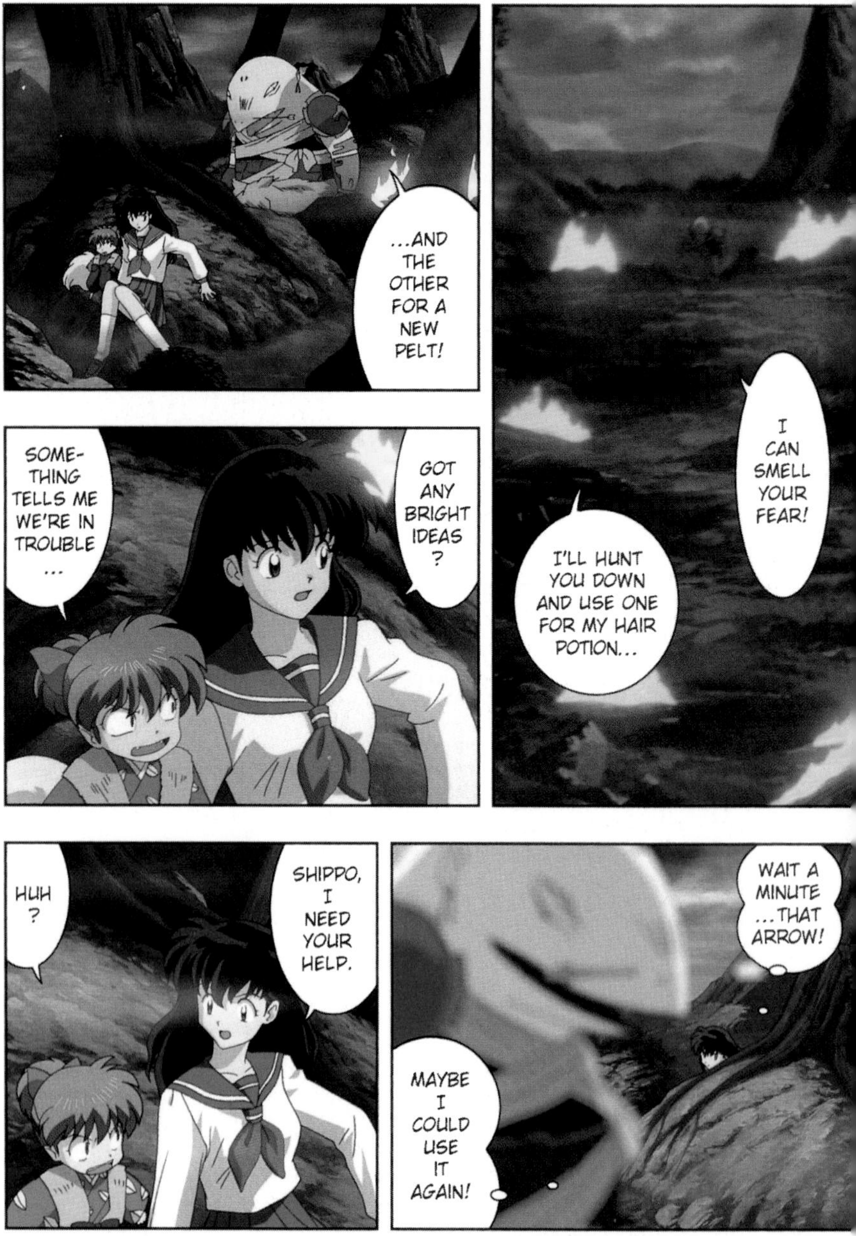
I CAN SMELL YOUR FEAR!
I'LL HUNT YOU DOWN AND USE ONE FOR MY HAIR POTION...
...AND THE OTHER FOR A NEW PELT!
GOT ANY BRIGHT IDEAS?
SOMETHING TELLS ME WE'RE IN TROUBLE...
WAIT A MINUTE ...THAT ARROW!
MAYBE I COULD USE IT AGAIN!
SHIPPO, I NEED YOUR HELP.
HUH?

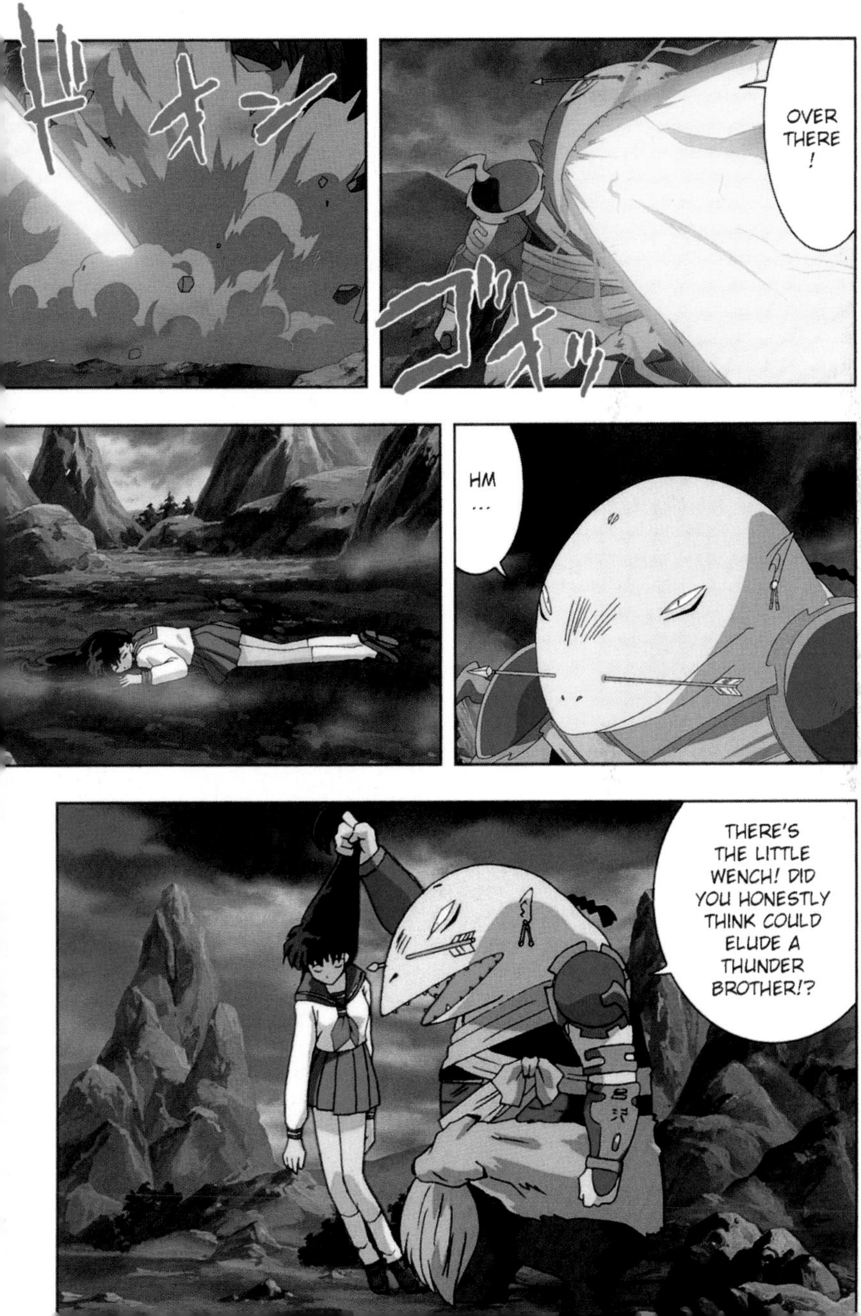
OVER THERE !
ゴキッ
HM ...
THERE'S THE LITTLE WENCH! DID YOU HONESTLY THINK COULD ELUDE A THUNDER BROTHER!?

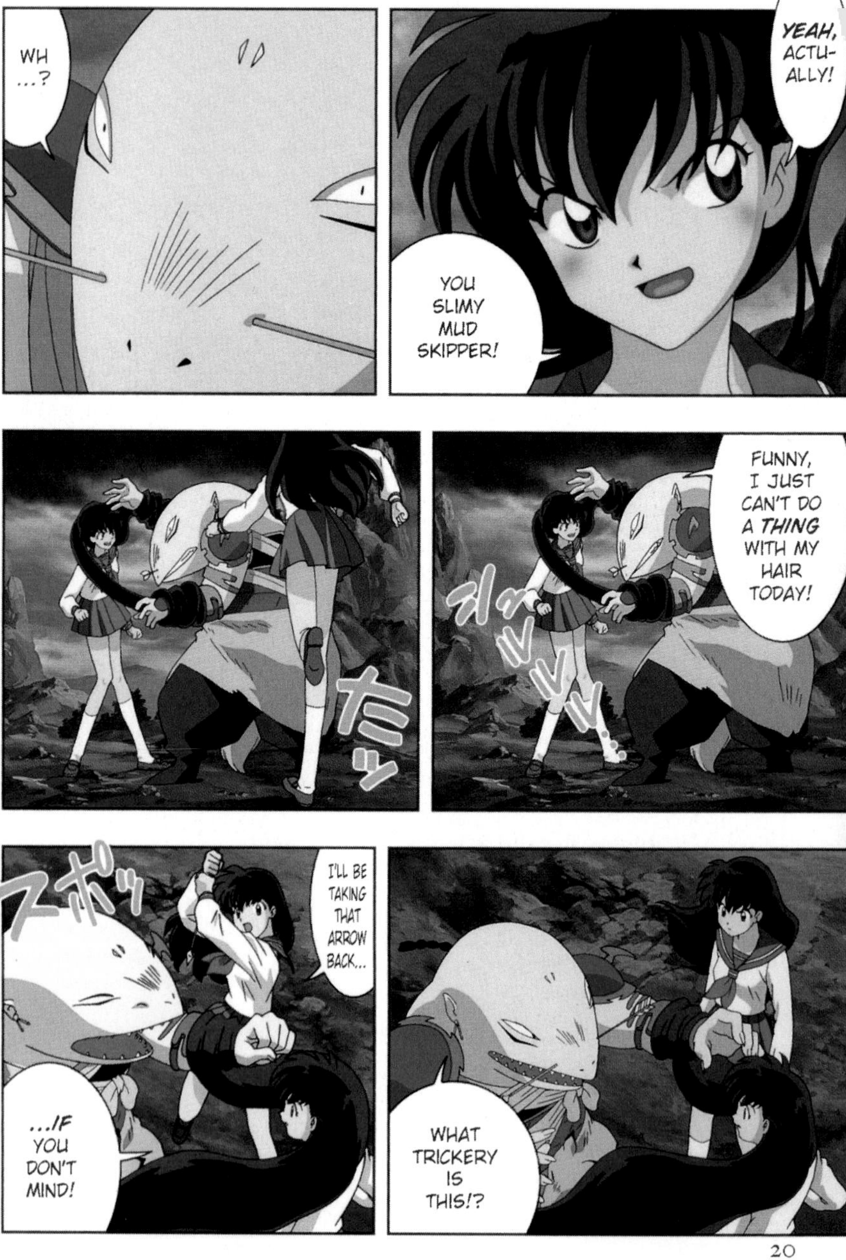
YEAH, ACTUALLY!
YOU SLIMY MUD SKIPPER!
WH ...?
FUNNY, I JUST CAN'T DO A THING WITH MY HAIR TODAY!
タッ
WHAT TRICKERY IS THIS!?
スポッ
I'LL BE TAKING THAT ARROW BACK...
...IF YOU DON'T MIND!

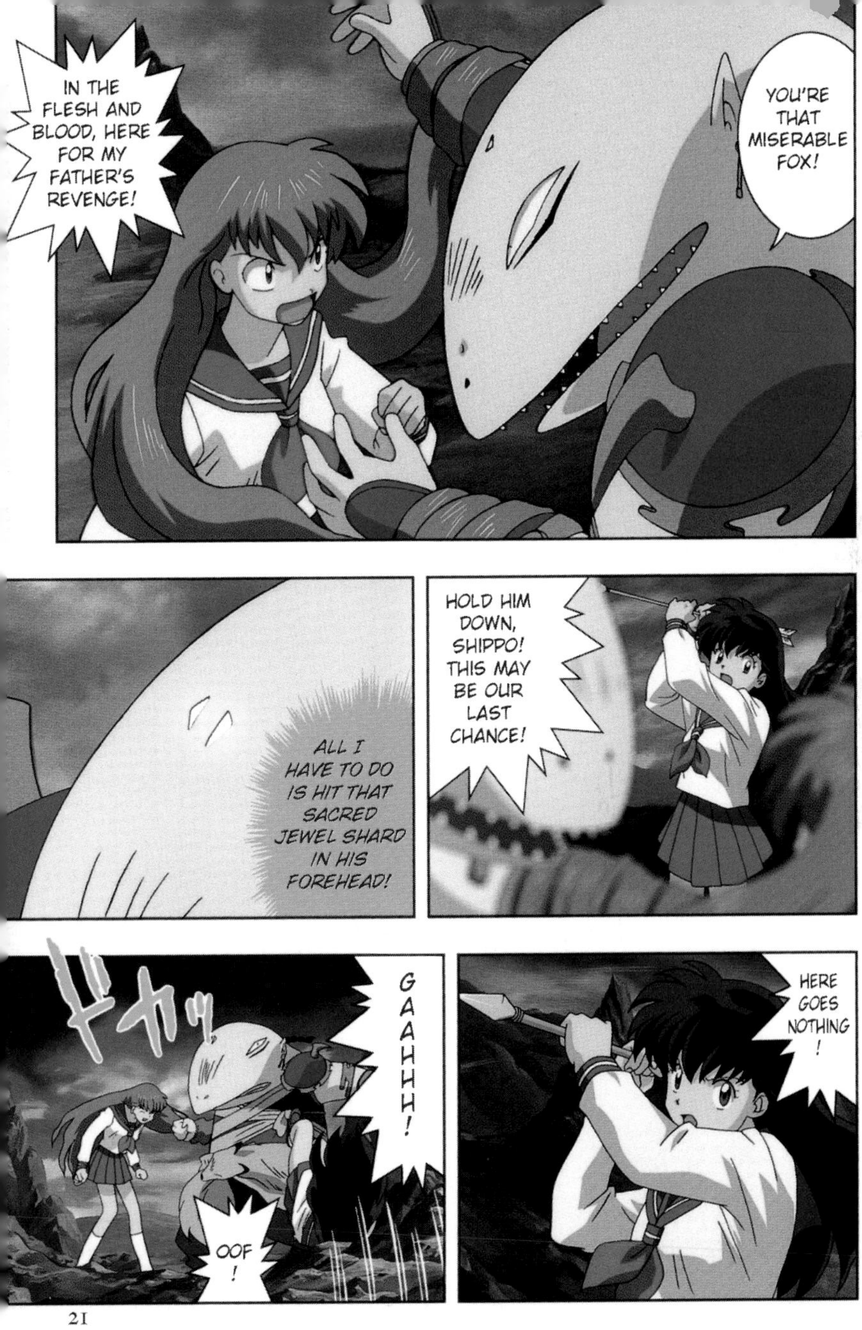
YOU'RE THAT MISERABLE FOX!
IN THE FLESH AND BLOOD, HERE FOR MY FATHER'S REVENGE!
HOLD HIM DOWN, SHIPPO! THIS MAY BE OUR LAST CHANCE!
ALL I HAVE TO DO IS HIT THAT SACRED JEWEL SHARD IN HIS FOREHEAD!
HERE GOES NOTHING!
GAAHHH!
ドカッ
OOF!

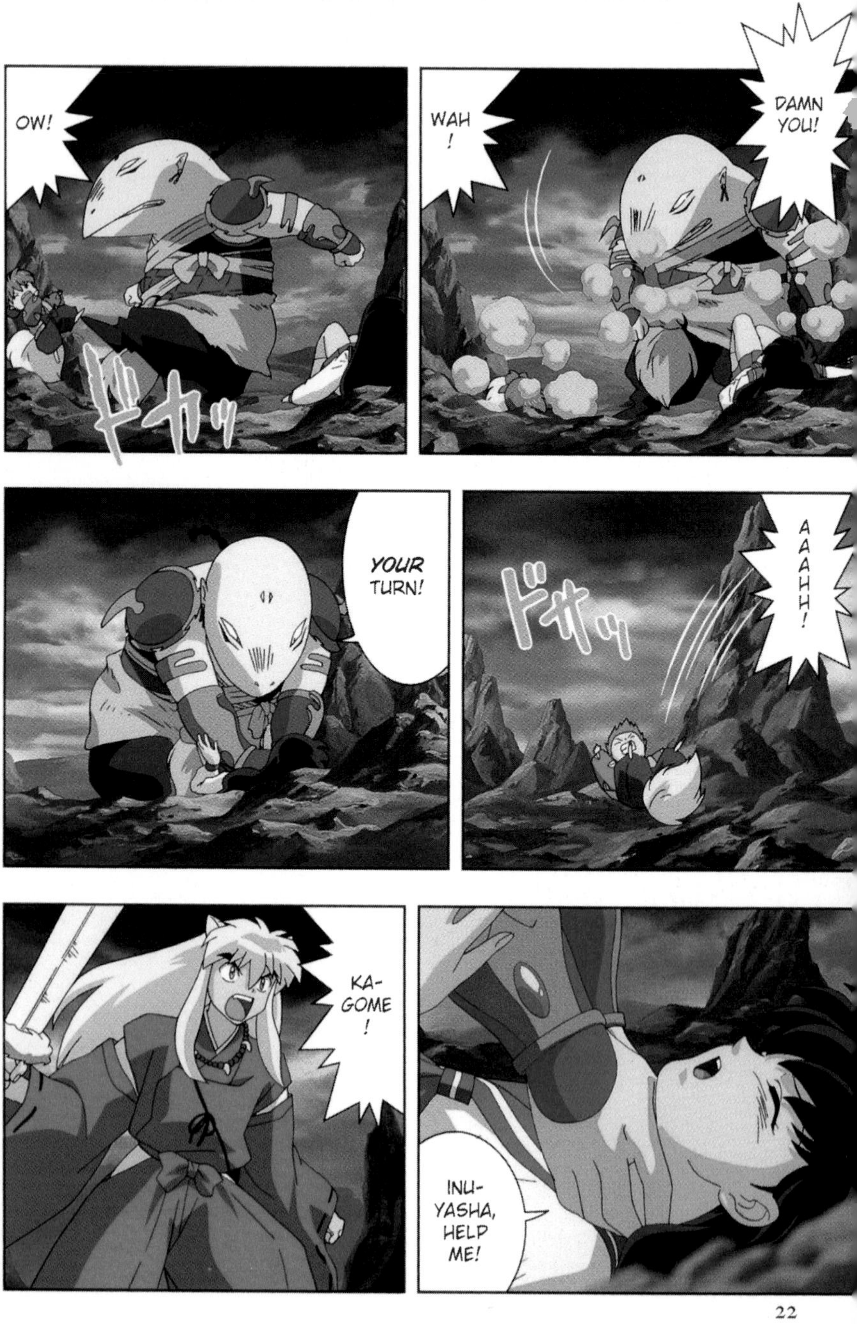
DAMN YOU!
WAH!
OW!
ドカッ
AAAHH!
ドサッ
YOUR TURN!
INU-YASHA, HELP ME!
KA-GOME!

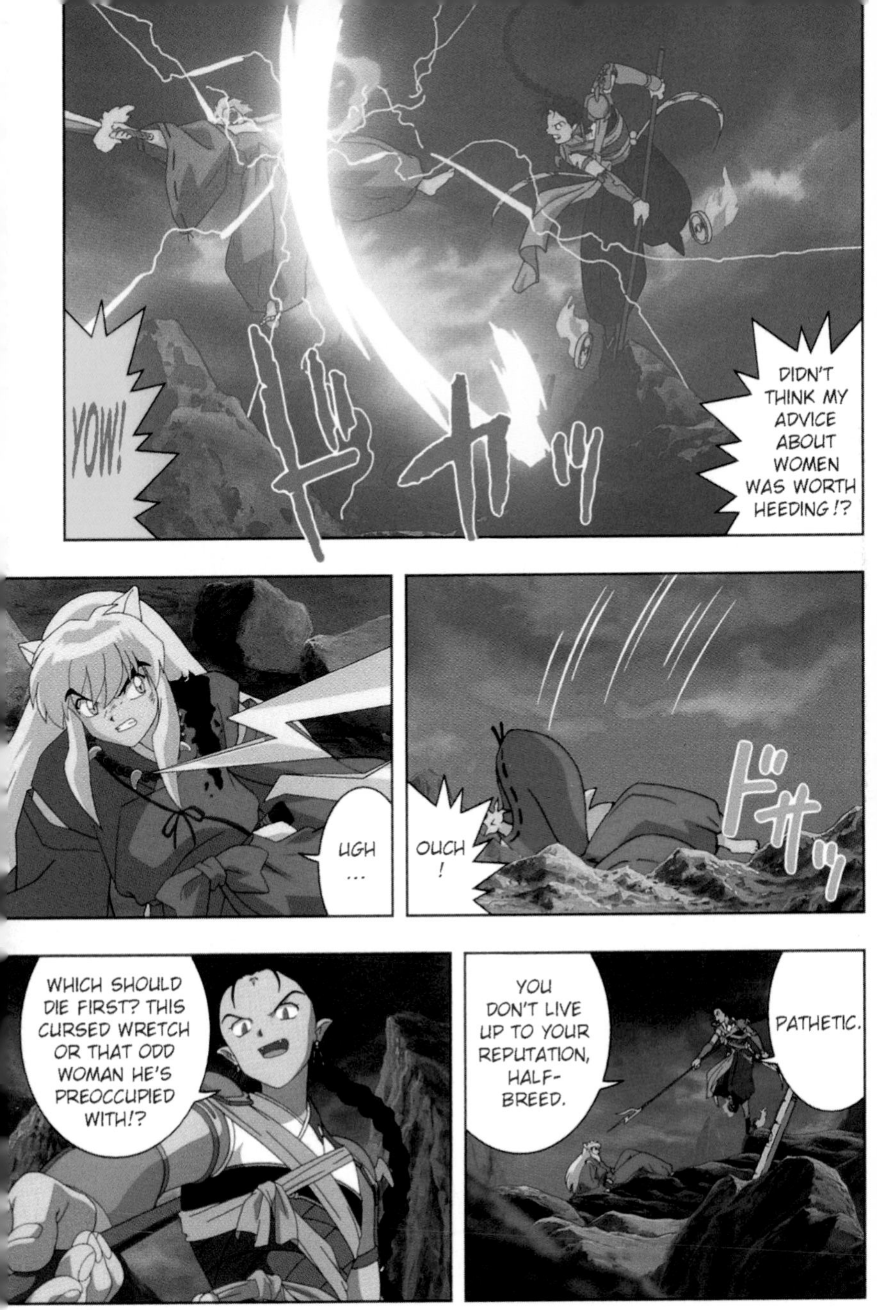
DIDN'T THINK MY ADVICE ABOUT WOMEN WAS WORTH HEEDING!?
ドカッ
YOW!
ドサッ
OUCH!
UGH ...
PATHETIC.
YOU DON'T LIVE UP TO YOUR REPUTATION, HALF-BREED.
WHICH SHOULD DIE FIRST? THIS CURSED WRETCH OR THAT ODD WOMAN HE'S PREOCCUPIED WITH!?

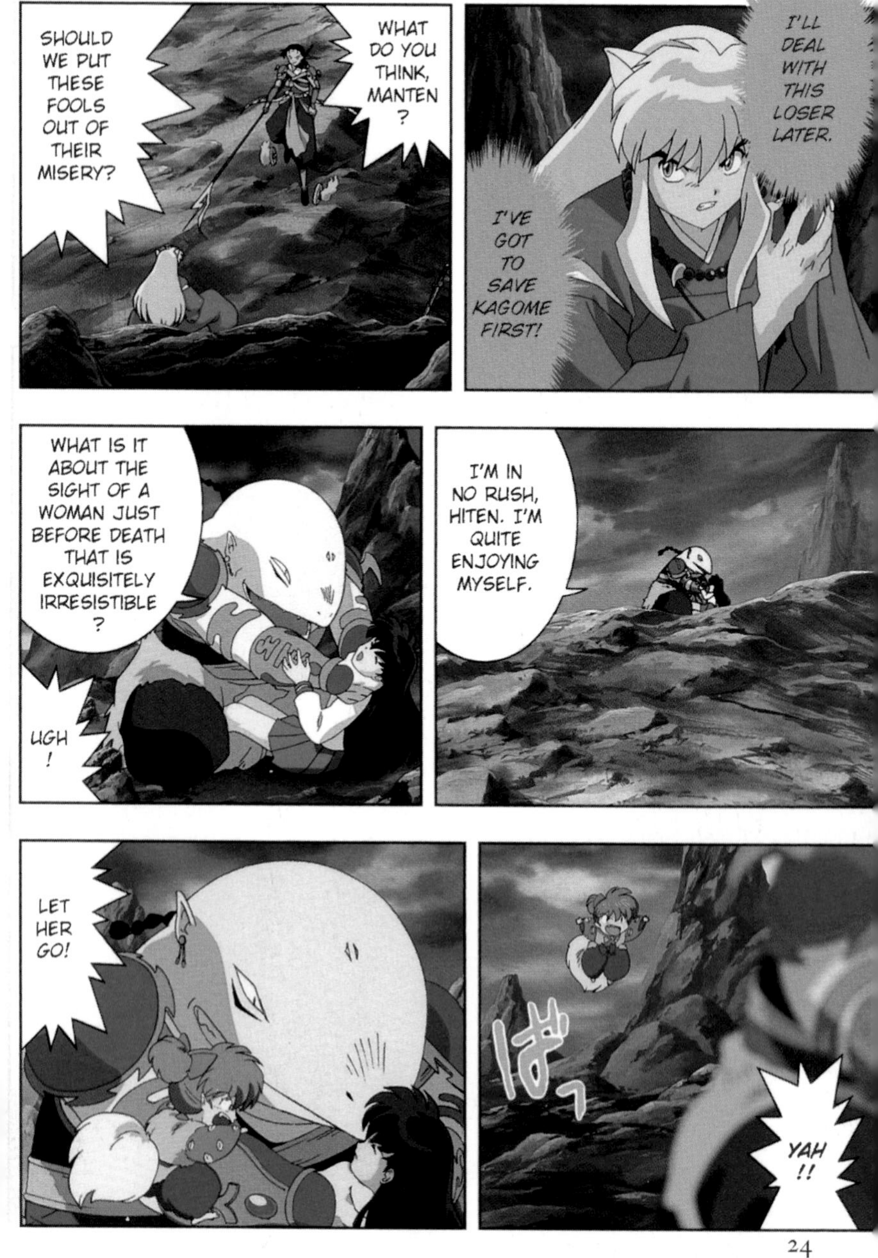
I'LL DEAL WITH THIS LOSER LATER.
I'VE GOT TO SAVE KAGOME FIRST!
WHAT DO YOU THINK, MANTEN?
SHOULD WE PUT THESE FOOLS OUT OF THEIR MISERY?
I'M IN NO RUSH, HITEN. I'M QUITE ENJOYING MYSELF.
WHAT IS IT ABOUT THE SIGHT OF A WOMAN JUST BEFORE DEATH THAT IS EXQUISITELY IRRESISTIBLE?
UGH!
ぱっ
YAH!!
LET HER GO!

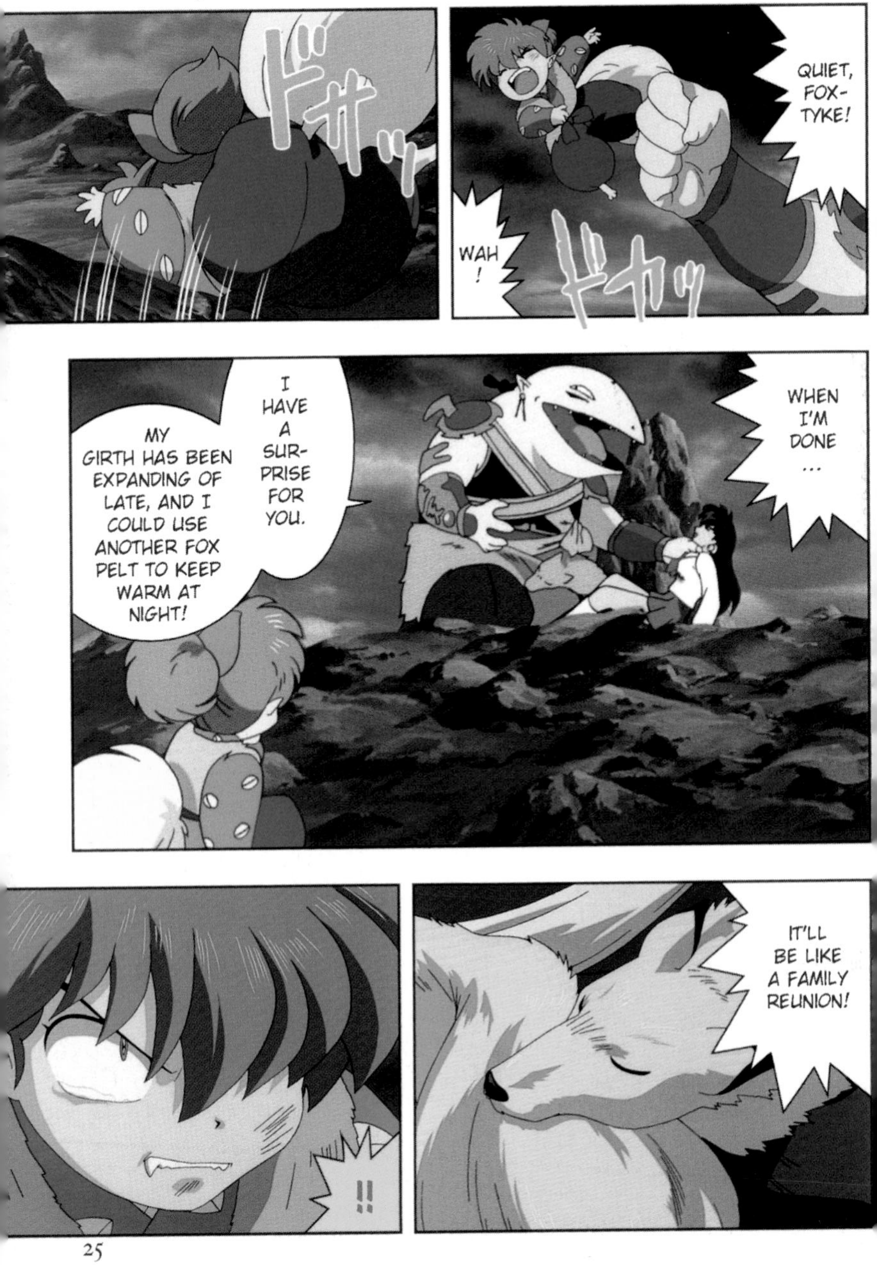

QUIET, FOX-TYKE!
WAH!
ドカッ
ドサッ
WHEN I'M DONE ...
I HAVE A SURPRISE FOR YOU.
MY GIRTH HAS BEEN EXPANDING OF LATE, AND I COULD USE ANOTHER FOX PELT TO KEEP WARM AT NIGHT!
IT'LL BE LIKE A FAMILY REUNION!
!!

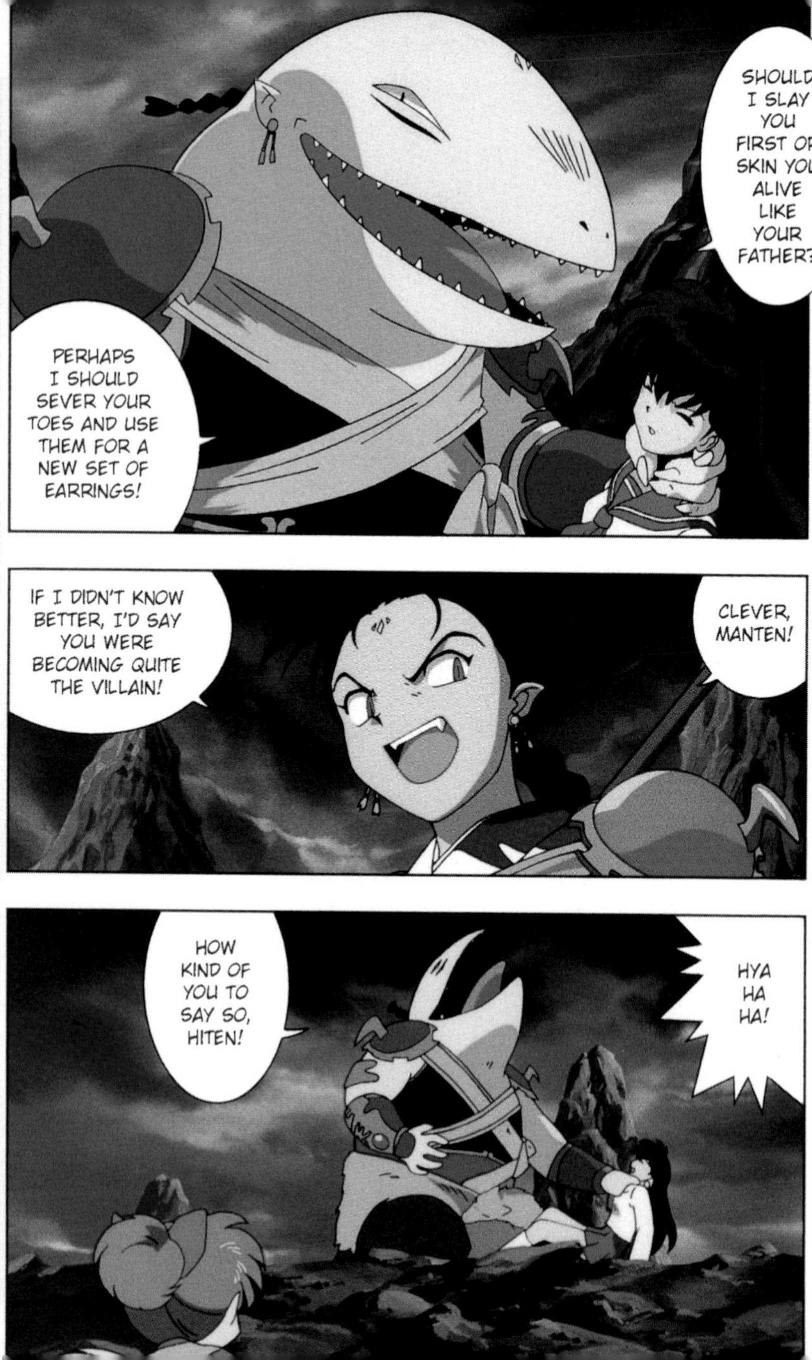
SHOULD I SLAY YOU FIRST OR SKIN YOU ALIVE LIKE YOUR FATHER?
PERHAPS I SHOULD SEVER YOUR TOES AND USE THEM FOR A NEW SET OF EARRINGS!
CLEVER, MANTEN!
IF I DIDN'T KNOW BETTER, I'D SAY YOU WERE BECOMING QUITE THE VILLAIN!
HYA HA HA!
HOW KIND OF YOU TO SAY SO, HITEN!

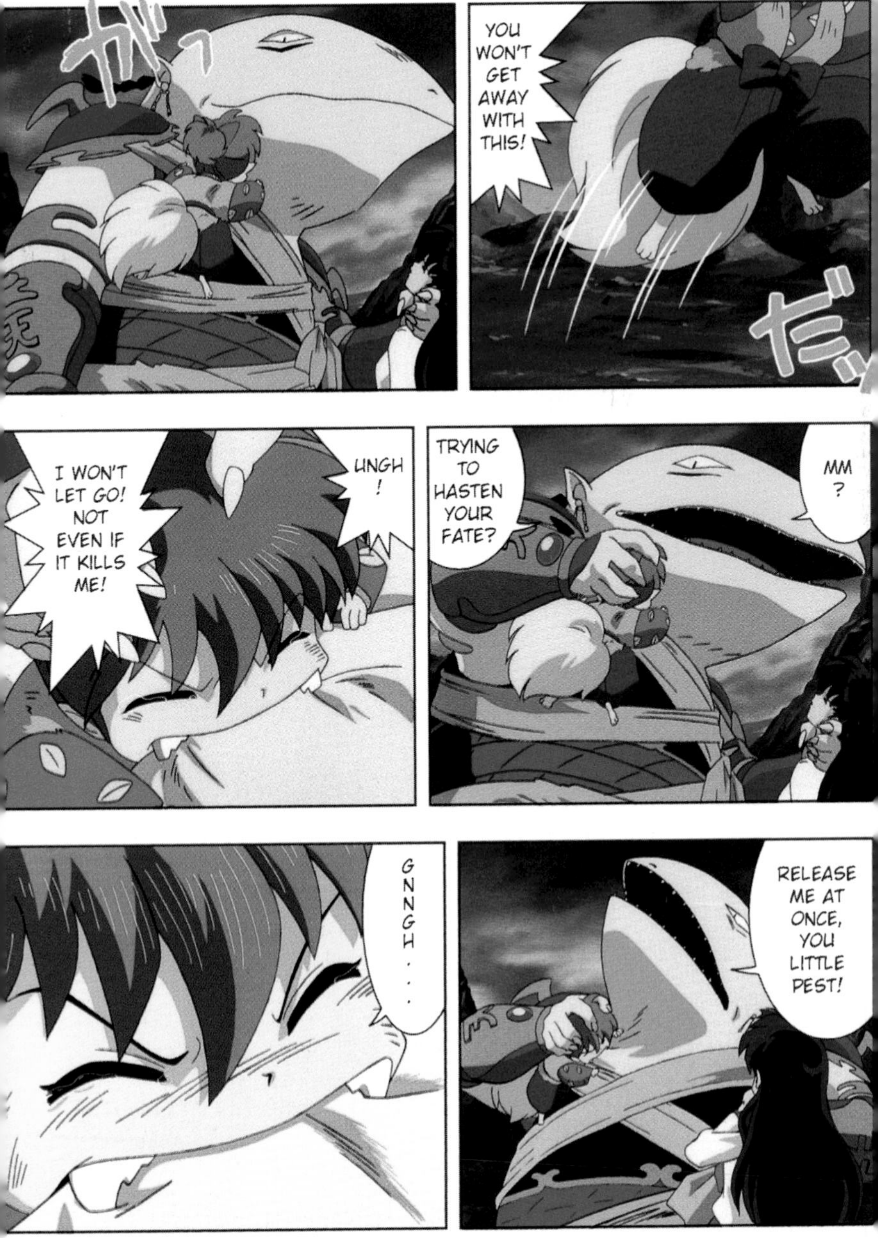
YOU WON'T GET AWAY WITH THIS!
ダッ
ガブッ
MM ?
TRYING TO HASTEN YOUR FATE?
UNGH !
I WON'T LET GO! NOT EVEN IF IT KILLS ME!
RELEASE ME AT ONCE, YOU LITTLE PEST!
GNNGH . . .

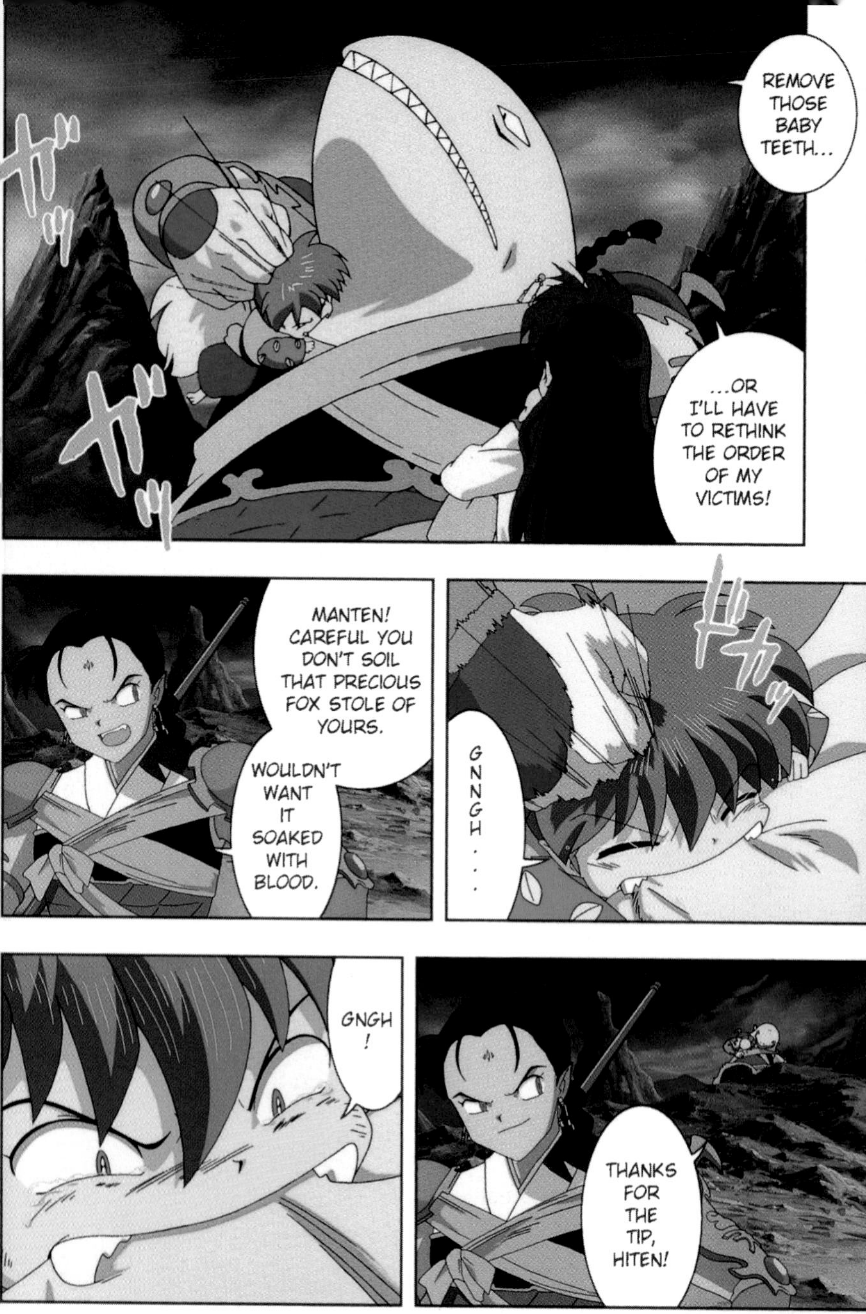
REMOVE THOSE BABY TEETH...
...OR I'LL HAVE TO RETHINK THE ORDER OF MY VICTIMS!
GNNGH . . .
MANTEN! CAREFUL YOU DON'T SOIL THAT PRECIOUS FOX STOLE OF YOURS.
WOULDN'T WANT IT SOAKED WITH BLOOD.
THANKS FOR THE TIP, HITEN!
GNGH!

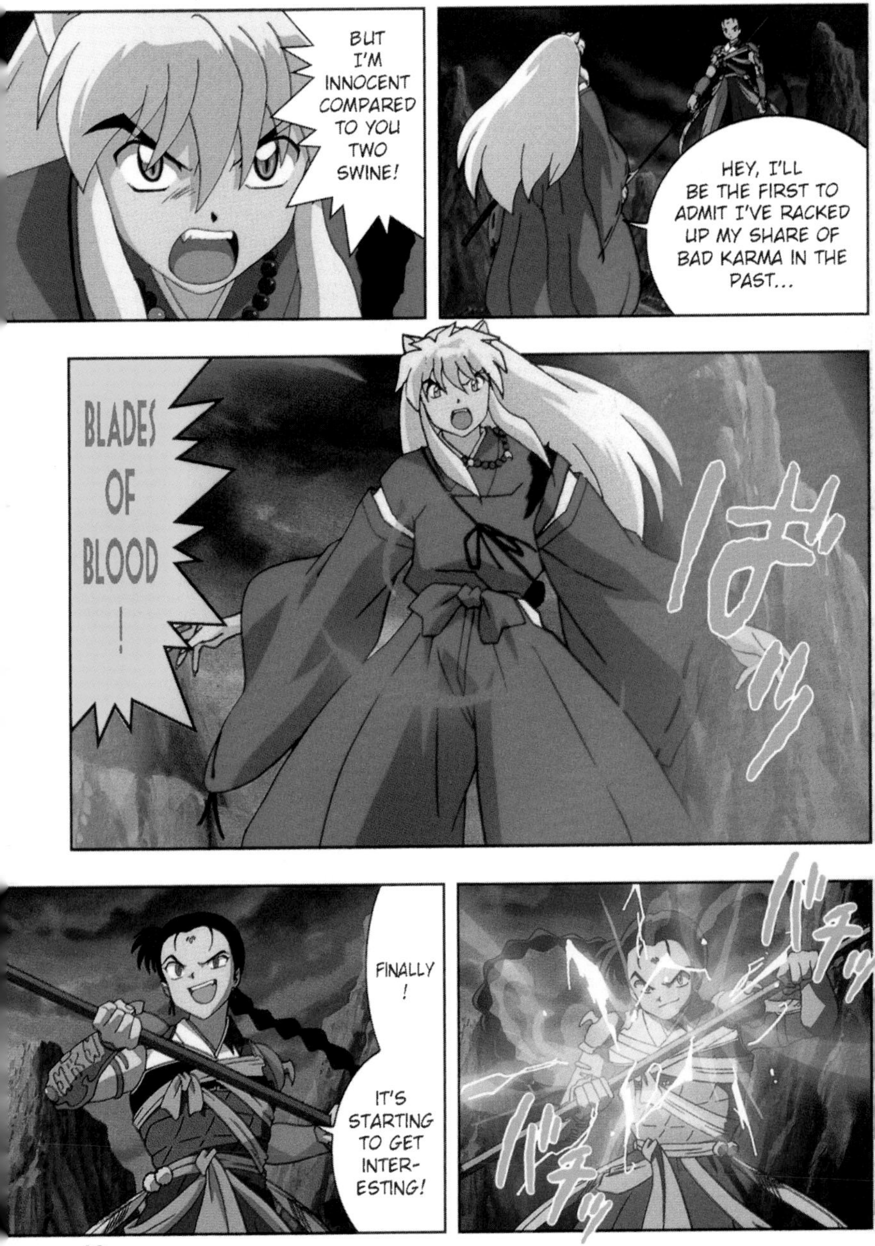
HEY, I'LL BE THE FIRST TO ADMIT I'VE RACKED UP MY SHARE OF BAD KARMA IN THE PAST...
BUT I'M INNOCENT COMPARED TO YOU TWO SWINE!
ぼッ
BLADES OF BLOOD!
バチッ
バチッ
FINALLY!
IT'S STARTING TO GET INTER-ESTING!

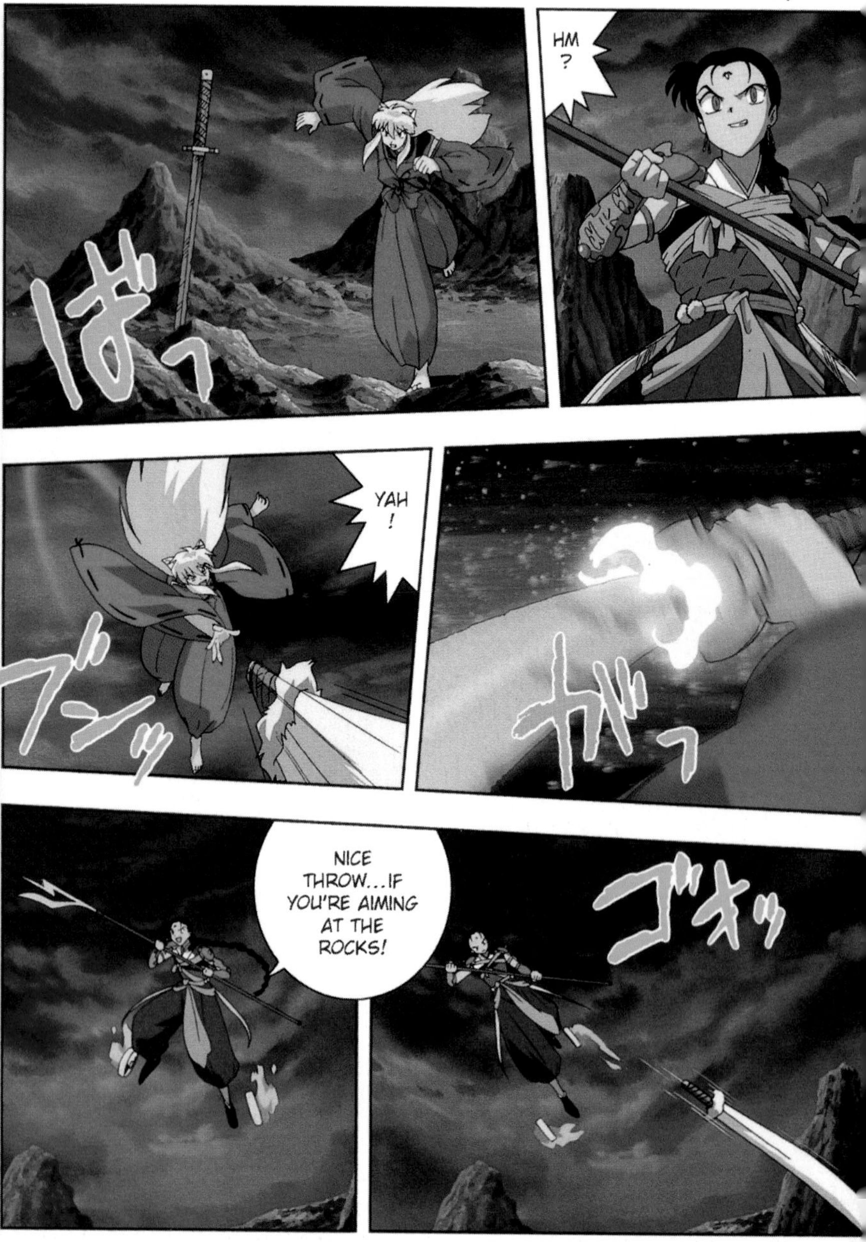
HM ?
ぼっ
ガッ
YAH !
ブシッ
ゴオッ
NICE THROW...IF YOU'RE AIMING AT THE ROCKS!

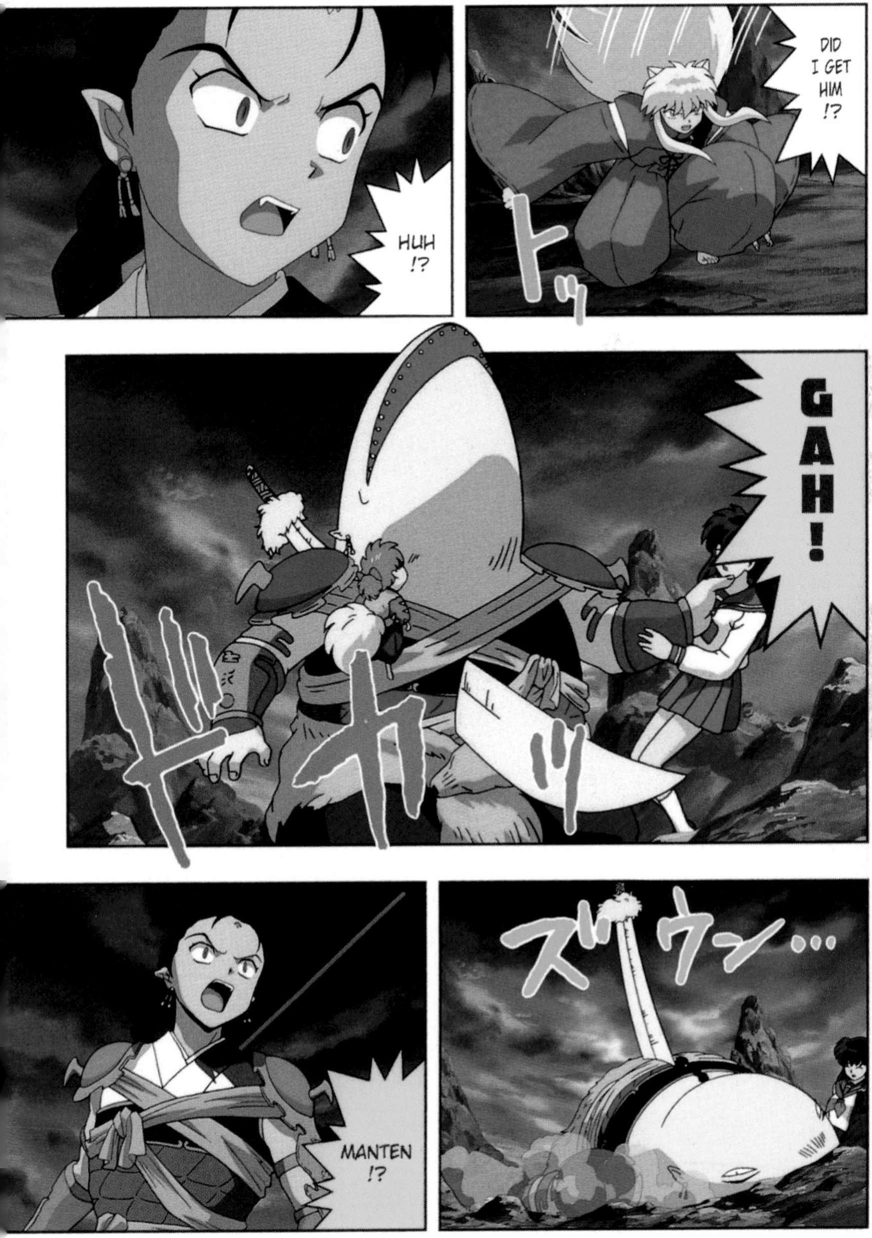
DID I GET HIM !?
トッ
HUH !?
GAH!
ドカッ
ズウン…
MANTEN !?

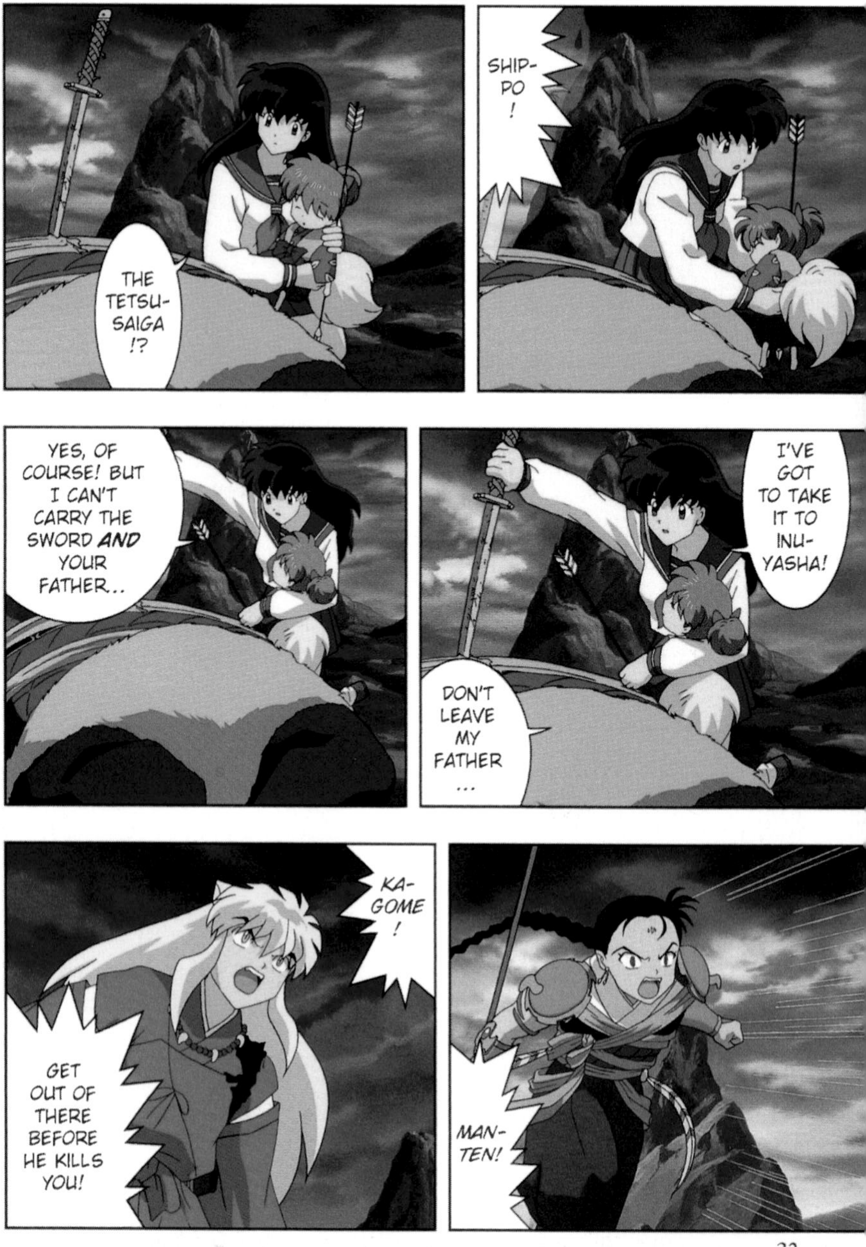
SHIP-PO!
THE TETSU-SAIGA!?
I'VE GOT TO TAKE IT TO INU-YASHA!
DON'T LEAVE MY FATHER...
YES, OF COURSE! BUT I CAN'T CARRY THE SWORD **AND** YOUR FATHER...
MAN-TEN!
KA-GOME!
GET OUT OF THERE BEFORE HE KILLS YOU!

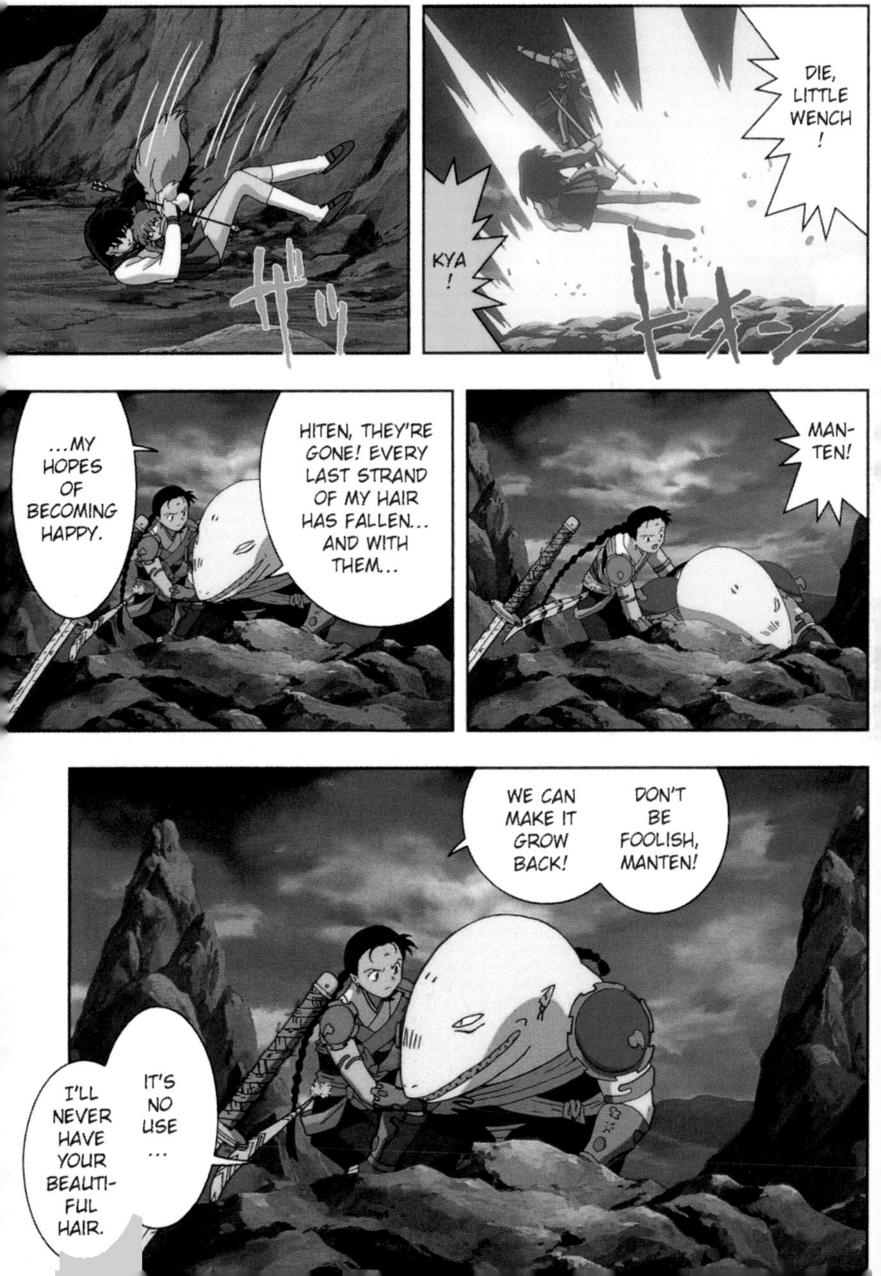
DIE, LITTLE WENCH!
KYA!
MAN-TEN!
HITEN, THEY'RE GONE! EVERY LAST STRAND OF MY HAIR HAS FALLEN... AND WITH THEM...
...MY HOPES OF BECOMING HAPPY.
DON'T BE FOOLISH, MANTEN!
WE CAN MAKE IT GROW BACK!
IT'S NO USE...
I'LL NEVER HAVE YOUR BEAUTIFUL HAIR.

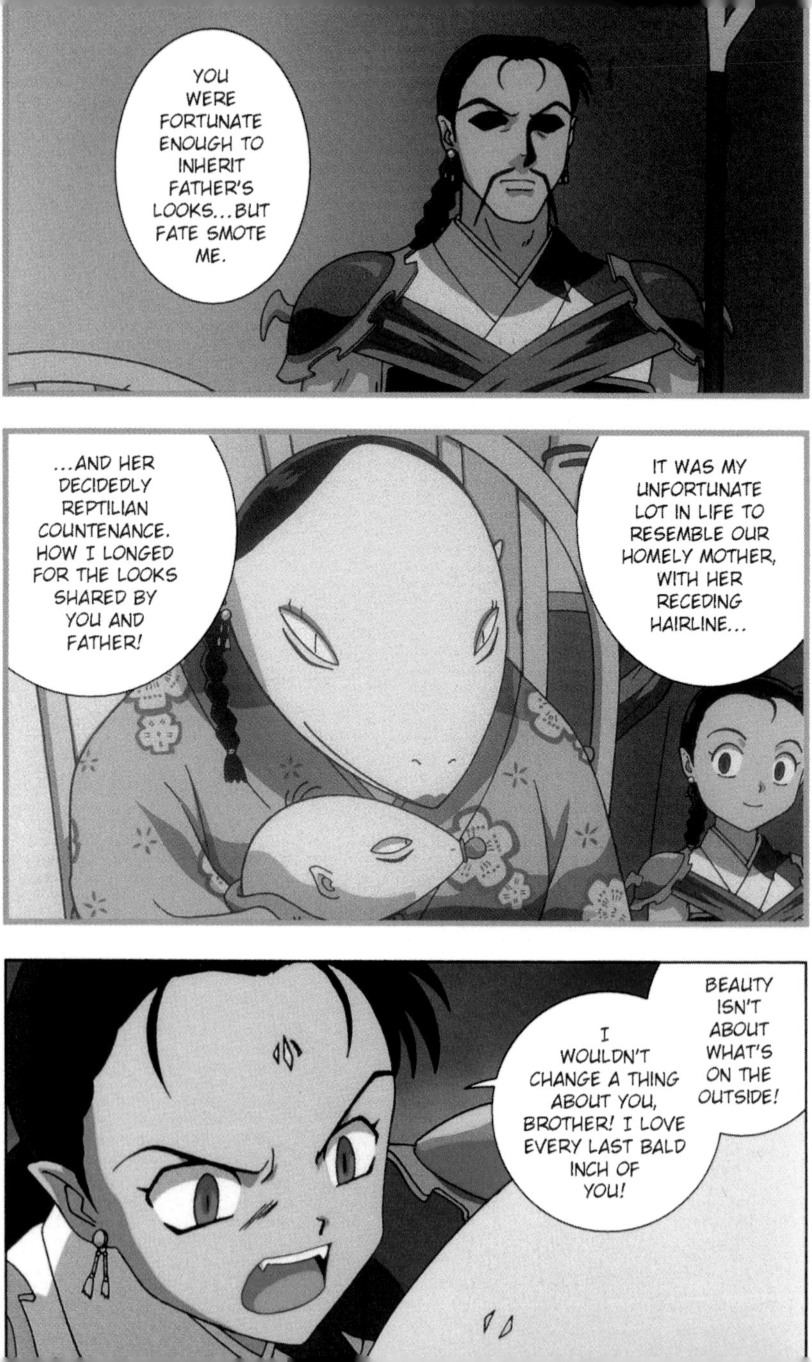
YOU WERE FORTUNATE ENOUGH TO INHERIT FATHER'S LOOKS...BUT FATE SMOTE ME.
IT WAS MY UNFORTUNATE LOT IN LIFE TO RESEMBLE OUR HOMELY MOTHER, WITH HER RECEDING HAIRLINE...
...AND HER DECIDEDLY REPTILIAN COUNTENANCE. HOW I LONGED FOR THE LOOKS SHARED BY YOU AND FATHER!
BEAUTY ISN'T ABOUT WHAT'S ON THE OUTSIDE!
I WOULDN'T CHANGE A THING ABOUT YOU, BROTHER! I LOVE EVERY LAST BALD INCH OF YOU!

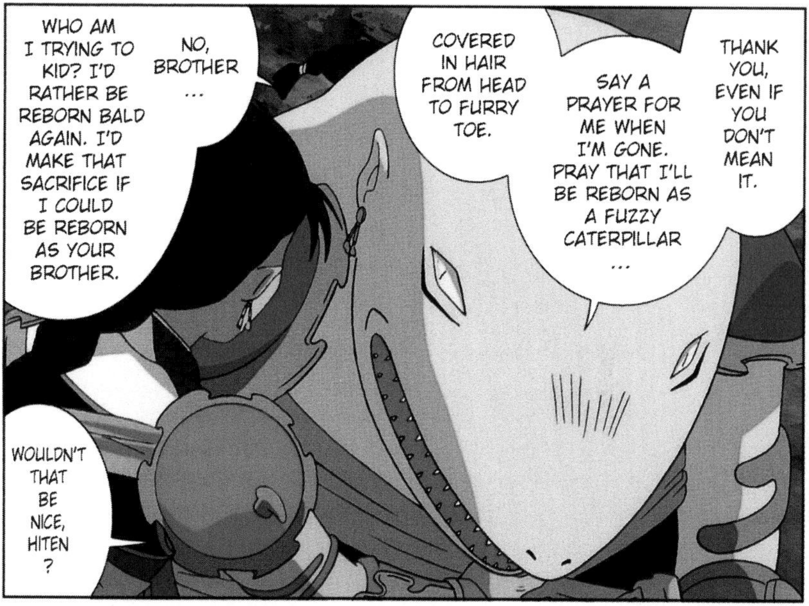
THANK YOU, EVEN IF YOU DON'T MEAN IT.
SAY A PRAYER FOR ME WHEN I'M GONE. PRAY THAT I'LL BE REBORN AS A FUZZY CATERPILLAR ...
COVERED IN HAIR FROM HEAD TO FURRY TOE.
NO, BROTHER ...
WHO AM I TRYING TO KID? I'D RATHER BE REBORN BALD AGAIN. I'D MAKE THAT SACRIFICE IF I COULD BE REBORN AS YOUR BROTHER.
WOULDN'T THAT BE NICE, HITEN?

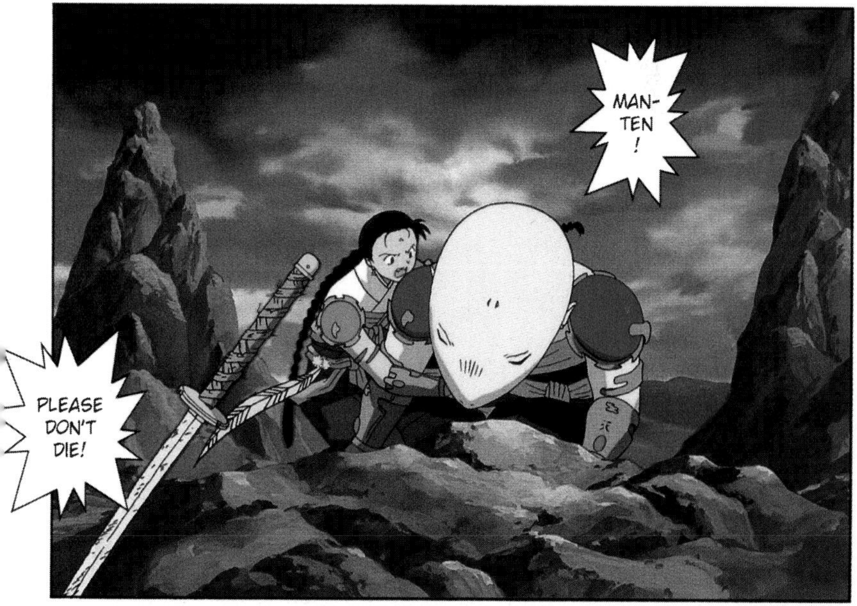
MAN-TEN!
PLEASE DON'T DIE!

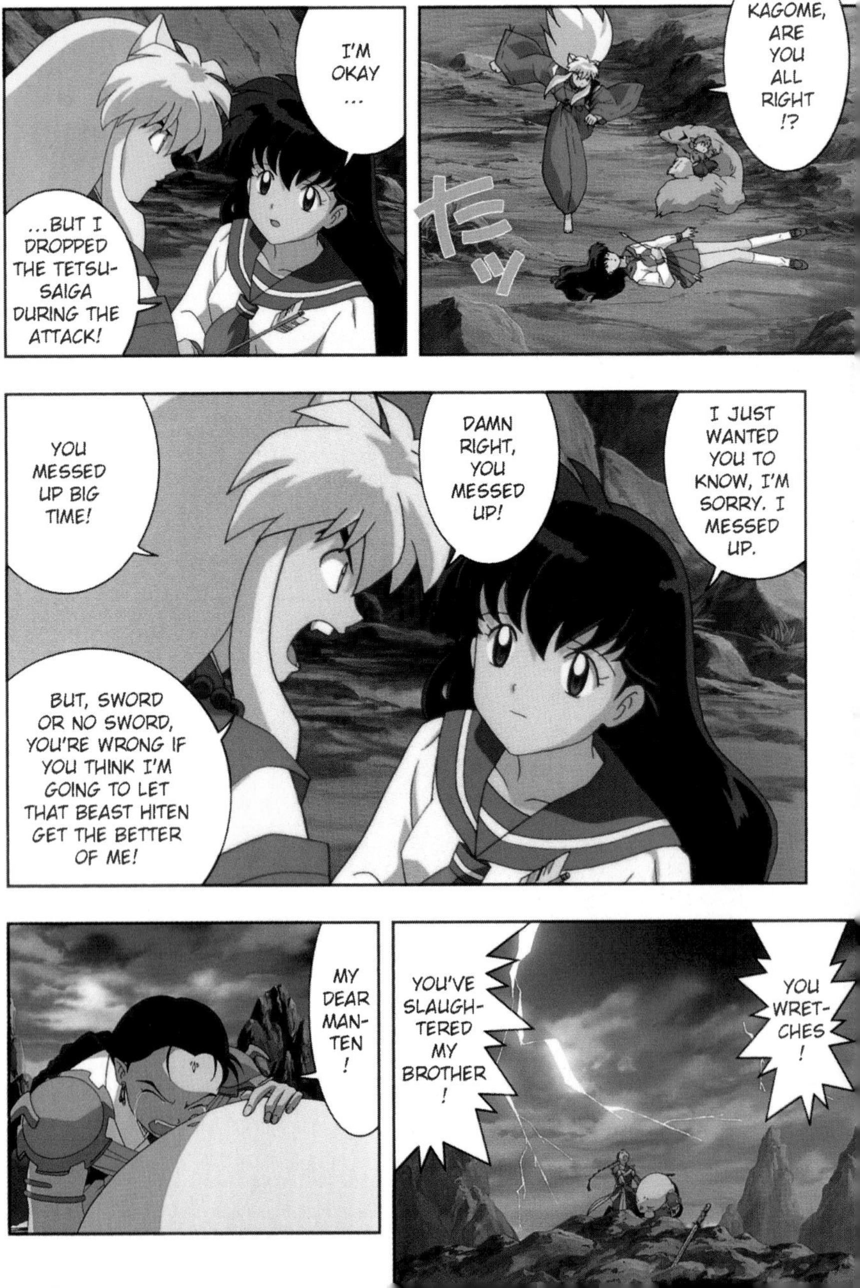
KAGOME, ARE YOU ALL RIGHT !?
ダッ
I'M OKAY ...
...BUT I DROPPED THE TETSU-SAIGA DURING THE ATTACK!
I JUST WANTED YOU TO KNOW, I'M SORRY. I MESSED UP.
DAMN RIGHT, YOU MESSED UP!
YOU MESSED UP BIG TIME!
BUT, SWORD OR NO SWORD, YOU'RE WRONG IF YOU THINK I'M GOING TO LET THAT BEAST HITEN GET THE BETTER OF ME!
YOU WRET-CHES !
YOU'VE SLAUGH-TERED MY BROTHER !
MY DEAR MAN-TEN !

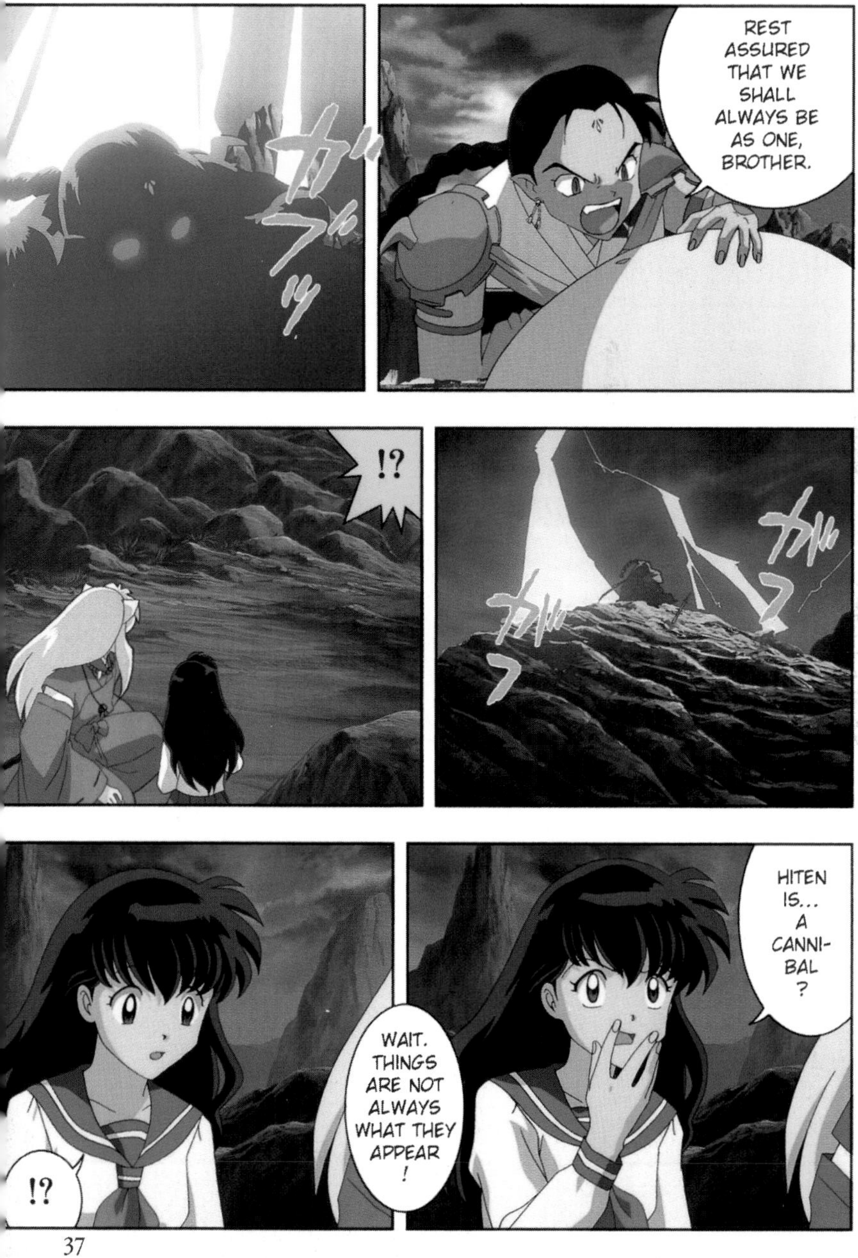
REST ASSURED THAT WE SHALL ALWAYS BE AS ONE, BROTHER.
!?
HITEN IS... A CANNI-BAL?
WAIT. THINGS ARE NOT ALWAYS WHAT THEY APPEAR!
!?

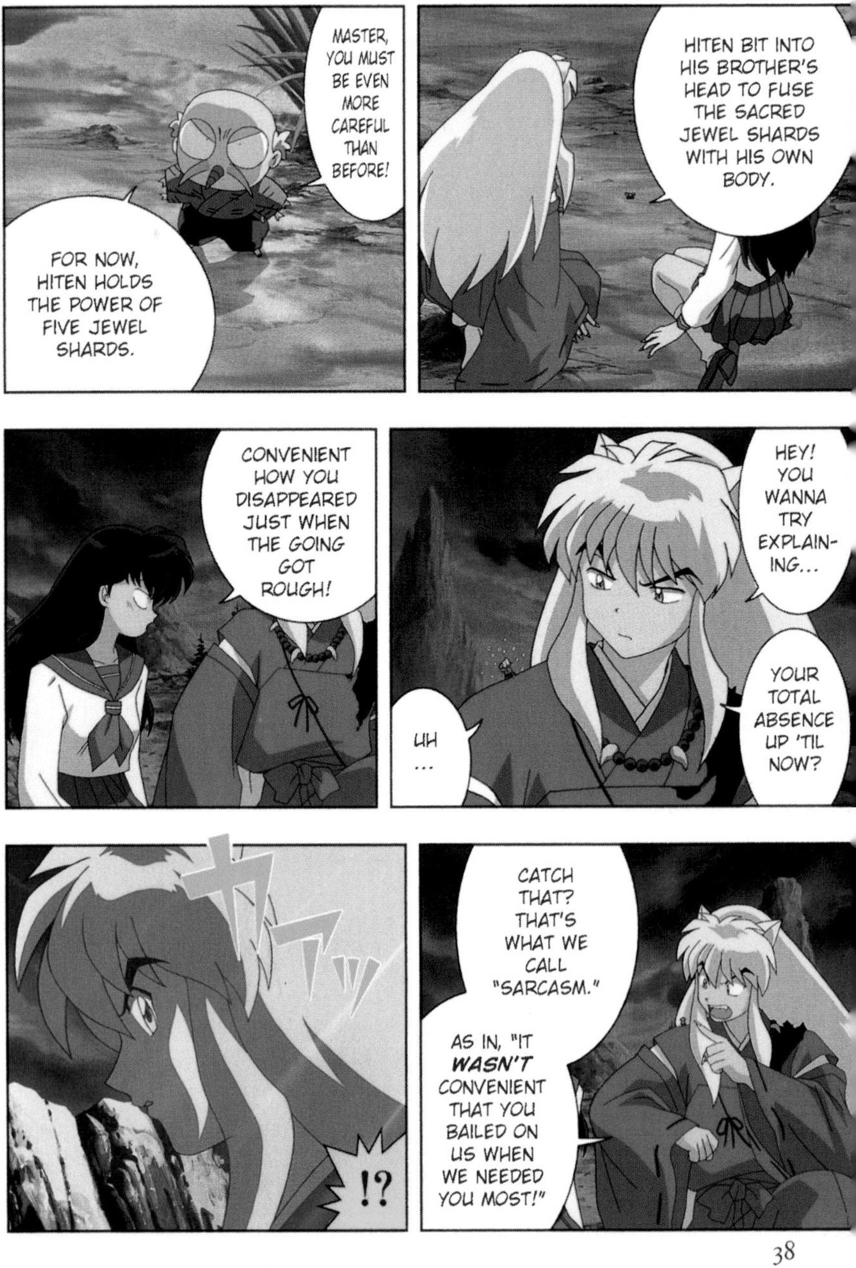
HITEN BIT INTO HIS BROTHER'S HEAD TO FUSE THE SACRED JEWEL SHARDS WITH HIS OWN BODY.
MASTER, YOU MUST BE EVEN MORE CAREFUL THAN BEFORE!
FOR NOW, HITEN HOLDS THE POWER OF FIVE JEWEL SHARDS.
HEY! YOU WANNA TRY EXPLAIN-ING...
YOUR TOTAL ABSENCE UP 'TIL NOW?
UH ...
CONVENIENT HOW YOU DISAPPEARED JUST WHEN THE GOING GOT ROUGH!
CATCH THAT? THAT'S WHAT WE CALL "SARCASM."
AS IN, "IT ***WASN'T*** CONVENIENT THAT YOU BAILED ON US WHEN WE NEEDED YOU MOST!"
!?

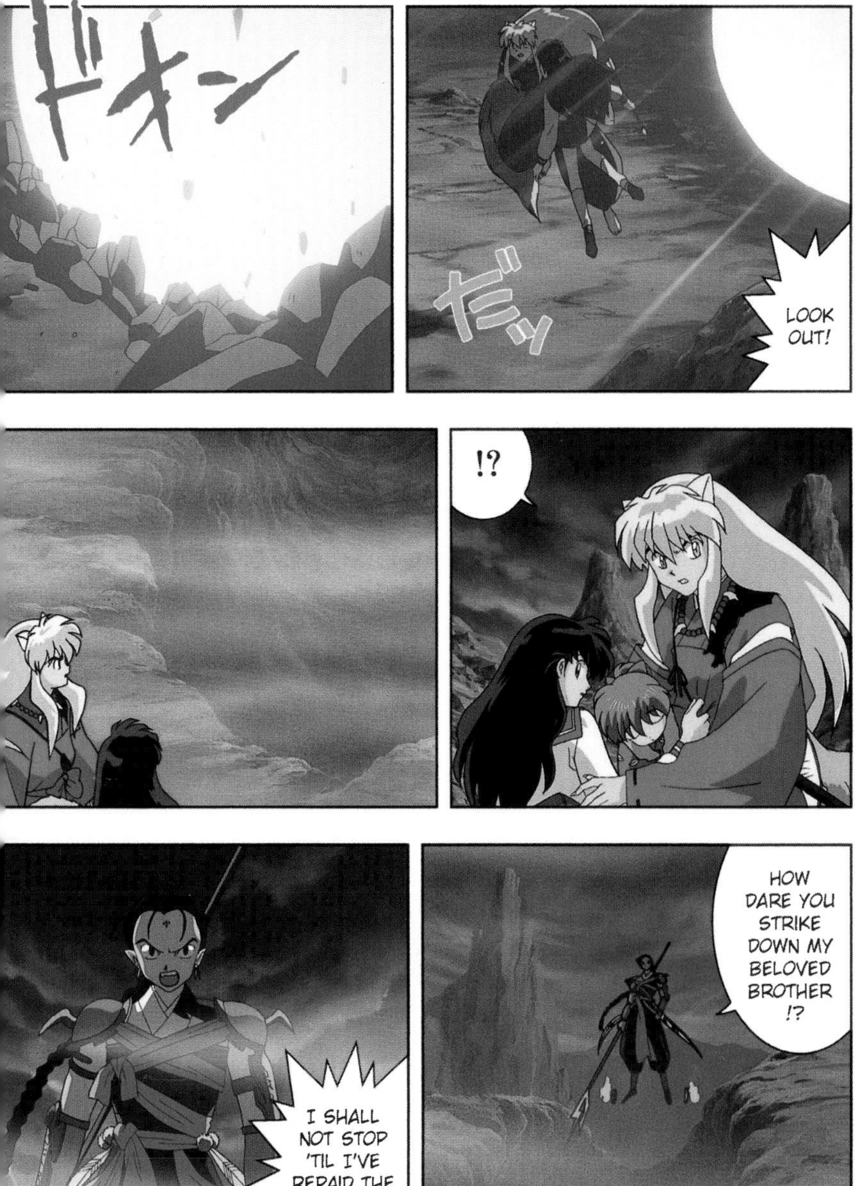
ダッ
LOOK OUT!
ドオン
!?
HOW DARE YOU STRIKE DOWN MY BELOVED BROTHER !?
I SHALL NOT STOP 'TIL I'VE REPAID THE DEED!

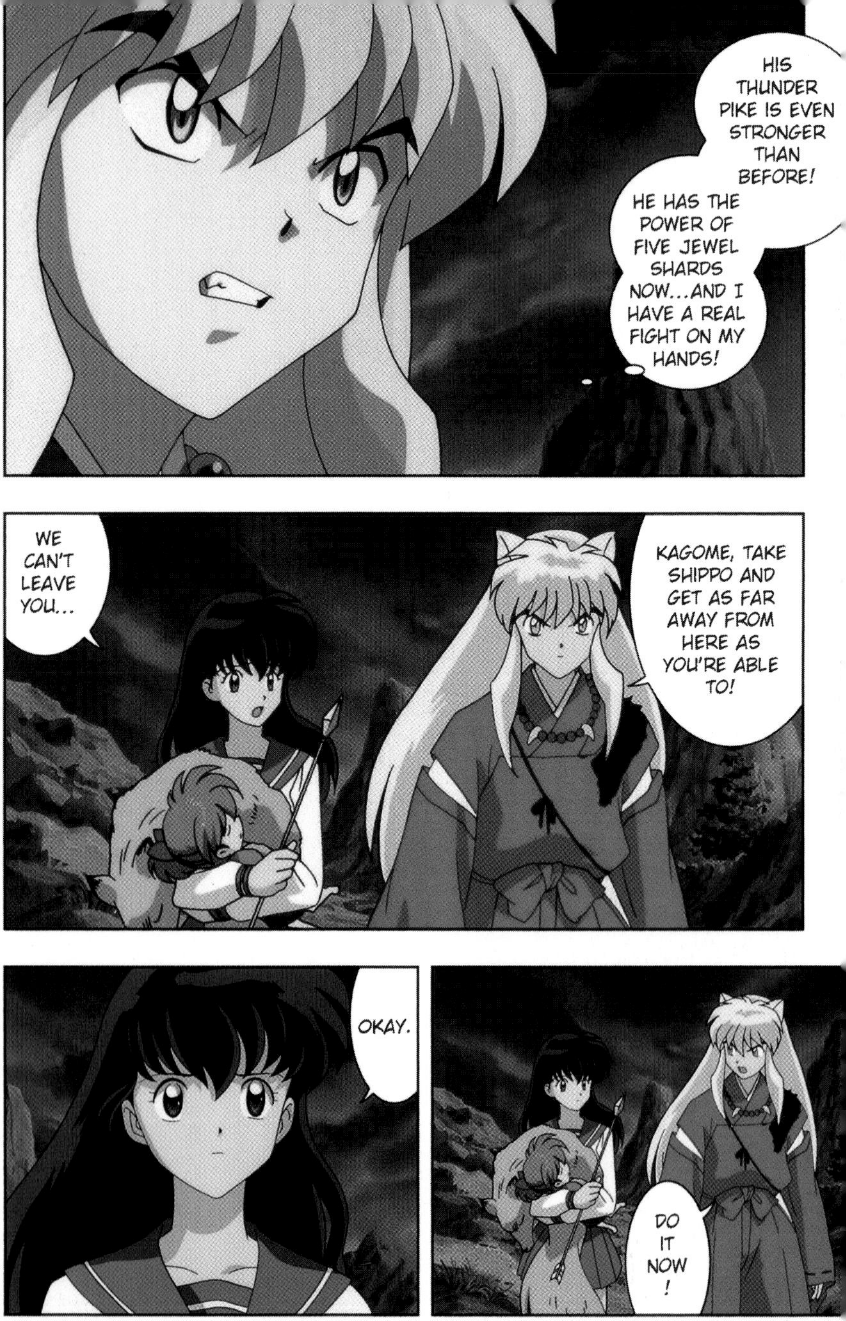
HIS THUNDER PIKE IS EVEN STRONGER THAN BEFORE!
HE HAS THE POWER OF FIVE JEWEL SHARDS NOW...AND I HAVE A REAL FIGHT ON MY HANDS!
KAGOME, TAKE SHIPPO AND GET AS FAR AWAY FROM HERE AS YOU'RE ABLE TO!
WE CAN'T LEAVE YOU...
DO IT NOW!
OKAY.

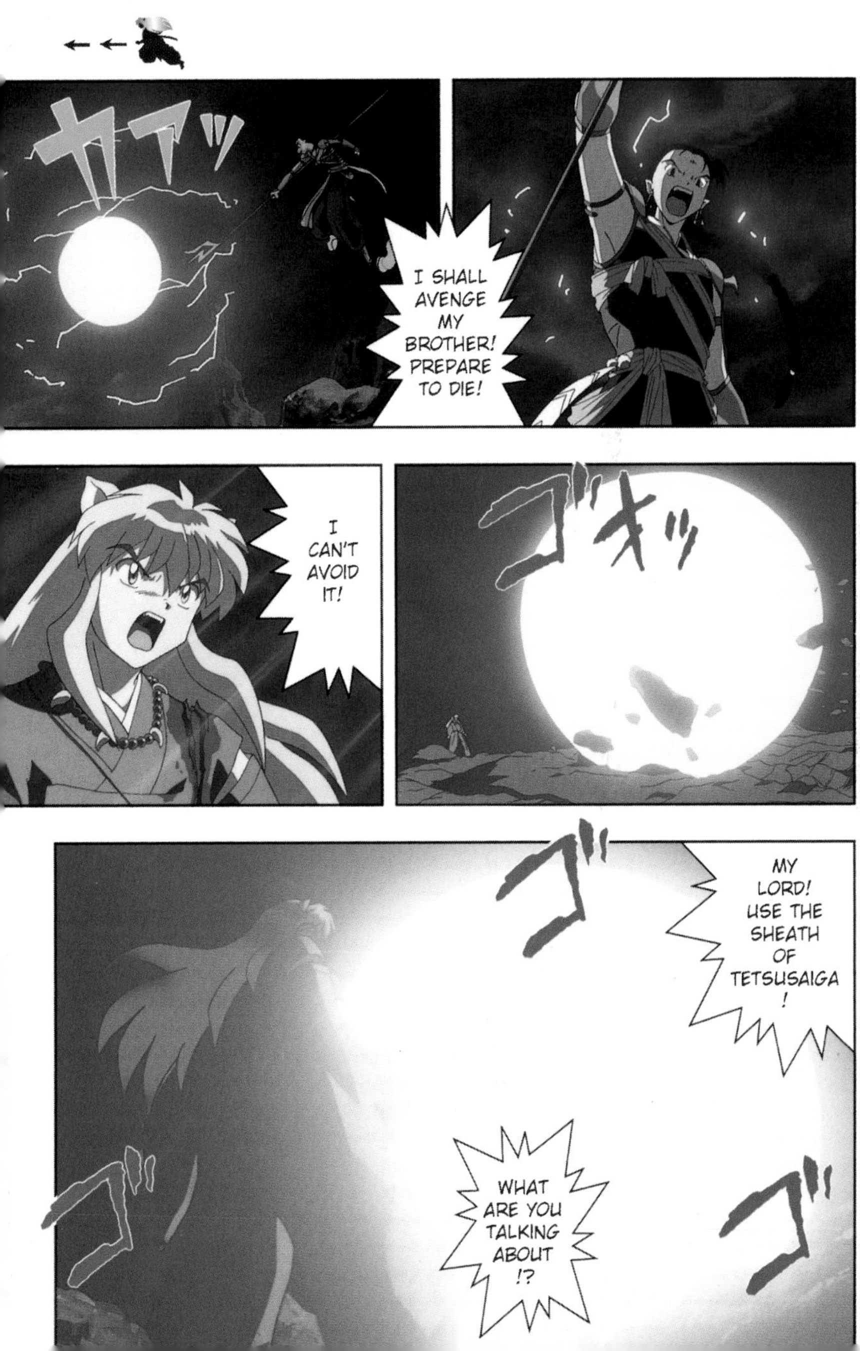
I SHALL AVENGE MY BROTHER! PREPARE TO DIE!
カァッ
ゴキッ
I CAN'T AVOID IT!
ゴゴ
MY LORD! USE THE SHEATH OF TETSUSAIGA!
WHAT ARE YOU TALKING ABOUT!?
ゴゴ
ゴゴ

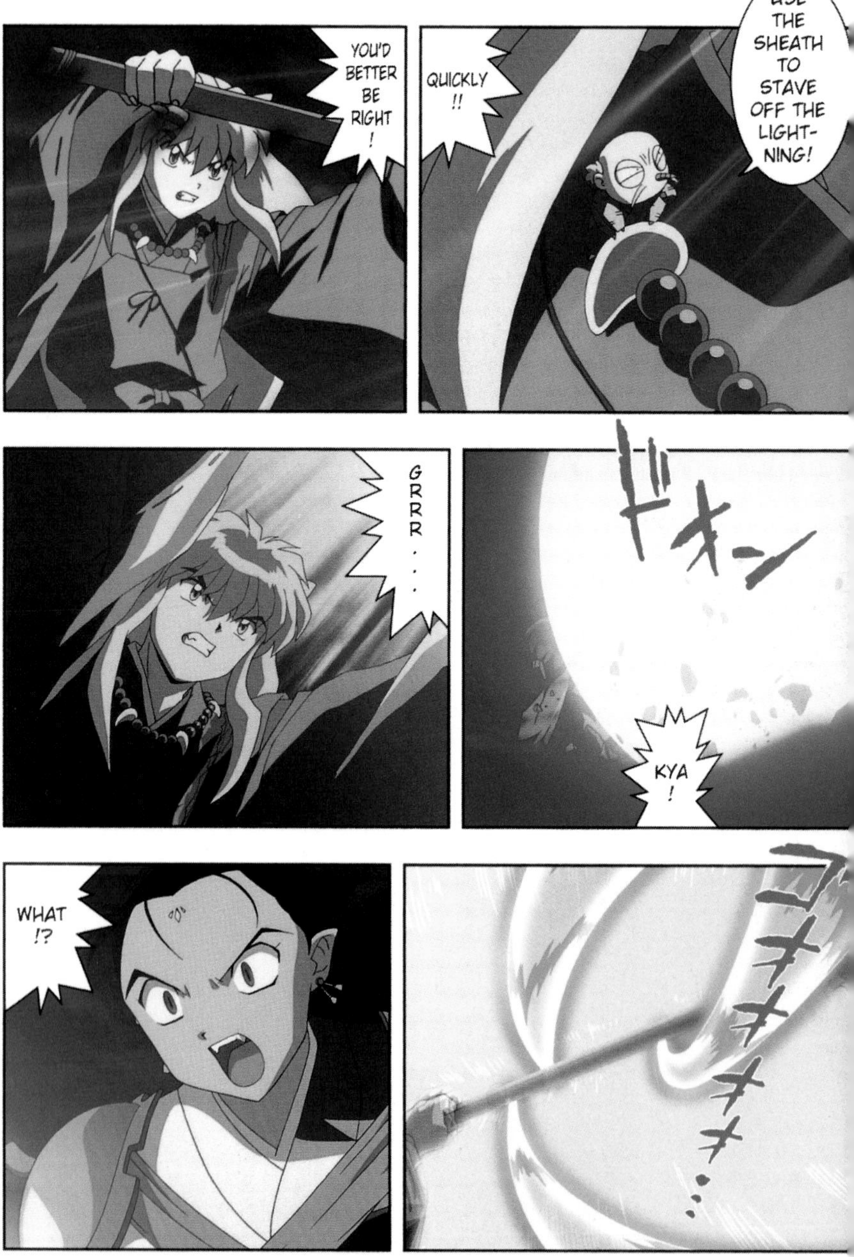
USE THE SHEATH TO STAVE OFF THE LIGHTNING!
QUICKLY!!
YOU'D BETTER BE RIGHT!
ドオン
KYA!
GRRR...
コォォォォォ…
WHAT!?

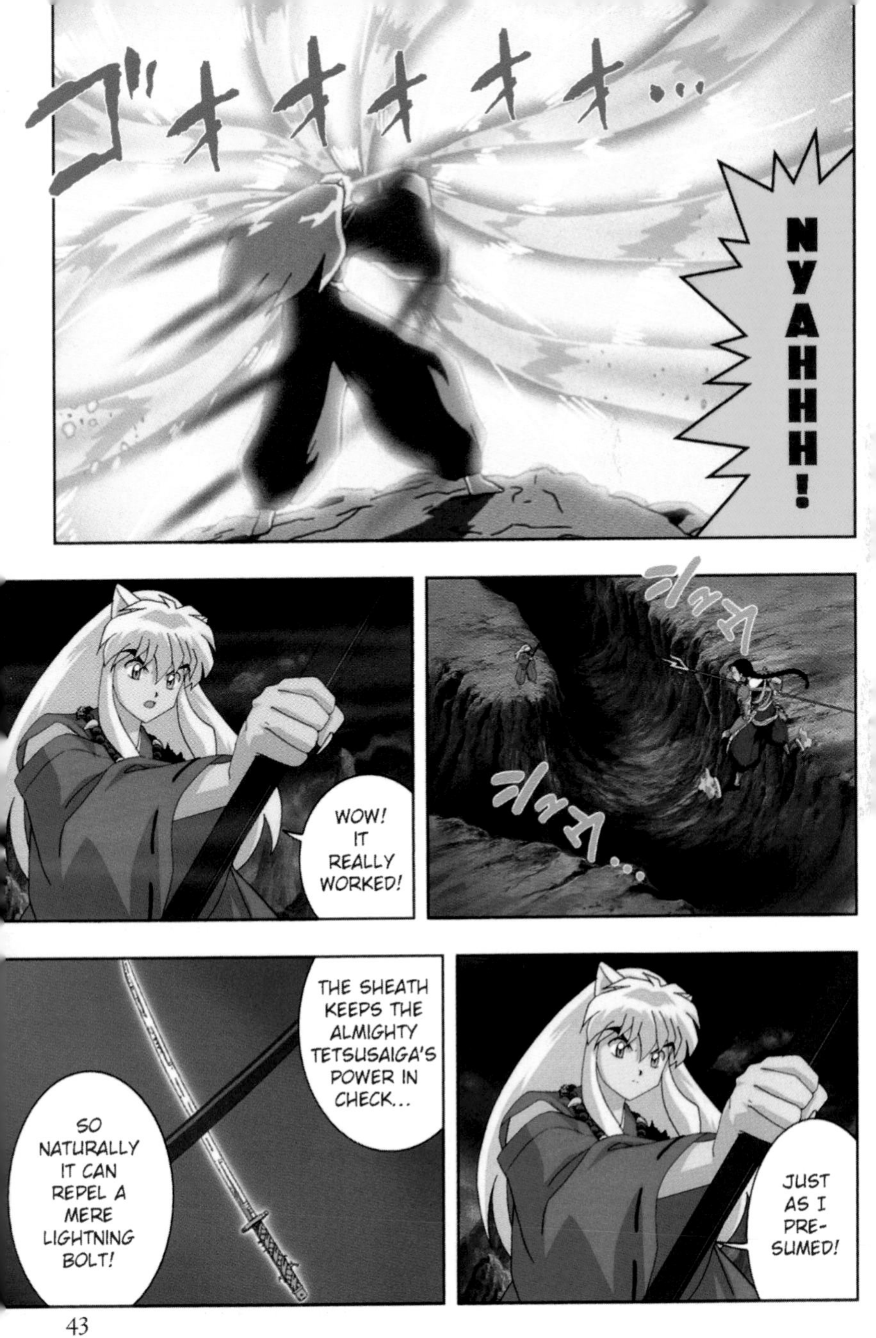
ゴオオオオオ…
NYAHHH!
シュウ
シュウ…
WOW! IT REALLY WORKED!
JUST AS I PRE-SUMED!
THE SHEATH KEEPS THE ALMIGHTY TETSUSAIGA'S POWER IN CHECK...
SO NATURALLY IT CAN REPEL A MERE LIGHTNING BOLT!

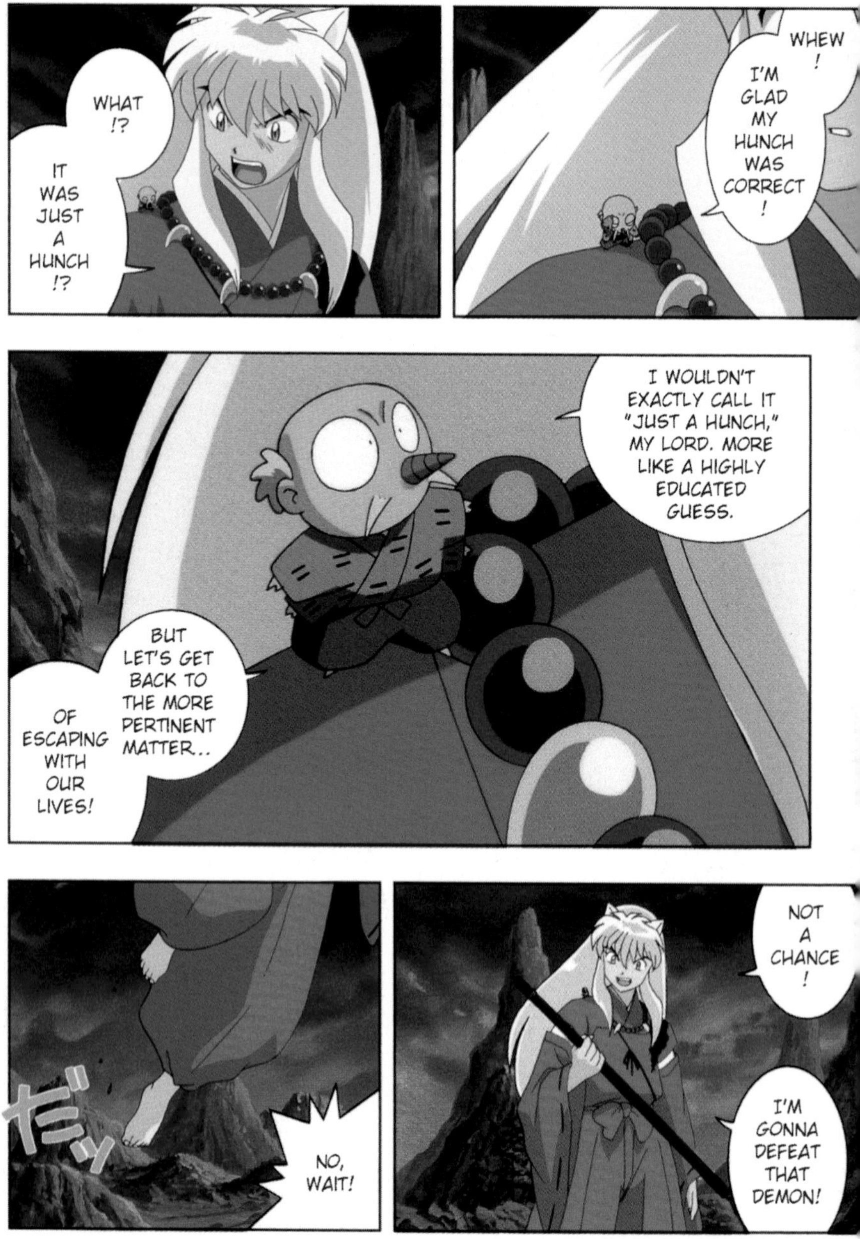
WHEW!
I'M GLAD MY HUNCH WAS CORRECT!
WHAT!?
IT WAS JUST A HUNCH!?
I WOULDN'T EXACTLY CALL IT "JUST A HUNCH," MY LORD. MORE LIKE A HIGHLY EDUCATED GUESS.
BUT LET'S GET BACK TO THE MORE PERTINENT MATTER...
OF ESCAPING WITH OUR LIVES!
NOT A CHANCE!
I'M GONNA DEFEAT THAT DEMON!
ダッ
NO, WAIT!

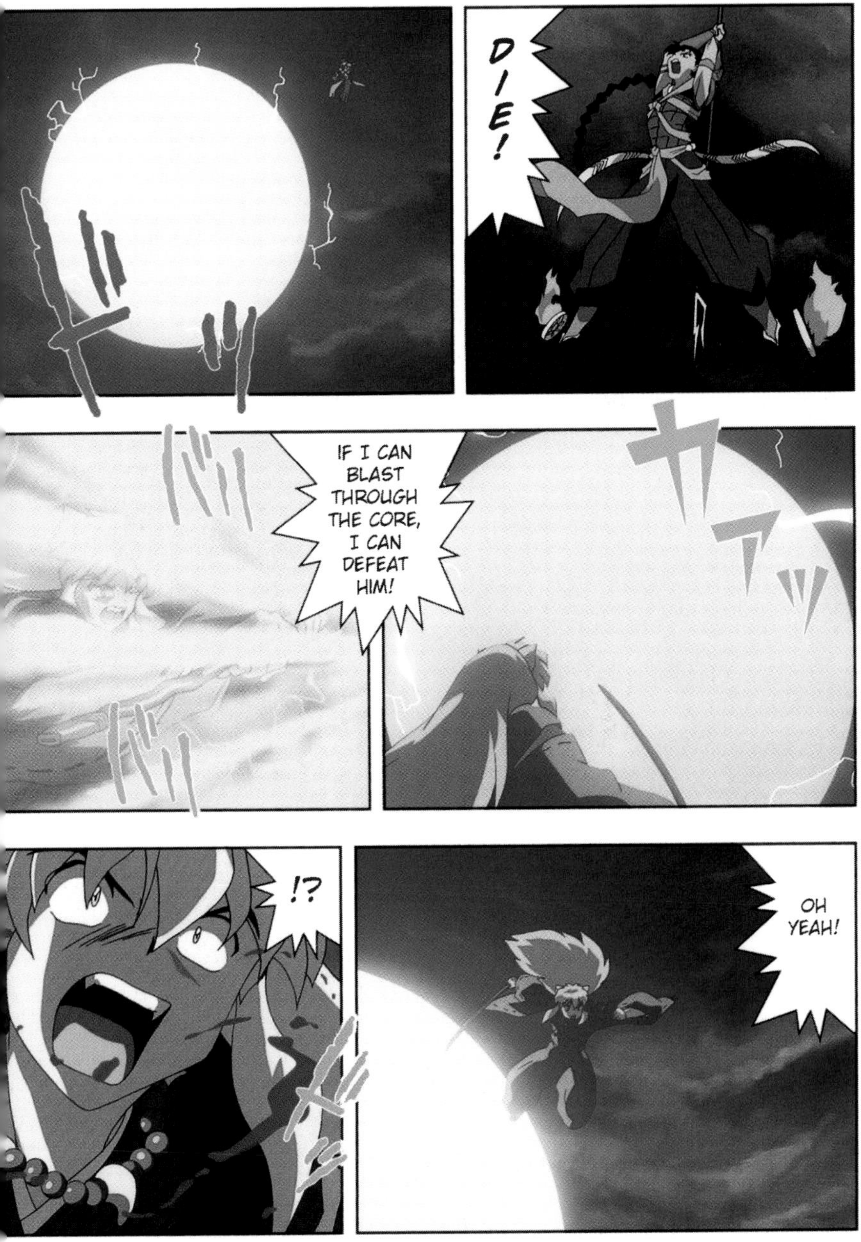
DIE!
IF I CAN BLAST THROUGH THE CORE, I CAN DEFEAT HIM!
OH YEAH!
!?

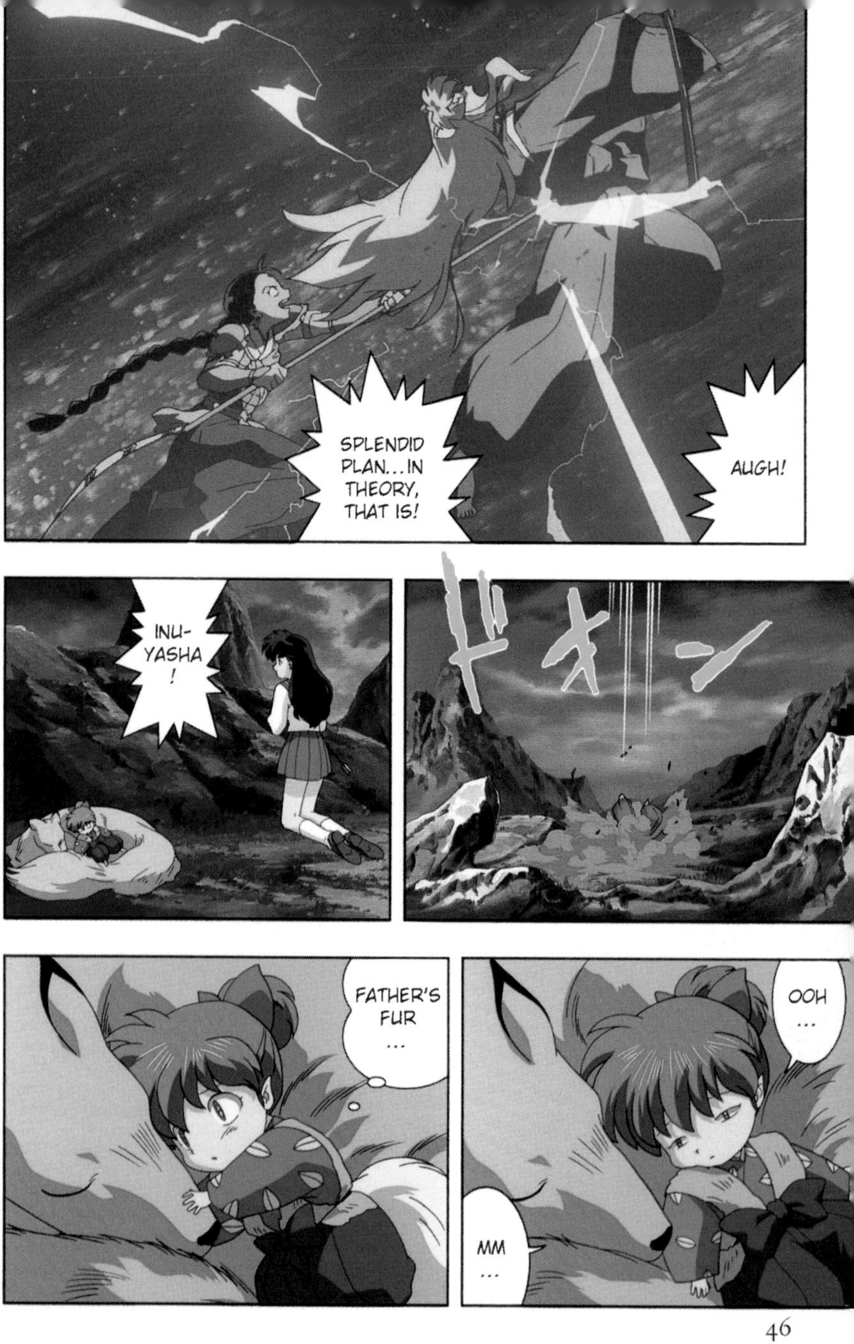
AUGH!
SPLENDID PLAN...IN THEORY, THAT IS!
ドオン
INU-YASHA!
OOH...
MM...
FATHER'S FUR...

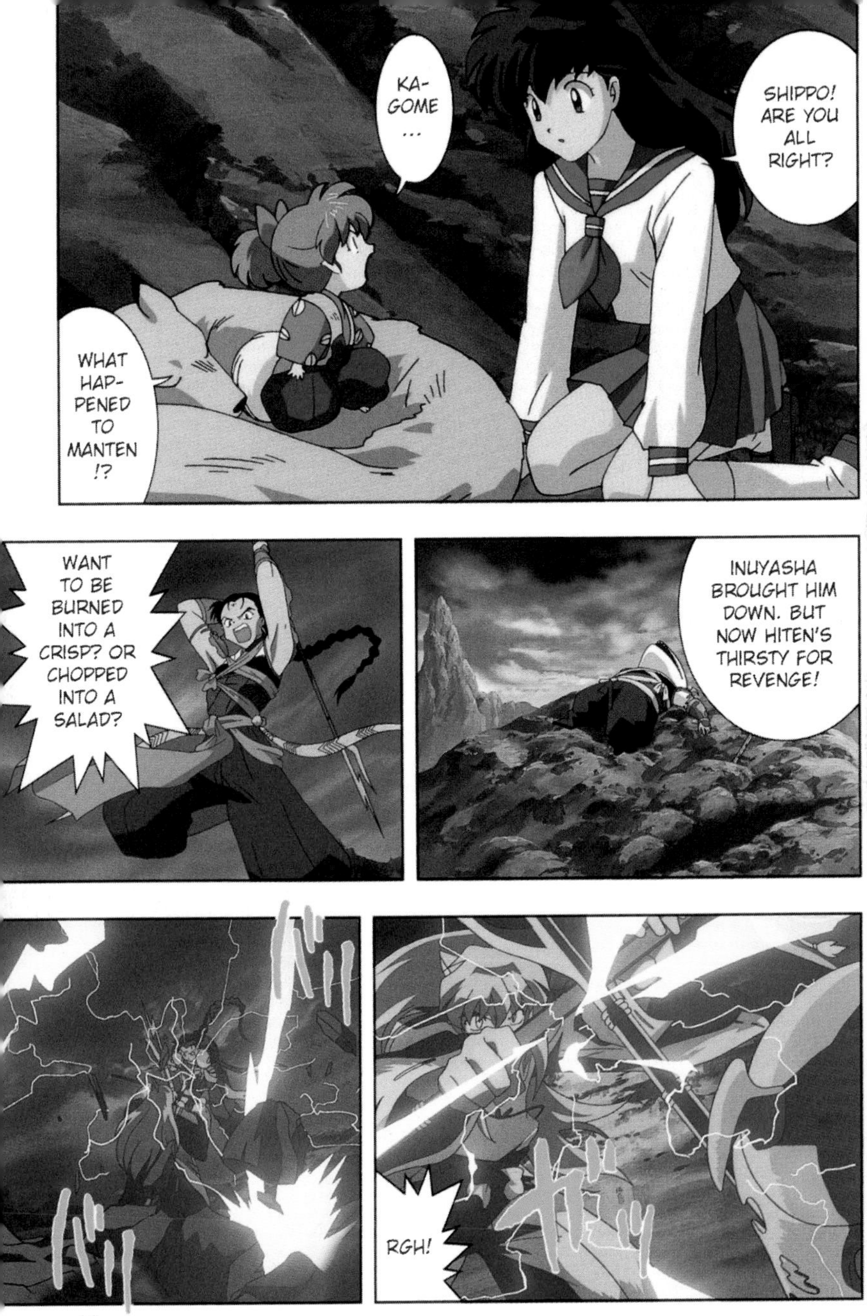
SHIPPO! ARE YOU ALL RIGHT?
KA-GOME ...
WHAT HAP-PENED TO MANTEN !?
INUYASHA BROUGHT HIM DOWN. BUT NOW HITEN'S THIRSTY FOR REVENGE!
WANT TO BE BURNED INTO A CRISP? OR CHOPPED INTO A SALAD?
RGH!

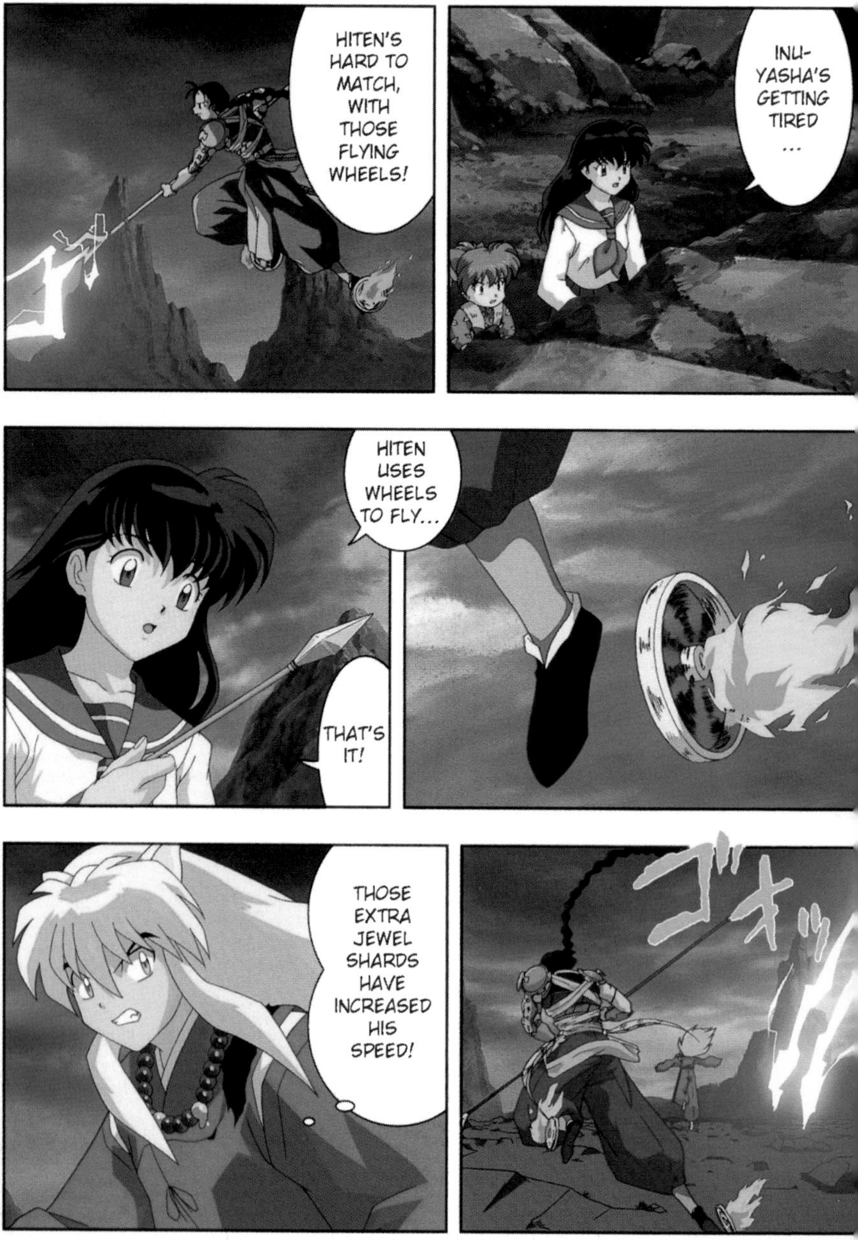
INU-YASHA'S GETTING TIRED ...
HITEN'S HARD TO MATCH, WITH THOSE FLYING WHEELS!
HITEN USES WHEELS TO FLY...
THAT'S IT!
ゴオッ
THOSE EXTRA JEWEL SHARDS HAVE INCREASED HIS SPEED!

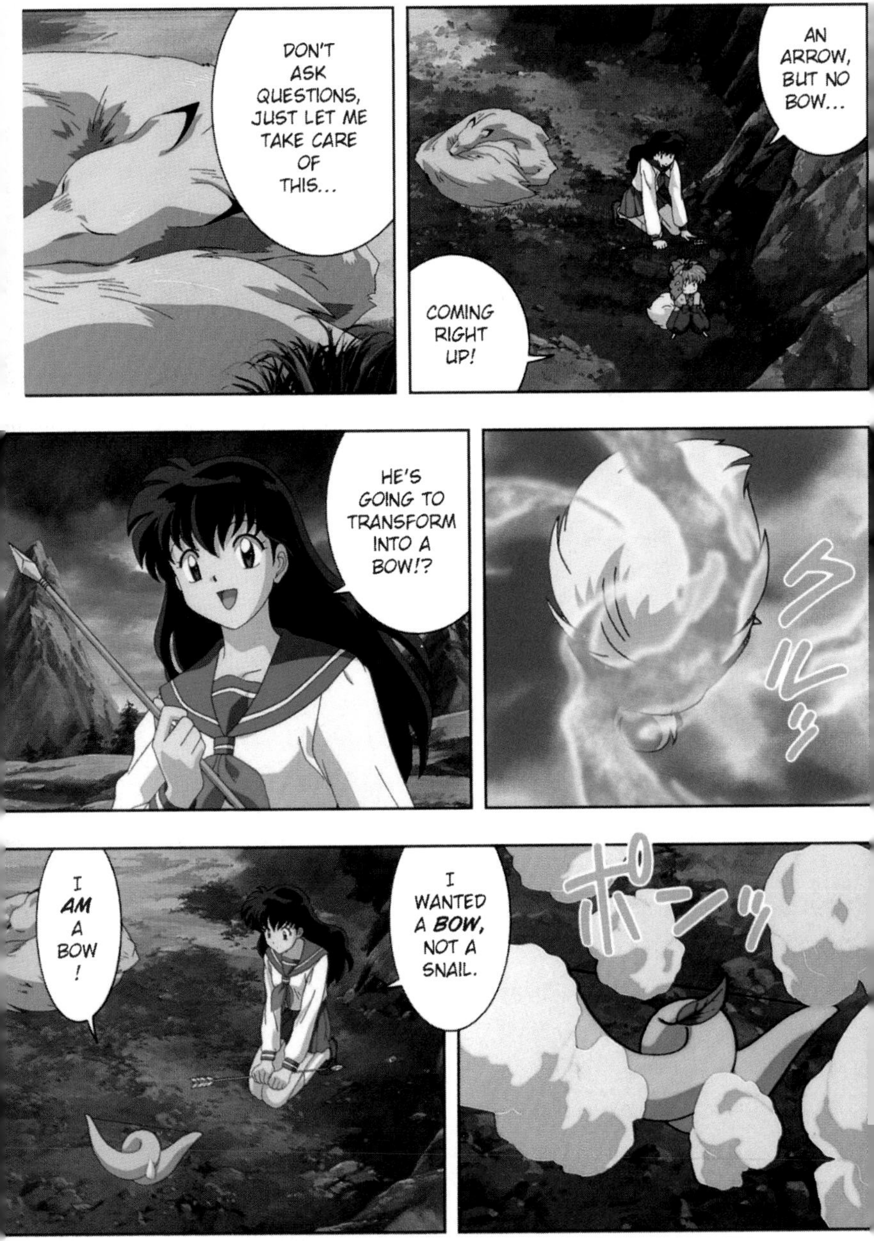
AN ARROW, BUT NO BOW...
COMING RIGHT UP!
DON'T ASK QUESTIONS, JUST LET ME TAKE CARE OF THIS...
クルッ
HE'S GOING TO TRANSFORM INTO A BOW!?
ポンッ
I WANTED A **BOW**, NOT A SNAIL.
I **AM** A BOW!

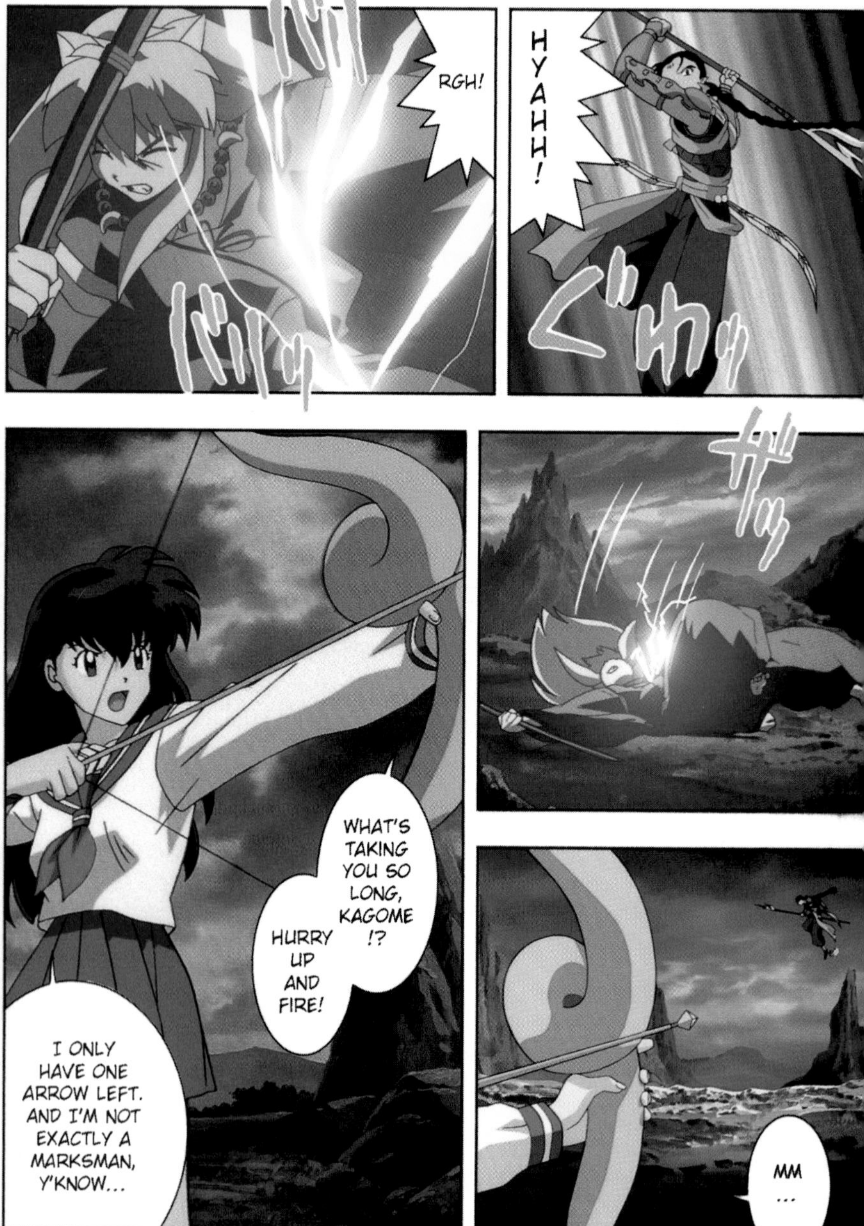
HYAHH!
ぐわッ
バリッ
RGH!
バリッ
ザッ
MM...
WHAT'S TAKING YOU SO LONG, KAGOME !?
HURRY UP AND FIRE!
I ONLY HAVE ONE ARROW LEFT. AND I'M NOT EXACTLY A MARKSMAN, Y'KNOW...

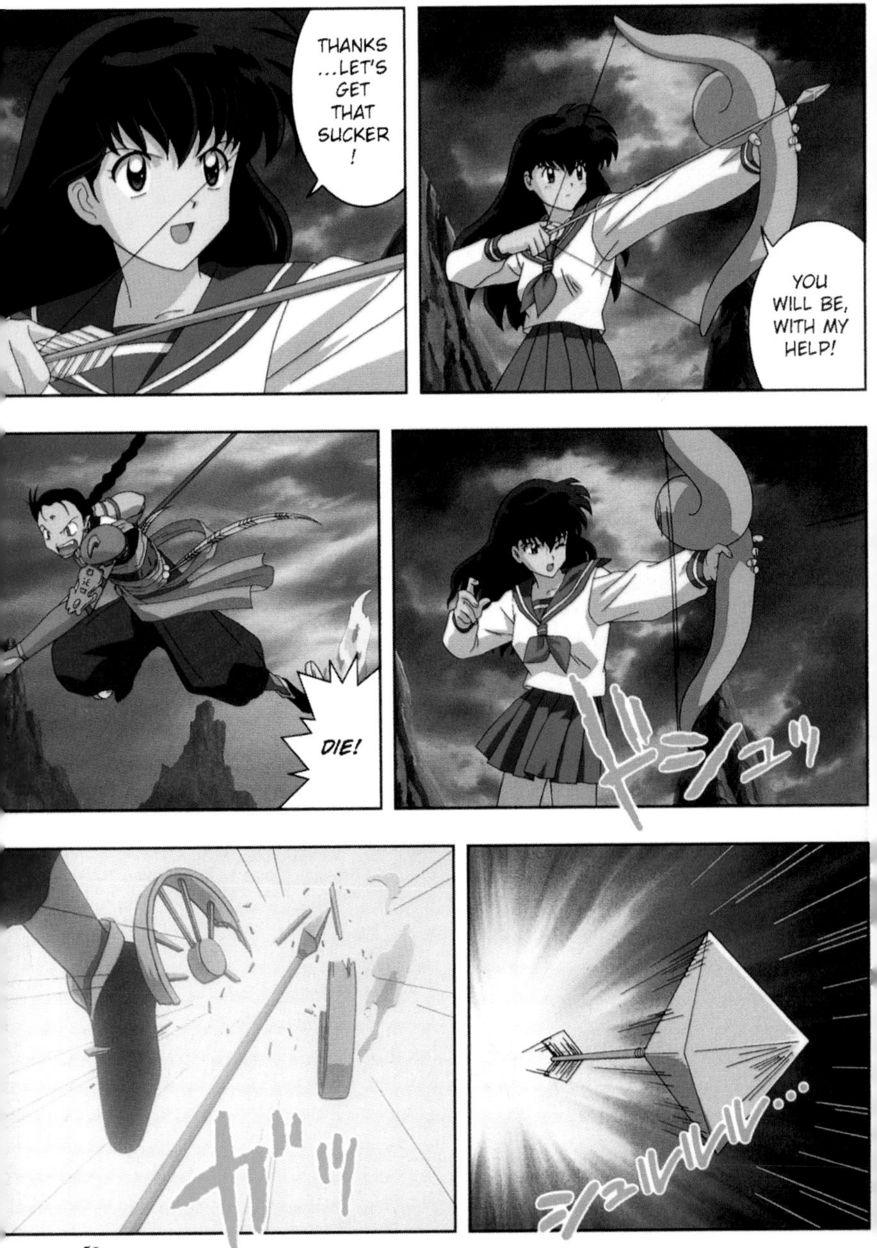
YOU WILL BE, WITH MY HELP!
THANKS ...LET'S GET THAT SUCKER!
ドシュッ
DIE!
シュルルルル…
ガッ

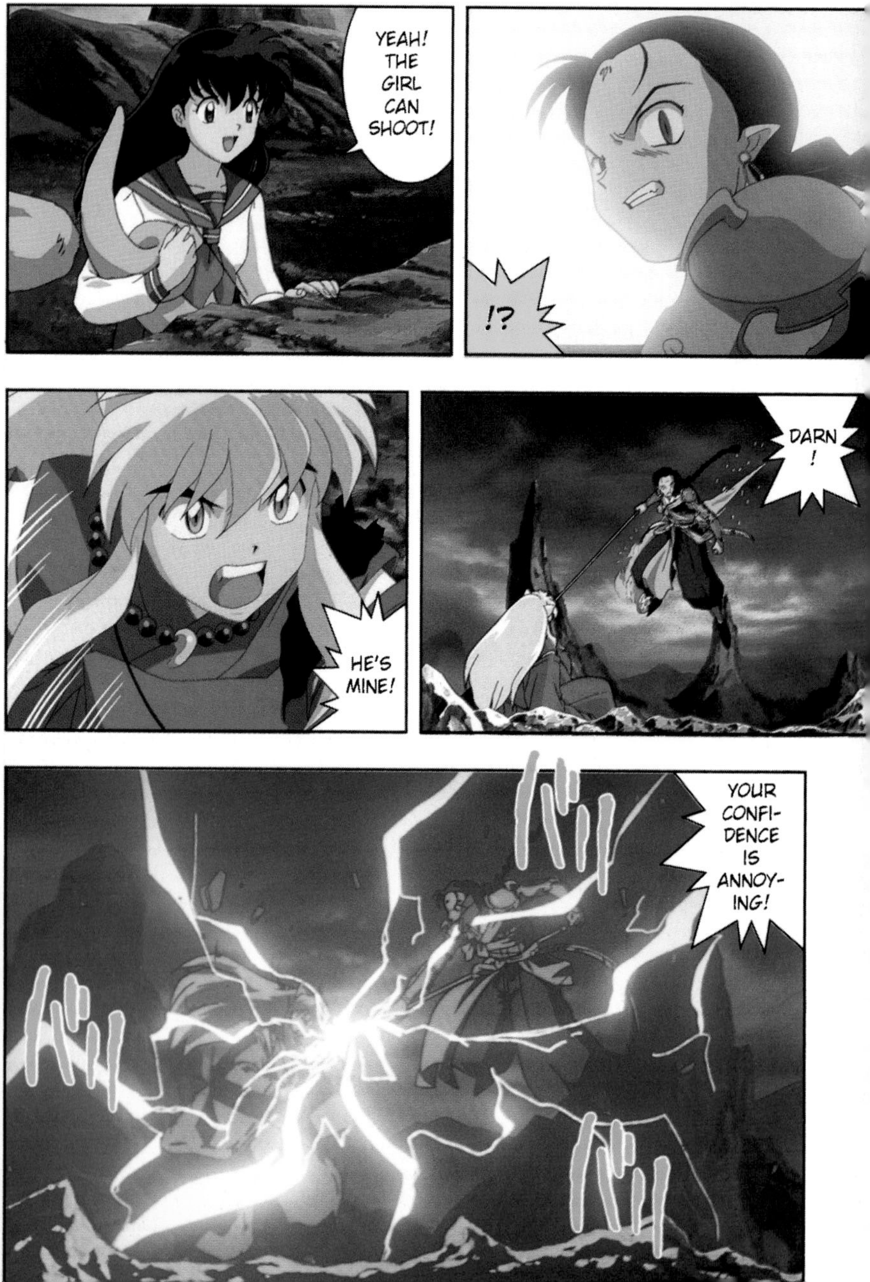
!?
YEAH! THE GIRL CAN SHOOT!
DARN!
HE'S MINE!
YOUR CONFIDENCE IS ANNOYING!

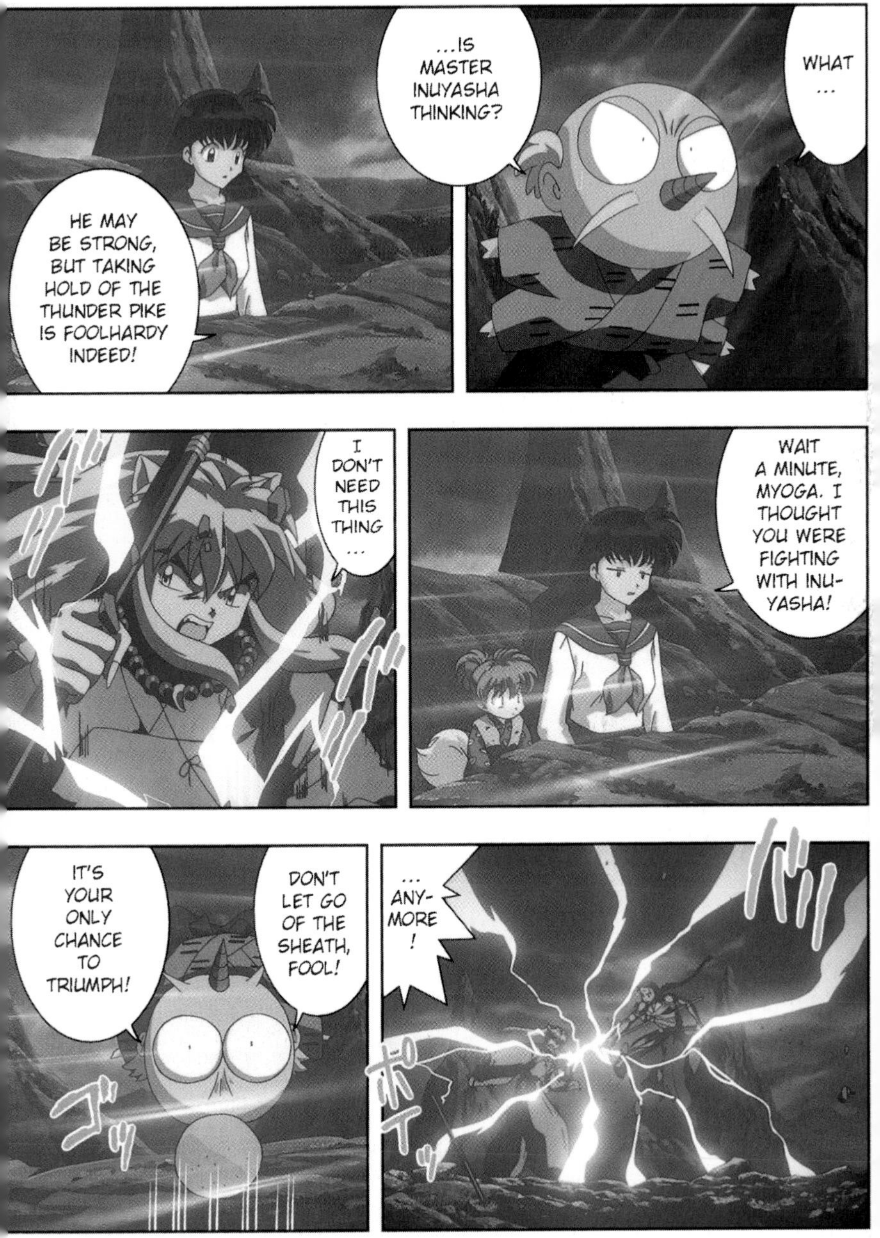
WHAT ...
...IS MASTER INUYASHA THINKING?
HE MAY BE STRONG, BUT TAKING HOLD OF THE THUNDER PIKE IS FOOLHARDY INDEED!
WAIT A MINUTE, MYOGA. I THOUGHT YOU WERE FIGHTING WITH INU-YASHA!
I DON'T NEED THIS THING ...
... ANY-MORE!
DON'T LET GO OF THE SHEATH, FOOL!
IT'S YOUR ONLY CHANCE TO TRIUMPH!

I'LL DO THINGS MY WAY!

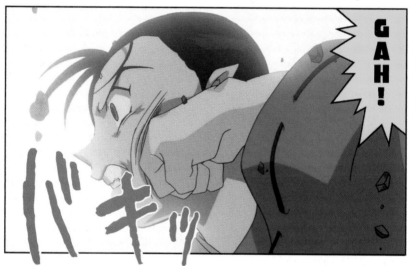

GAH!

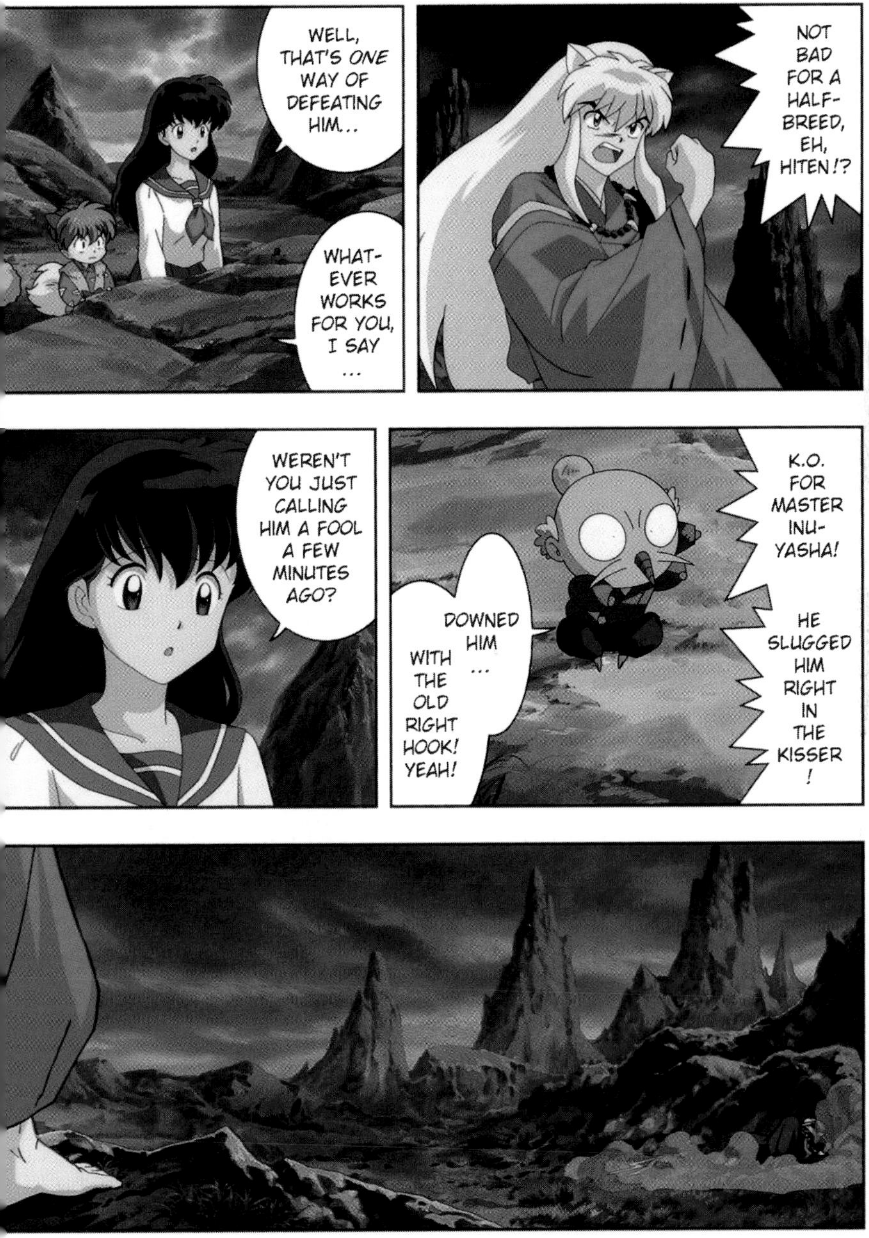
NOT BAD FOR A HALF-BREED, EH, HITEN!?
WELL, THAT'S *ONE* WAY OF DEFEATING HIM...
WHAT-EVER WORKS FOR YOU, I SAY...
K.O. FOR MASTER INU-YASHA!
HE SLUGGED HIM RIGHT IN THE KISSER!
DOWNED HIM...
WITH THE OLD RIGHT HOOK! YEAH!
WEREN'T YOU JUST CALLING HIM A FOOL A FEW MINUTES AGO?

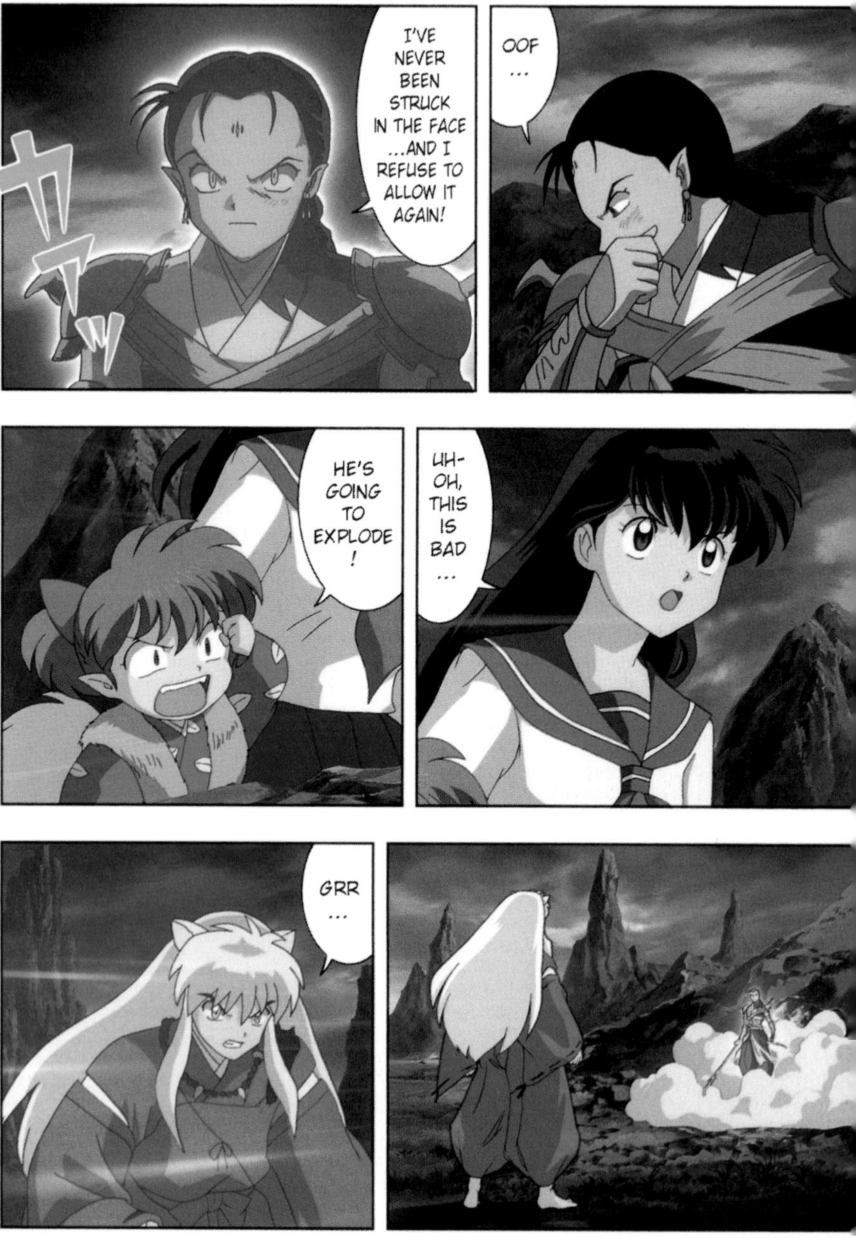
OOF ...
I'VE NEVER BEEN STRUCK IN THE FACE ...AND I REFUSE TO ALLOW IT AGAIN!
UH-OH, THIS IS BAD ...
HE'S GOING TO EXPLODE!
GRR ...

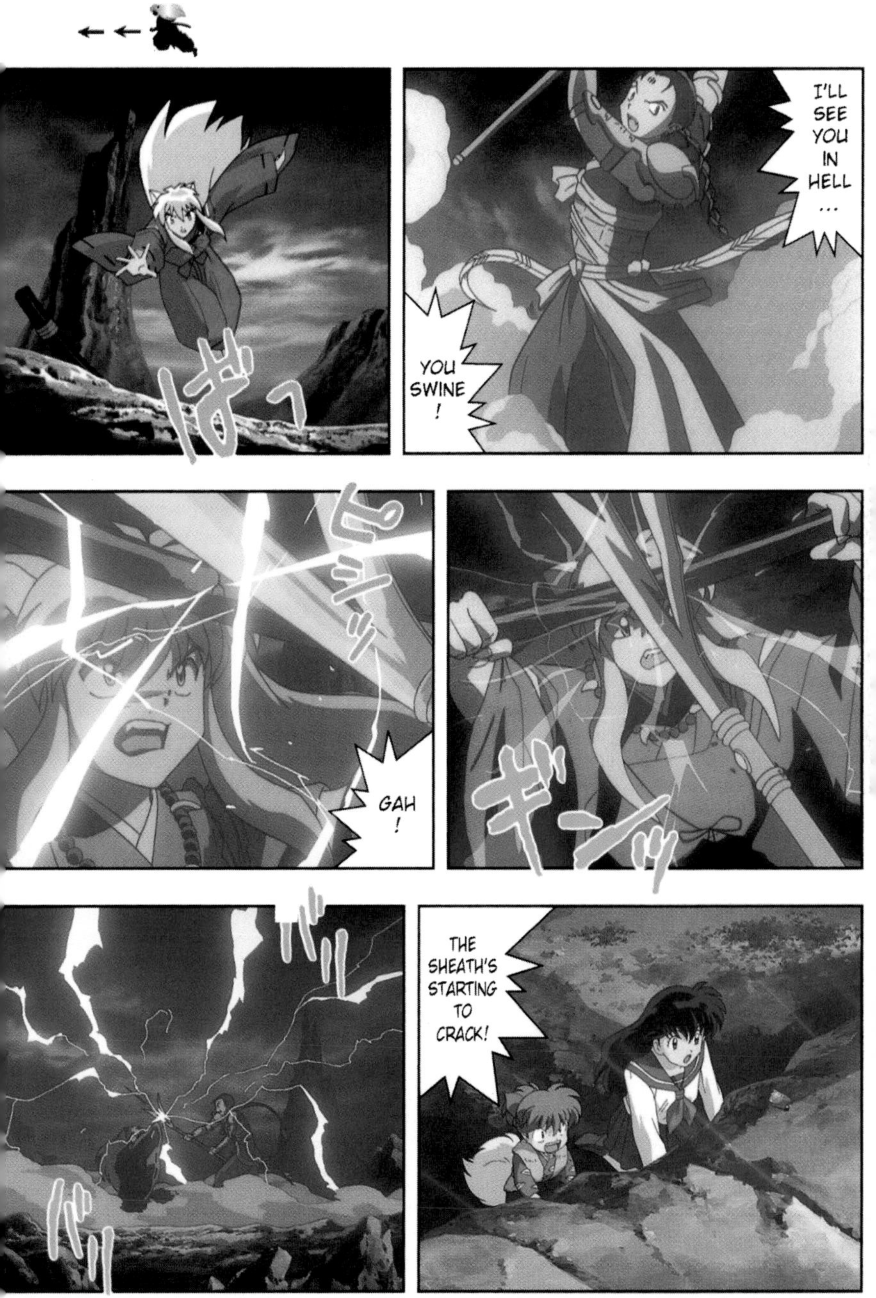
I'LL SEE YOU IN HELL...
YOU SWINE!
ばっ
ギーンッ
ピシッ
GAH!
THE SHEATH'S STARTING TO CRACK!
バリ
バリ

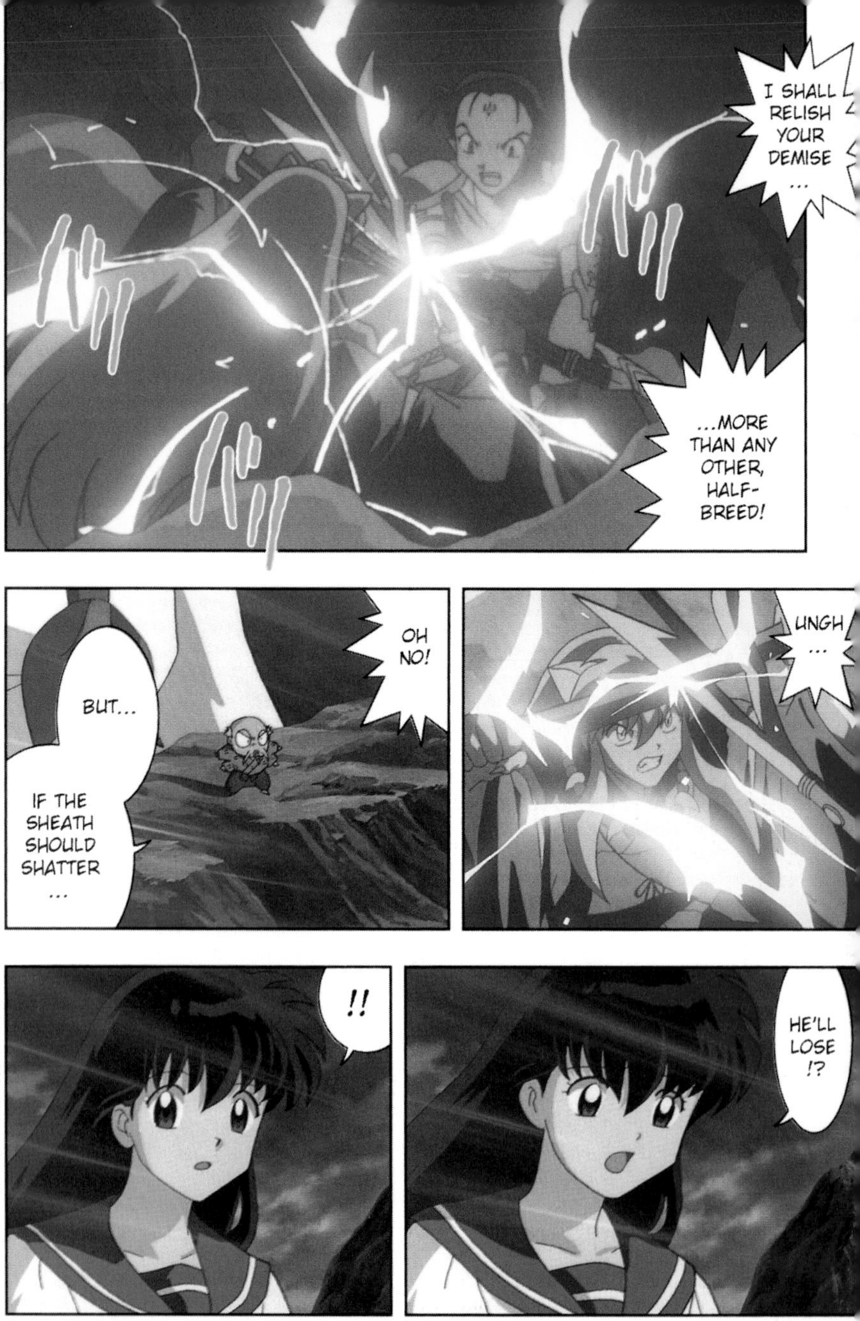
I SHALL RELISH YOUR DEMISE ...
...MORE THAN ANY OTHER, HALF-BREED!
UNGH ...
OH NO!
BUT...
IF THE SHEATH SHOULD SHATTER ...
HE'LL LOSE !?
!!

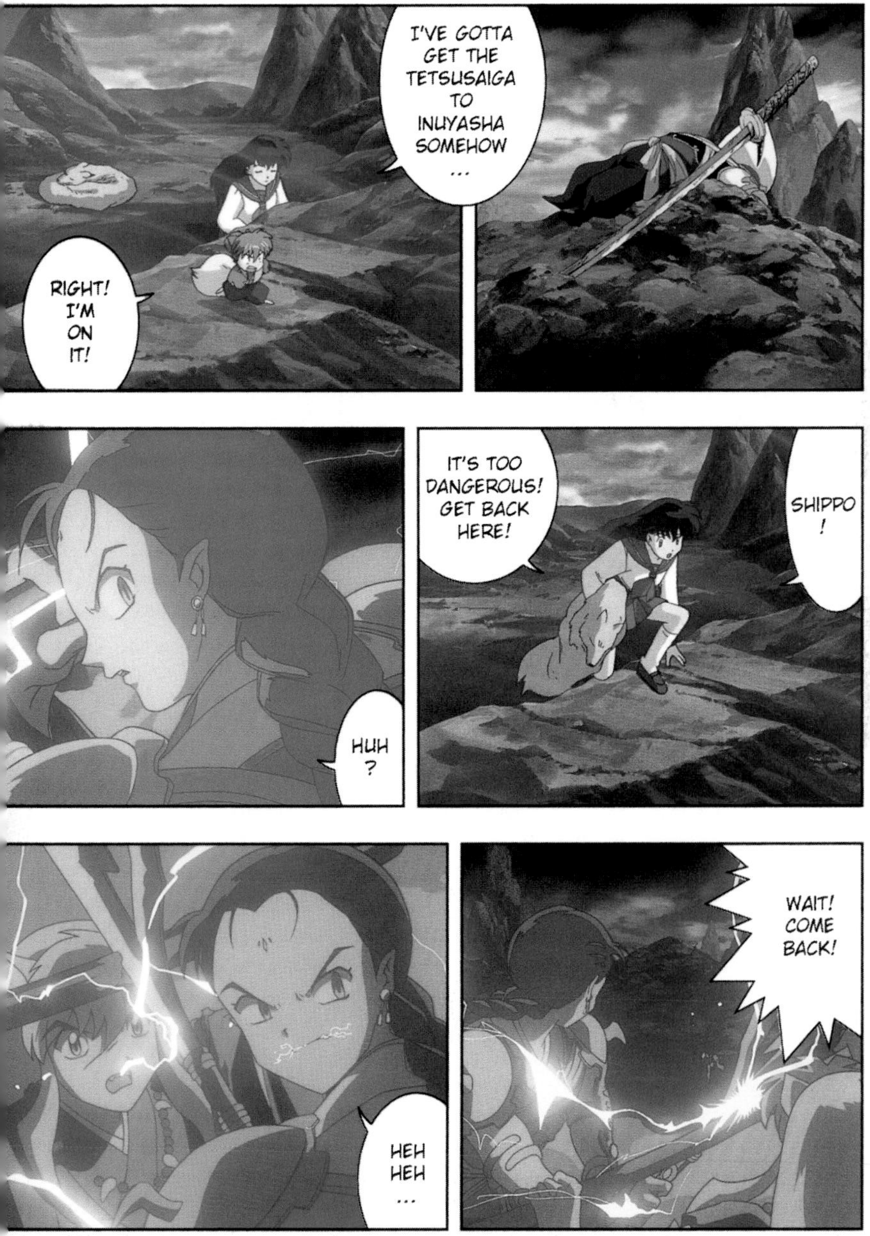
I'VE GOTTA GET THE TETSUSAIGA TO INUYASHA SOMEHOW ...
RIGHT! I'M ON IT!
SHIPPO!
IT'S TOO DANGEROUS! GET BACK HERE!
HUH?
WAIT! COME BACK!
HEH HEH ...

HITEN MUST'VE GAINED MANTEN'S ABILITIES ...

...AS **WELL** AS HIS JEWEL SHARDS!

KAGOME! RUN FOR IT!

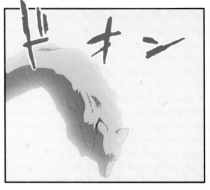

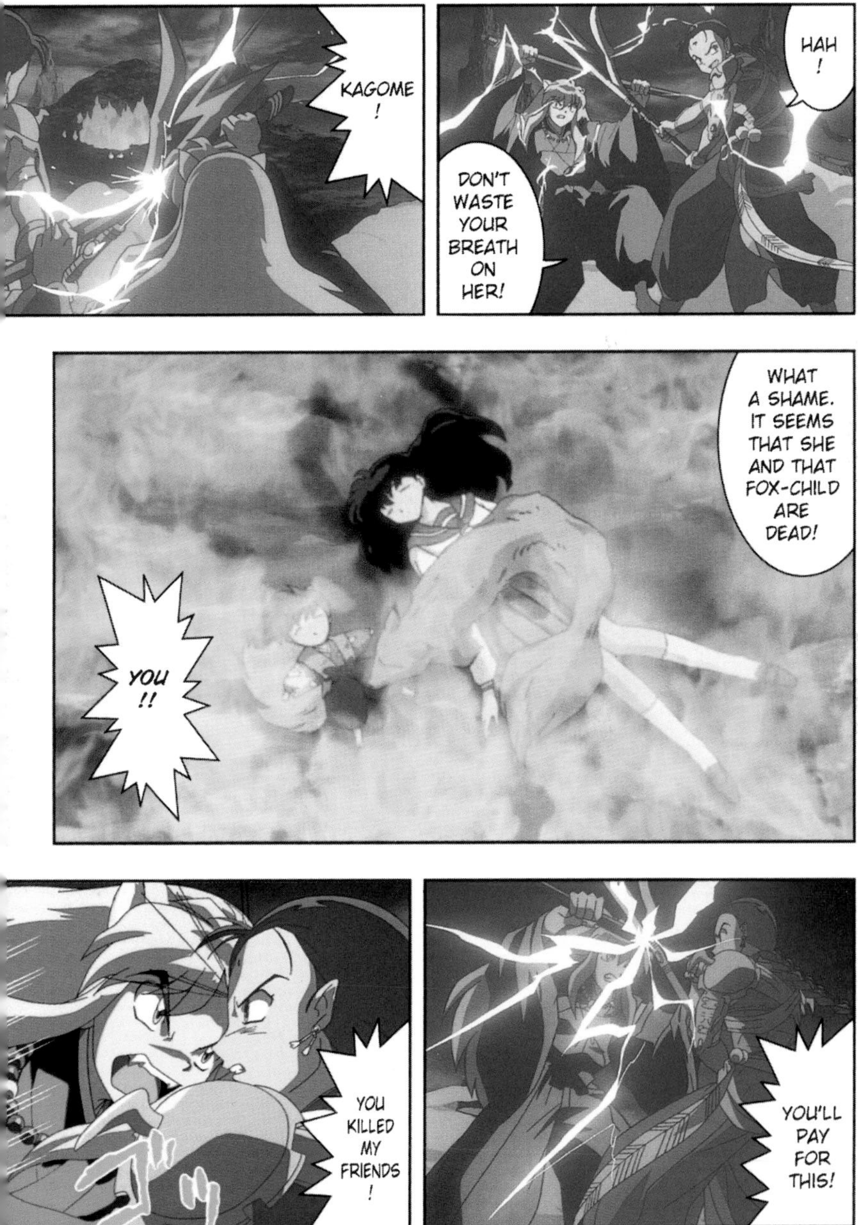

HAH!
DON'T WASTE YOUR BREATH ON HER!
KAGOME!
WHAT A SHAME. IT SEEMS THAT SHE AND THAT FOX-CHILD ARE DEAD!
YOU!!
YOU'LL PAY FOR THIS!
YOU KILLED MY FRIENDS!

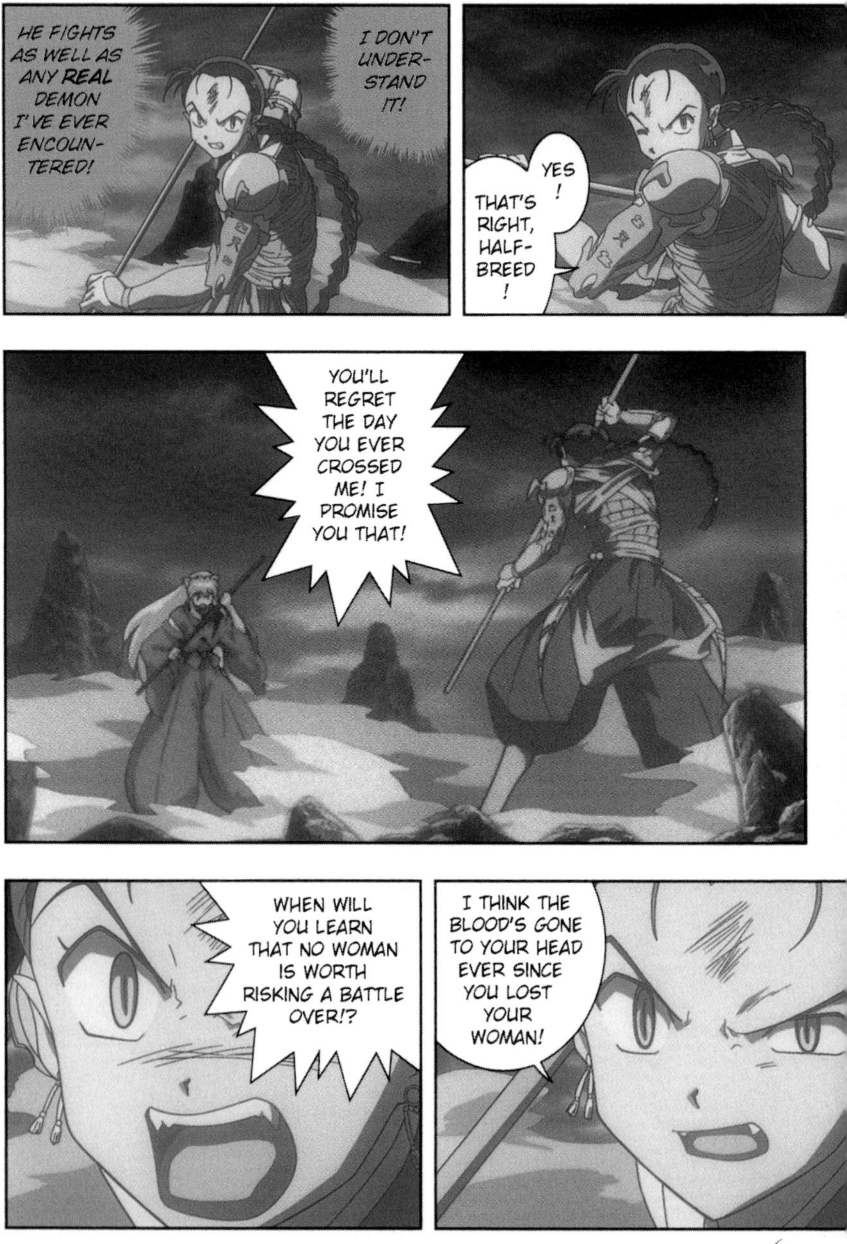
YES! THAT'S RIGHT, HALF-BREED!
I DON'T UNDER-STAND IT!
HE FIGHTS AS WELL AS ANY **REAL** DEMON I'VE EVER ENCOUN-TERED!
YOU'LL REGRET THE DAY YOU EVER CROSSED ME! I PROMISE YOU THAT!
I THINK THE BLOOD'S GONE TO YOUR HEAD EVER SINCE YOU LOST YOUR WOMAN!
WHEN WILL YOU LEARN THAT NO WOMAN IS WORTH RISKING A BATTLE OVER!?

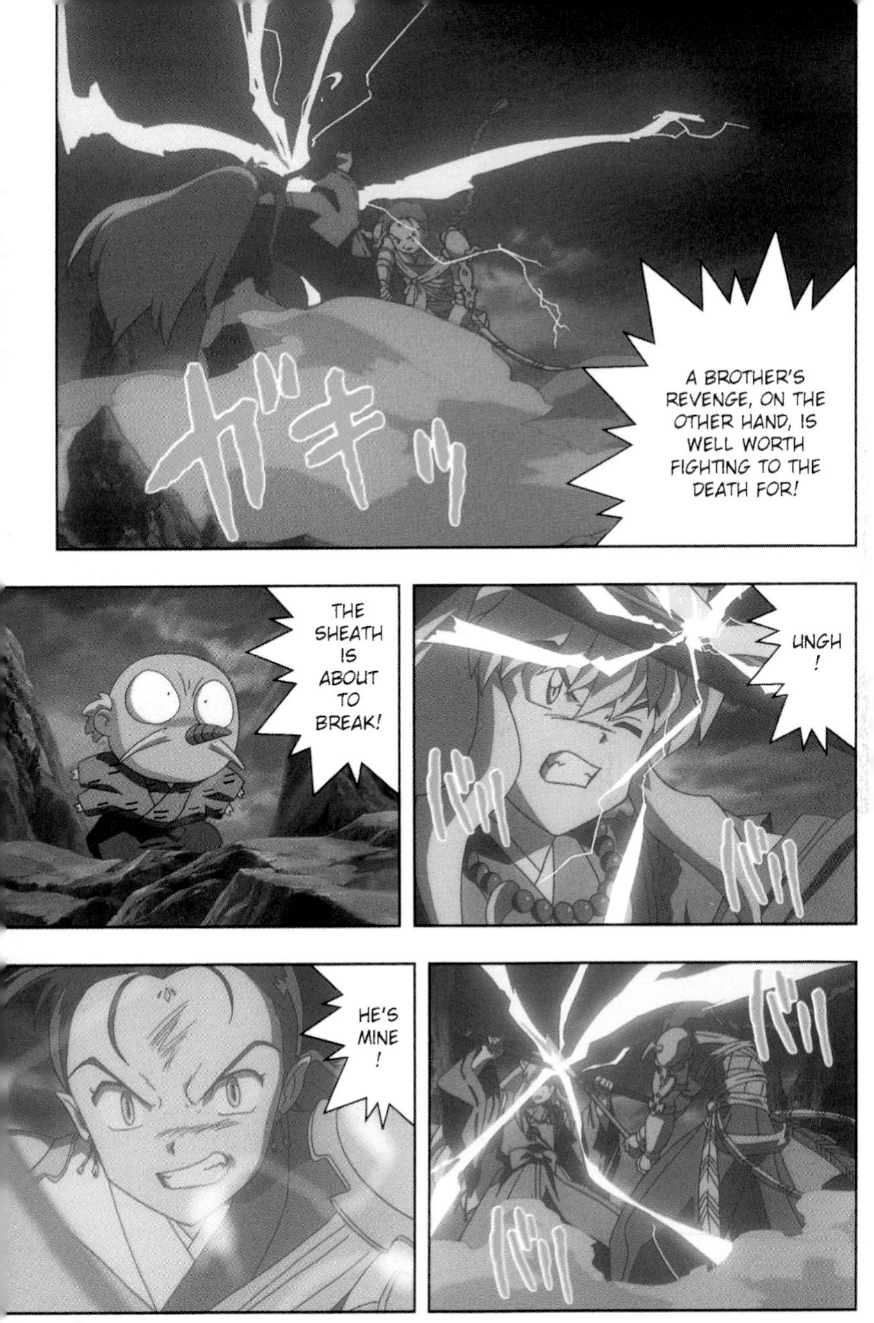
A BROTHER'S REVENGE, ON THE OTHER HAND, IS WELL WORTH FIGHTING TO THE DEATH FOR!
ガギッ
UNGH!
バリ
バリ
THE SHEATH IS ABOUT TO BREAK!
バリ
バリ
HE'S MINE!

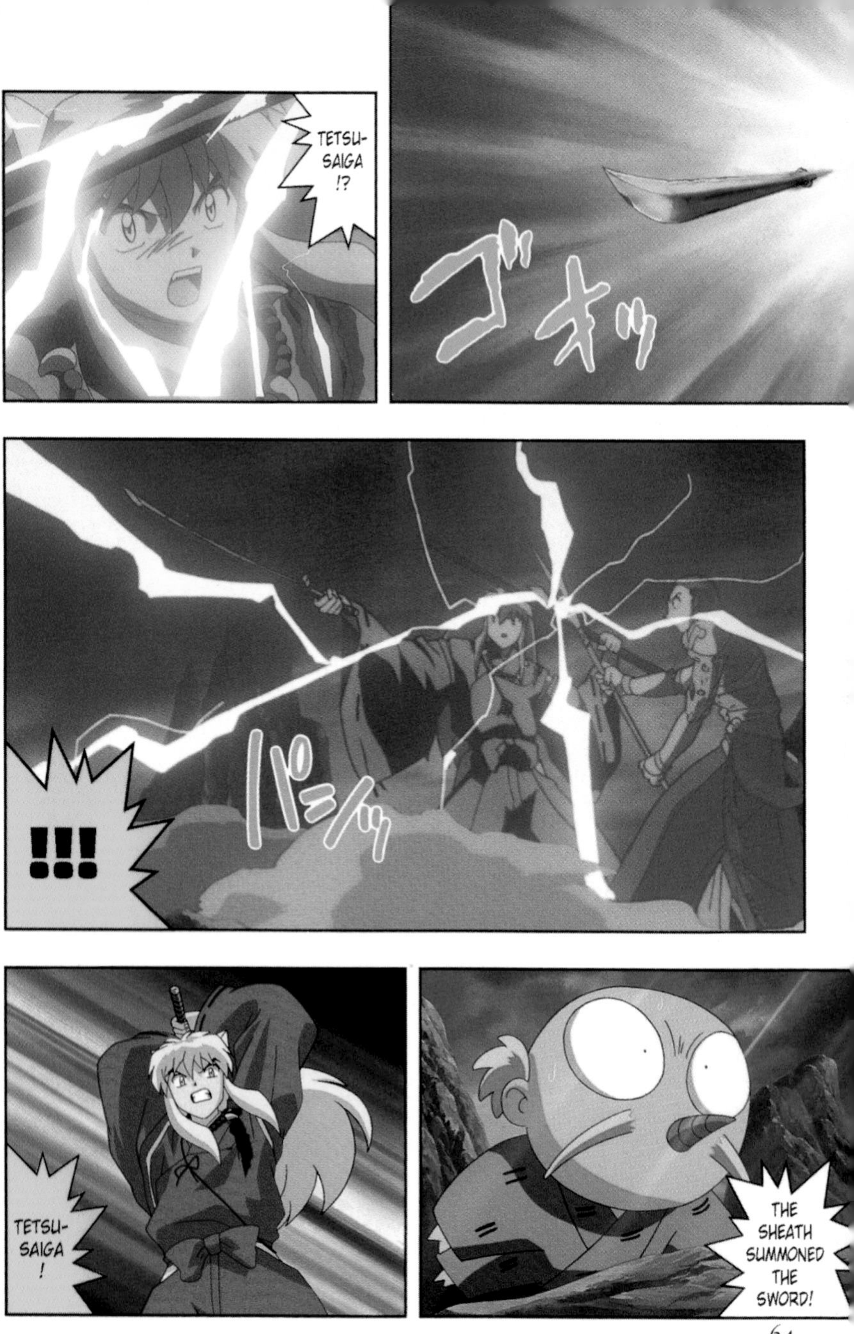
ゴオッ
TETSU-SAIGA !?
パシッ
!!!
THE SHEATH SUMMONED THE SWORD!
TETSU-SAIGA !

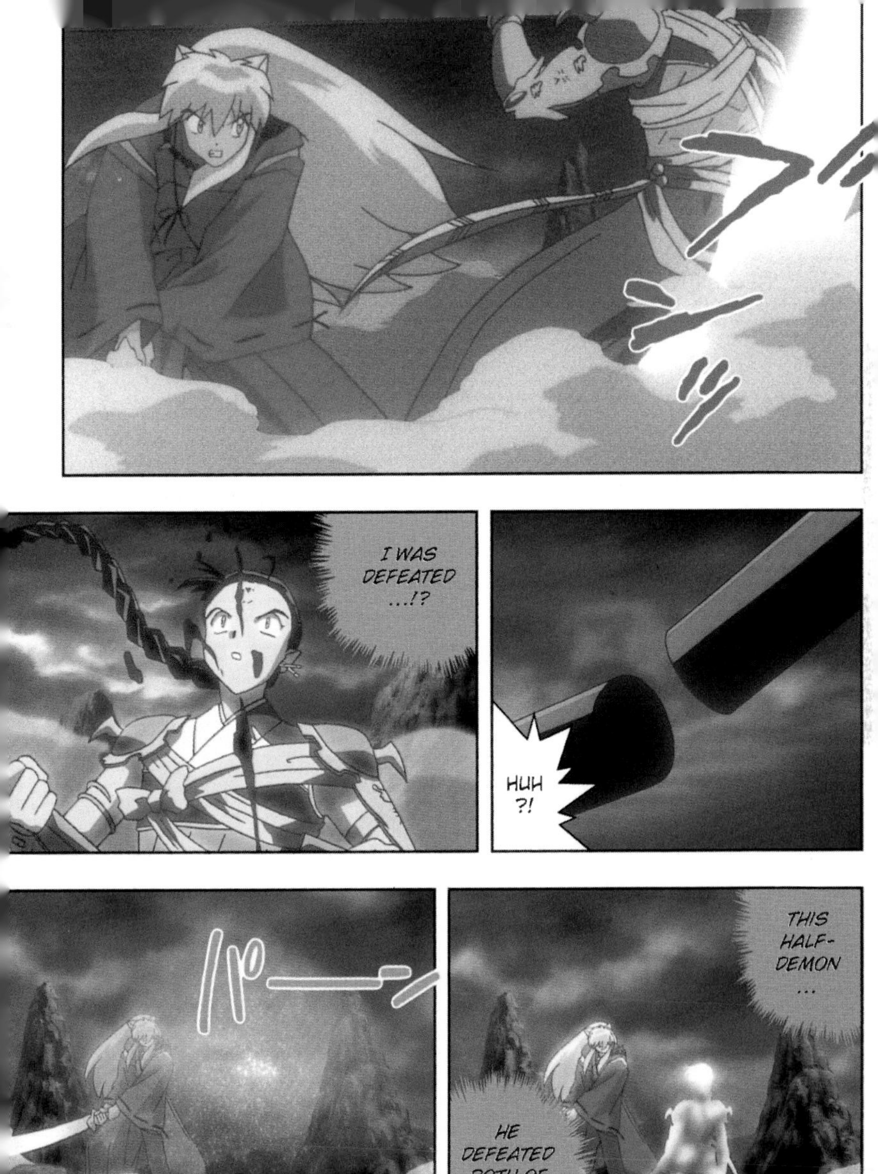
HUH ?!
I WAS DEFEATED ...!?
THIS HALF-DEMON ...
HE DEFEATED BOTH OF US!?

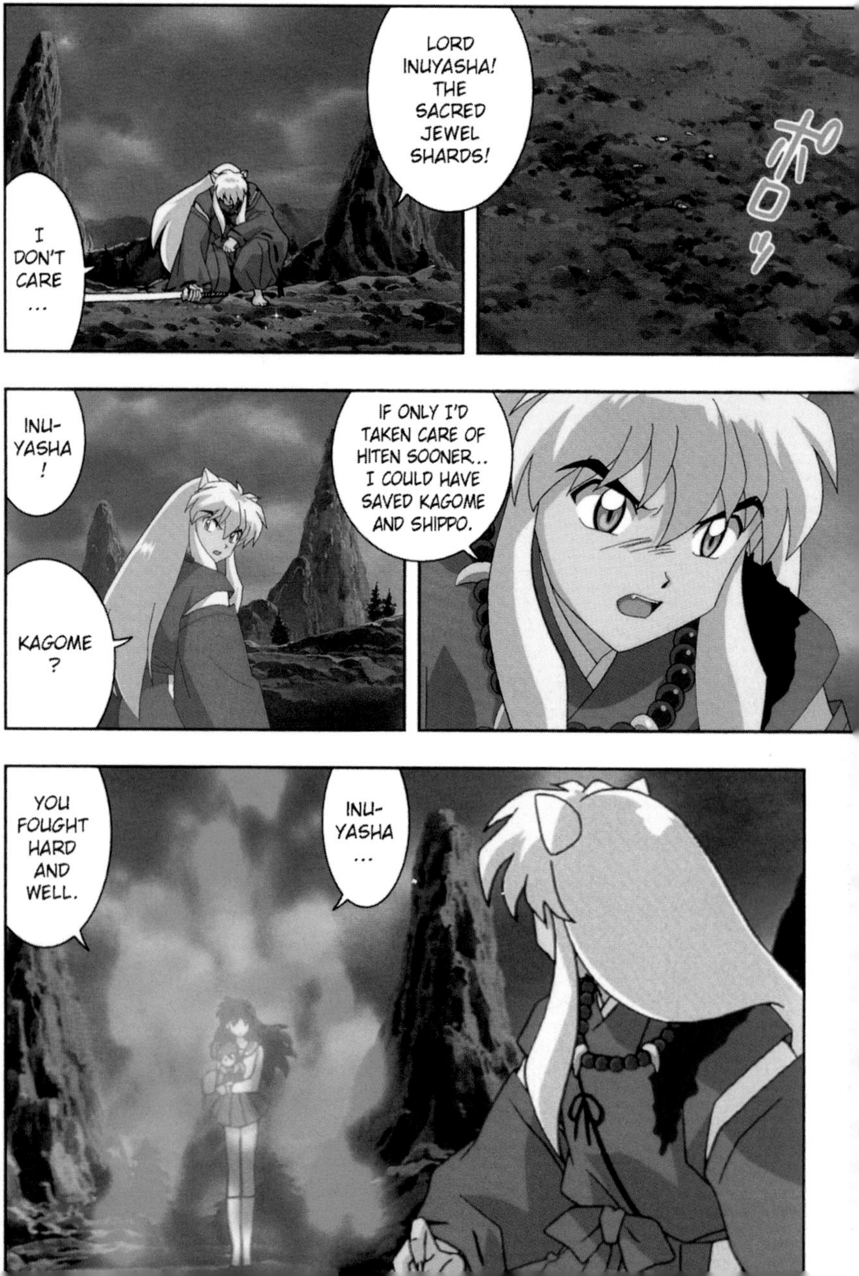

ポロッ
LORD INUYASHA! THE SACRED JEWEL SHARDS!
I DON'T CARE ...
IF ONLY I'D TAKEN CARE OF HITEN SOONER... I COULD HAVE SAVED KAGOME AND SHIPPO.
INU-YASHA!
KAGOME?
INU-YASHA ...
YOU FOUGHT HARD AND WELL.

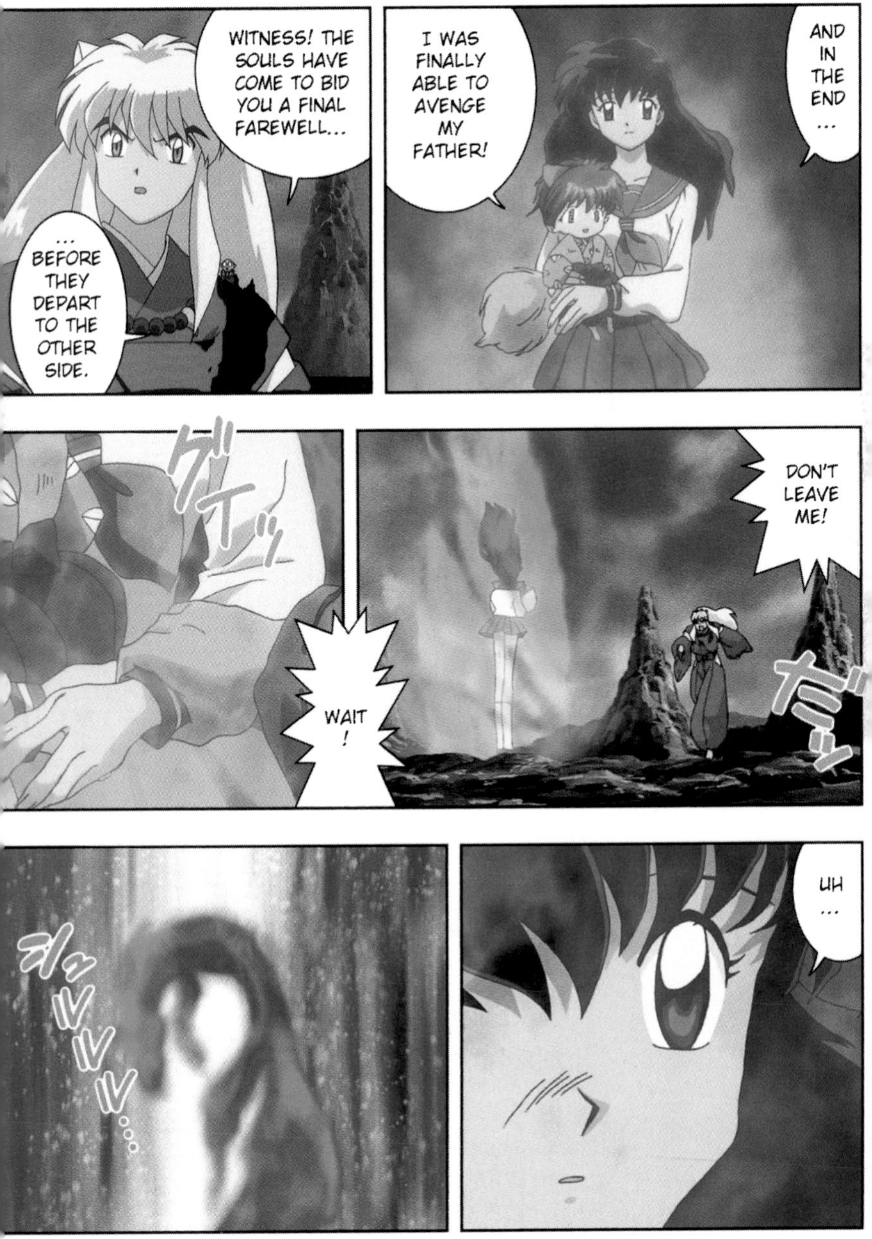
AND IN THE END ...
I WAS FINALLY ABLE TO AVENGE MY FATHER!
WITNESS! THE SOULS HAVE COME TO BID YOU A FINAL FAREWELL...
... BEFORE THEY DEPART TO THE OTHER SIDE.
DON'T LEAVE ME!
ダッ
グイッ
WAIT!
UH ...
シュゥゥゥゥ...

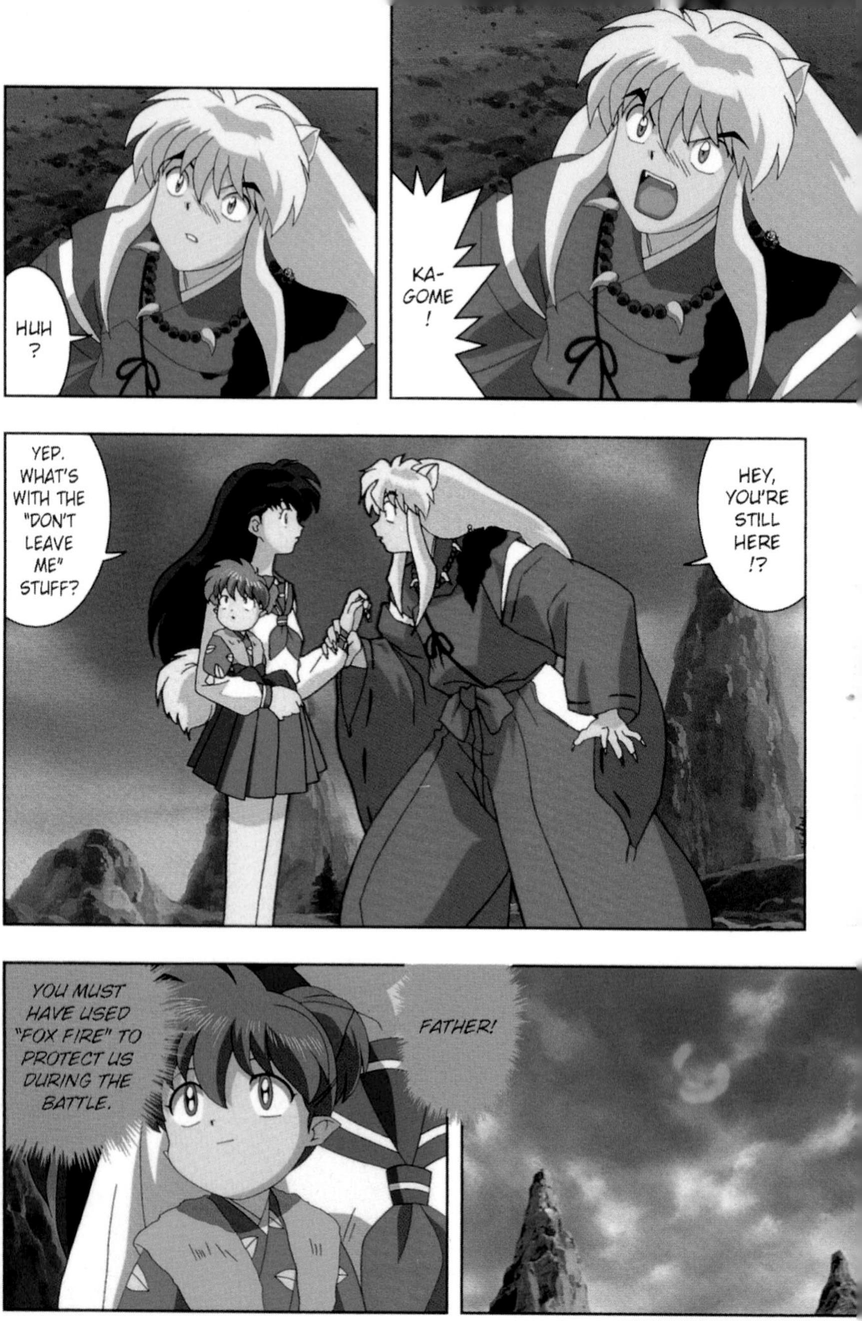
KA-GOME!
HUH?
HEY, YOU'RE STILL HERE!?
YEP. WHAT'S WITH THE "DON'T LEAVE ME" STUFF?
FATHER!
YOU MUST HAVE USED "FOX FIRE" TO PROTECT US DURING THE BATTLE.

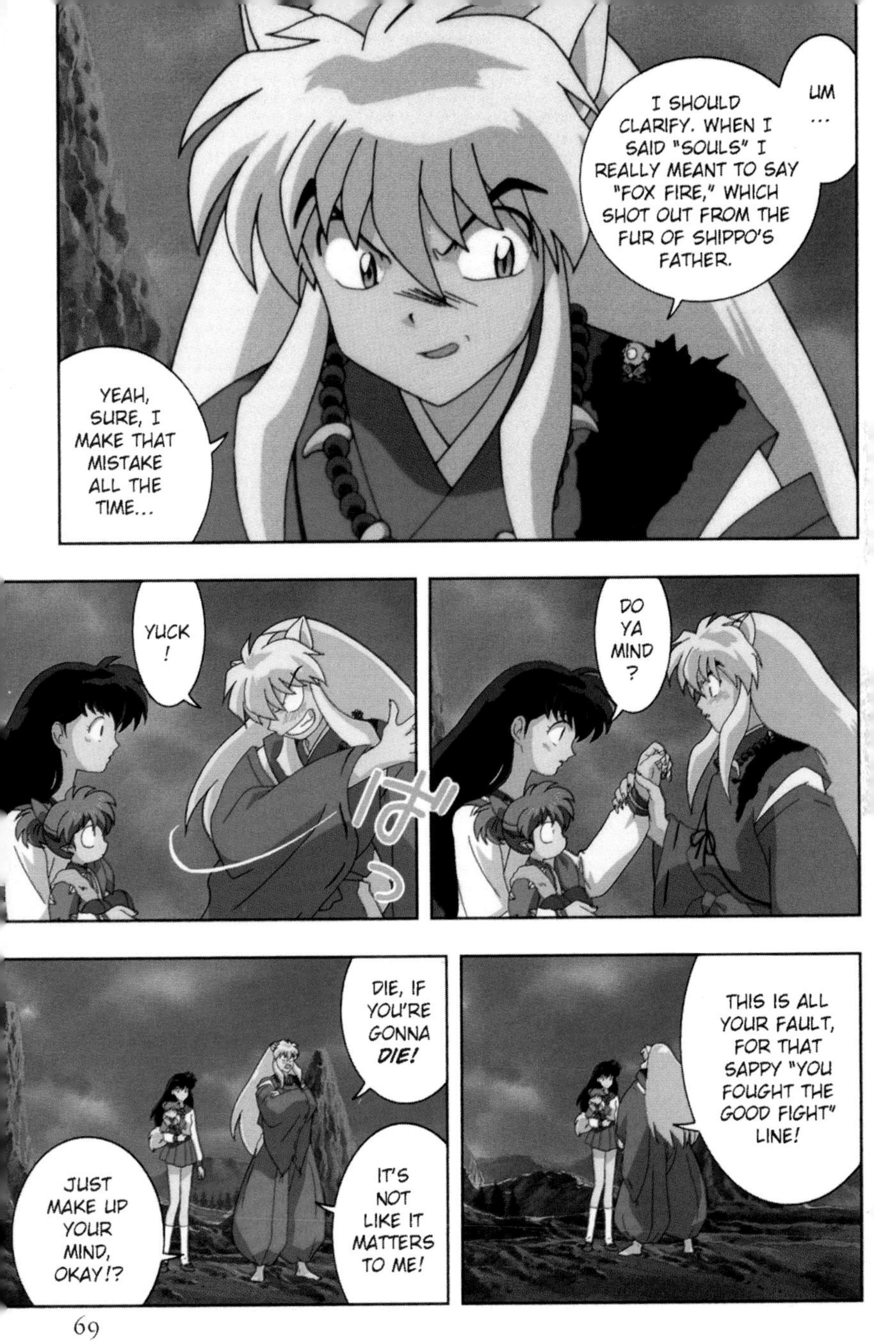
UM...
I SHOULD CLARIFY. WHEN I SAID "SOULS" I REALLY MEANT TO SAY "FOX FIRE," WHICH SHOT OUT FROM THE FUR OF SHIPPO'S FATHER.
YEAH, SURE, I MAKE THAT MISTAKE ALL THE TIME...
DO YA MIND?
YUCK!
ぱっ
THIS IS ALL YOUR FAULT, FOR THAT SAPPY "YOU FOUGHT THE GOOD FIGHT" LINE!
DIE, IF YOU'RE GONNA *DIE!*
IT'S NOT LIKE IT MATTERS TO ME!
JUST MAKE UP YOUR MIND, OKAY!?

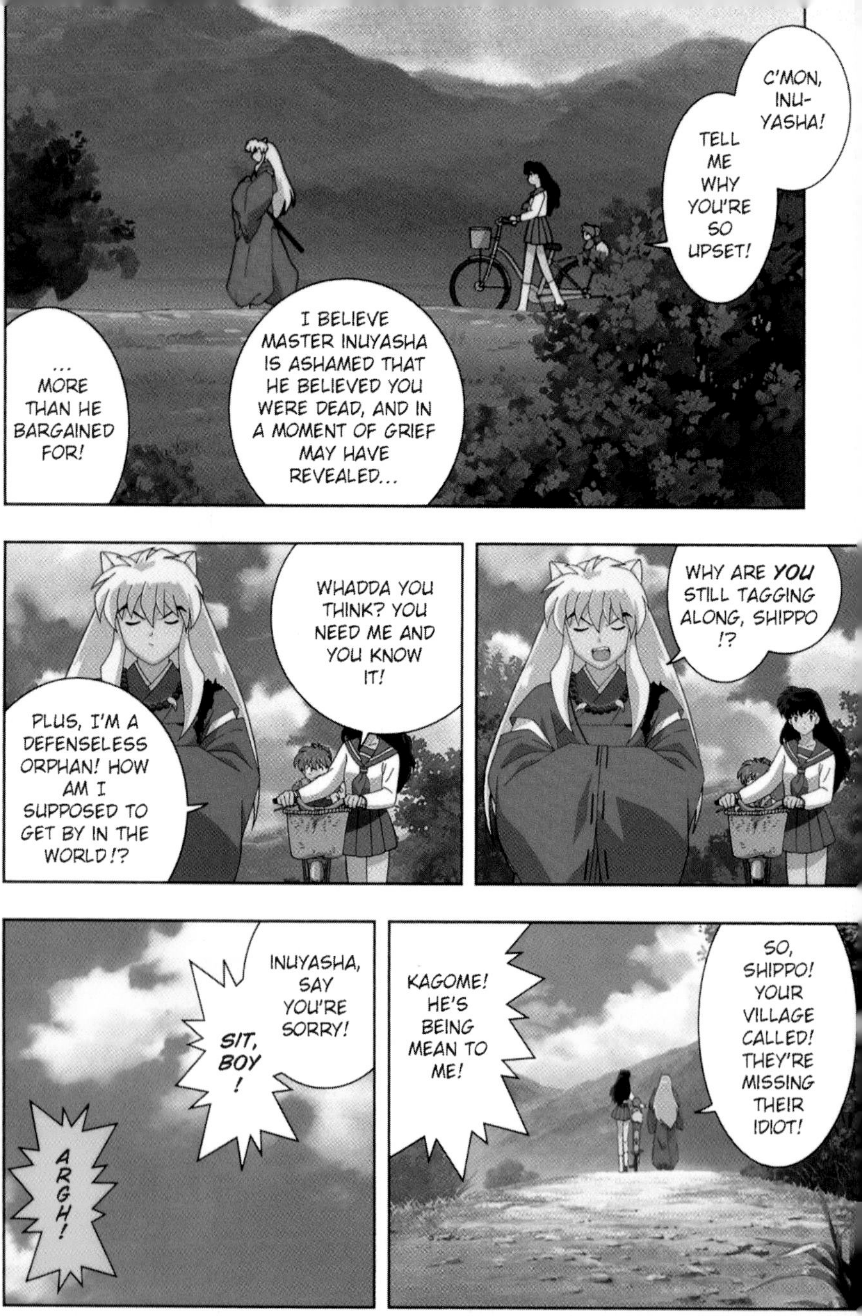
C'MON, INU-YASHA!
TELL ME WHY YOU'RE SO UPSET!
I BELIEVE MASTER INUYASHA IS ASHAMED THAT HE BELIEVED YOU WERE DEAD, AND IN A MOMENT OF GRIEF MAY HAVE REVEALED...
... MORE THAN HE BARGAINED FOR!
WHY ARE *YOU* STILL TAGGING ALONG, SHIPPO !?
WHADDA YOU THINK? YOU NEED ME AND YOU KNOW IT!
PLUS, I'M A DEFENSELESS ORPHAN! HOW AM I SUPPOSED TO GET BY IN THE WORLD!?
SO, SHIPPO! YOUR VILLAGE CALLED! THEY'RE MISSING THEIR IDIOT!
KAGOME! HE'S BEING MEAN TO ME!
INUYASHA, SAY YOU'RE SORRY!
SIT, BOY!
ARGH!

11
Terror of the Ancient Noh Mask

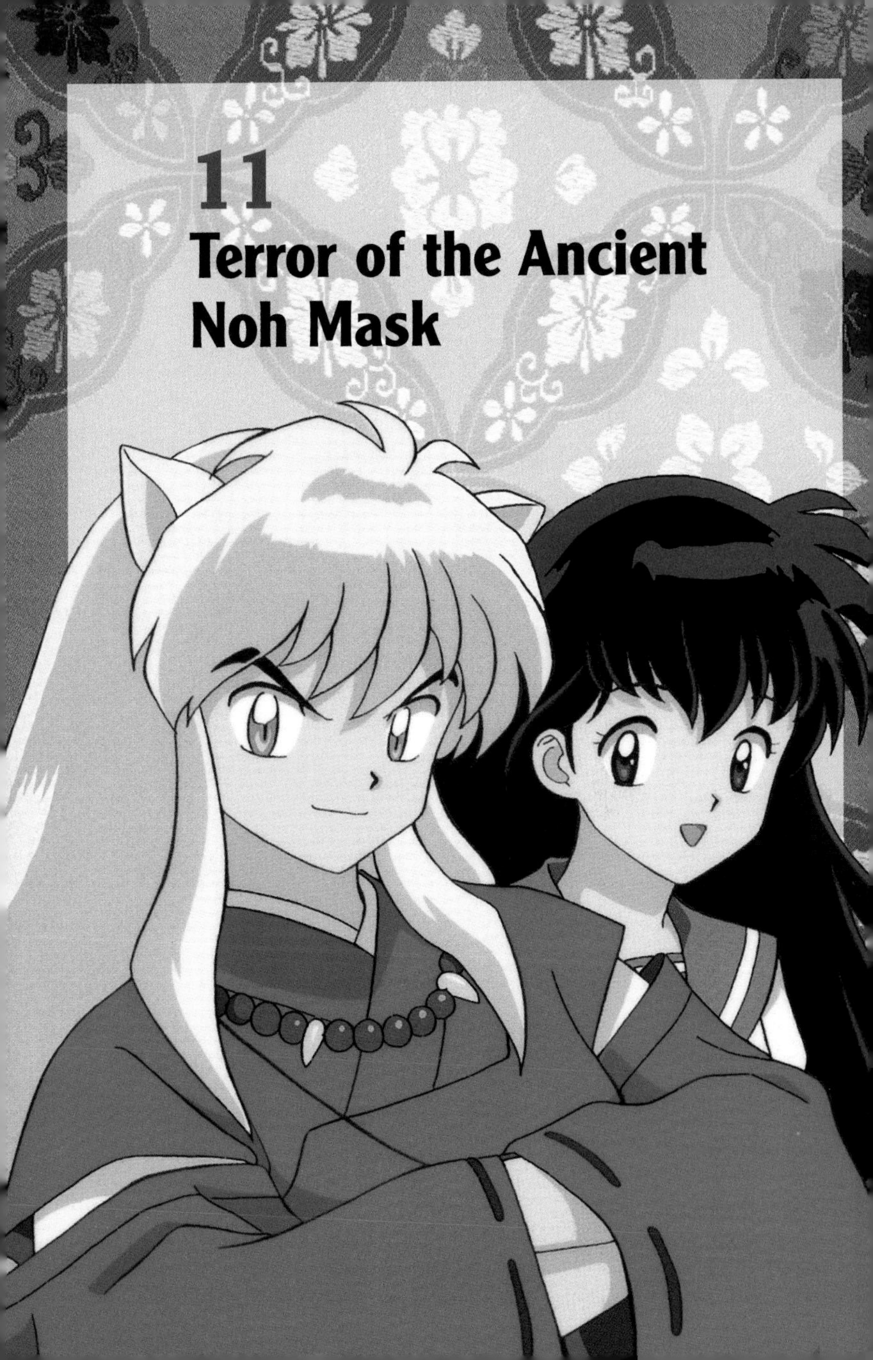

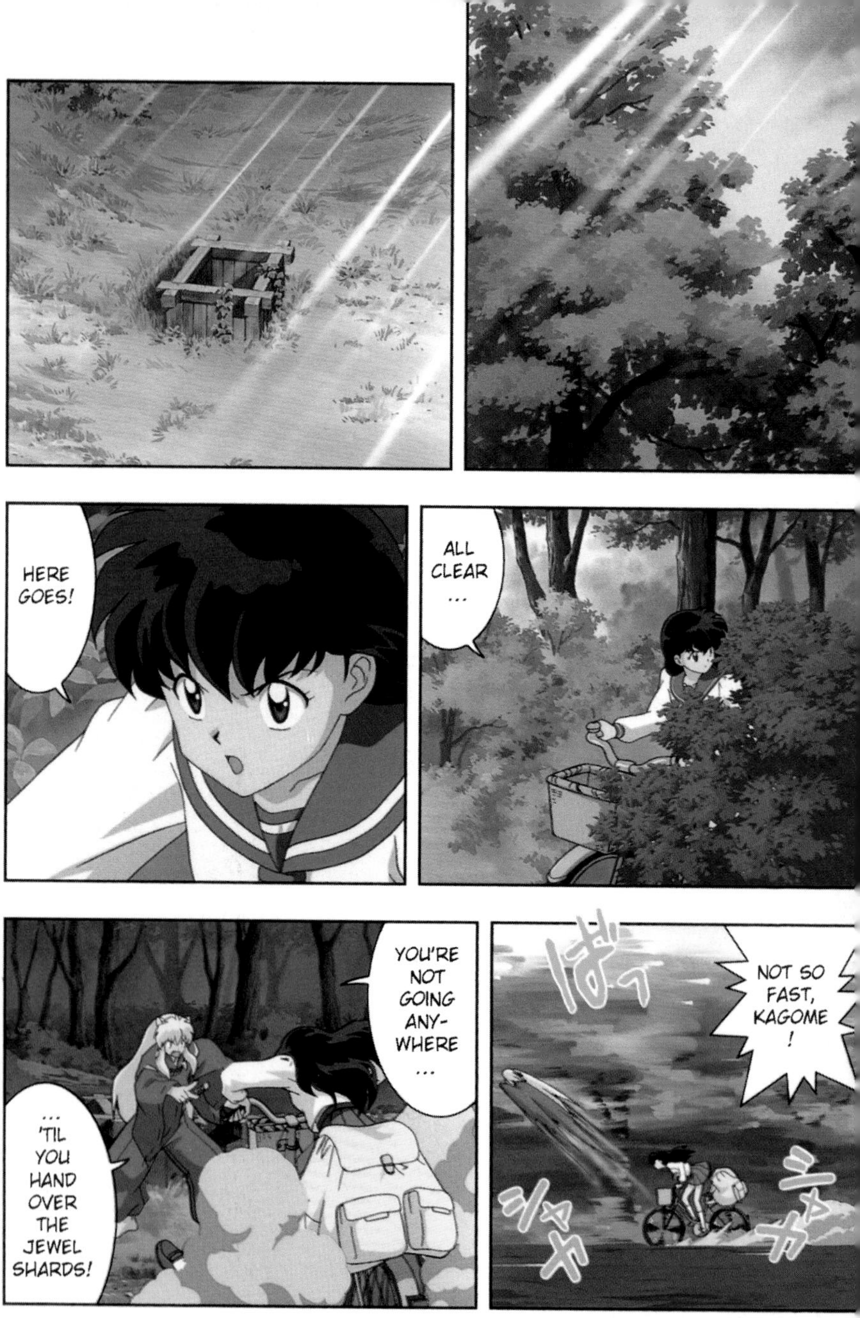
ALL CLEAR ...
HERE GOES!
ばっ
NOT SO FAST, KAGOME !
シャカ
シャカ
YOU'RE NOT GOING ANY-WHERE ...
... 'TIL YOU HAND OVER THE JEWEL SHARDS!

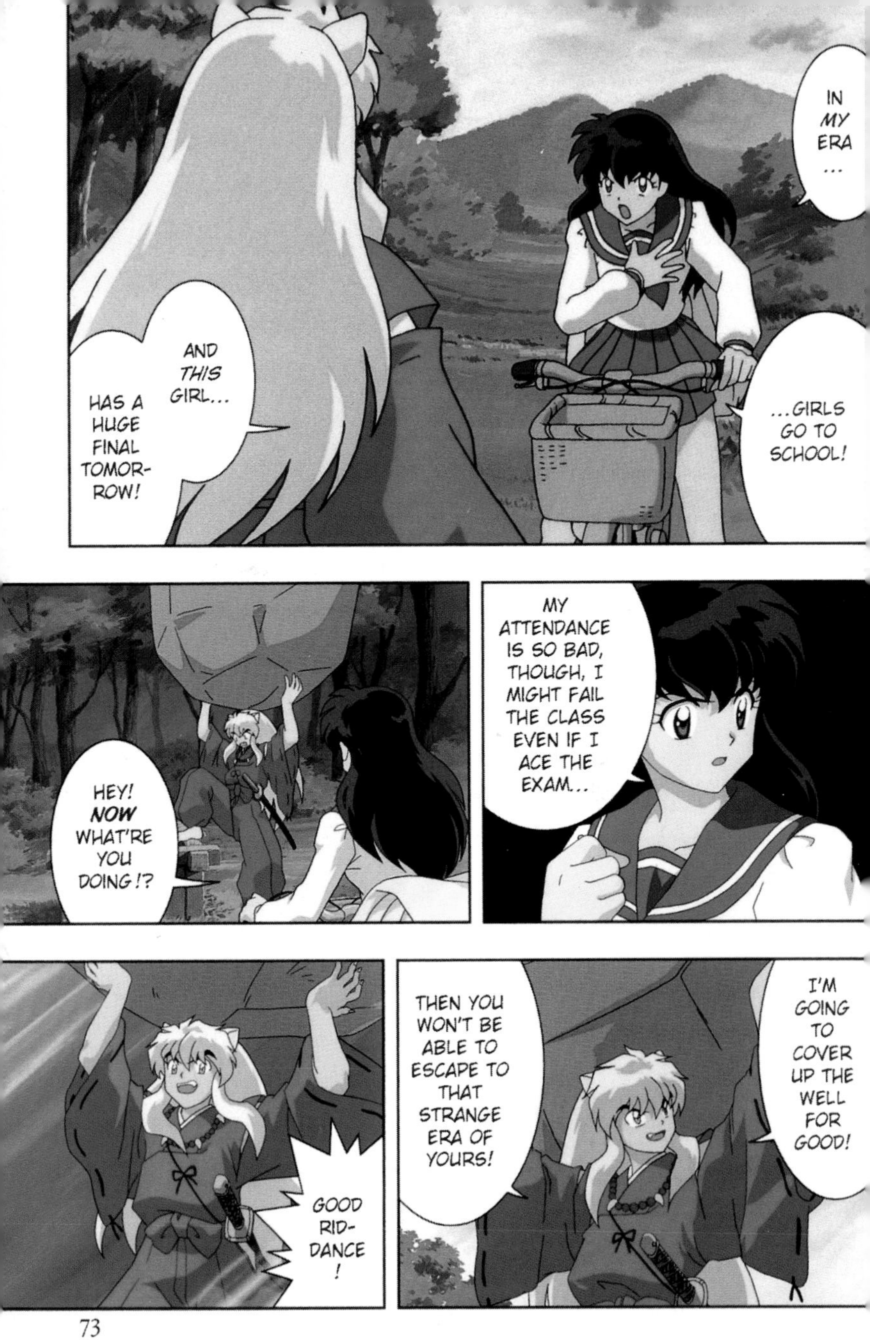
IN MY ERA...
...GIRLS GO TO SCHOOL!
AND THIS GIRL... HAS A HUGE FINAL TOMORROW!
MY ATTENDANCE IS SO BAD, THOUGH, I MIGHT FAIL THE CLASS EVEN IF I ACE THE EXAM...
HEY! NOW WHAT'RE YOU DOING!?
I'M GOING TO COVER UP THE WELL FOR GOOD!
THEN YOU WON'T BE ABLE TO ESCAPE TO THAT STRANGE ERA OF YOURS!
GOOD RIDDANCE!

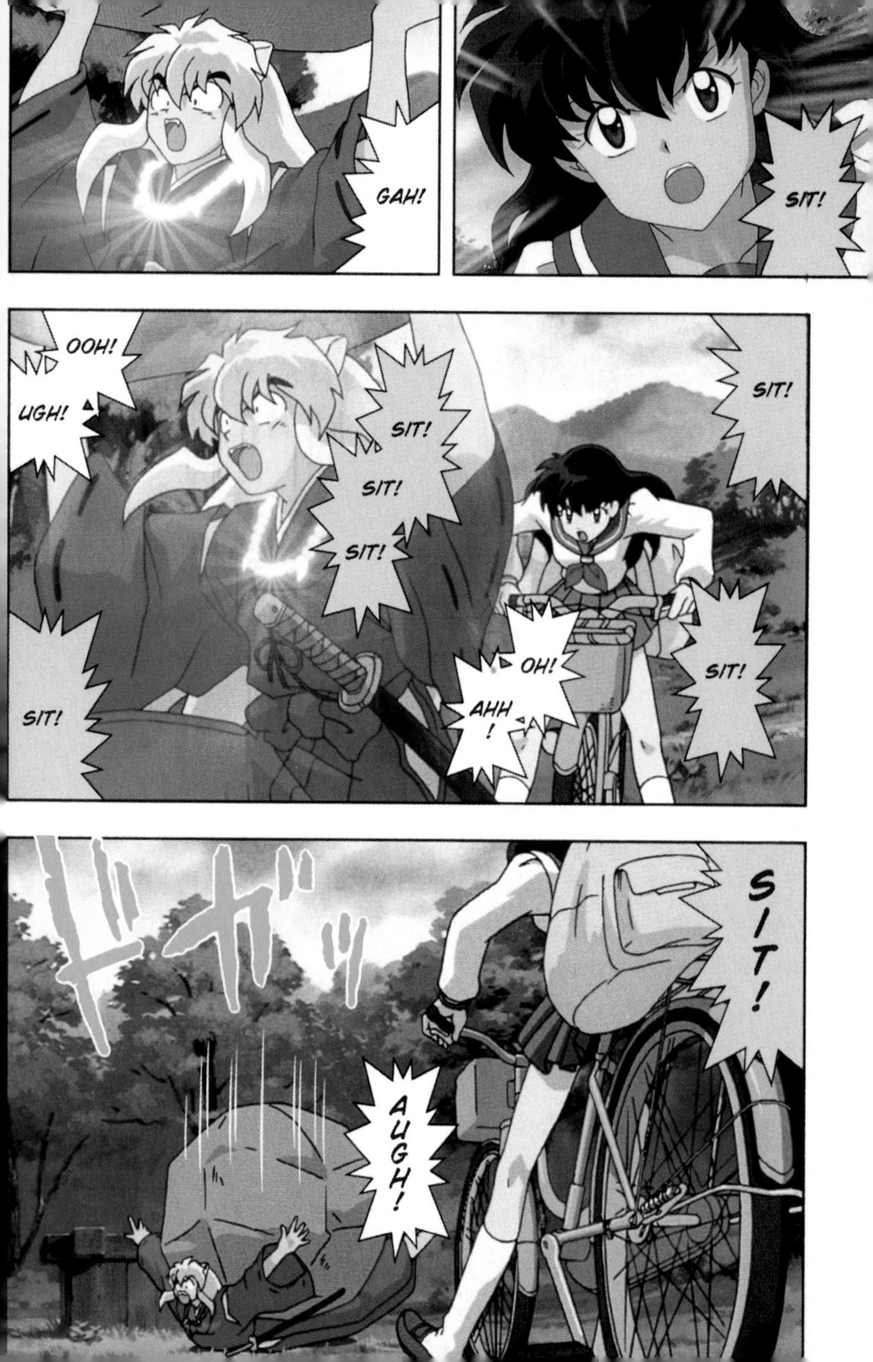
SIT!
GAH!
SIT!
SIT!
SIT!
SIT!
SIT!
OH!
AHH!
OOH!
UGH!
SIT!
SIT!
AUGH!
ドガッ

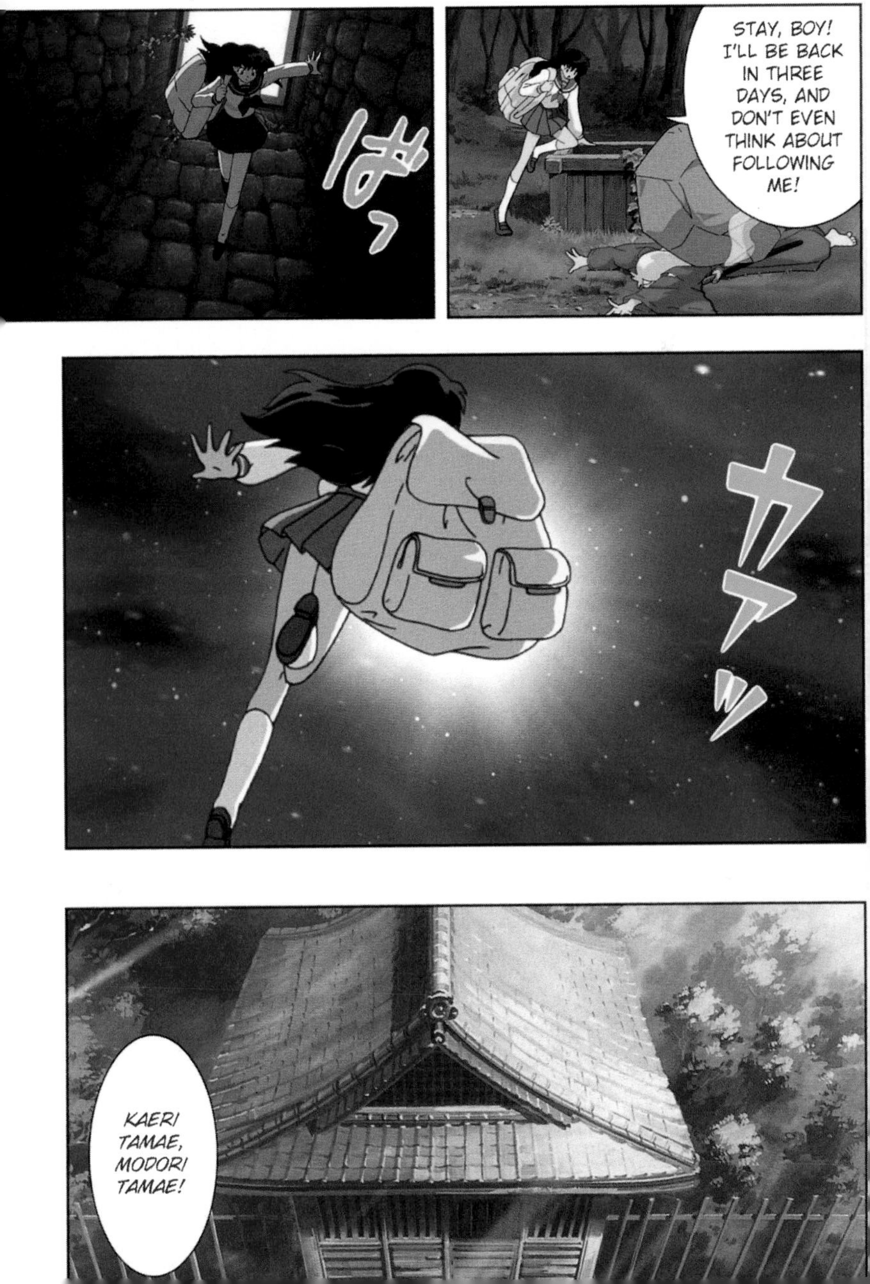
STAY, BOY! I'LL BE BACK IN THREE DAYS, AND DON'T EVEN THINK ABOUT FOLLOWING ME!
ぱっ
カァッ
KAERI TAMAE, MODORI TAMAE!

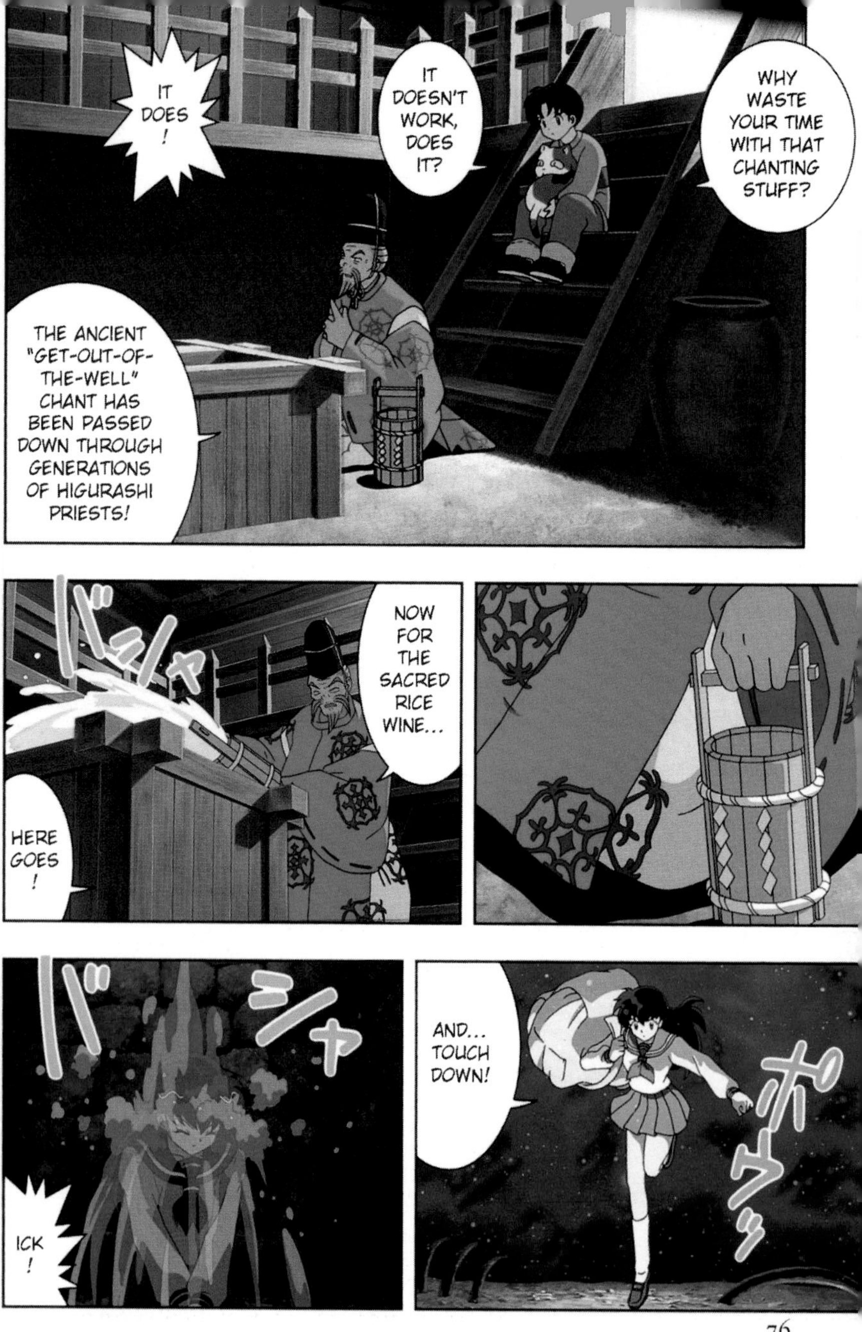
WHY WASTE YOUR TIME WITH THAT CHANTING STUFF?
IT DOESN'T WORK, DOES IT?
IT DOES!
THE ANCIENT "GET-OUT-OF-THE-WELL" CHANT HAS BEEN PASSED DOWN THROUGH GENERATIONS OF HIGURASHI PRIESTS!
NOW FOR THE SACRED RICE WINE...
バシャ
HERE GOES!
ポウッ
AND... TOUCH DOWN!
バシャ
ICK!

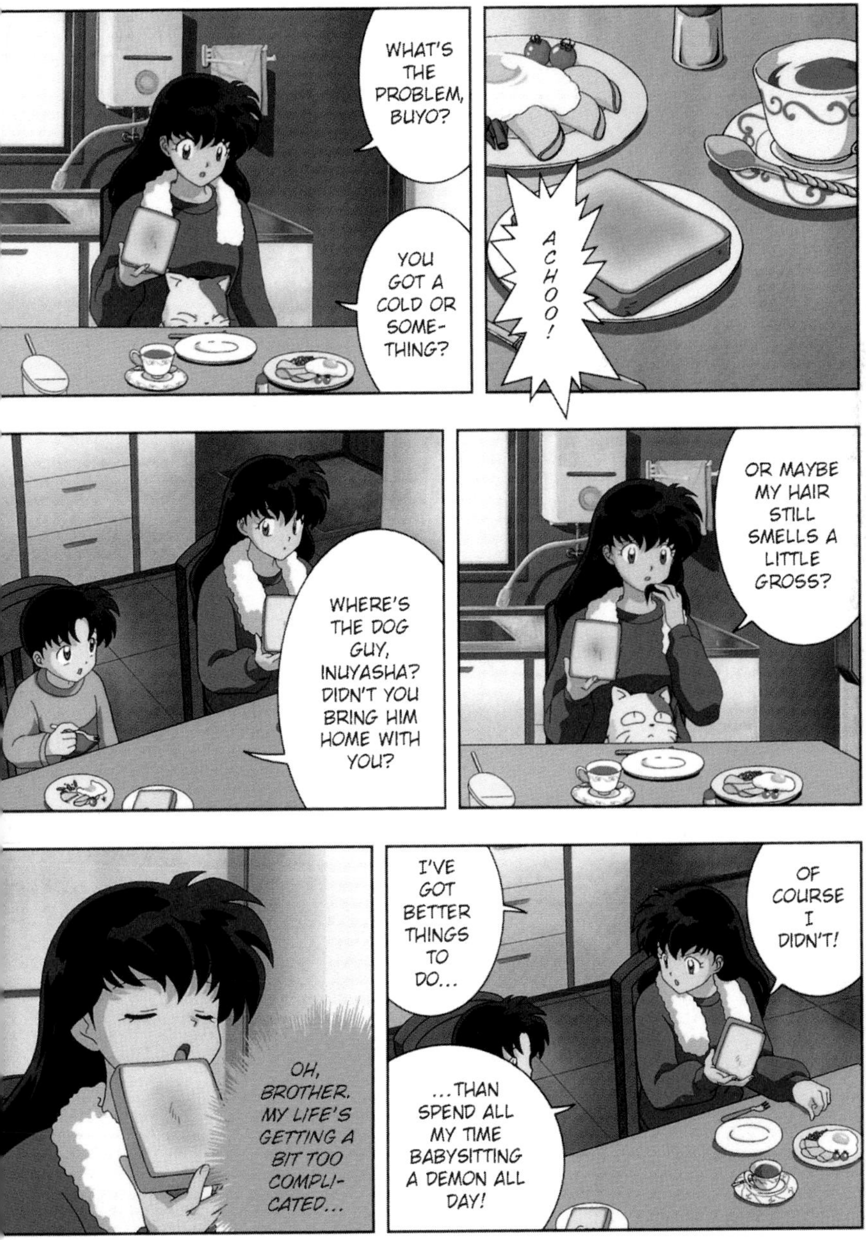
ACHOO!
WHAT'S THE PROBLEM, BUYO?
YOU GOT A COLD OR SOME-THING?
OR MAYBE MY HAIR STILL SMELLS A LITTLE GROSS?
WHERE'S THE DOG GUY, INUYASHA? DIDN'T YOU BRING HIM HOME WITH YOU?
OF COURSE I DIDN'T!
I'VE GOT BETTER THINGS TO DO...
...THAN SPEND ALL MY TIME BABYSITTING A DEMON ALL DAY!
OH, BROTHER. MY LIFE'S GETTING A BIT TOO COMPLI-CATED...

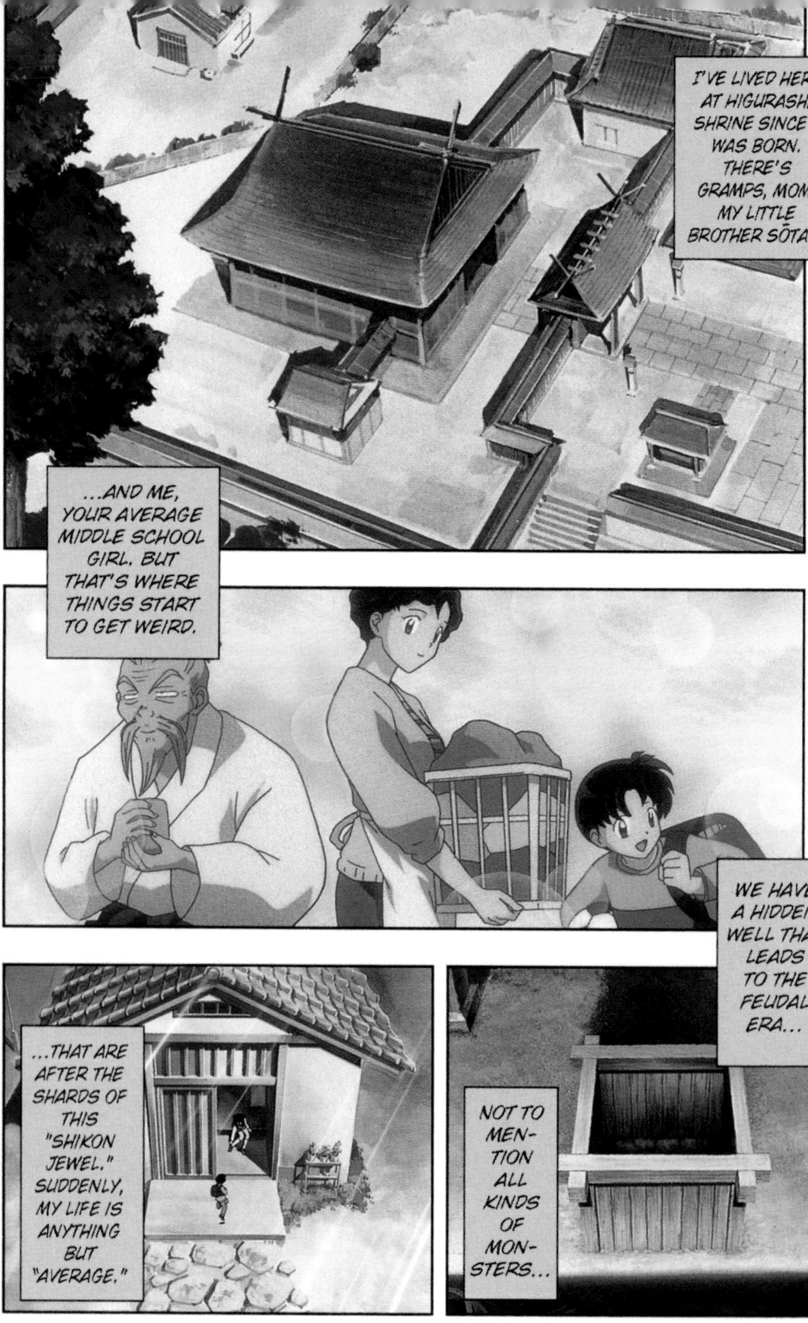
I'VE LIVED HERE AT HIGURASHI SHRINE SINCE I WAS BORN. THERE'S GRAMPS, MOM, MY LITTLE BROTHER SŌTA...
...AND ME, YOUR AVERAGE MIDDLE SCHOOL GIRL. BUT THAT'S WHERE THINGS START TO GET WEIRD.
WE HAVE A HIDDEN WELL THAT LEADS TO THE FEUDAL ERA...
NOT TO MEN-TION ALL KINDS OF MON-STERS...
...THAT ARE AFTER THE SHARDS OF THIS "SHIKON JEWEL." SUDDENLY, MY LIFE IS ANYTHING BUT "AVERAGE."

I KEEP THINKING I'M GOING TO WAKE UP TO FIND OUT IT'S ALL A BAD DREAM OR SOMETHING. BUT IT'S NOT A DREAM...

...AND I HAVE TO FIND A WAY TO DEAL WITH IT.

HERE I GO!

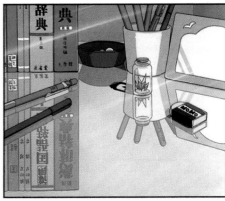

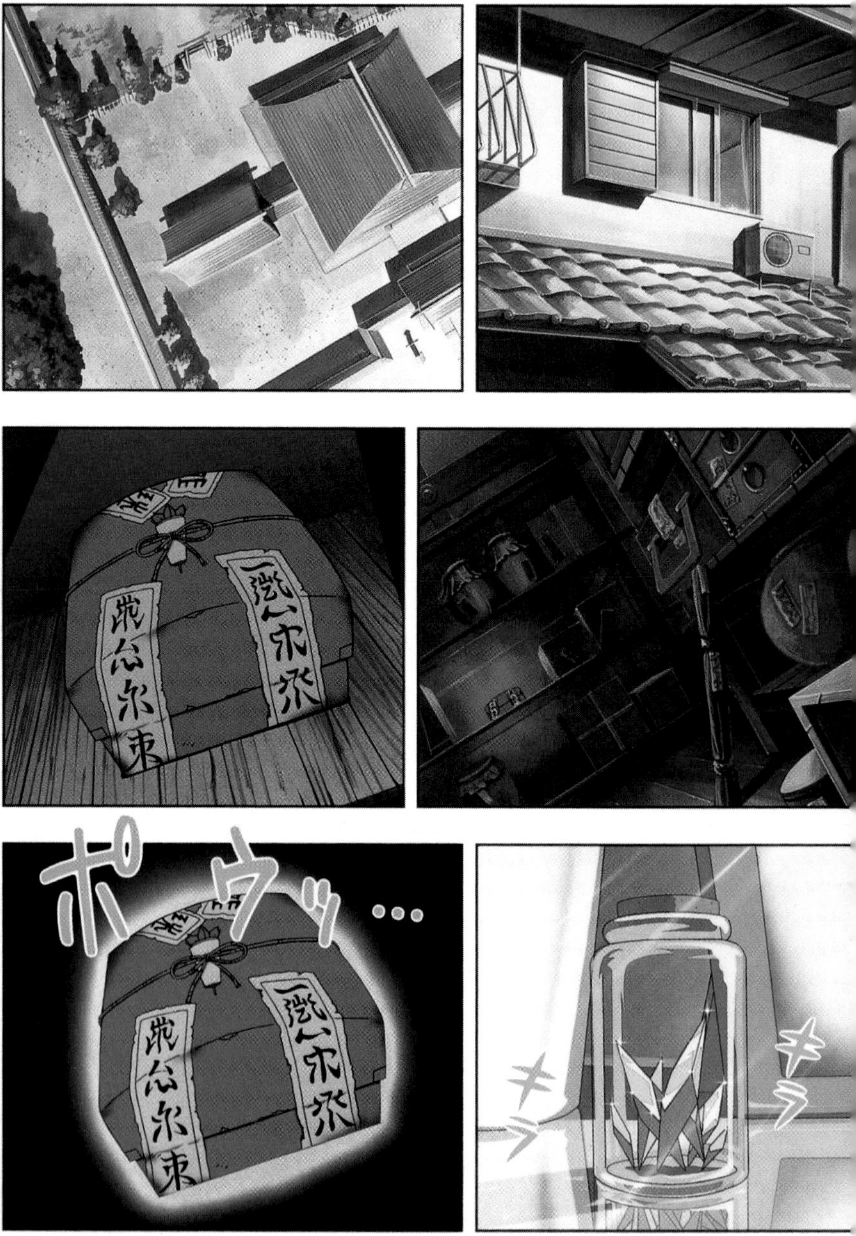
キラ
キラ
ポウッ...

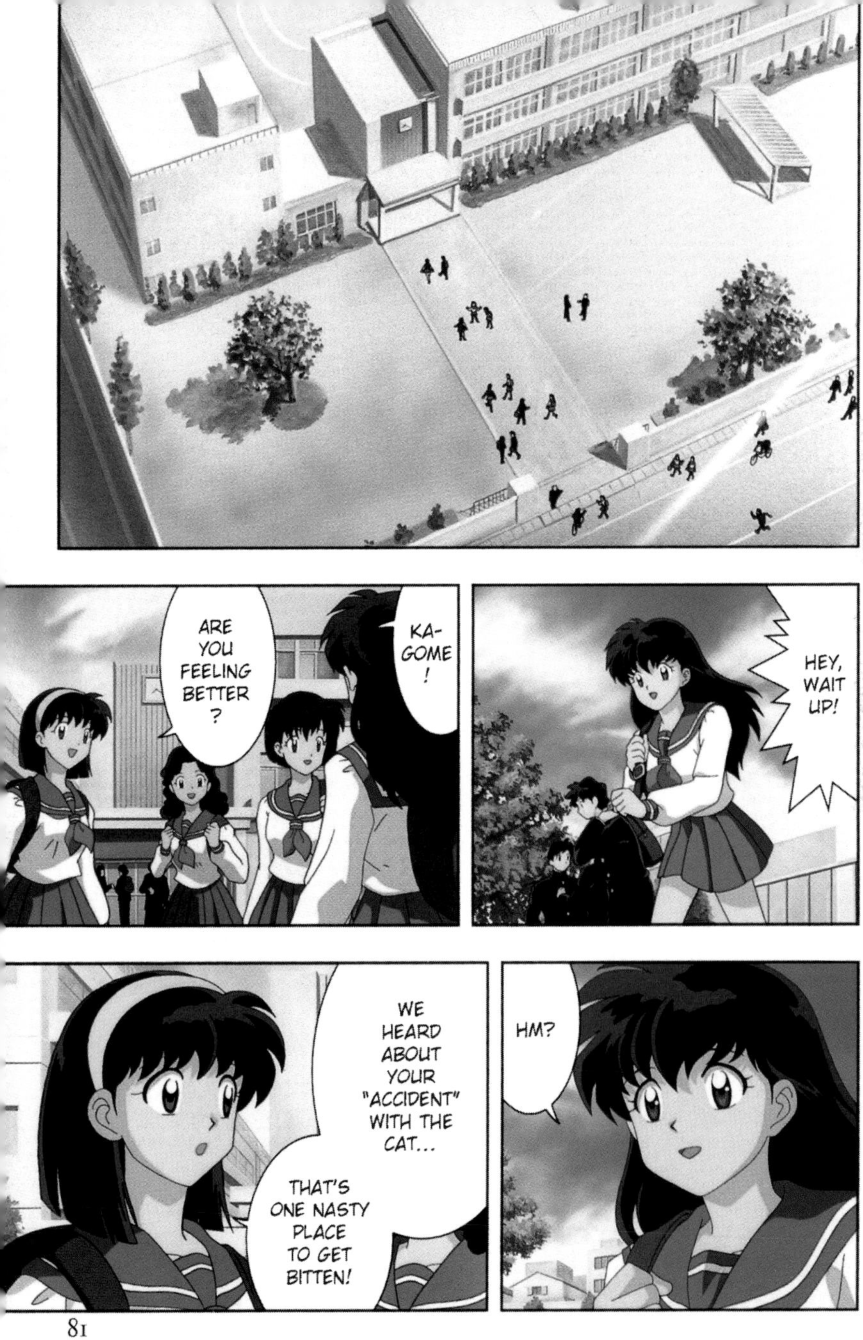
HEY, WAIT UP!
KA-GOME!
ARE YOU FEELING BETTER?
HM?
WE HEARD ABOUT YOUR "ACCIDENT" WITH THE CAT...
THAT'S ONE NASTY PLACE TO GET BITTEN!

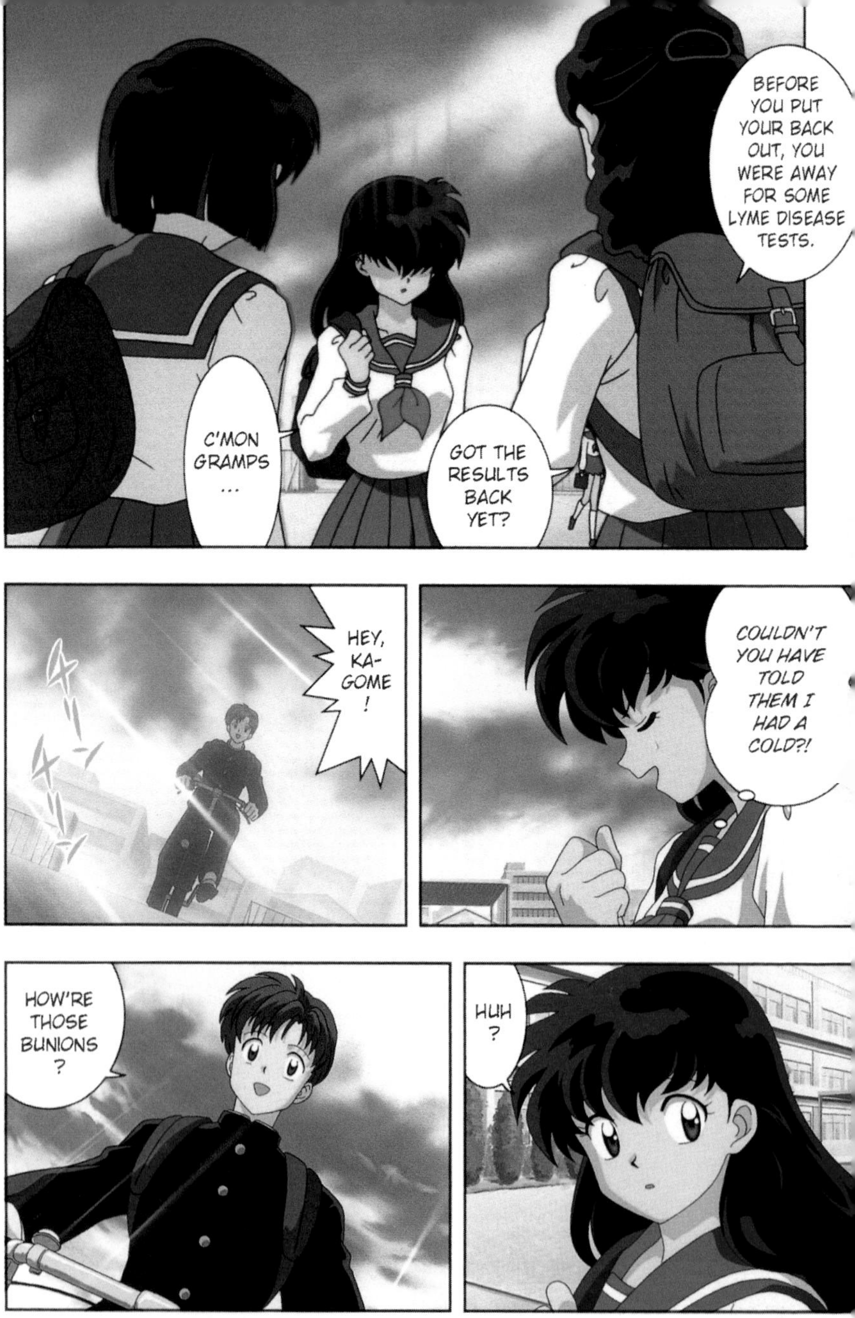
BEFORE YOU PUT YOUR BACK OUT, YOU WERE AWAY FOR SOME LYME DISEASE TESTS.
GOT THE RESULTS BACK YET?
C'MON GRAMPS ...
COULDN'T YOU HAVE TOLD THEM I HAD A COLD?!
HEY, KA-GOME!
HUH?
HOW'RE THOSE BUNIONS?

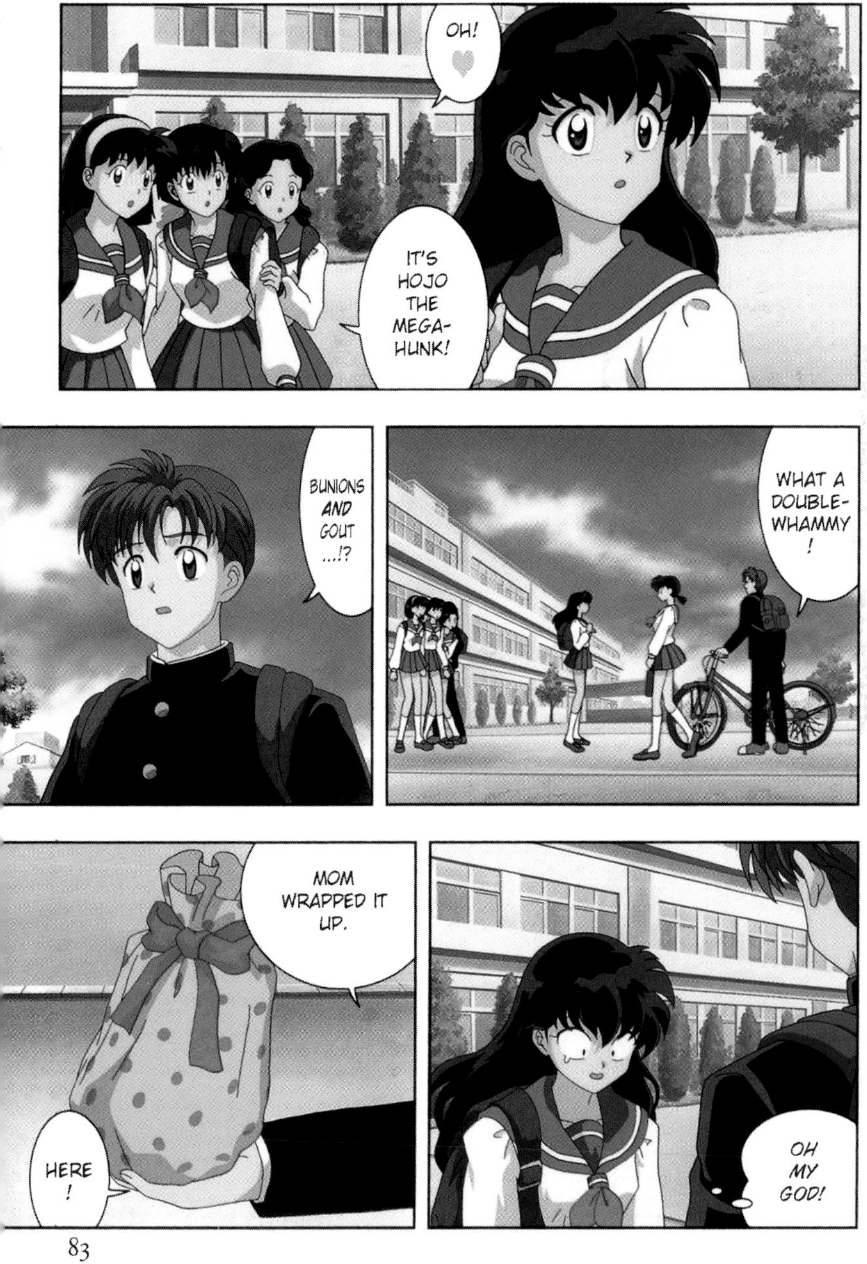
OH! ♥
IT'S HOJO THE MEGA-HUNK!
WHAT A DOUBLE-WHAMMY!
BUNIONS AND GOUT ...!?
OH MY GOD!
MOM WRAPPED IT UP.
HERE!

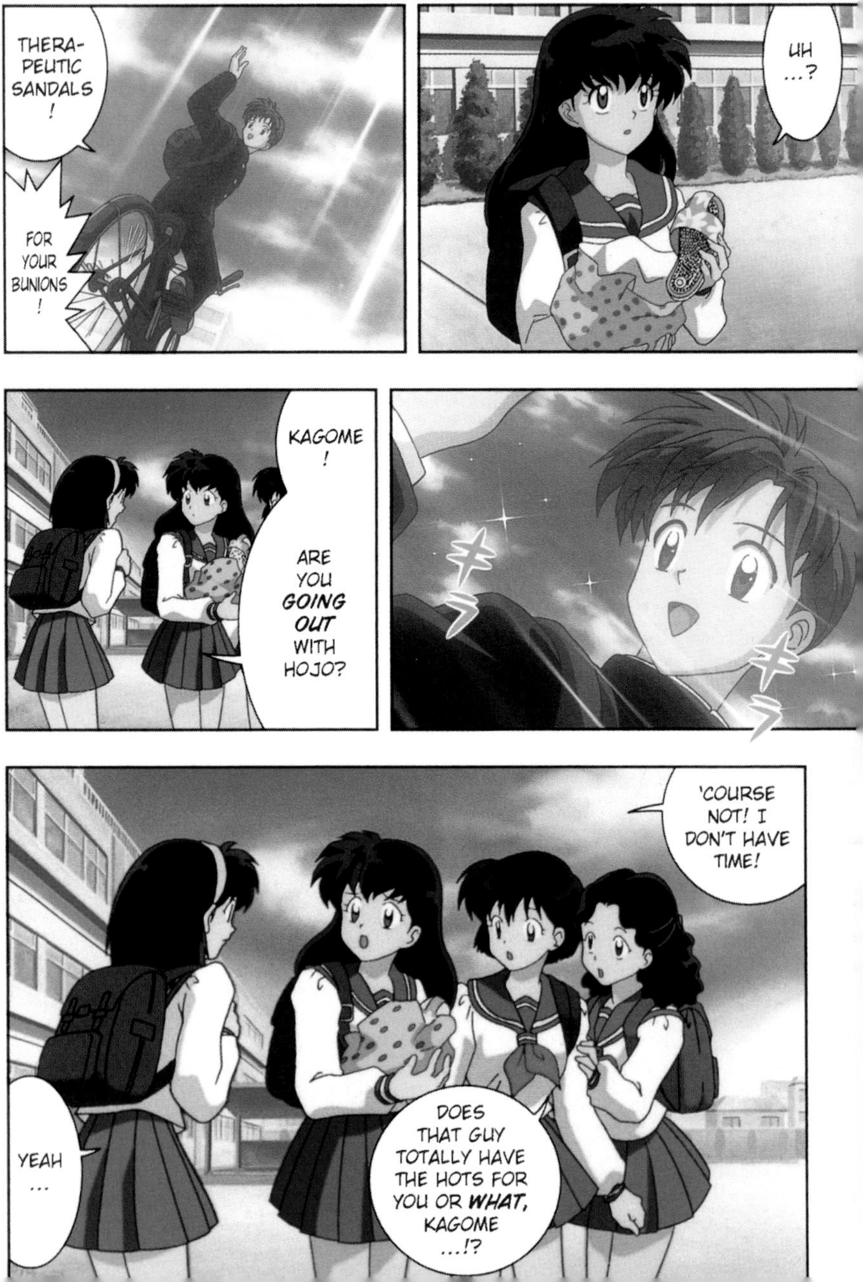
UH ...?
THERA-PEUTIC SANDALS!
FOR YOUR BUNIONS!
KAGOME!
ARE YOU GOING OUT WITH HOJO?
'COURSE NOT! I DON'T HAVE TIME!
DOES THAT GUY TOTALLY HAVE THE HOTS FOR YOU OR WHAT, KAGOME ...!?
YEAH ...

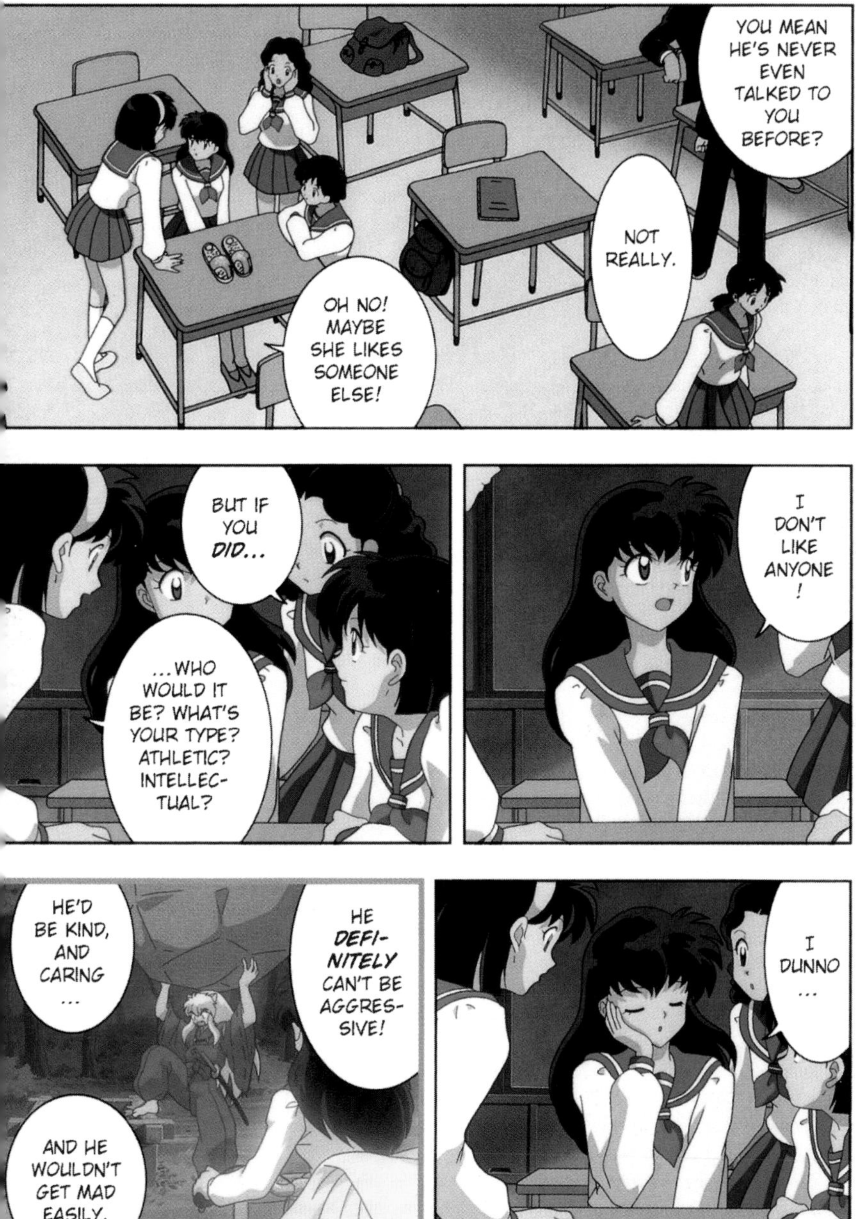
YOU MEAN HE'S NEVER EVEN TALKED TO YOU BEFORE?
NOT REALLY.
OH NO! MAYBE SHE LIKES SOMEONE ELSE!
I DON'T LIKE ANYONE!
BUT IF YOU *DID...*
...WHO WOULD IT BE? WHAT'S YOUR TYPE? ATHLETIC? INTELLEC-TUAL?
I DUNNO...
HE *DEFI-NITELY* CAN'T BE AGGRES-SIVE!
HE'D BE KIND, AND CARING...
AND HE WOULDN'T GET MAD EASILY.

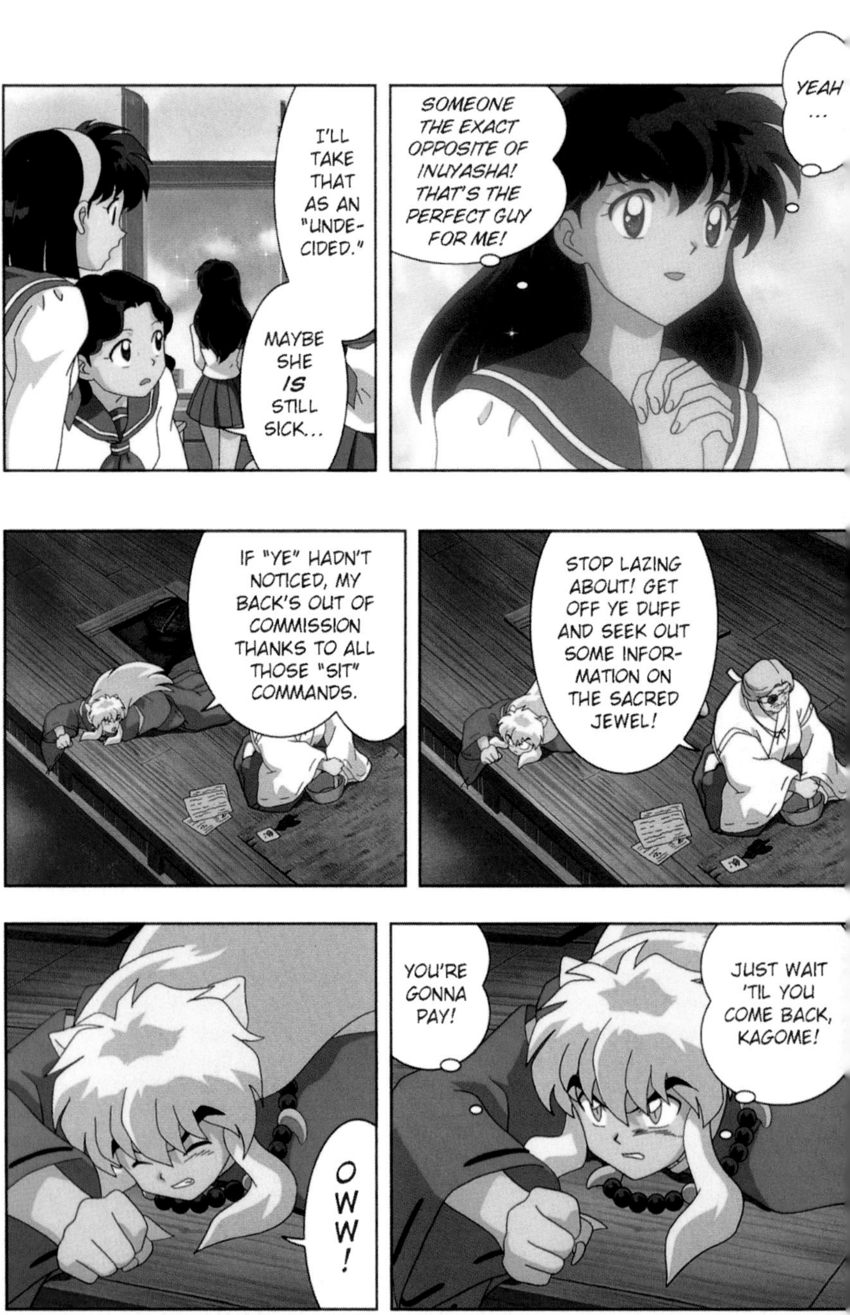
YEAH ...
SOMEONE THE EXACT OPPOSITE OF INUYASHA! THAT'S THE PERFECT GUY FOR ME!
I'LL TAKE THAT AS AN "UNDECIDED."
MAYBE SHE *IS* STILL SICK...
STOP LAZING ABOUT! GET OFF YE DUFF AND SEEK OUT SOME INFORMATION ON THE SACRED JEWEL!
IF "YE" HADN'T NOTICED, MY BACK'S OUT OF COMMISSION THANKS TO ALL THOSE "SIT" COMMANDS.
JUST WAIT 'TIL YOU COME BACK, KAGOME!
YOU'RE GONNA PAY!
OWW!

EH ?

A FIRE !?

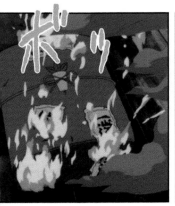

THE STORE-HOUSE !

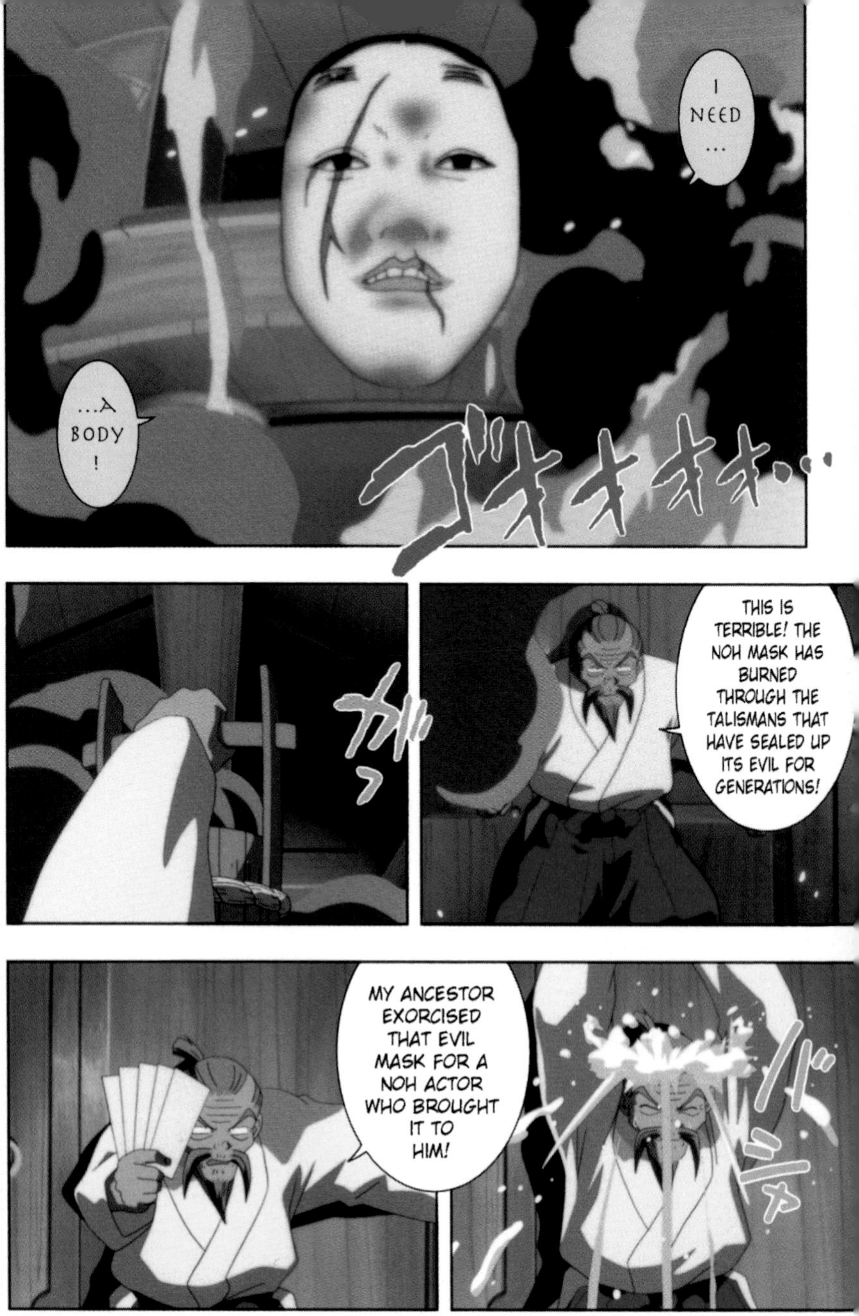
I NEED ...
...A BODY!
ゴオオオオ…
THIS IS TERRIBLE! THE NOH MASK HAS BURNED THROUGH THE TALISMANS THAT HAVE SEALED UP ITS EVIL FOR GENERATIONS!
ガッ
MY ANCESTOR EXORCISED THAT EVIL MASK FOR A NOH ACTOR WHO BROUGHT IT TO HIM!

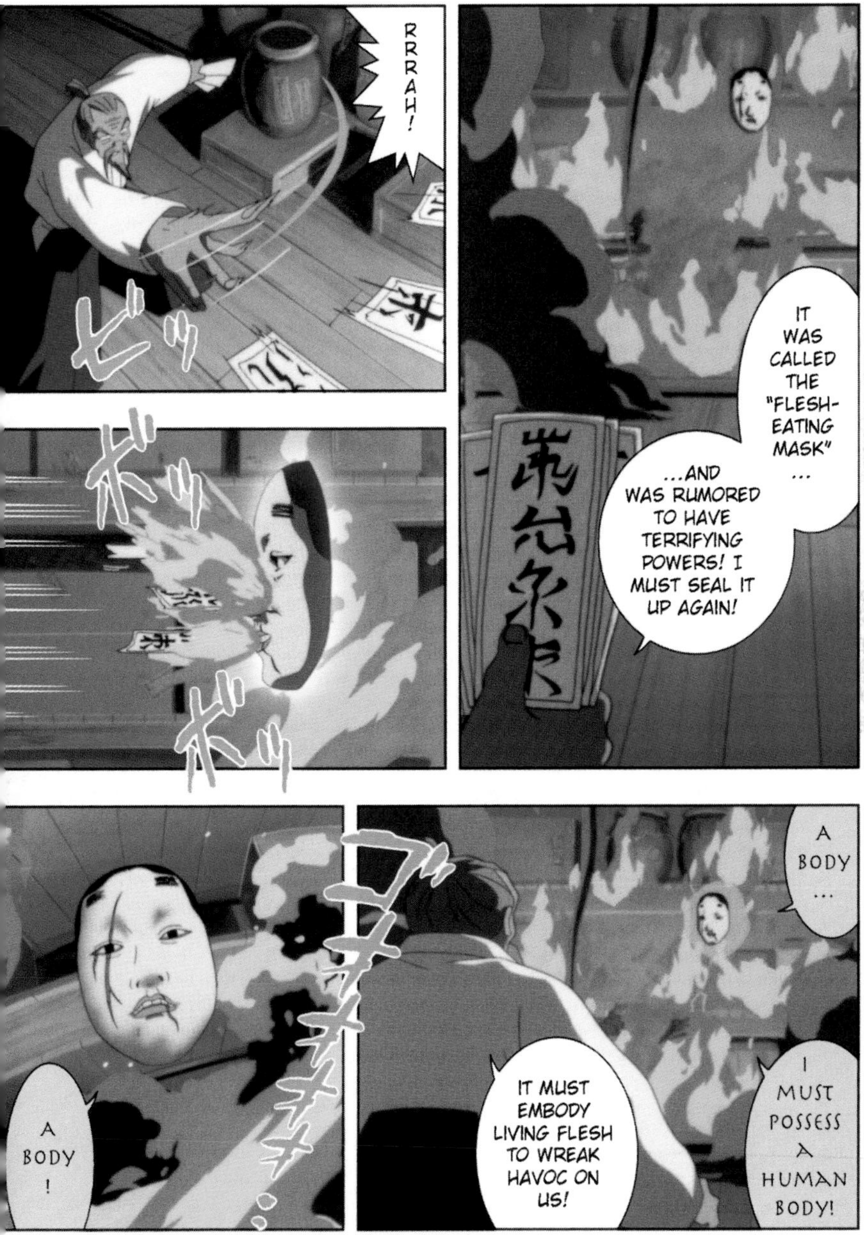
IT WAS CALLED THE "FLESH-EATING MASK"...
...AND WAS RUMORED TO HAVE TERRIFYING POWERS! I MUST SEAL IT UP AGAIN!
RRRAH!
ビッ
ボッ
ボッ
A BODY...
I MUST POSSESS A HUMAN BODY!
IT MUST EMBODY LIVING FLESH TO WREAK HAVOC ON US!
A BODY!

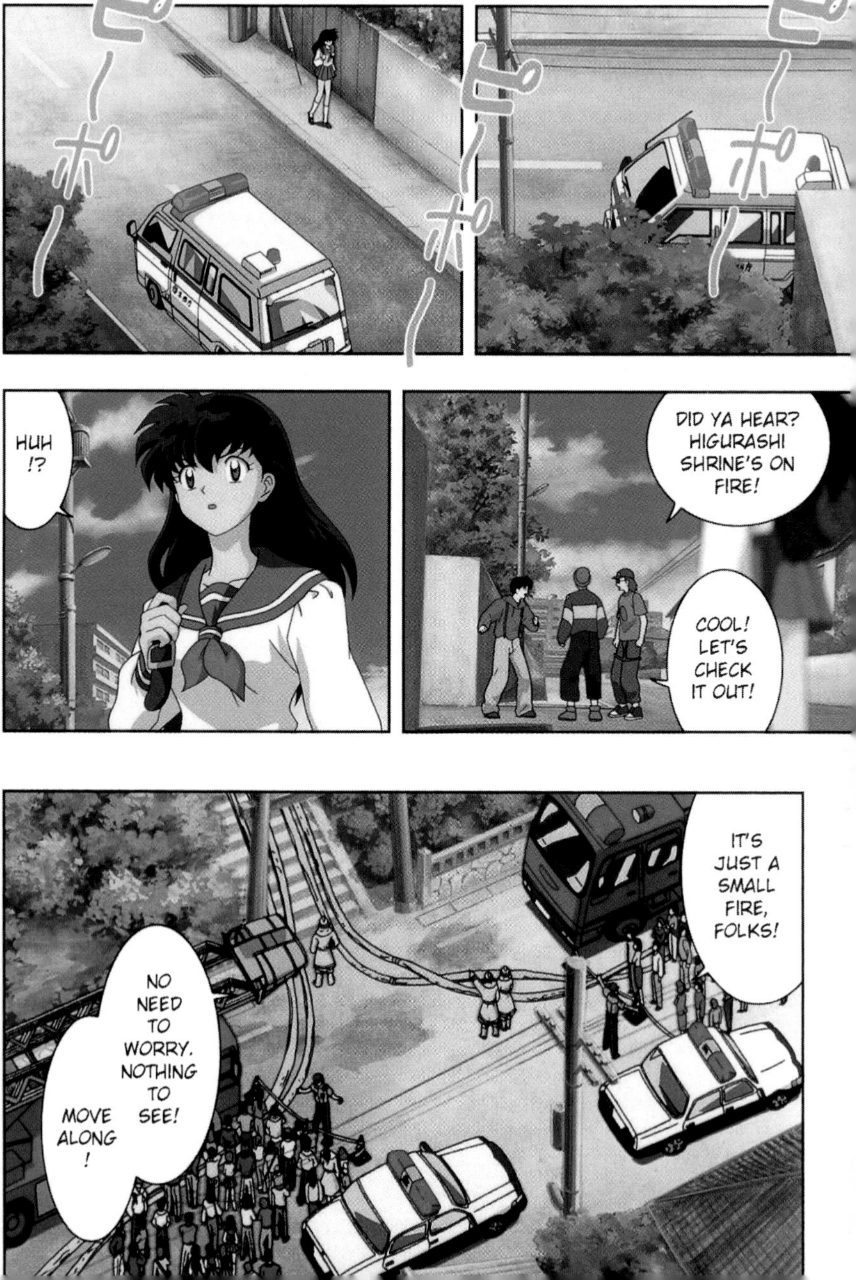
ピーポー
ピーポー
ピーポー
DID YA HEAR? HIGURASHI SHRINE'S ON FIRE!
COOL! LET'S CHECK IT OUT!
HUH !?
IT'S JUST A SMALL FIRE, FOLKS!
NO NEED TO WORRY. NOTHING TO SEE!
MOVE ALONG !

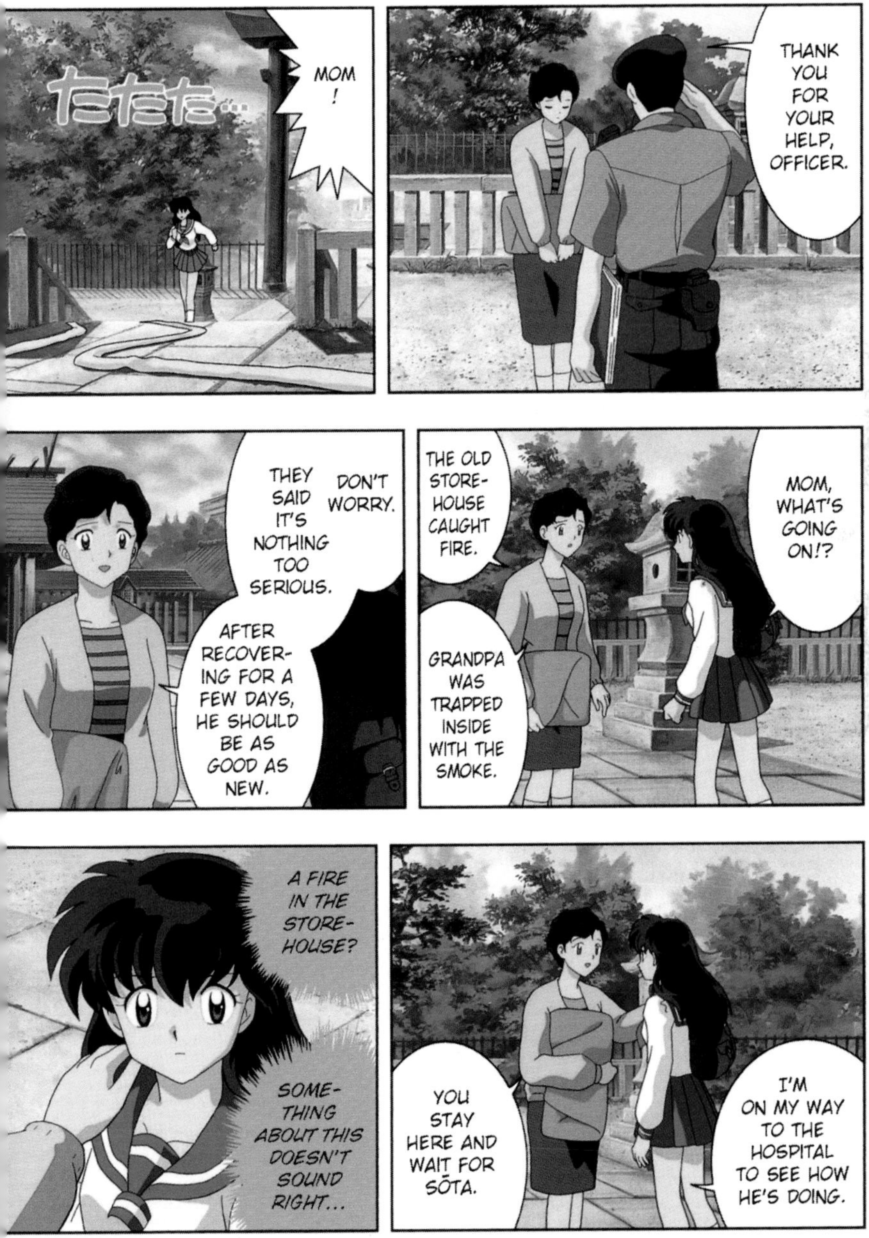
THANK YOU FOR YOUR HELP, OFFICER.
MOM!
たたた…
MOM, WHAT'S GOING ON!?
THE OLD STORE-HOUSE CAUGHT FIRE.
GRANDPA WAS TRAPPED INSIDE WITH THE SMOKE.
DON'T WORRY.
THEY SAID IT'S NOTHING TOO SERIOUS.
AFTER RECOVERING FOR A FEW DAYS, HE SHOULD BE AS GOOD AS NEW.
I'M ON MY WAY TO THE HOSPITAL TO SEE HOW HE'S DOING.
YOU STAY HERE AND WAIT FOR SŌTA.
A FIRE IN THE STORE-HOUSE?
SOME-THING ABOUT THIS DOESN'T SOUND RIGHT...

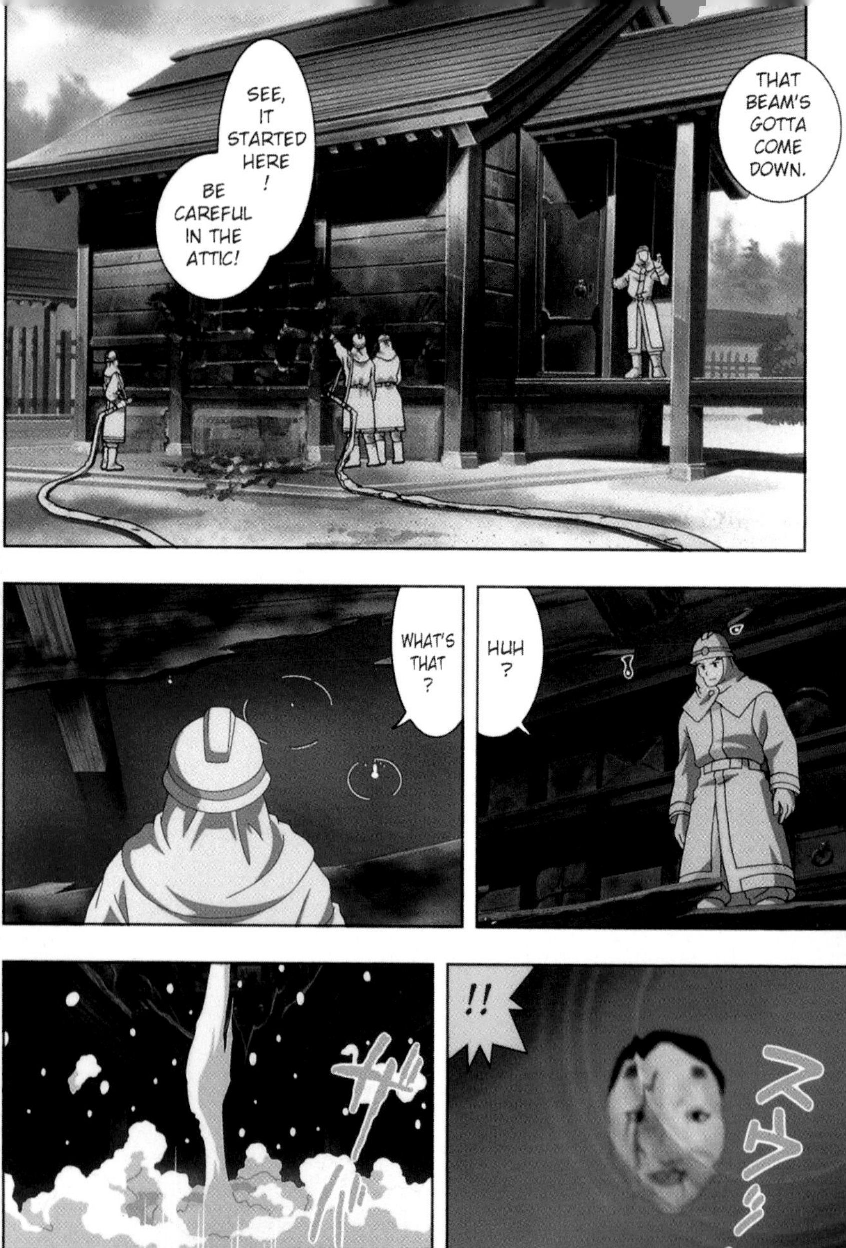
THAT BEAM'S GOTTA COME DOWN.
SEE, IT STARTED HERE!
BE CAREFUL IN THE ATTIC!
HUH?
WHAT'S THAT?
!!
スゥッ…

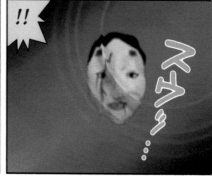

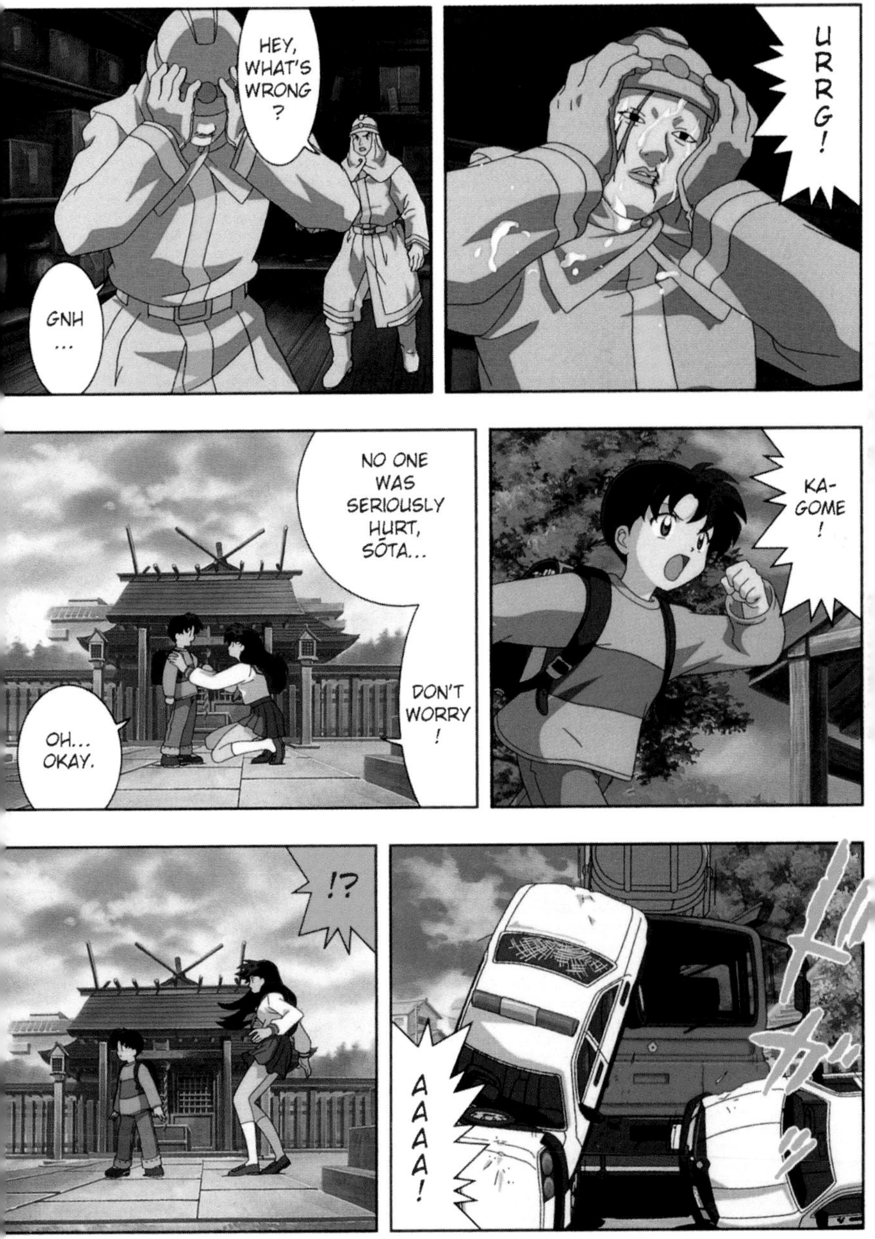
URRG!
HEY, WHAT'S WRONG?
GNH...
KA-GOME!
NO ONE WAS SERIOUSLY HURT, SŌTA...
DON'T WORRY!
OH... OKAY.
AAAAA!
!?

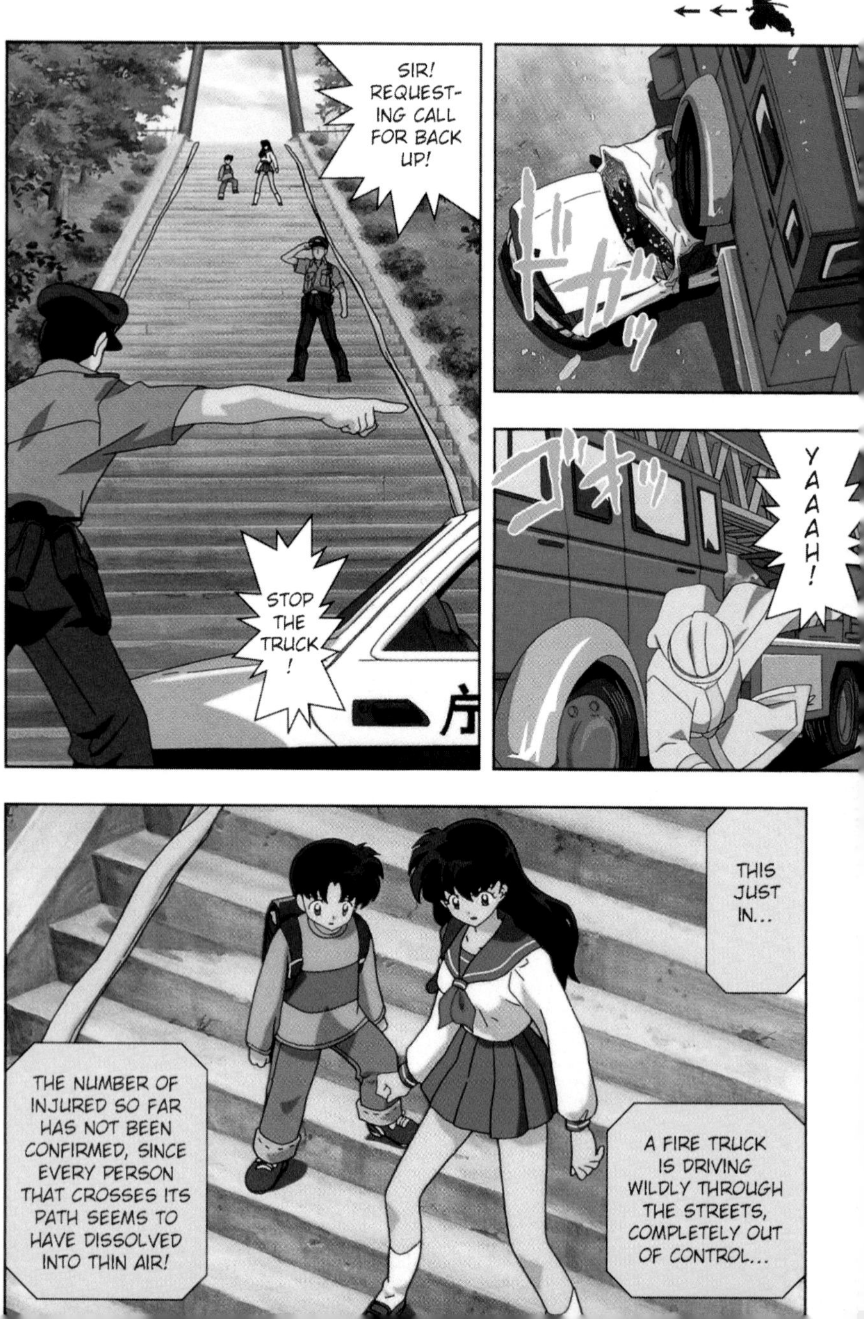
ドガッ
ゴオッ
YAAAAH!
SIR! REQUESTING CALL FOR BACK UP!
STOP THE TRUCK!
庁
THIS JUST IN...
A FIRE TRUCK IS DRIVING WILDLY THROUGH THE STREETS, COMPLETELY OUT OF CONTROL...
THE NUMBER OF INJURED SO FAR HAS NOT BEEN CONFIRMED, SINCE EVERY PERSON THAT CROSSES ITS PATH SEEMS TO HAVE DISSOLVED INTO THIN AIR!

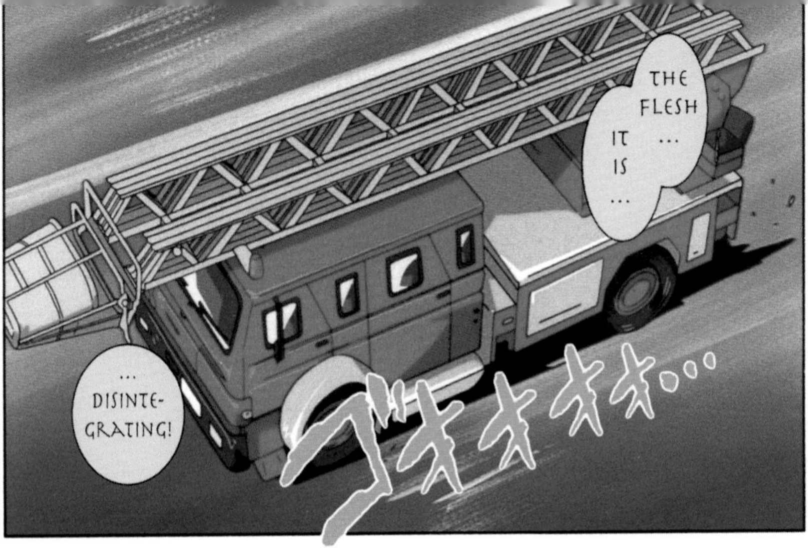
THE FLESH ...
IT IS ...
... DISINTE-GRATING!

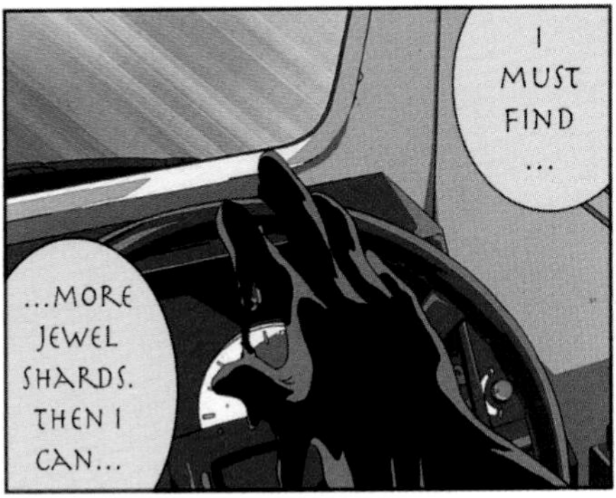
I MUST FIND ...
...MORE JEWEL SHARDS. THEN I CAN...

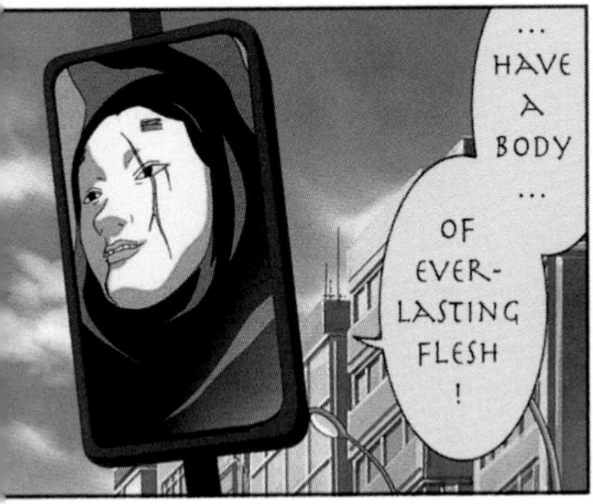
... HAVE A BODY ...
OF EVER-LASTING FLESH !

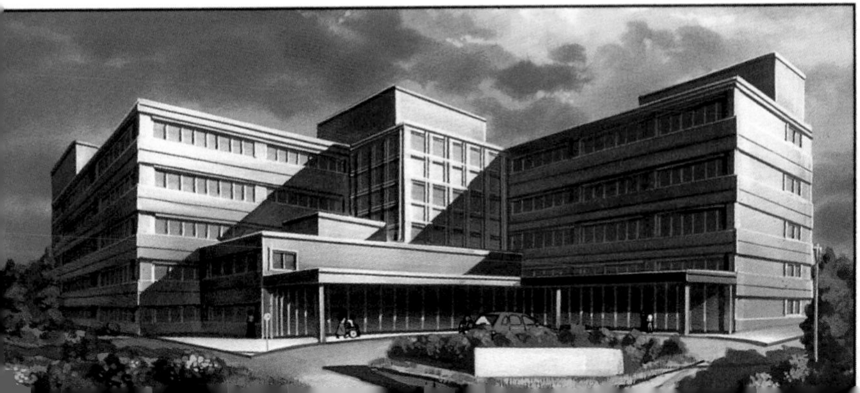

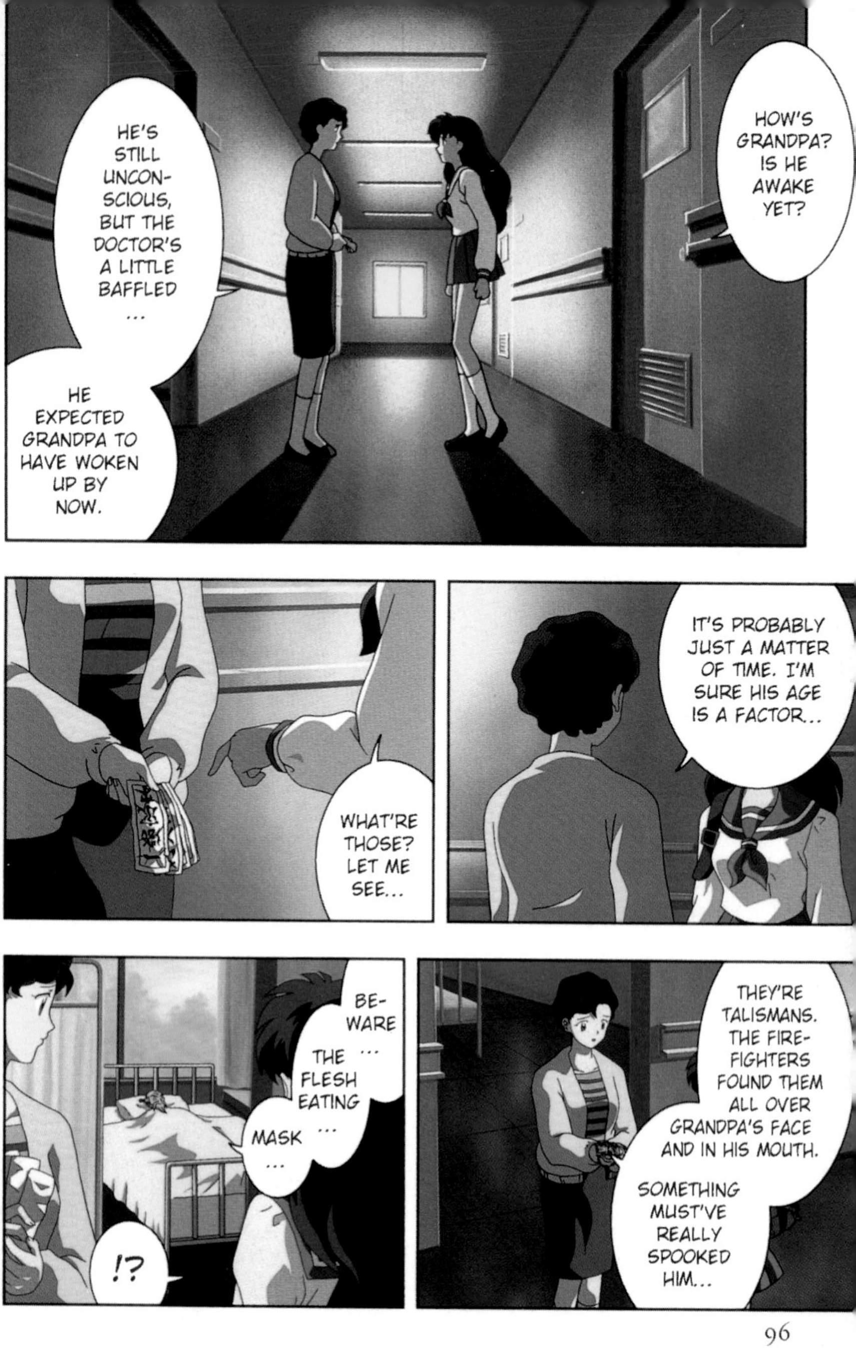
HOW'S GRANDPA? IS HE AWAKE YET?
HE'S STILL UNCON-SCIOUS, BUT THE DOCTOR'S A LITTLE BAFFLED ...
HE EXPECTED GRANDPA TO HAVE WOKEN UP BY NOW.
IT'S PROBABLY JUST A MATTER OF TIME. I'M SURE HIS AGE IS A FACTOR...
WHAT'RE THOSE? LET ME SEE...
THEY'RE TALISMANS. THE FIRE-FIGHTERS FOUND THEM ALL OVER GRANDPA'S FACE AND IN HIS MOUTH.
SOMETHING MUST'VE REALLY SPOOKED HIM...
BE-WARE ...
THE FLESH EATING ...
MASK ...
!?

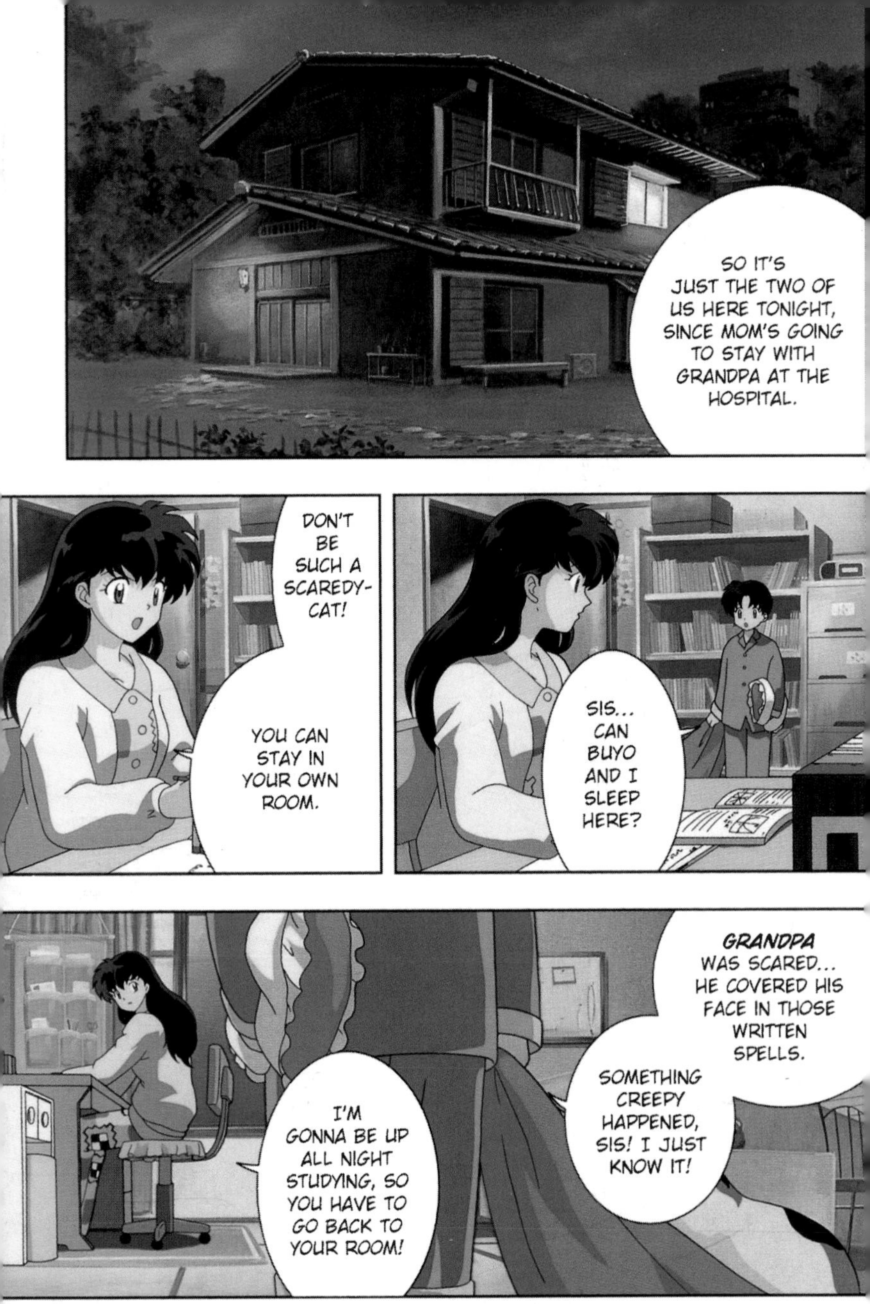
SO IT'S JUST THE TWO OF US HERE TONIGHT, SINCE MOM'S GOING TO STAY WITH GRANDPA AT THE HOSPITAL.
SIS... CAN BUYO AND I SLEEP HERE?
DON'T BE SUCH A SCAREDY-CAT!
YOU CAN STAY IN YOUR OWN ROOM.
GRANDPA WAS SCARED... HE COVERED HIS FACE IN THOSE WRITTEN SPELLS.
SOMETHING CREEPY HAPPENED, SIS! I JUST KNOW IT!
I'M GONNA BE UP ALL NIGHT STUDYING, SO YOU HAVE TO GO BACK TO YOUR ROOM!

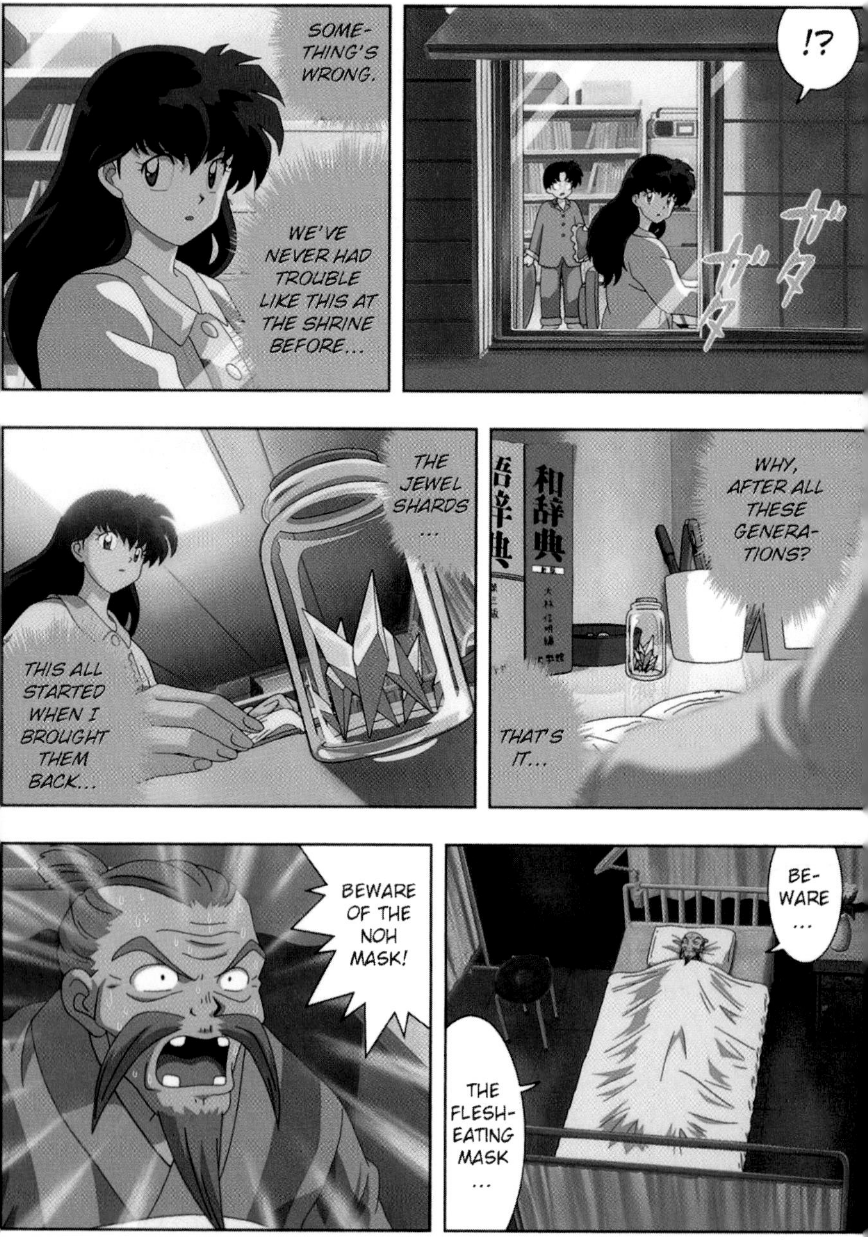
!?
ガタガタ
SOME-THING'S WRONG.
WE'VE NEVER HAD TROUBLE LIKE THIS AT THE SHRINE BEFORE...
WHY, AFTER ALL THESE GENERA-TIONS?
和辞典
THAT'S IT...
THE JEWEL SHARDS...
THIS ALL STARTED WHEN I BROUGHT THEM BACK...
BE-WARE...
THE FLESH-EATING MASK...
BEWARE OF THE NOH MASK!

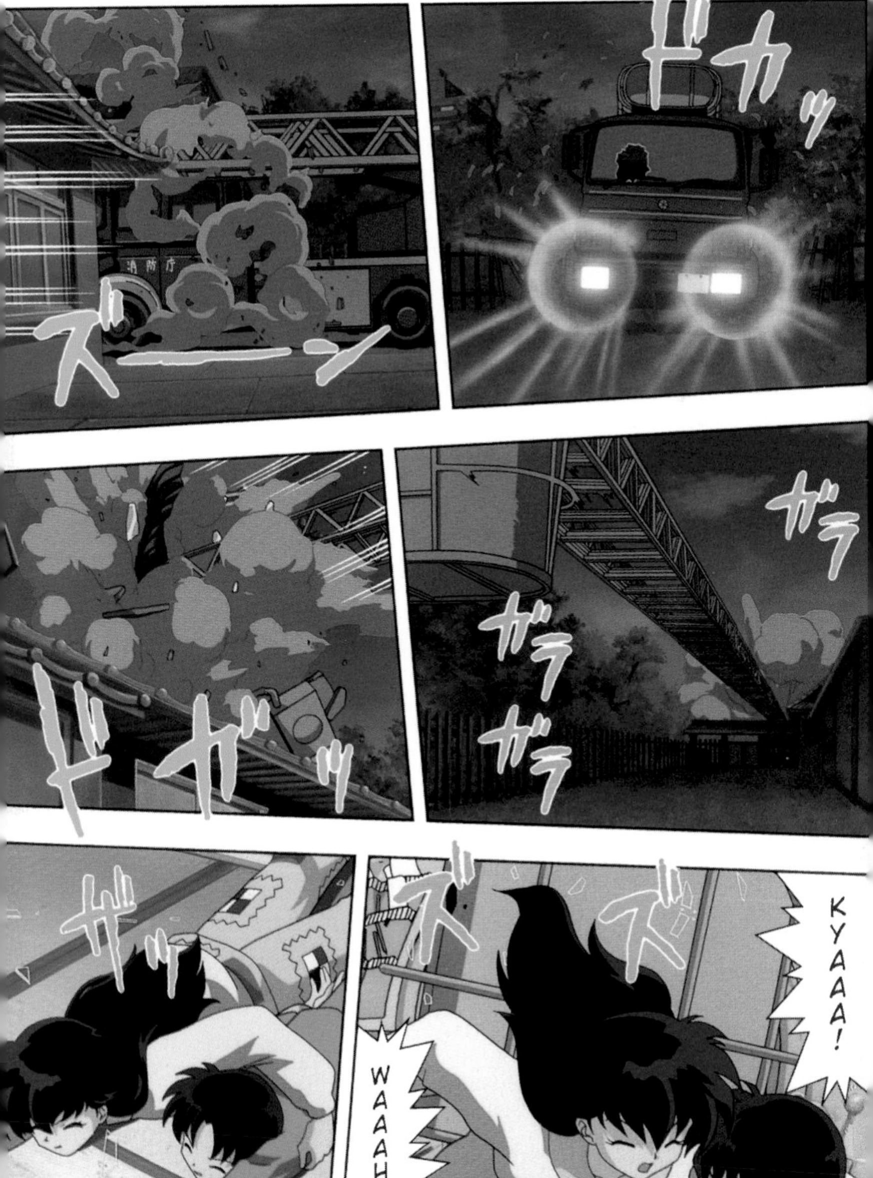
ドカッ
ズーン
ガラ
ガラ
ガラ
ドガッ
ズ
ズ
KYAAAA!
WAAAAH!
ザッ

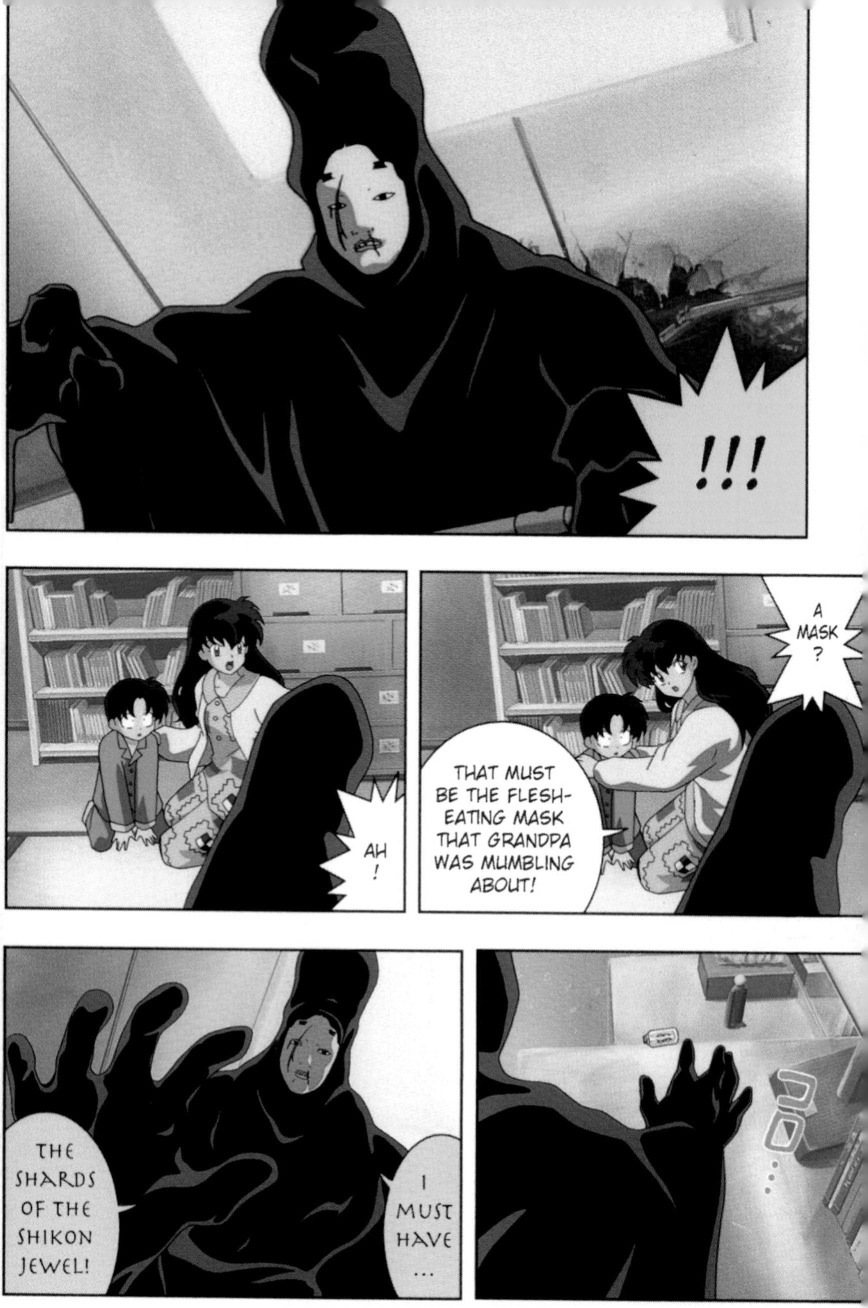
!!!
A MASK?
THAT MUST BE THE FLESH-EATING MASK THAT GRANDPA WAS MUMBLING ABOUT!
AH!
コロ…
I MUST HAVE...
THE SHARDS OF THE SHIKON JEWEL!

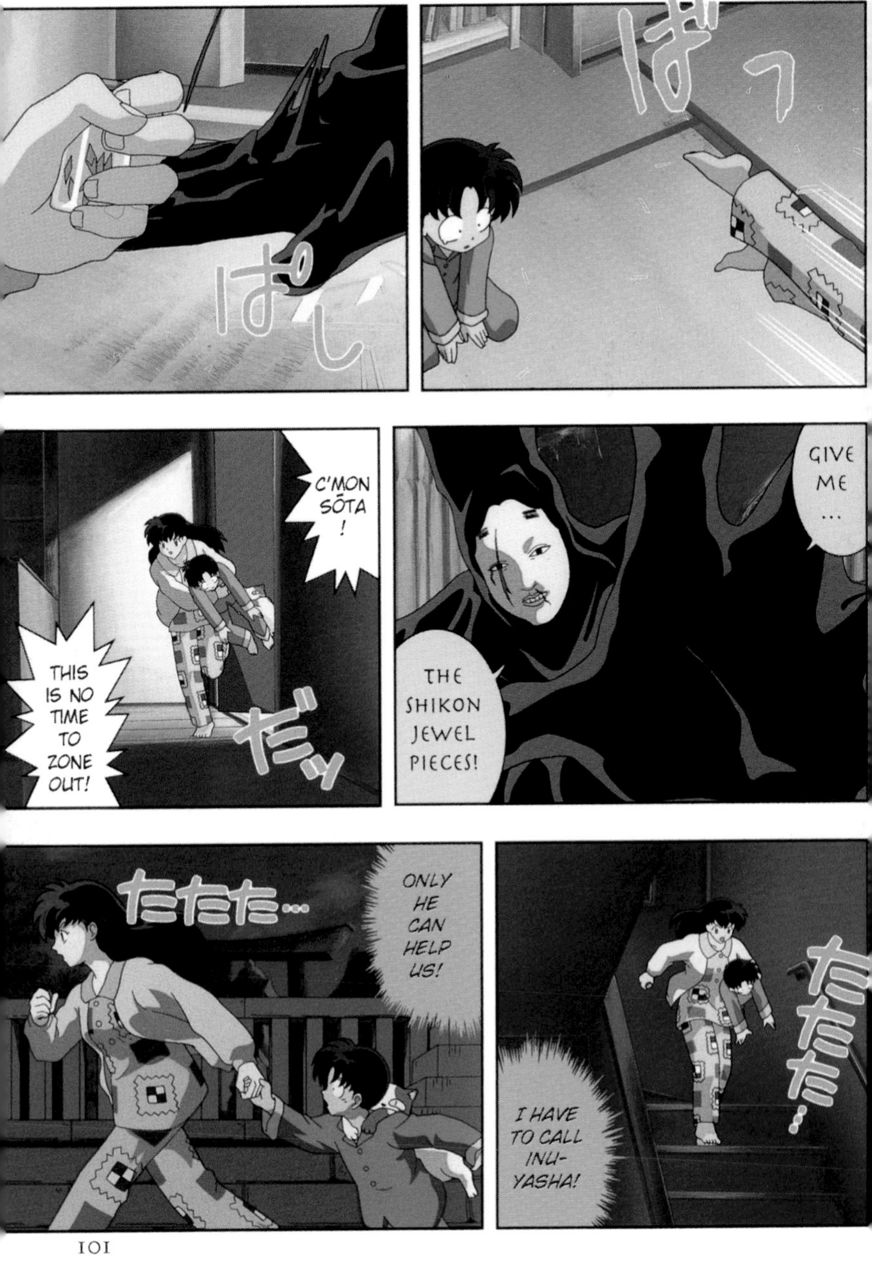
ぱっ
ぱし
GIVE ME ...
THE SHIKON JEWEL PIECES!
C'MON SŌTA!
THIS IS NO TIME TO ZONE OUT!
だッ
たたた…
I HAVE TO CALL INU-YASHA!
たたた…
ONLY HE CAN HELP US!

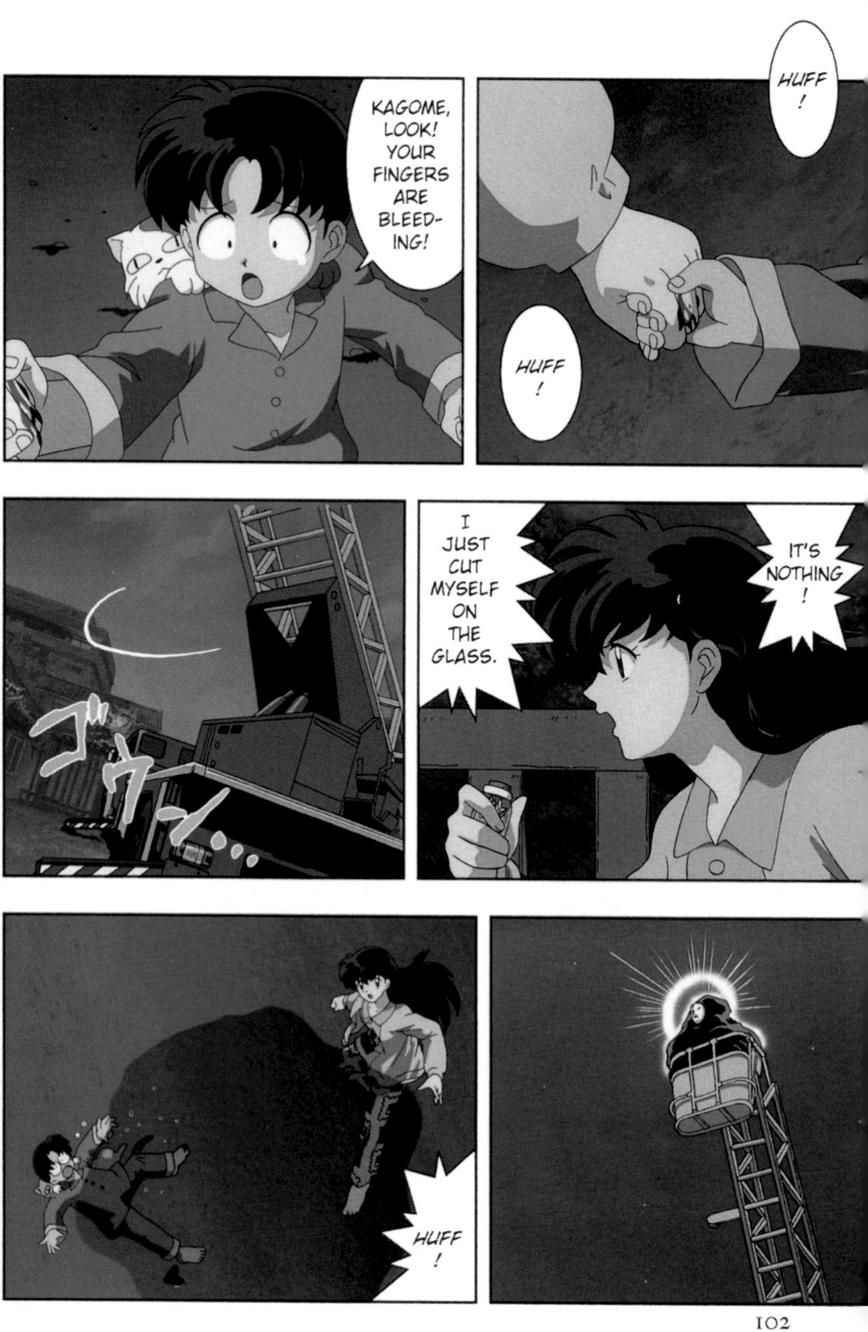
HUFF!
HUFF!
KAGOME, LOOK! YOUR FINGERS ARE BLEEDING!
IT'S NOTHING!
I JUST CUT MYSELF ON THE GLASS.
ゴウーッ…
HUFF!

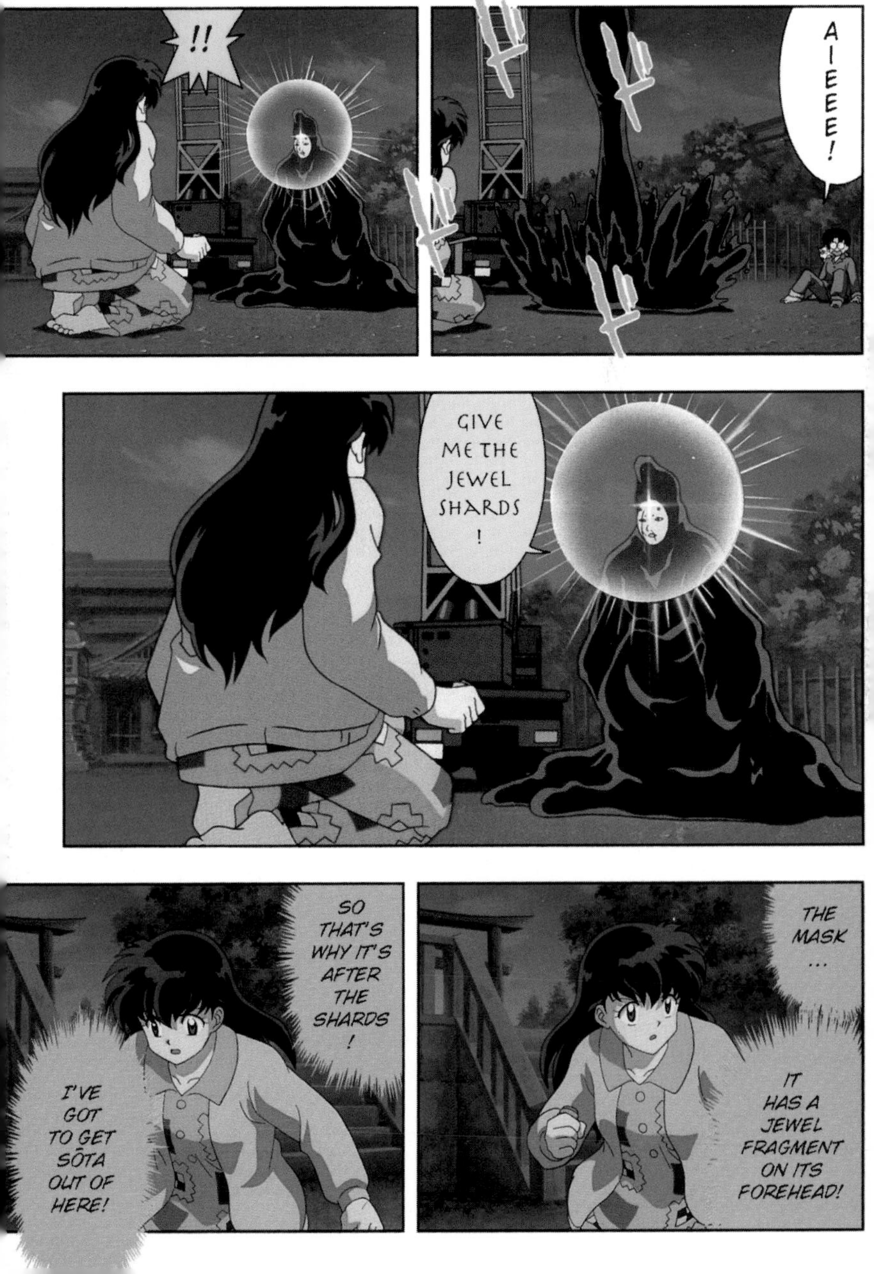
AIEEEE!
!!
GIVE ME THE JEWEL SHARDS!
THE MASK...
IT HAS A JEWEL FRAGMENT ON ITS FOREHEAD!
SO THAT'S WHY IT'S AFTER THE SHARDS!
I'VE GOT TO GET SŌTA OUT OF HERE!

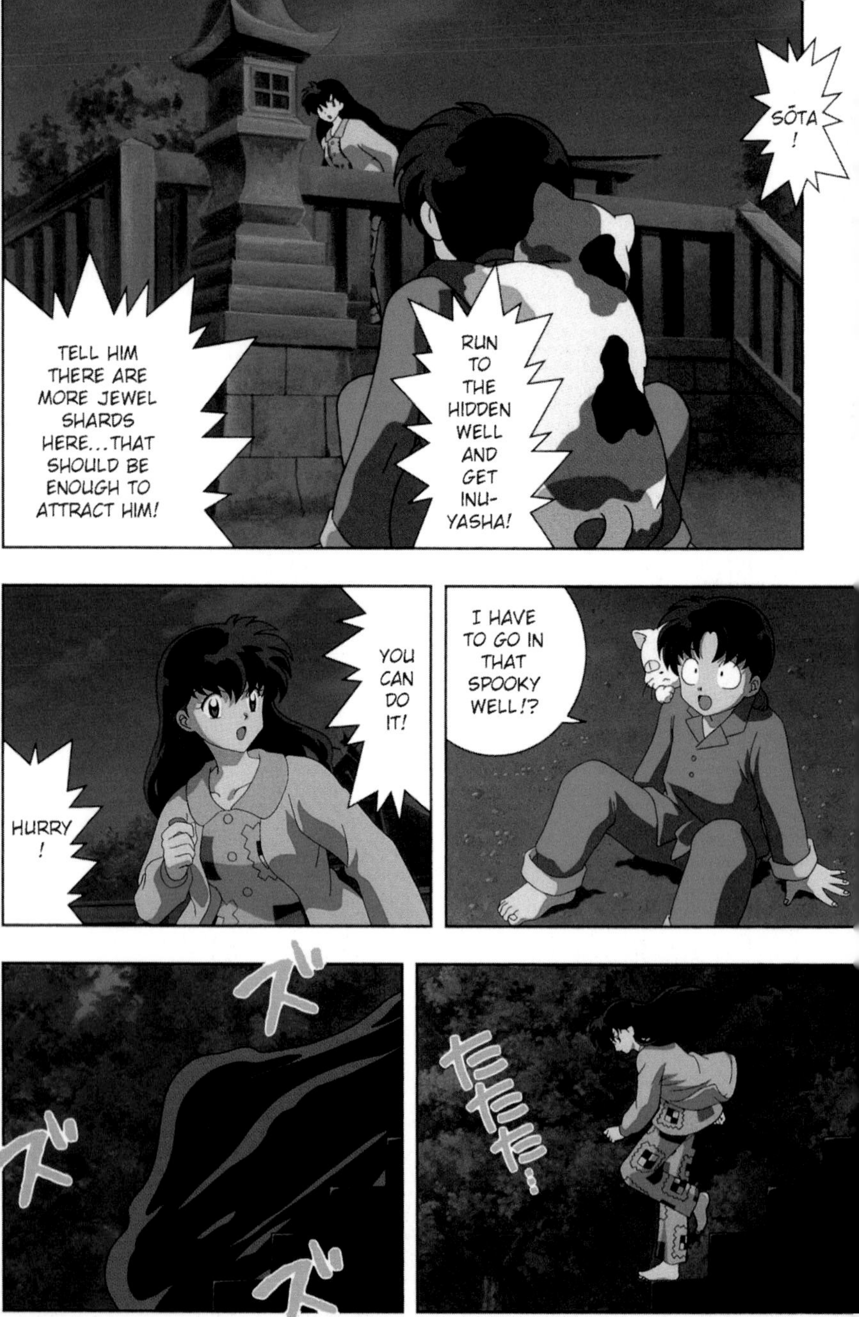
SŌTA!
RUN TO THE HIDDEN WELL AND GET INU-YASHA!
TELL HIM THERE ARE MORE JEWEL SHARDS HERE...THAT SHOULD BE ENOUGH TO ATTRACT HIM!
I HAVE TO GO IN THAT SPOOKY WELL!?
YOU CAN DO IT!
HURRY!
たたた…
ズ
ズ
ズ

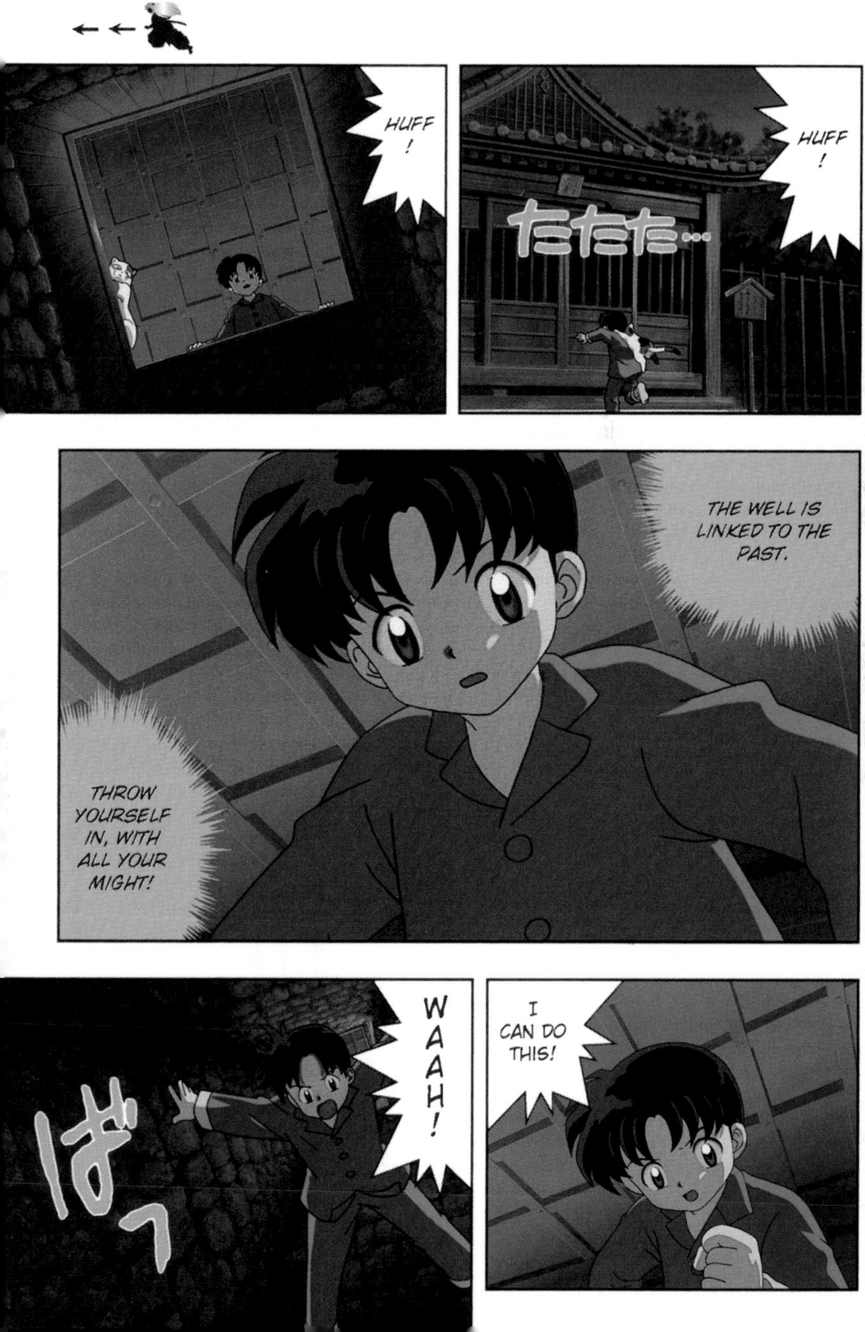
HUFF!
たたた…
HUFF!
THE WELL IS LINKED TO THE PAST.
THROW YOURSELF IN, WITH ALL YOUR MIGHT!
I CAN DO THIS!
WAAH!
ばっ

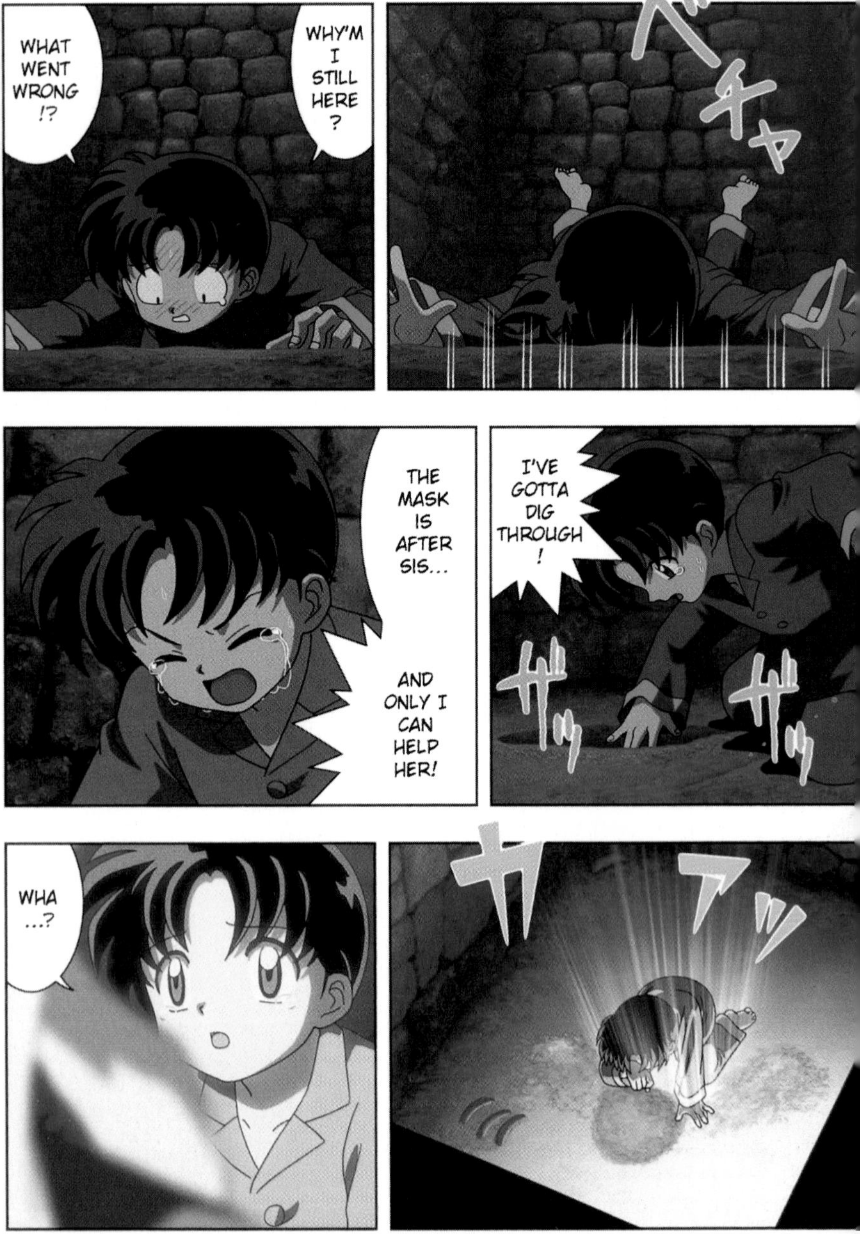
ベチャ
WHY'M I STILL HERE?
WHAT WENT WRONG!?
I'VE GOTTA DIG THROUGH!
ザッ
ザッ
THE MASK IS AFTER SIS...
AND ONLY I CAN HELP HER!
カアッ
WHA...?

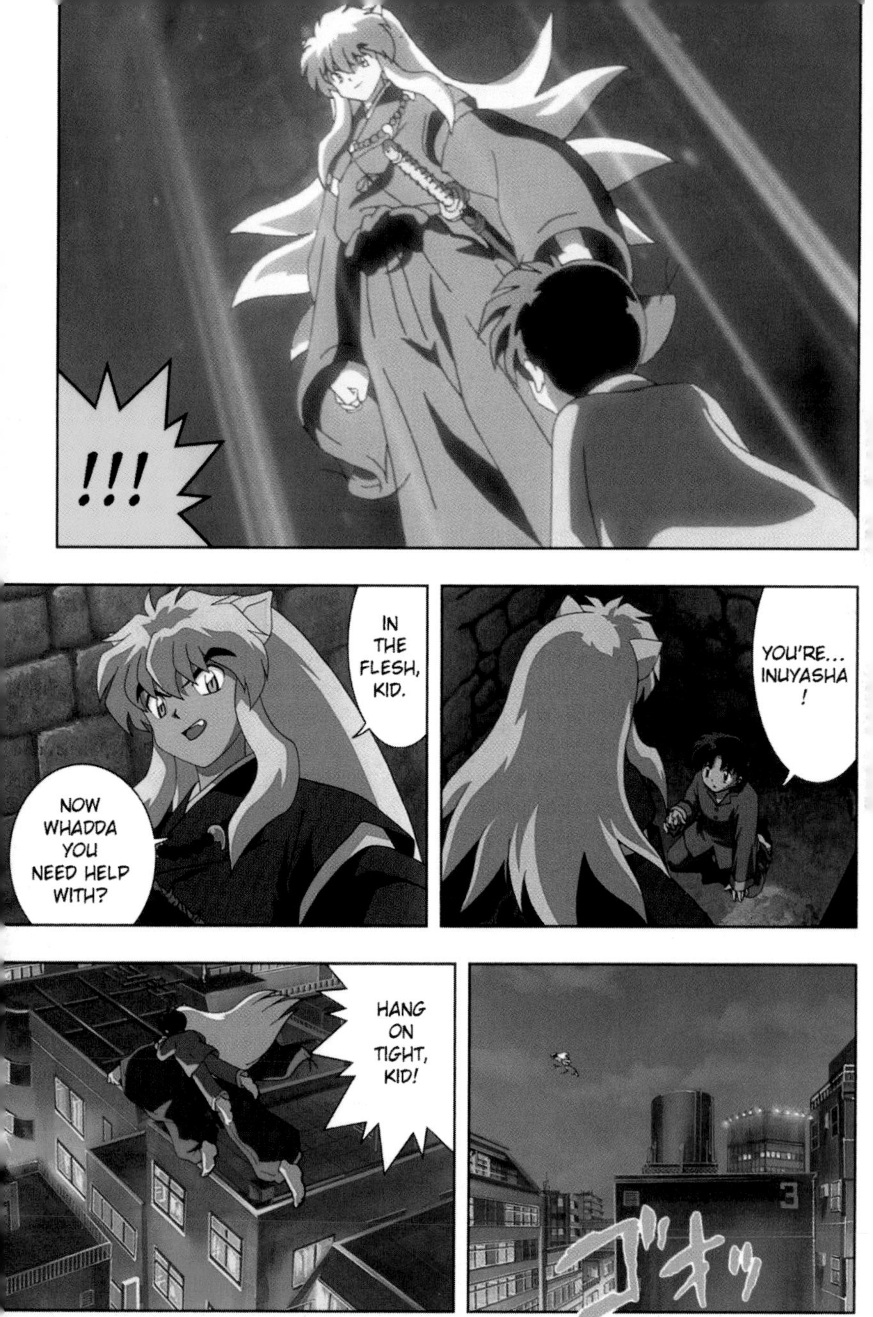
!!!
YOU'RE... INUYASHA!
IN THE FLESH, KID.
NOW WHADDA YOU NEED HELP WITH?
ゴオッ
HANG ON TIGHT, KID!

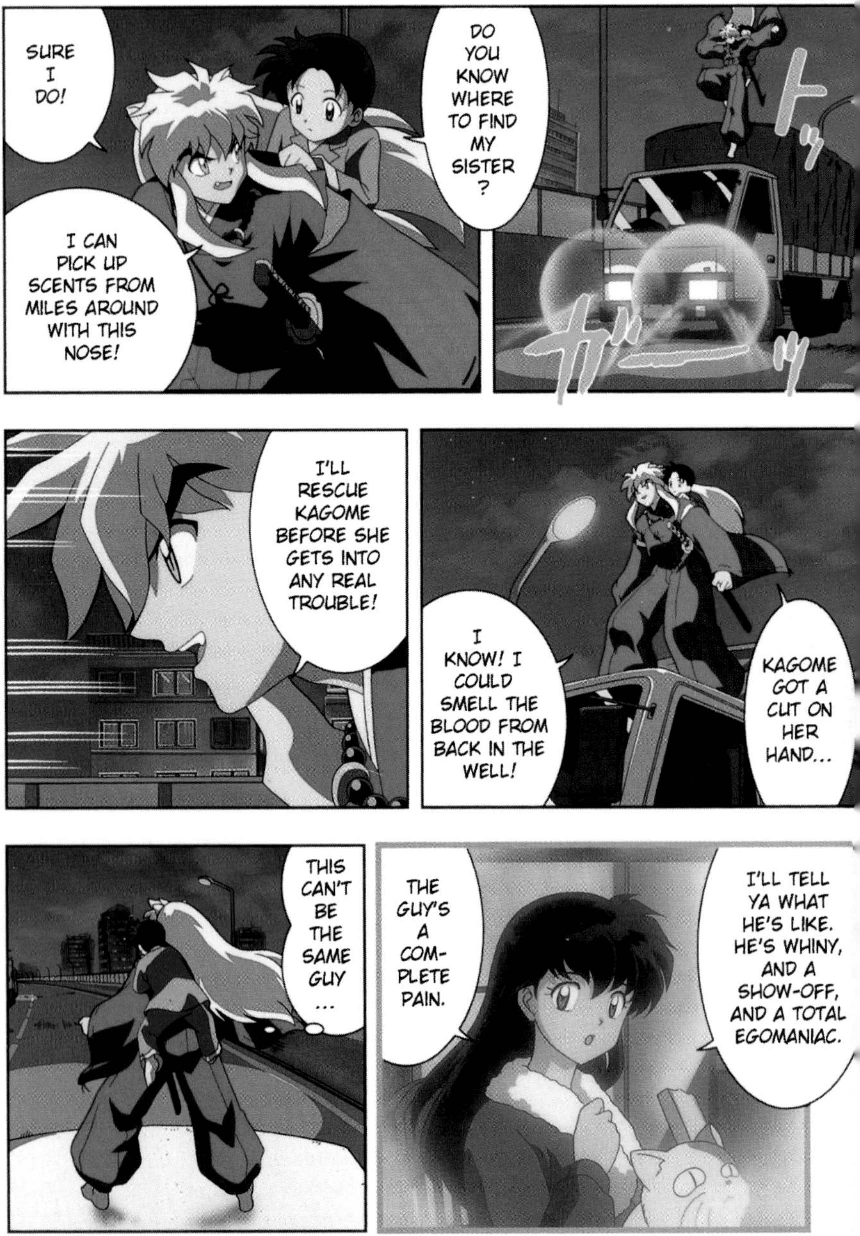
トッ
ガーッ
DO YOU KNOW WHERE TO FIND MY SISTER?
SURE I DO!
I CAN PICK UP SCENTS FROM MILES AROUND WITH THIS NOSE!
KAGOME GOT A CUT ON HER HAND...
I KNOW! I COULD SMELL THE BLOOD FROM BACK IN THE WELL!
I'LL RESCUE KAGOME BEFORE SHE GETS INTO ANY REAL TROUBLE!
I'LL TELL YA WHAT HE'S LIKE. HE'S WHINY, AND A SHOW-OFF, AND A TOTAL EGOMANIAC.
THE GUY'S A COMPLETE PAIN.
THIS CAN'T BE THE SAME GUY...

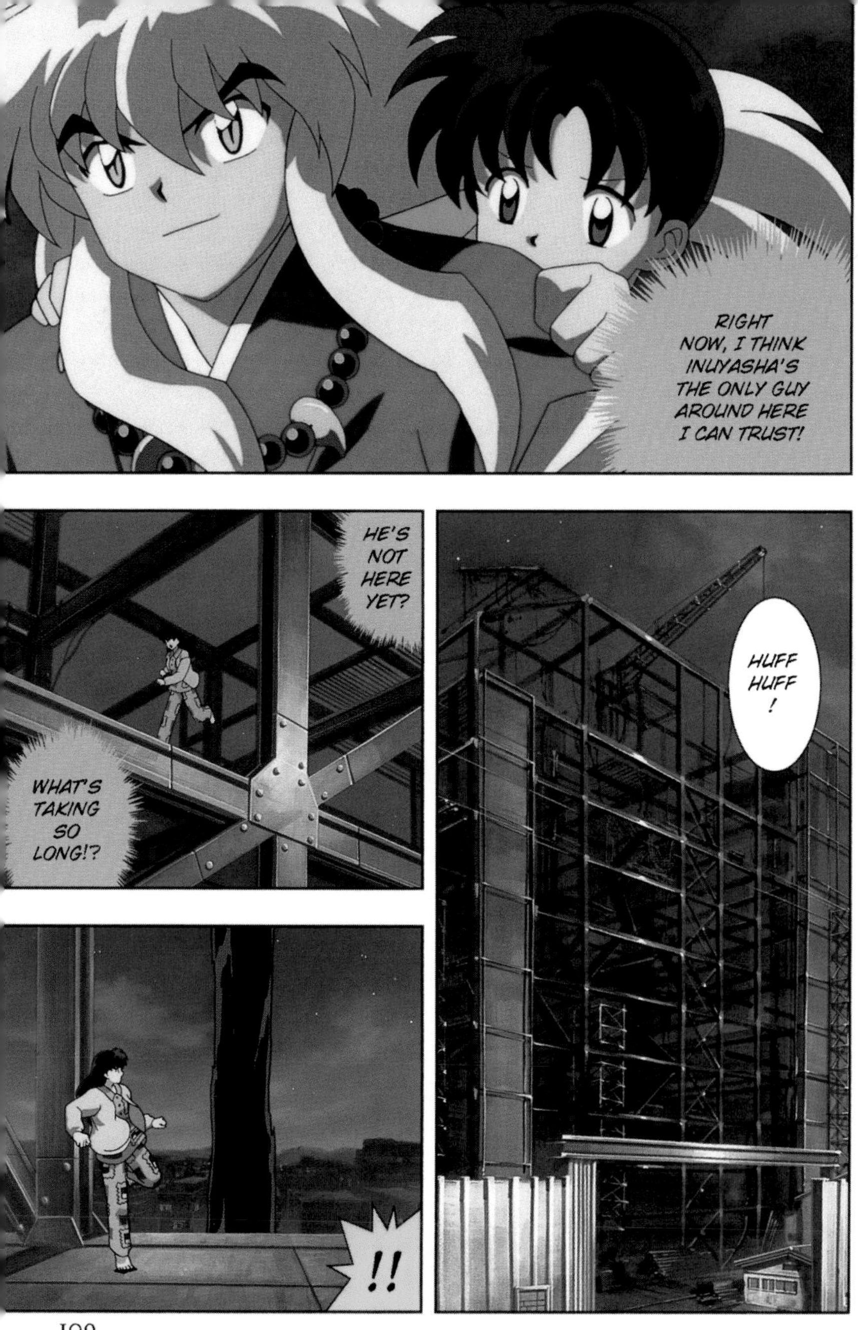
RIGHT NOW, I THINK INUYASHA'S THE ONLY GUY AROUND HERE I CAN TRUST!
HUFF HUFF !
HE'S NOT HERE YET?
WHAT'S TAKING SO LONG!?
!!

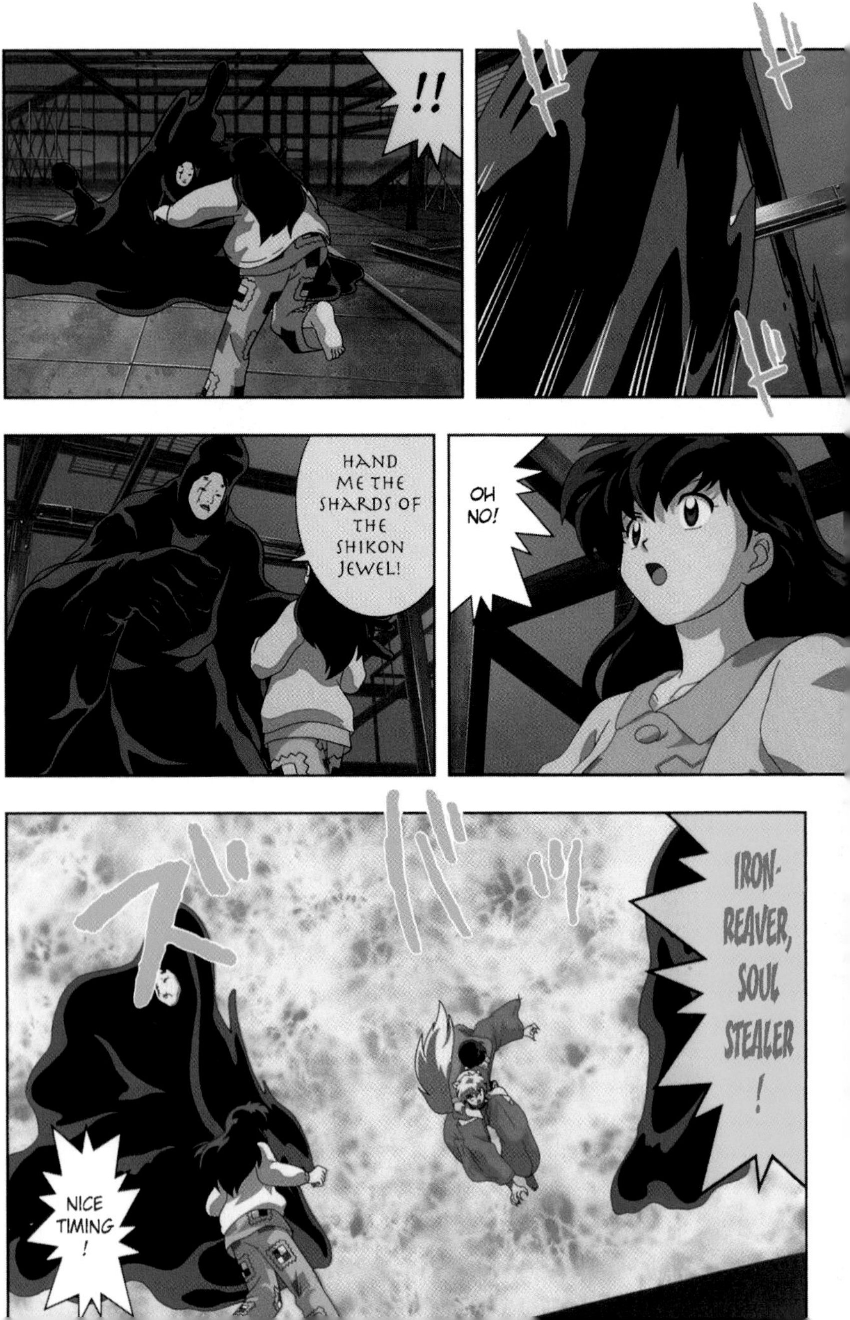
!!
OH NO!
HAND ME THE SHARDS OF THE SHIKON JEWEL!
IRON-REAVER, SOUL STEALER!
ズバッ
NICE TIMING!

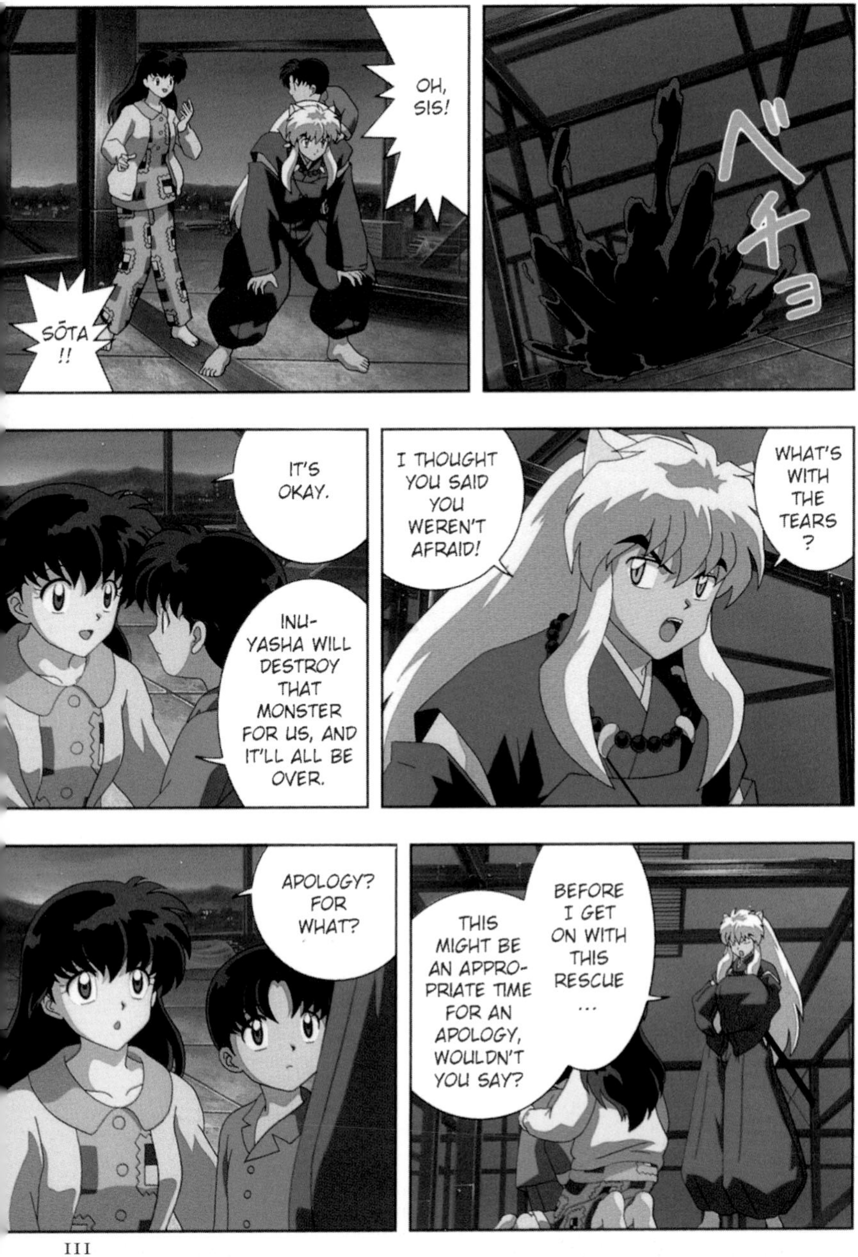
ベチョ
OH, SIS!
SŌTA !!
WHAT'S WITH THE TEARS ?
I THOUGHT YOU SAID YOU WEREN'T AFRAID!
IT'S OKAY.
INU-YASHA WILL DESTROY THAT MONSTER FOR US, AND IT'LL ALL BE OVER.
BEFORE I GET ON WITH THIS RESCUE ...
THIS MIGHT BE AN APPROPRIATE TIME FOR AN APOLOGY, WOULDN'T YOU SAY?
APOLOGY? FOR WHAT?

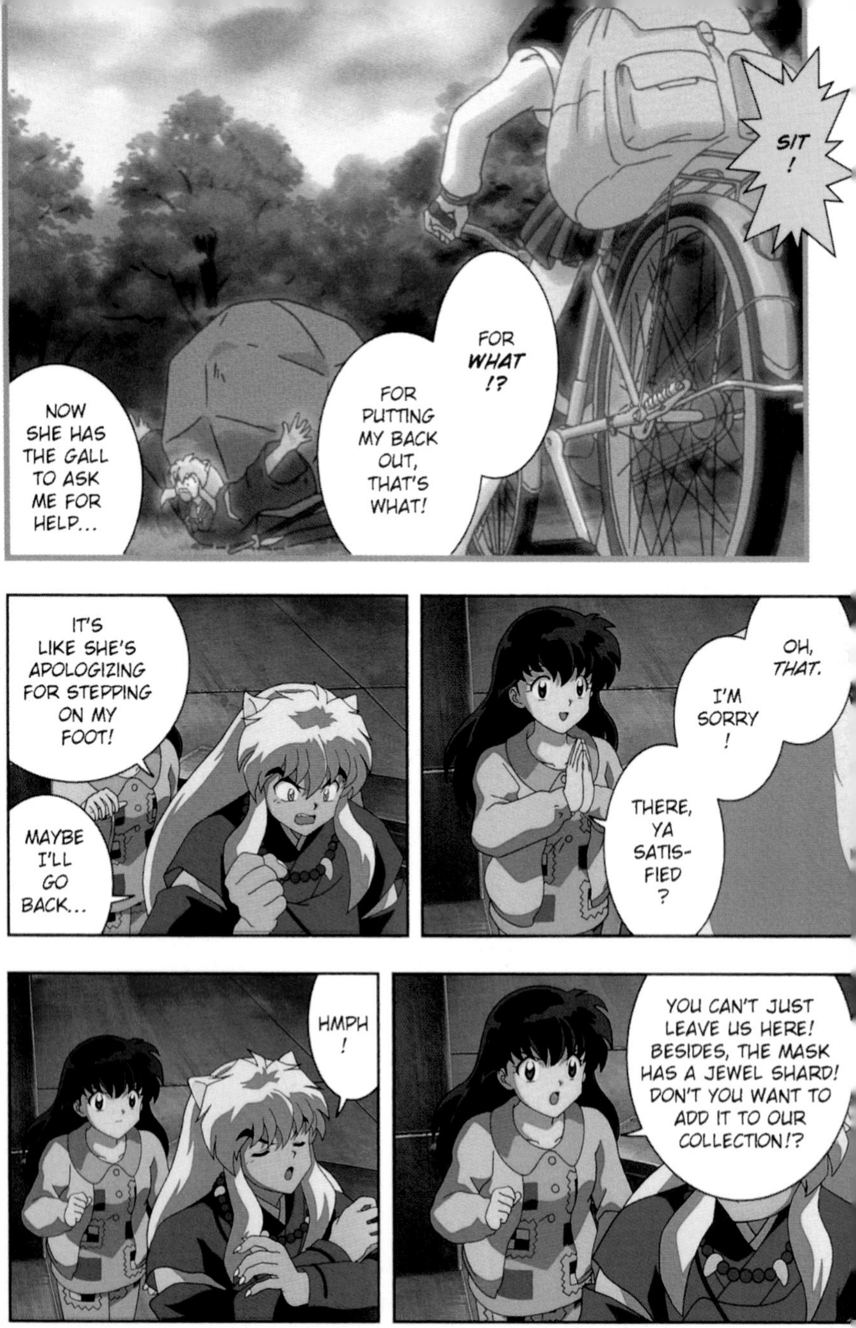
SIT!
FOR WHAT!?
FOR PUTTING MY BACK OUT, THAT'S WHAT!
NOW SHE HAS THE GALL TO ASK ME FOR HELP...
OH, THAT.
I'M SORRY!
THERE, YA SATISFIED?
IT'S LIKE SHE'S APOLOGIZING FOR STEPPING ON MY FOOT!
MAYBE I'LL GO BACK...
YOU CAN'T JUST LEAVE US HERE! BESIDES, THE MASK HAS A JEWEL SHARD! DON'T YOU WANT TO ADD IT TO OUR COLLECTION!?
HMPH!

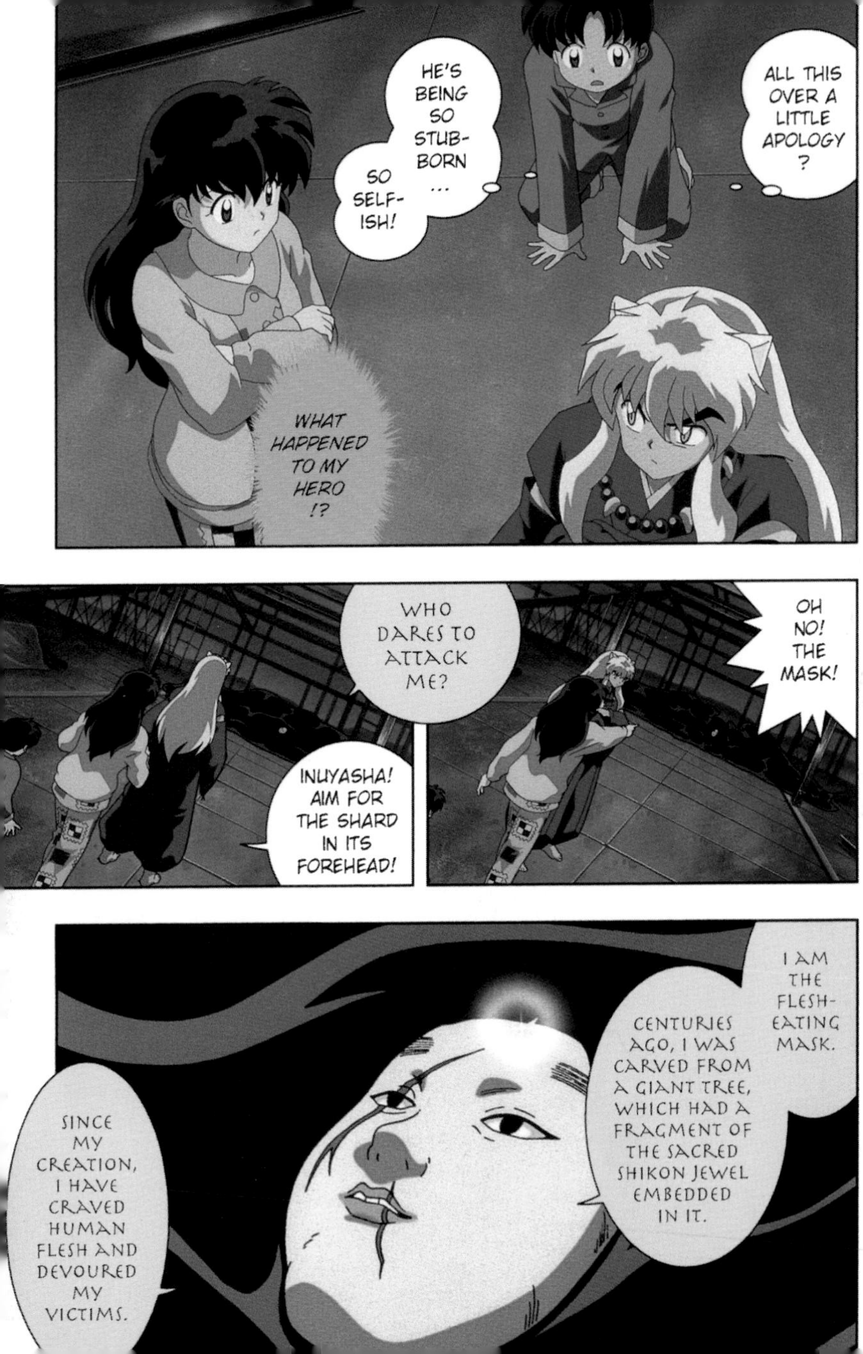
ALL THIS OVER A LITTLE APOLOGY?
HE'S BEING SO STUBBORN...
SO SELFISH!
WHAT HAPPENED TO MY HERO!?
OH NO! THE MASK!
WHO DARES TO ATTACK ME?
INUYASHA! AIM FOR THE SHARD IN ITS FOREHEAD!
I AM THE FLESH-EATING MASK.
CENTURIES AGO, I WAS CARVED FROM A GIANT TREE, WHICH HAD A FRAGMENT OF THE SACRED SHIKON JEWEL EMBEDDED IN IT.
SINCE MY CREATION, I HAVE CRAVED HUMAN FLESH AND DEVOURED MY VICTIMS.

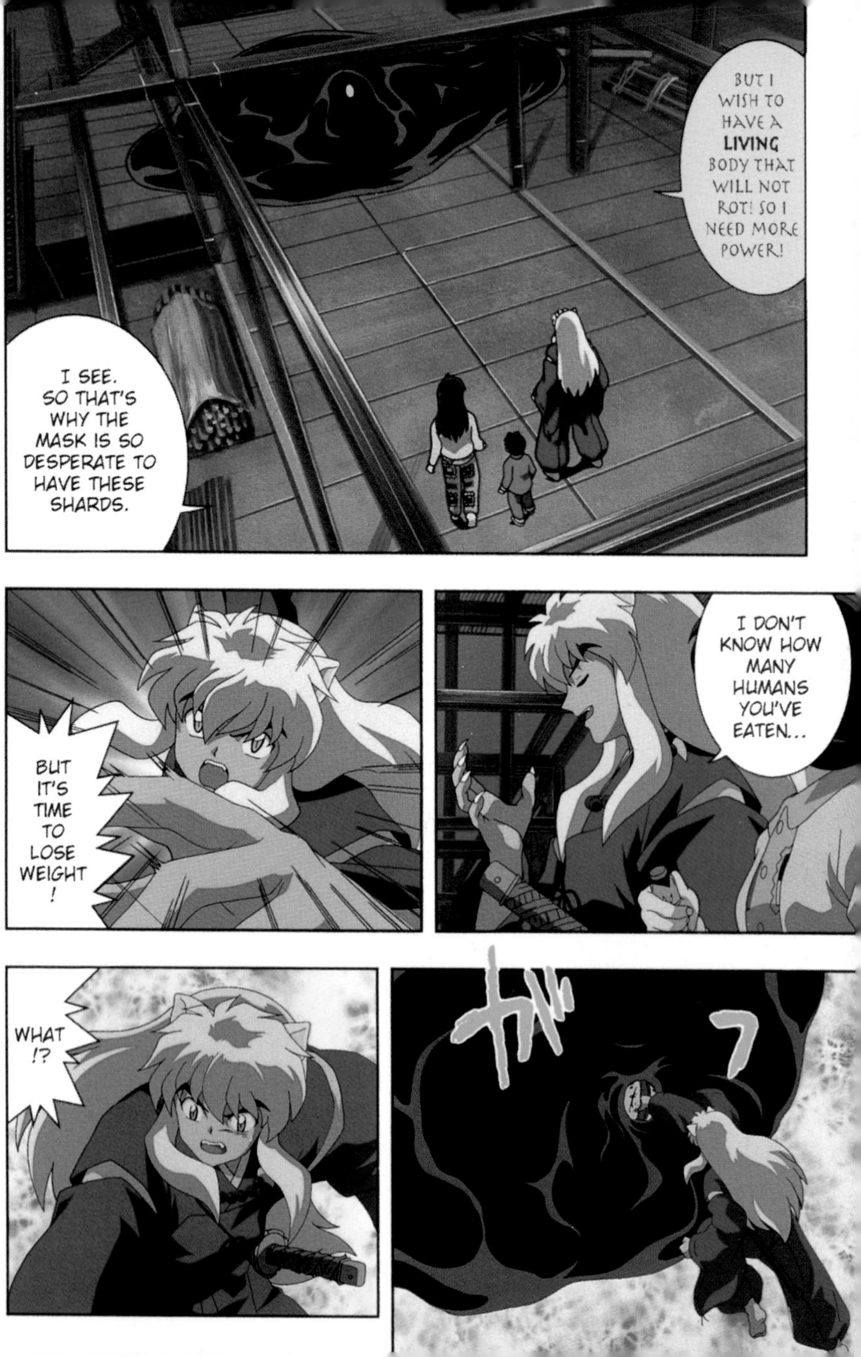
BUT I WISH TO HAVE A **LIVING** BODY THAT WILL NOT ROT! SO I NEED MORE POWER!
I SEE. SO THAT'S WHY THE MASK IS SO DESPERATE TO HAVE THESE SHARDS.
I DON'T KNOW HOW MANY HUMANS YOU'VE EATEN...
BUT IT'S TIME TO LOSE WEIGHT!
WHAT!?

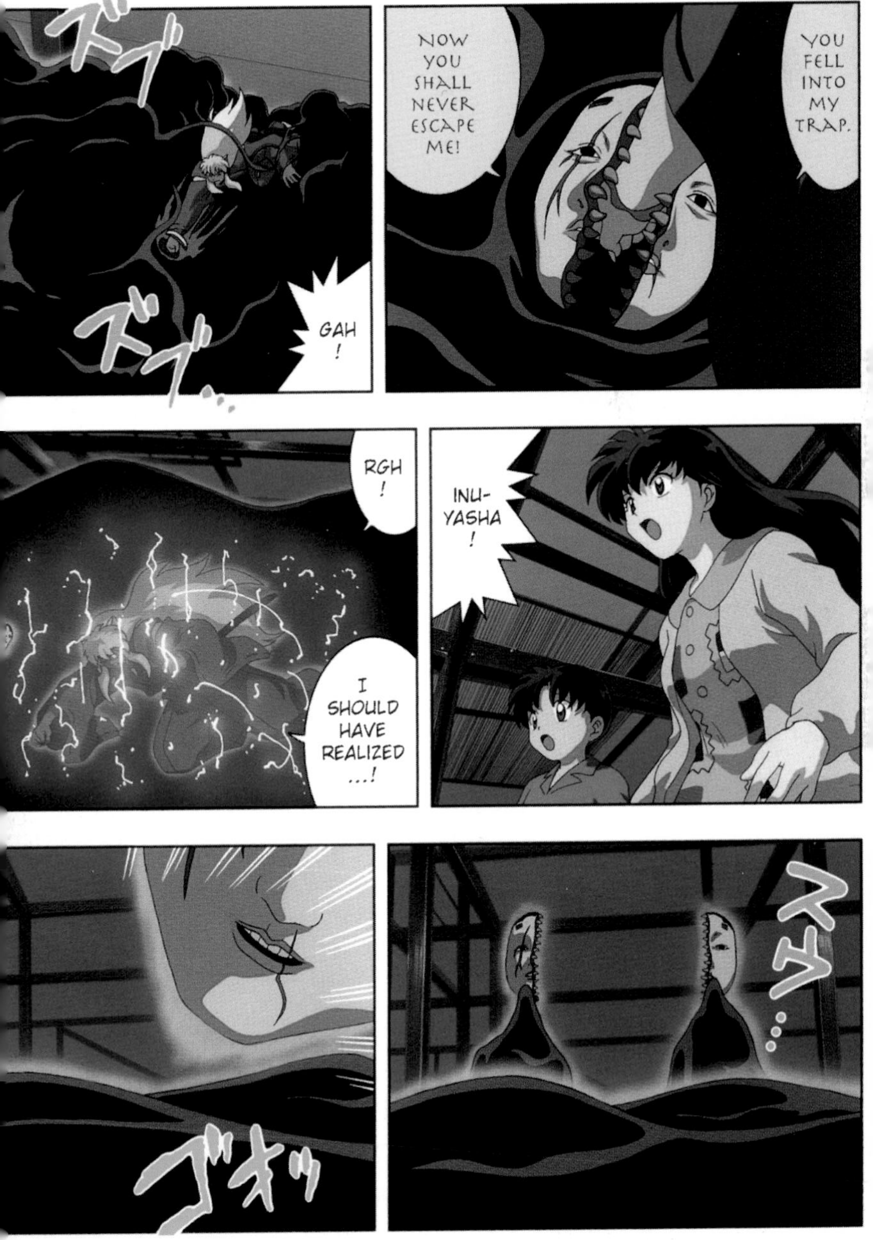
YOU FELL INTO MY TRAP.
NOW YOU SHALL NEVER ESCAPE ME!
ズブ
ズブ…
GAH!
INU-YASHA!
RGH!
I SHOULD HAVE REALIZED…!
スゥ…
ゴオッ

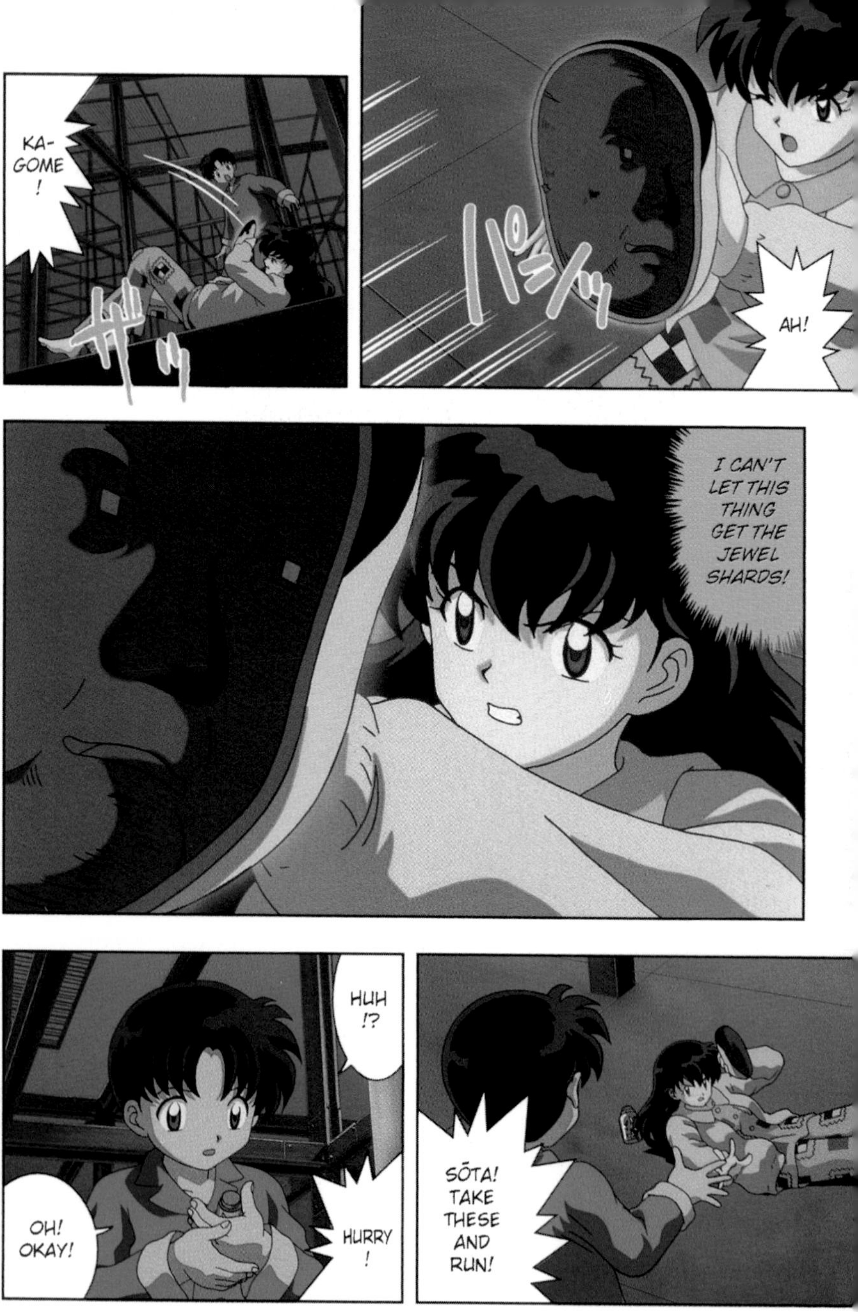
パシッ
AH!
KA-GOME!
ザッ
I CAN'T LET THIS THING GET THE JEWEL SHARDS!
SŌTA! TAKE THESE AND RUN!
HUH!?
HURRY!
OH! OKAY!

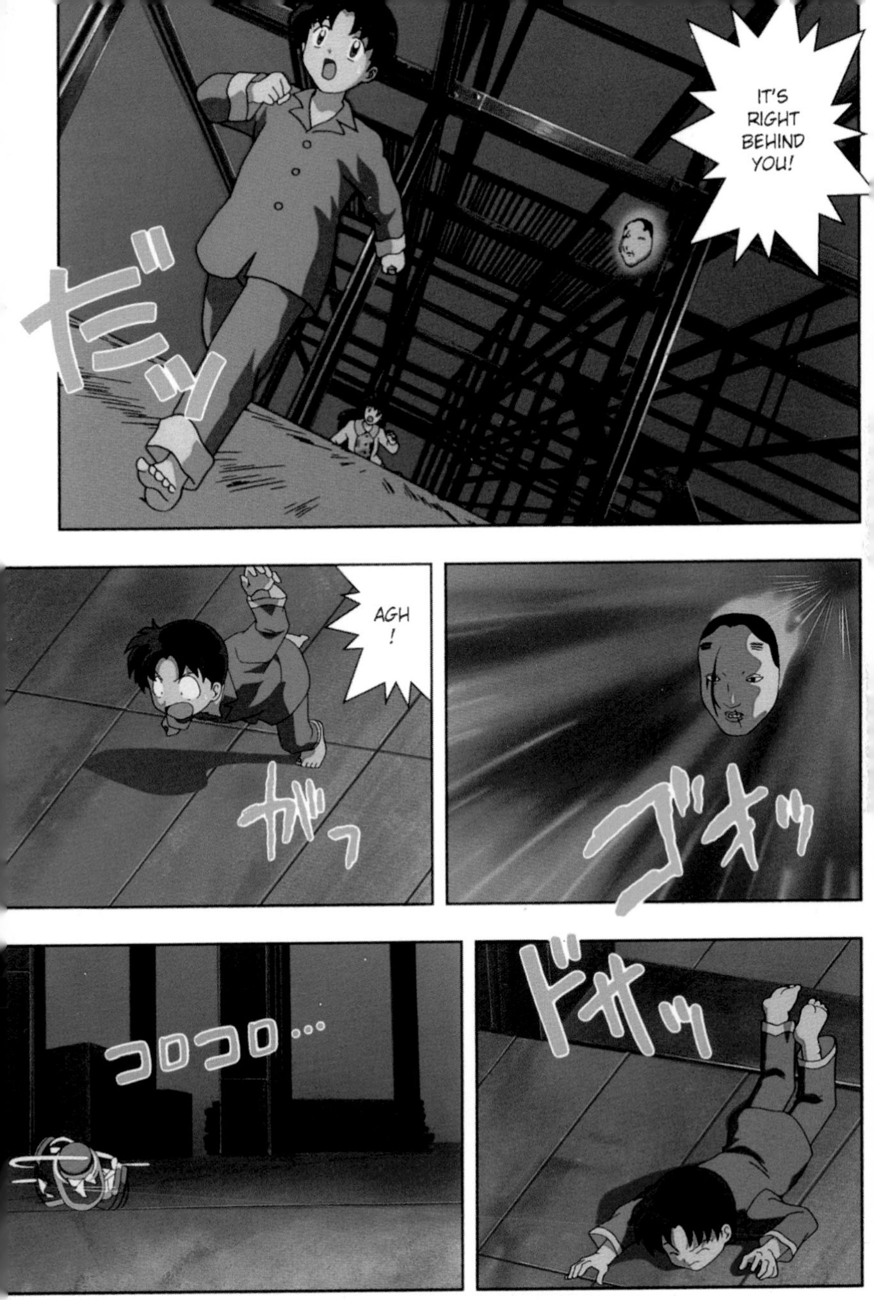
IT'S RIGHT BEHIND YOU!
ダッ
ゴオッ
AGH!
ガバッ
ドサッ
コロコロ…

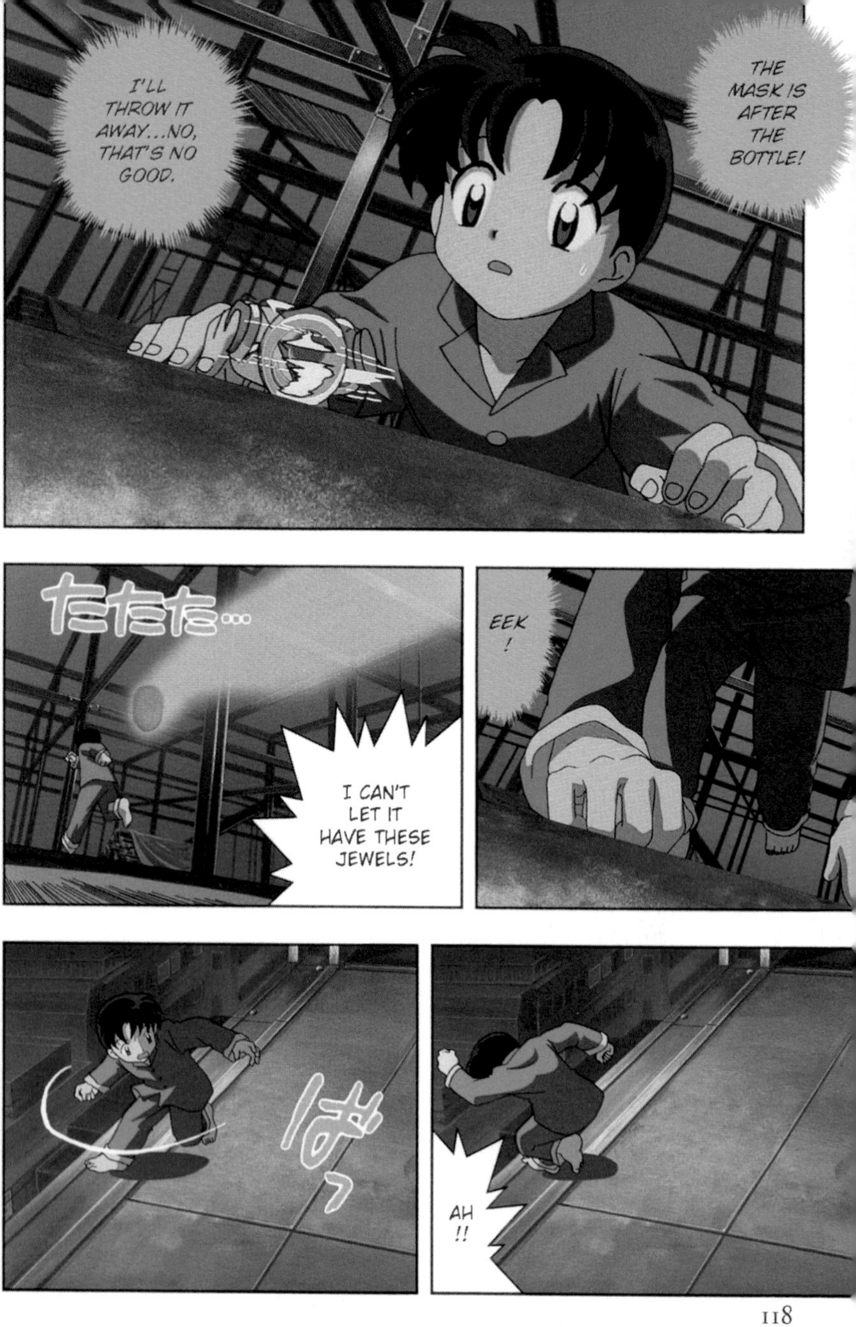
THE MASK IS AFTER THE BOTTLE!
I'LL THROW IT AWAY...NO, THAT'S NO GOOD.
EEK!
たたたた…
I CAN'T LET IT HAVE THESE JEWELS!
AH!!
ばっ

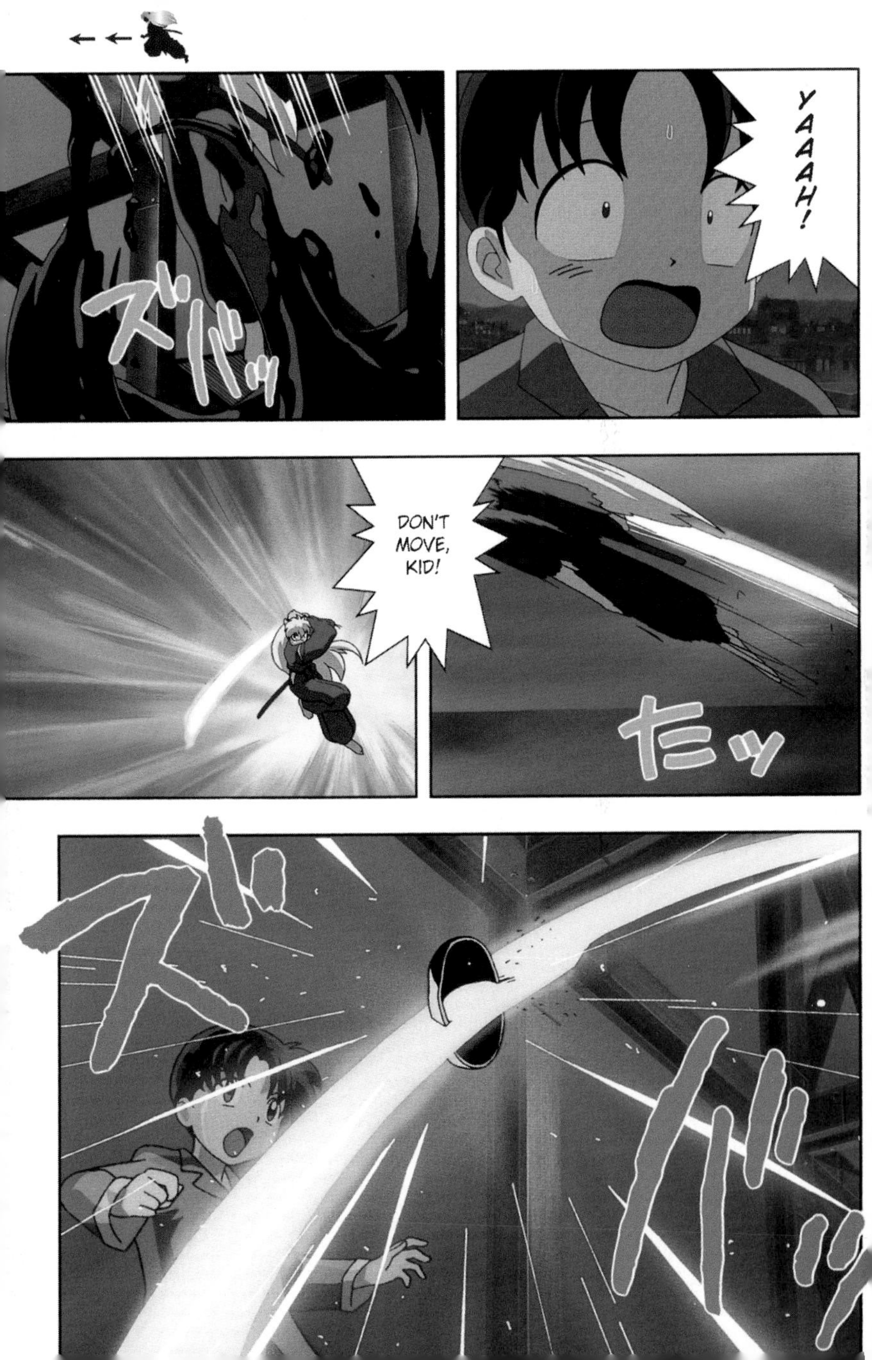
YAAAH!
ズバッ
たッ
DON'T MOVE, KID!
ズバッ

パーン
カァァァァ…
シュウゥ…
コロン…
YOU DID IT!
YOU DES-TROYED IT!

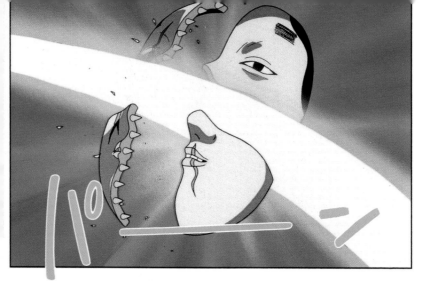

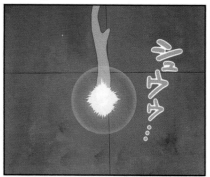

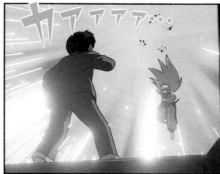

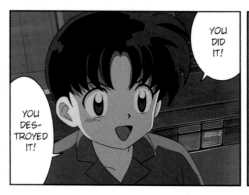

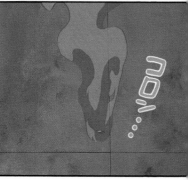

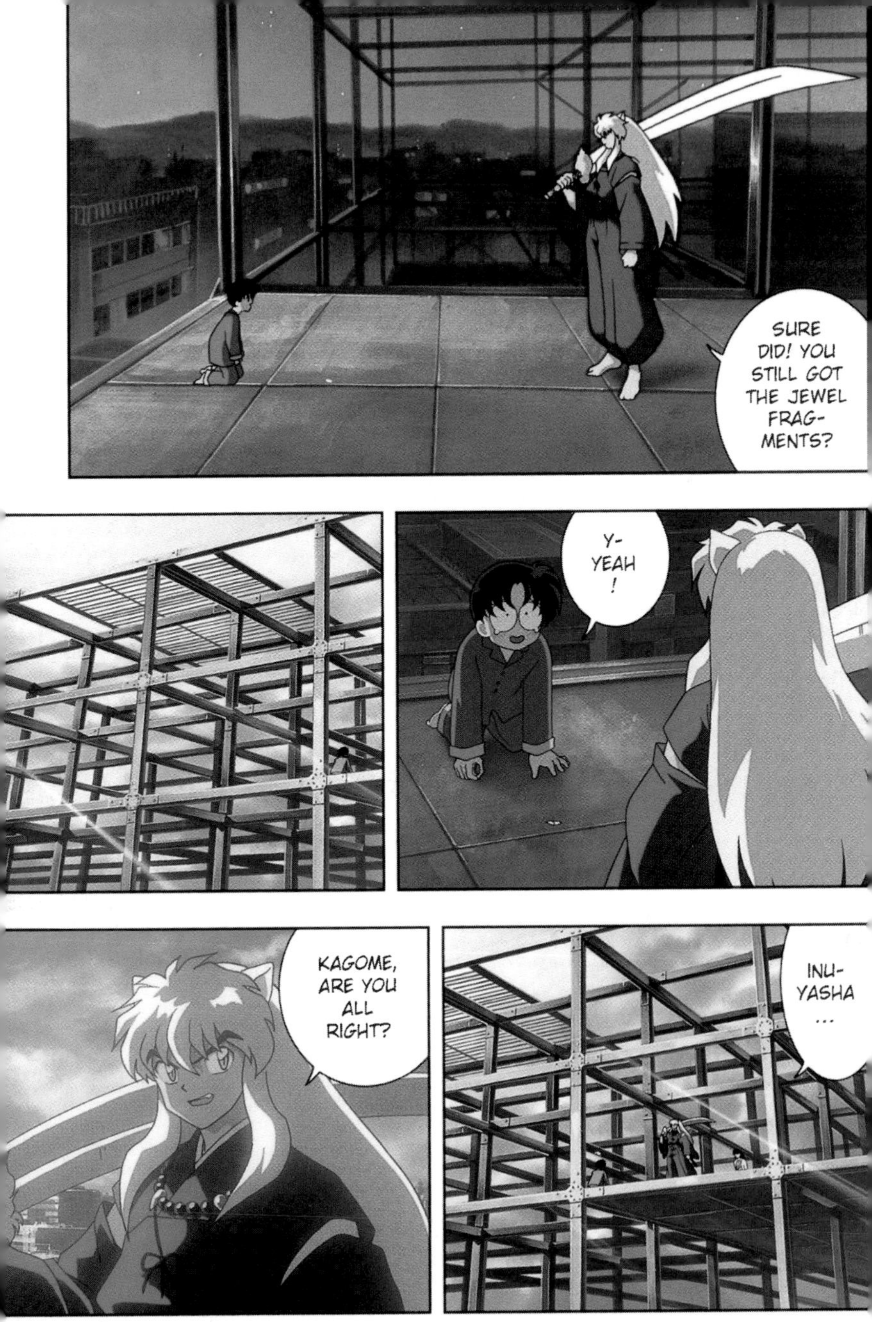

SURE DID! YOU STILL GOT THE JEWEL FRAG- MENTS?
Y- YEAH !
INU- YASHA ...
KAGOME, ARE YOU ALL RIGHT?

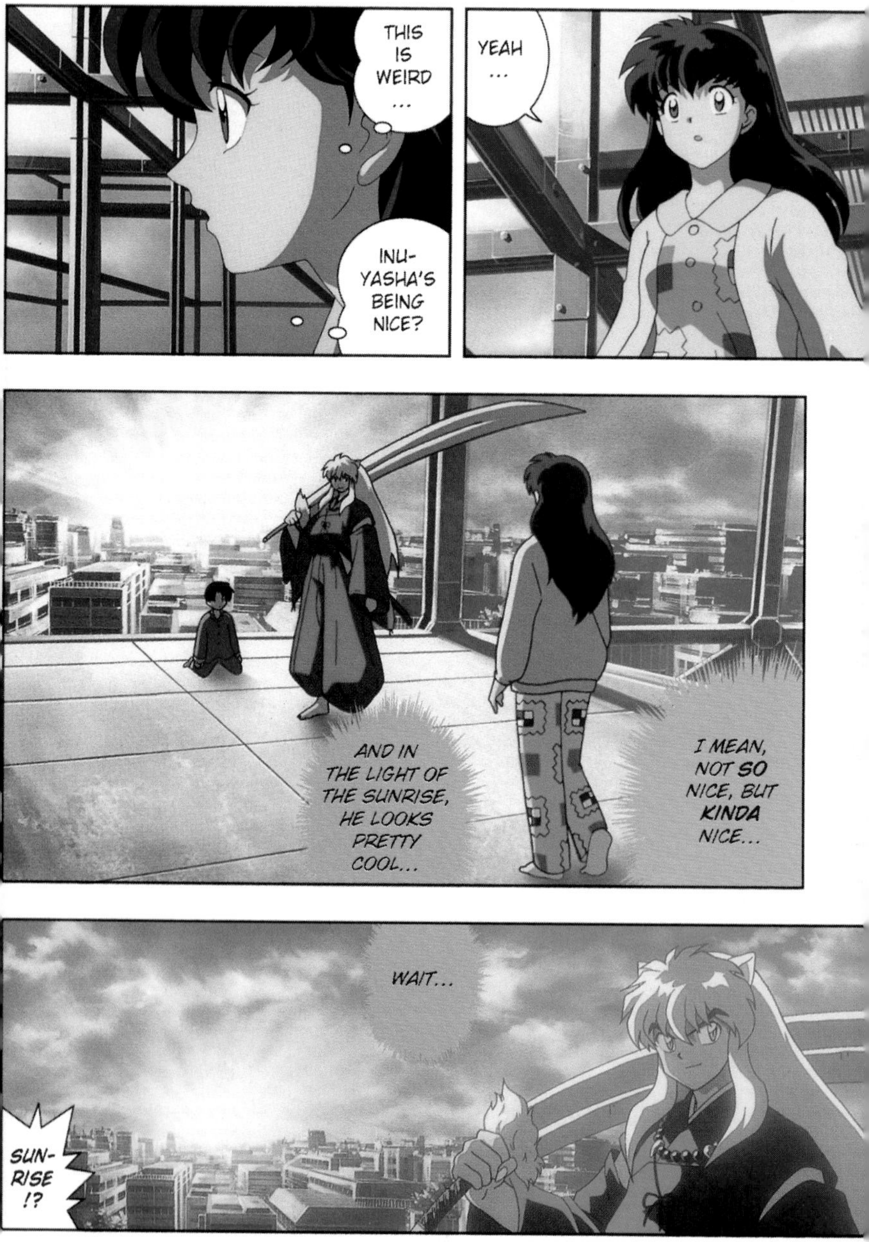
YEAH …
THIS IS WEIRD …
INU-YASHA'S BEING NICE?
I MEAN, NOT SO NICE, BUT KINDA NICE…
AND IN THE LIGHT OF THE SUNRISE, HE LOOKS PRETTY COOL…
WAIT…
SUN-RISE !?

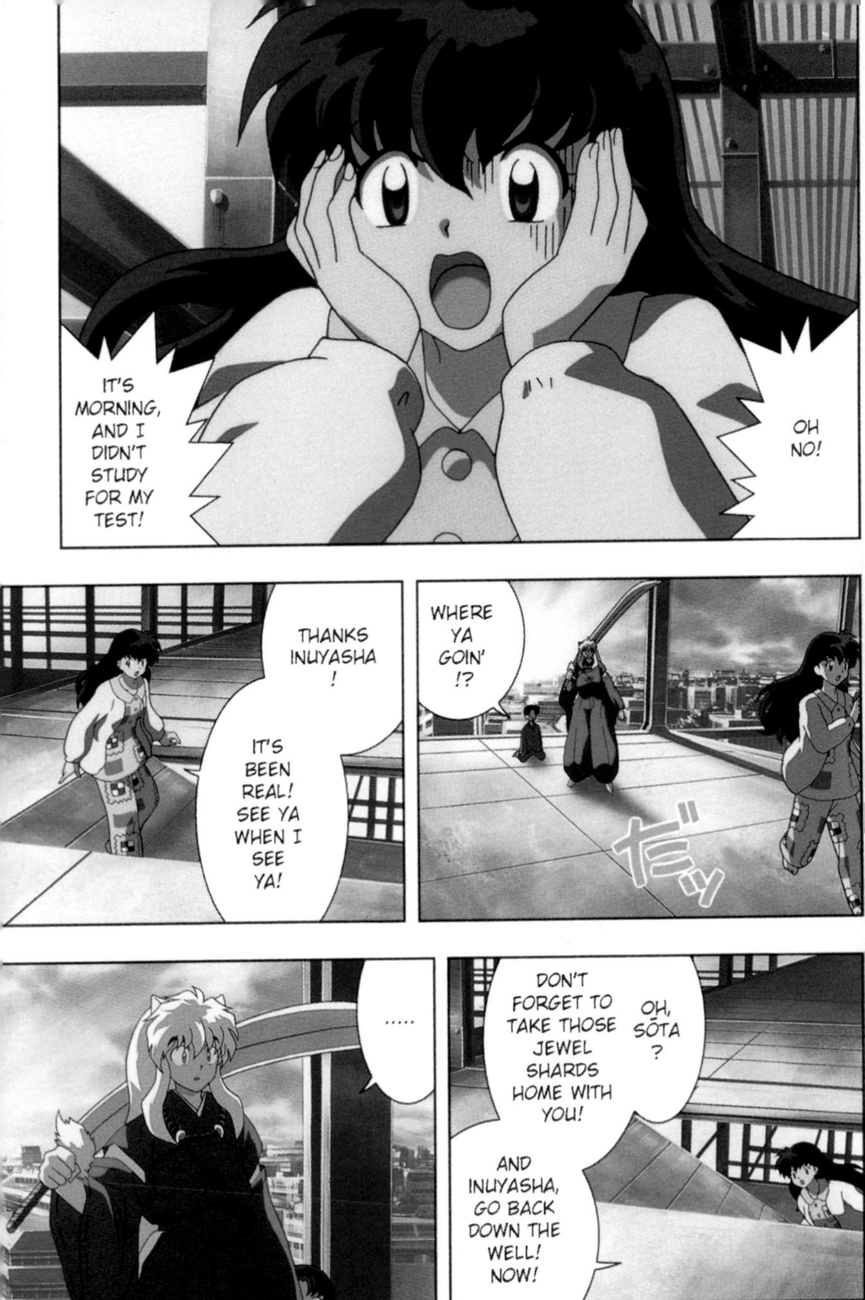
OH NO!
IT'S MORNING, AND I DIDN'T STUDY FOR MY TEST!
WHERE YA GOIN' !?
ダッ
THANKS INUYASHA !
IT'S BEEN REAL! SEE YA WHEN I SEE YA!
OH, SŌTA ?
DON'T FORGET TO TAKE THOSE JEWEL SHARDS HOME WITH YOU!
AND INUYASHA, GO BACK DOWN THE WELL! NOW!
.....

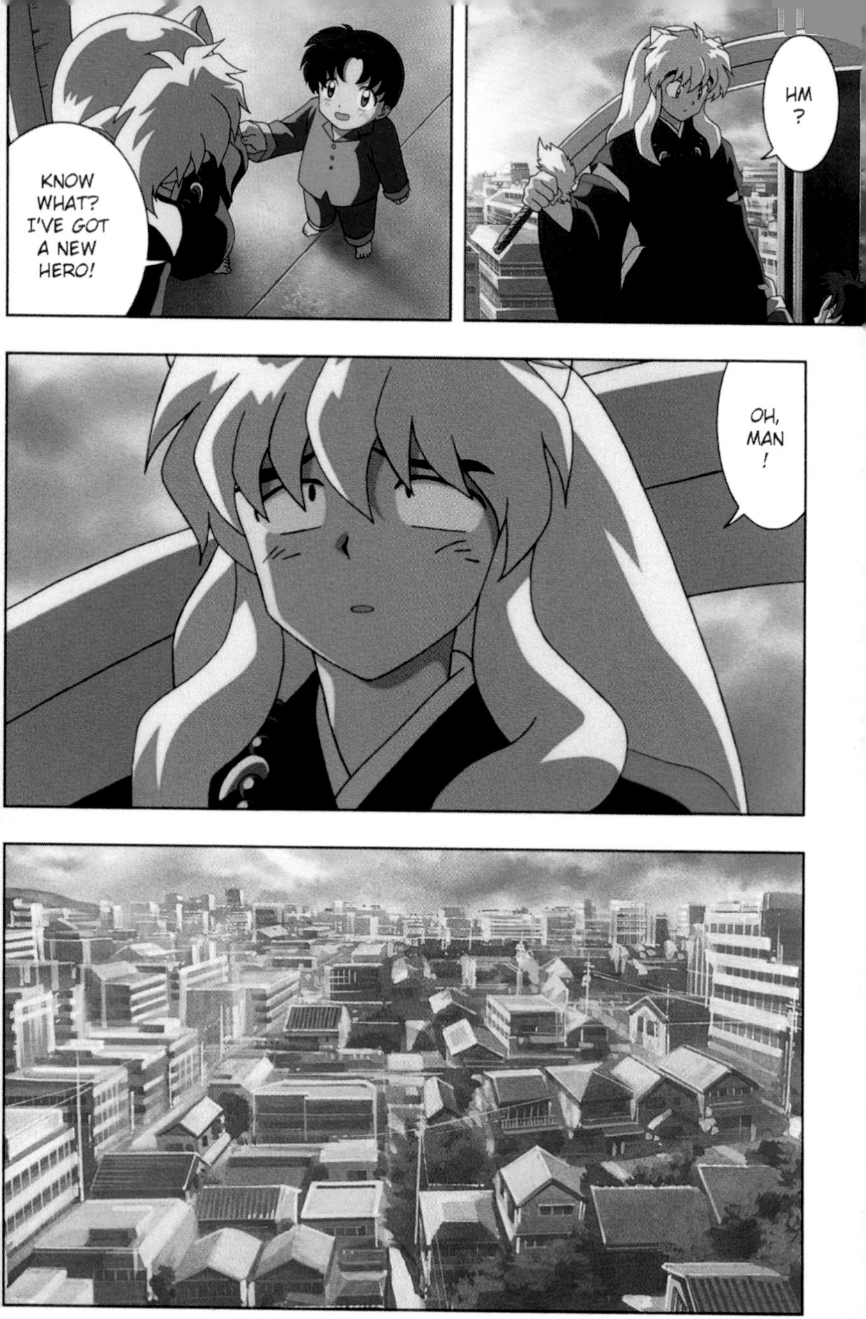
HM?
KNOW WHAT? I'VE GOT A NEW HERO!
OH, MAN!

12
The Soul Piper and the Mischievous Little Soul

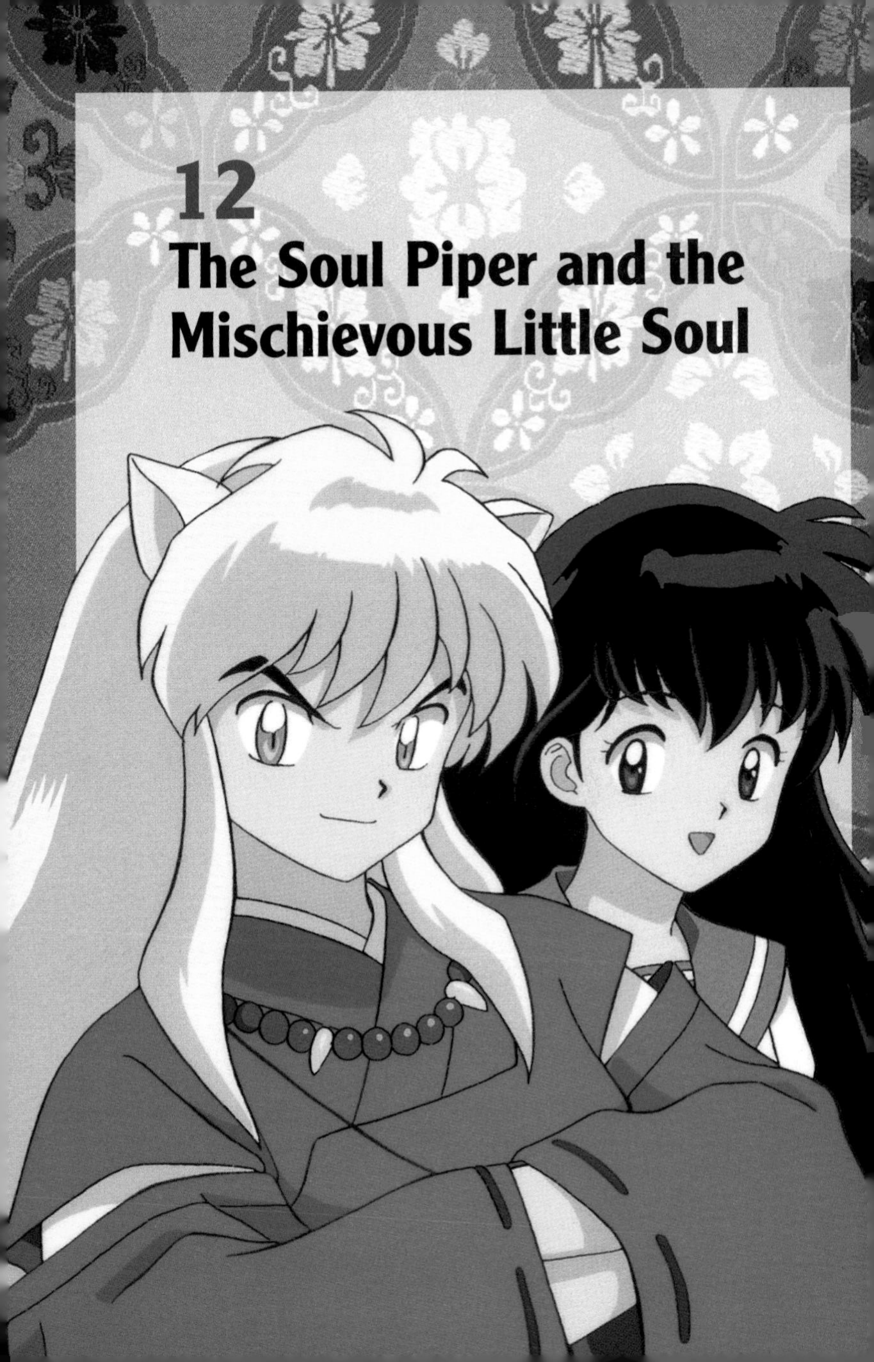

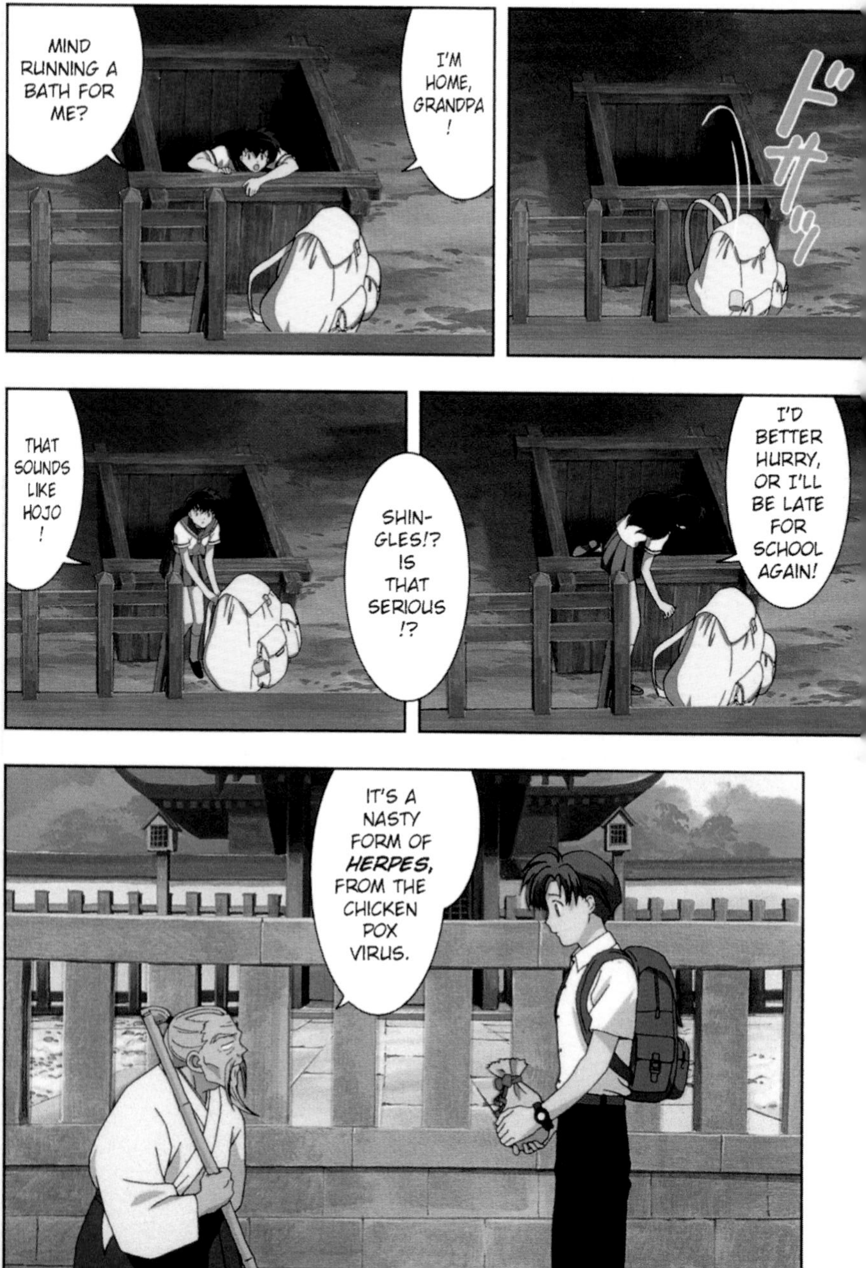
ドサッ
I'M HOME, GRANDPA!
MIND RUNNING A BATH FOR ME?
I'D BETTER HURRY, OR I'LL BE LATE FOR SCHOOL AGAIN!
SHIN-GLES!? IS THAT SERIOUS!?
THAT SOUNDS LIKE HOJO!
IT'S A NASTY FORM OF ***HERPES,*** FROM THE CHICKEN POX VIRUS.

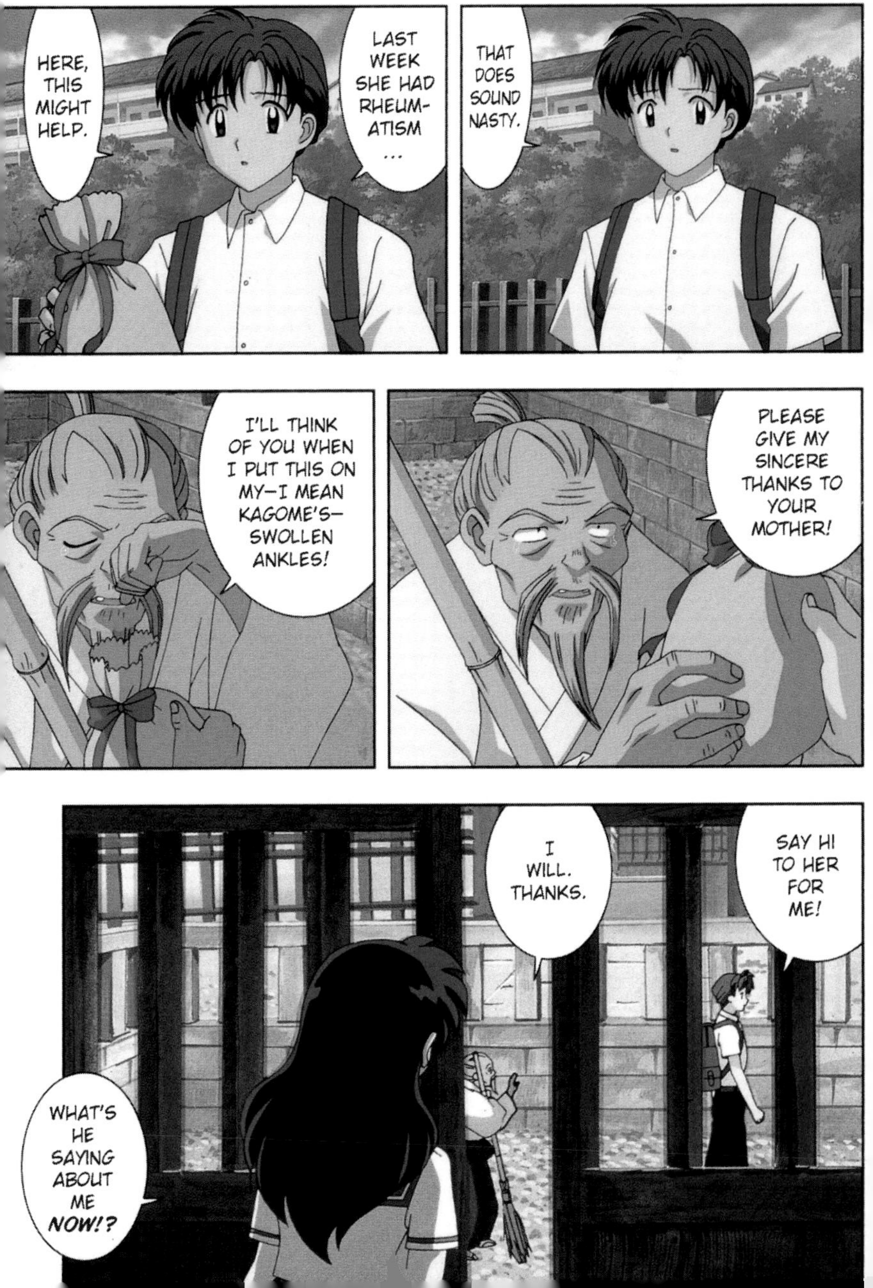
THAT DOES SOUND NASTY.
LAST WEEK SHE HAD RHEUM-ATISM ...
HERE, THIS MIGHT HELP.
PLEASE GIVE MY SINCERE THANKS TO YOUR MOTHER!
I'LL THINK OF YOU WHEN I PUT THIS ON MY—I MEAN KAGOME'S—SWOLLEN ANKLES!
SAY HI TO HER FOR ME!
I WILL. THANKS.
WHAT'S HE SAYING ABOUT ME NOW!?

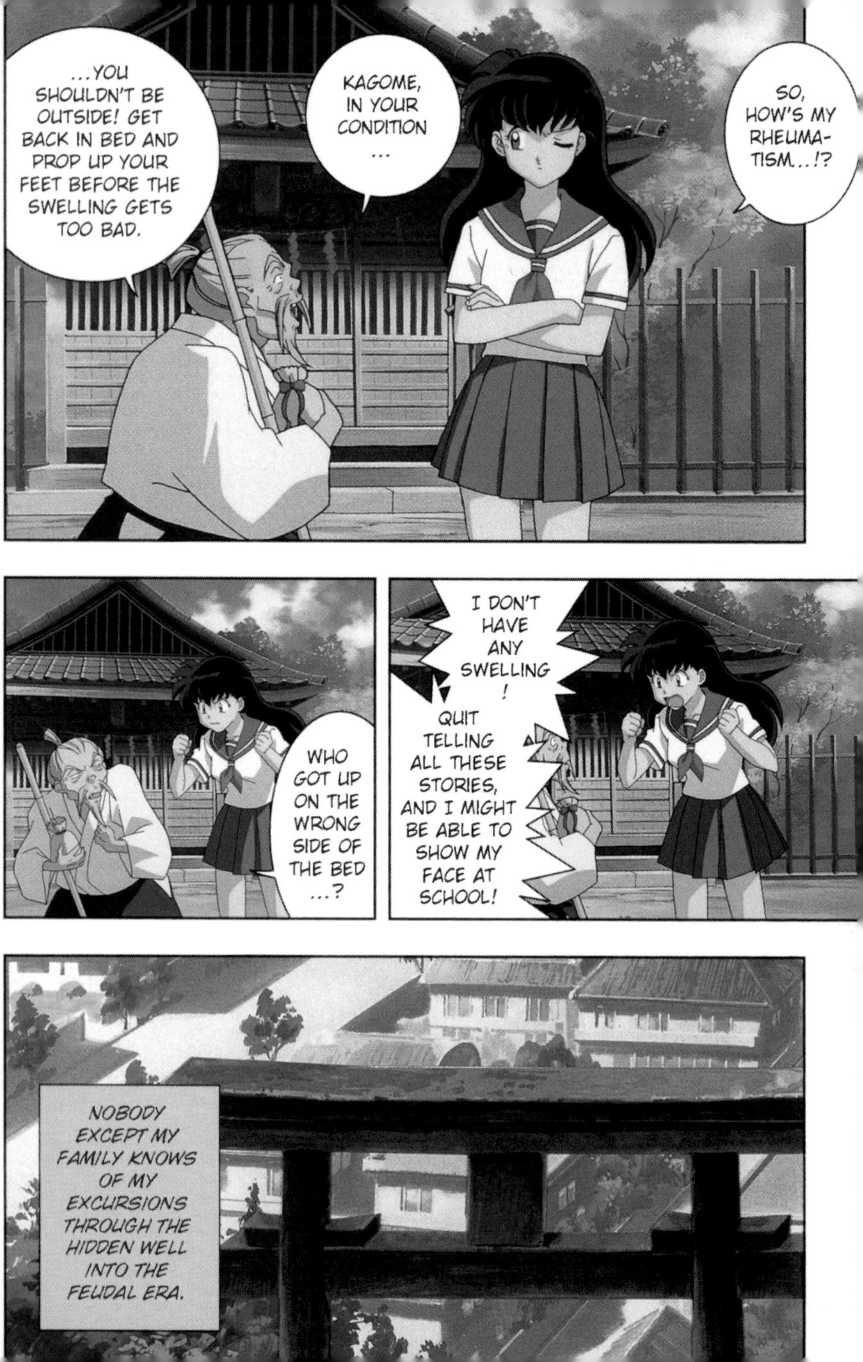
SO, HOW'S MY RHEUMA-TISM...!?
KAGOME, IN YOUR CONDITION ...
...YOU SHOULDN'T BE OUTSIDE! GET BACK IN BED AND PROP UP YOUR FEET BEFORE THE SWELLING GETS TOO BAD.
I DON'T HAVE ANY SWELLING!
QUIT TELLING ALL THESE STORIES, AND I MIGHT BE ABLE TO SHOW MY FACE AT SCHOOL!
WHO GOT UP ON THE WRONG SIDE OF THE BED ...?
NOBODY EXCEPT MY FAMILY KNOWS OF MY EXCURSIONS THROUGH THE HIDDEN WELL INTO THE FEUDAL ERA.

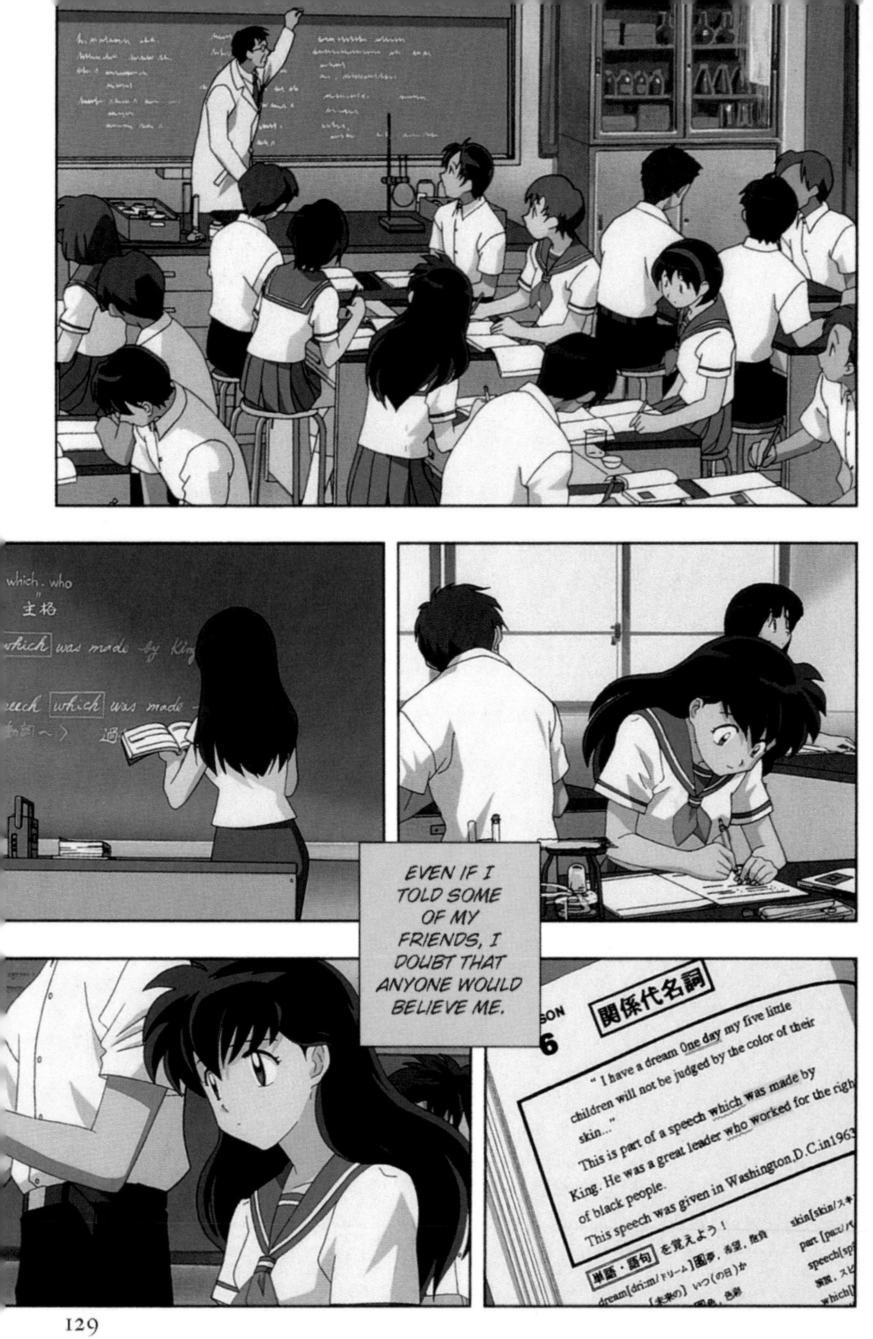

which. who
主格
which was made by Kin
eech which was made
EVEN IF I TOLD SOME OF MY FRIENDS, I DOUBT THAT ANYONE WOULD BELIEVE ME.
関係代名詞
" I have a dream One day my five little
children will not be judged by the color of their
skin... "
This is part of a speech which was made by
King. He was a great leader who worked for the righ
of black people.
This speech was given in Washington,D.C.in1963
単語・語句 を覚えよう！

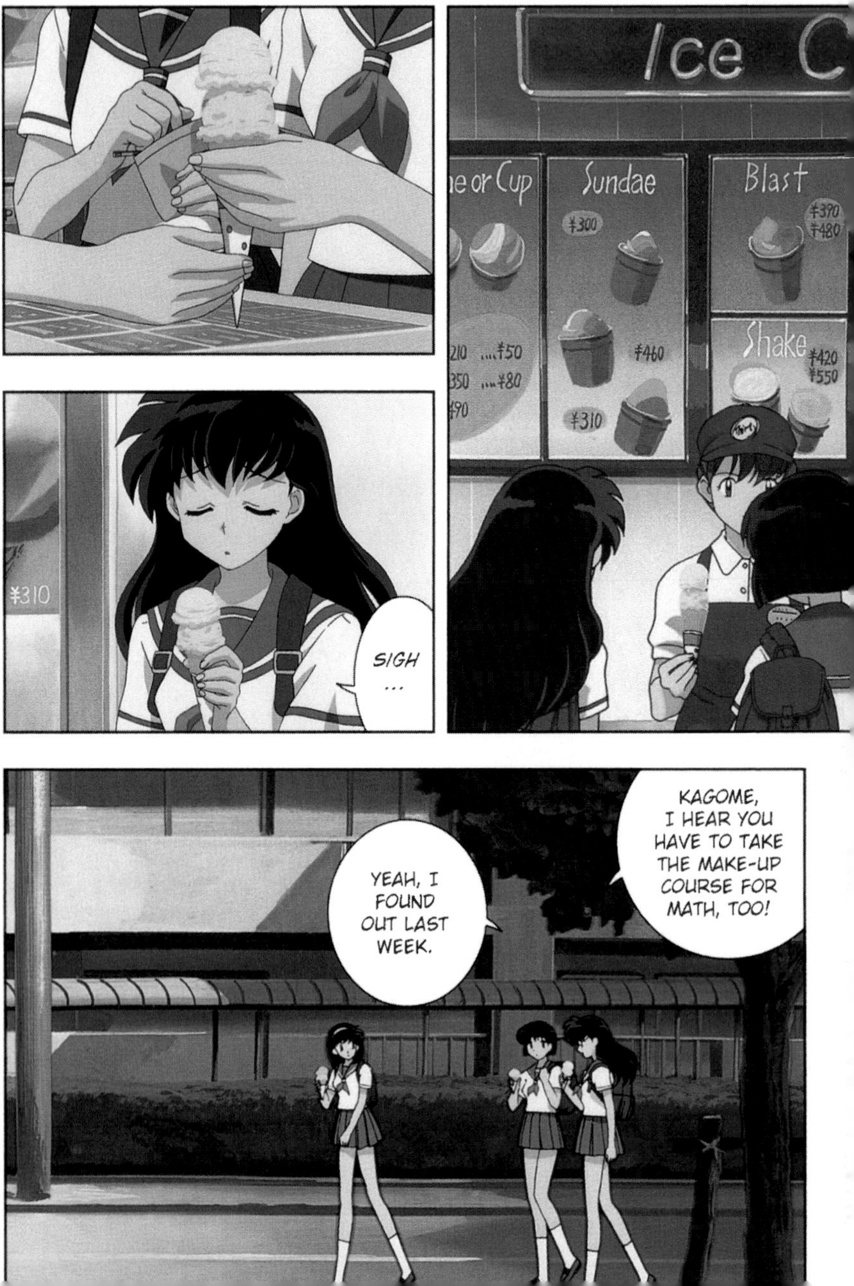
Ice C
ne or Cup
Sundae
Blast
Shake
¥300
¥460
¥310
¥390
¥480
¥420
¥550
¥310
SIGH ...
KAGOME, I HEAR YOU HAVE TO TAKE THE MAKE-UP COURSE FOR MATH, TOO!
YEAH, I FOUND OUT LAST WEEK.

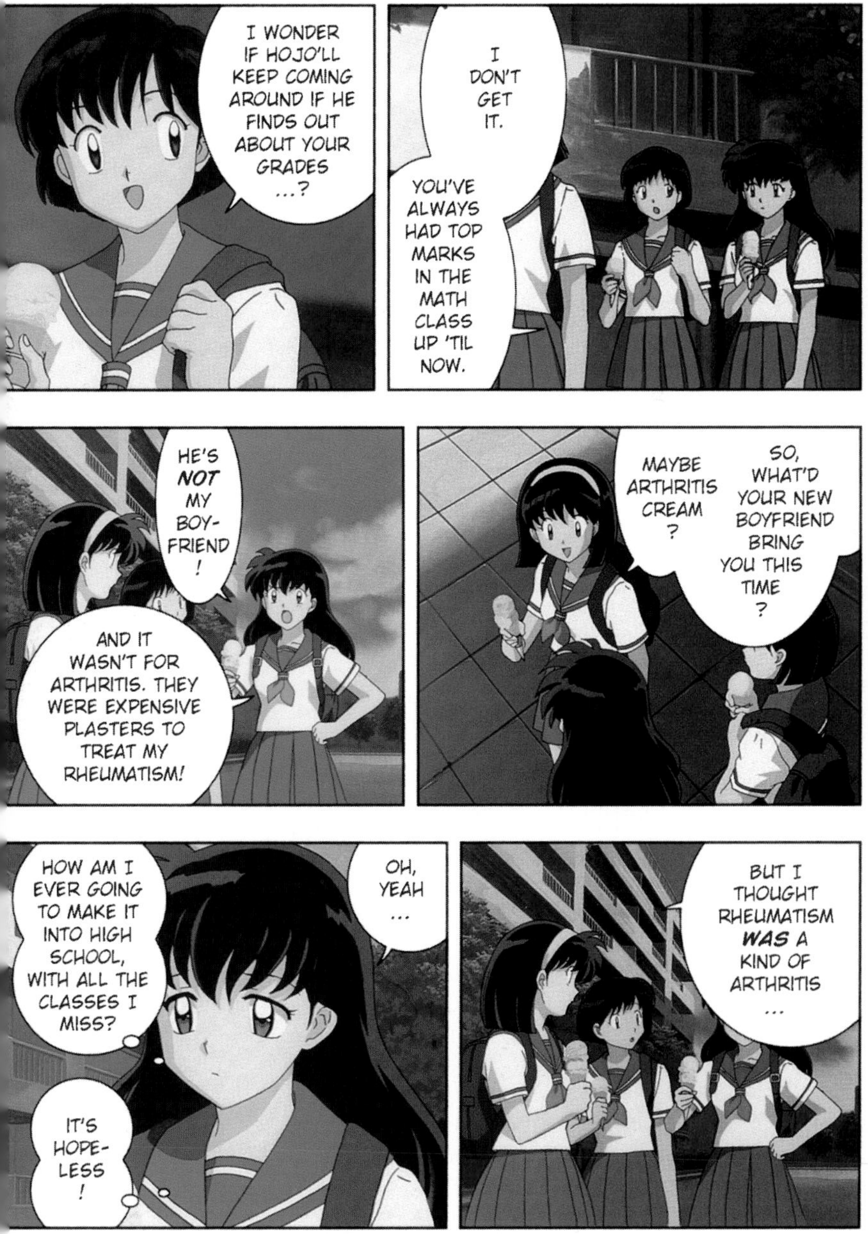

I DON'T GET IT.
YOU'VE ALWAYS HAD TOP MARKS IN THE MATH CLASS UP 'TIL NOW.
I WONDER IF HOJO'LL KEEP COMING AROUND IF HE FINDS OUT ABOUT YOUR GRADES ...?
SO, WHAT'D YOUR NEW BOYFRIEND BRING YOU THIS TIME?
MAYBE ARTHRITIS CREAM?
HE'S NOT MY BOY-FRIEND!
AND IT WASN'T FOR ARTHRITIS. THEY WERE EXPENSIVE PLASTERS TO TREAT MY RHEUMATISM!
BUT I THOUGHT RHEUMATISM WAS A KIND OF ARTHRITIS ...
OH, YEAH ...
HOW AM I EVER GOING TO MAKE IT INTO HIGH SCHOOL, WITH ALL THE CLASSES I MISS?
IT'S HOPE-LESS!

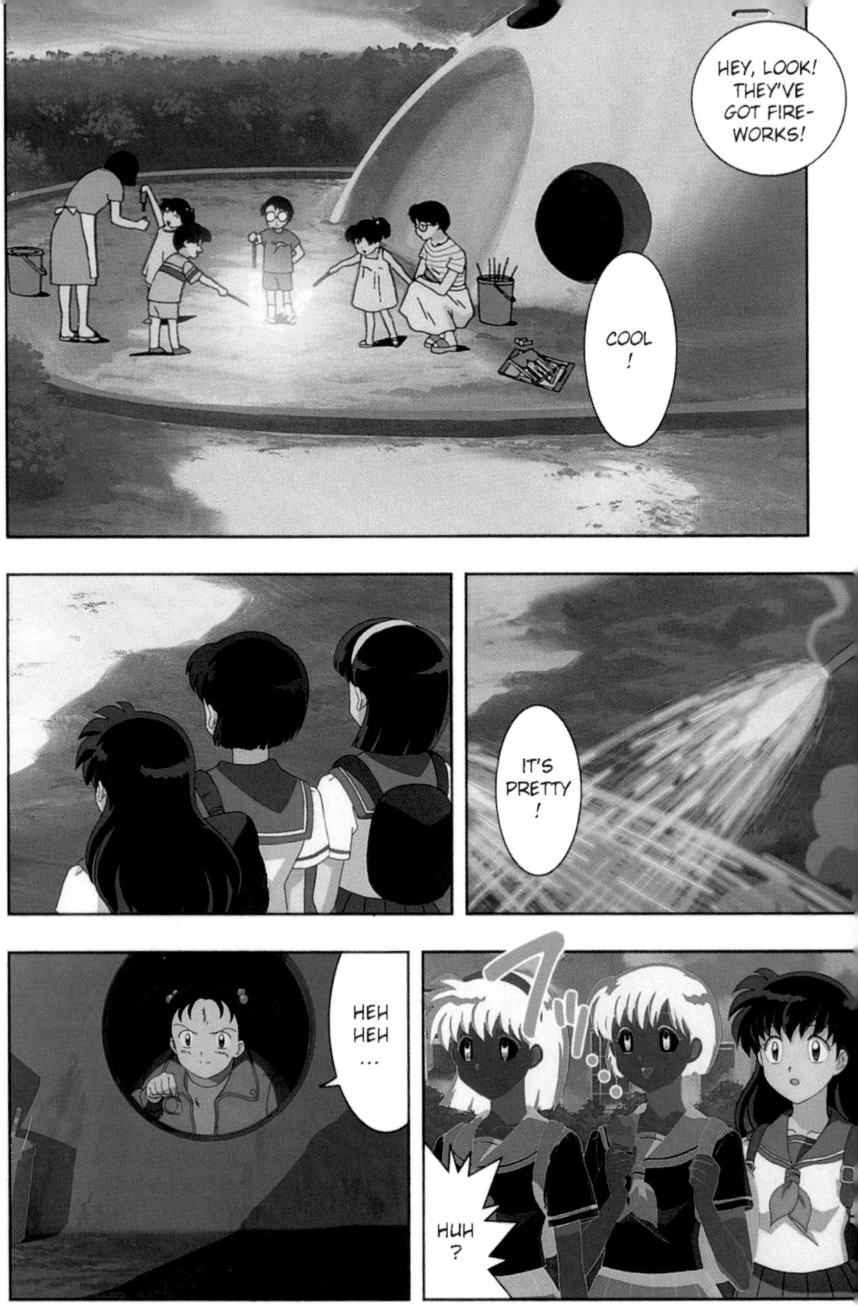
HEY, LOOK! THEY'VE GOT FIRE-WORKS!
COOL!
IT'S PRETTY!
HUH?
HEH HEH ...

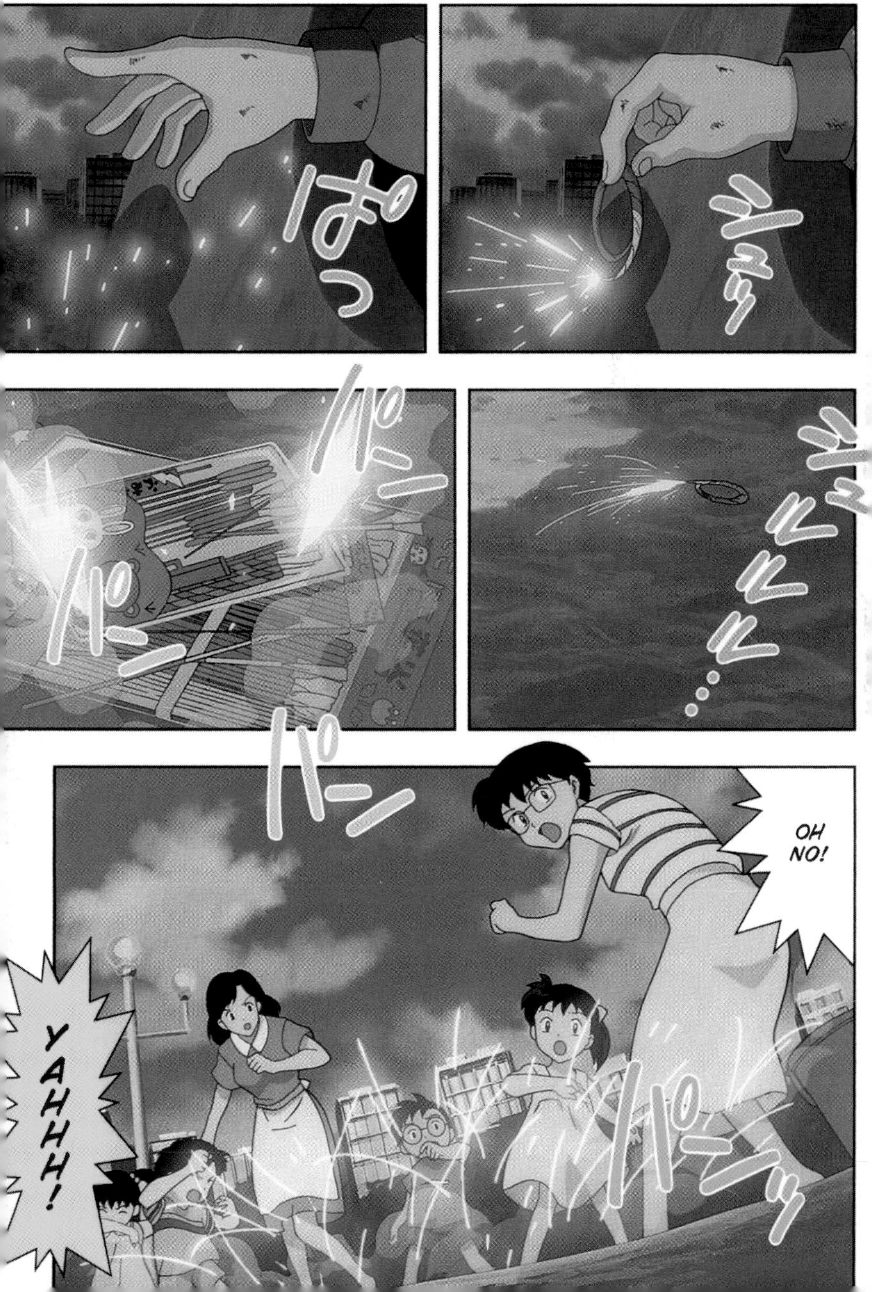
シュッ
ぱっ
シュルルルル…
パーン
パーン
パン
OH NO!
パーンッ
YAHHH!

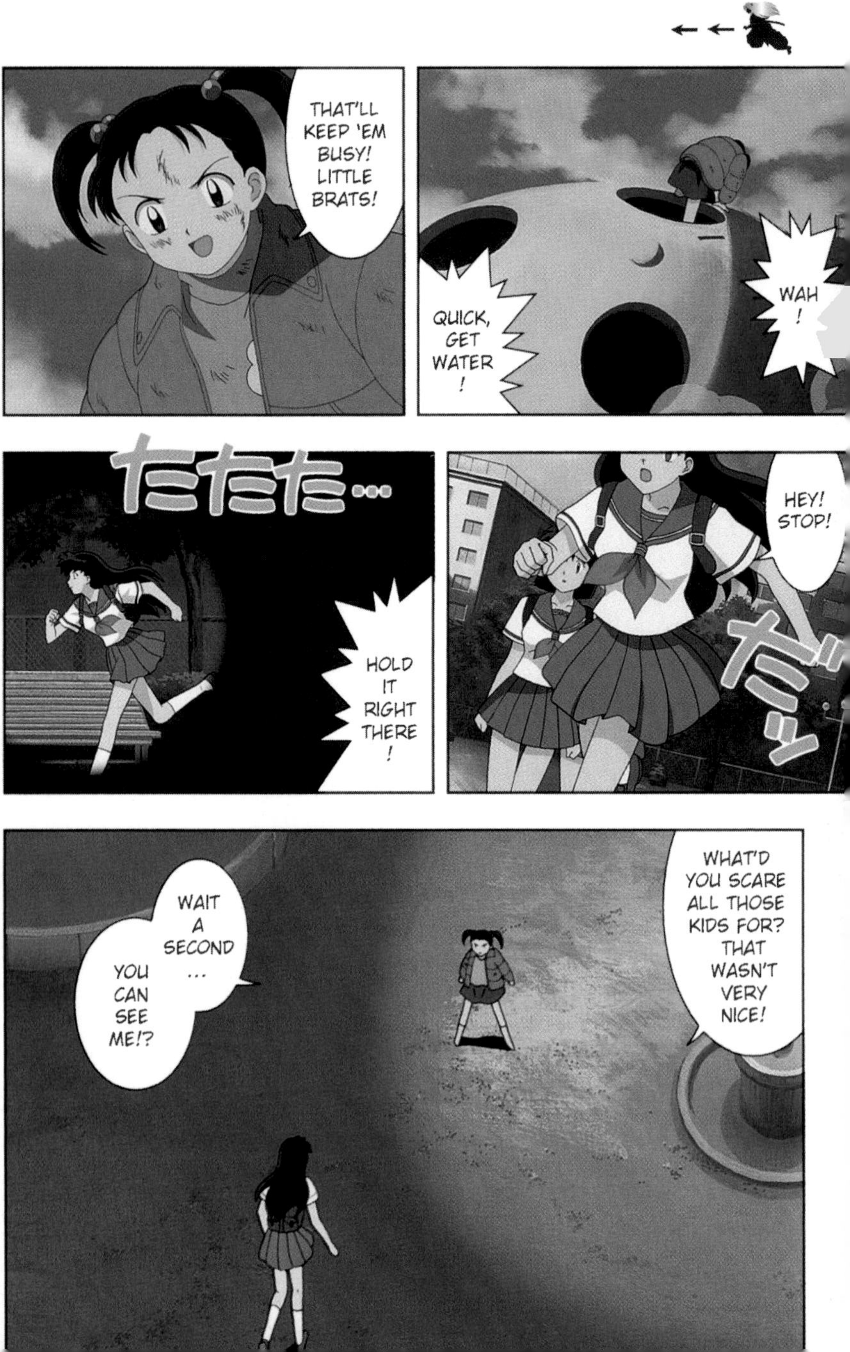
WAH!
QUICK, GET WATER!
THAT'LL KEEP 'EM BUSY! LITTLE BRATS!
HEY! STOP!
ダッ
たたた…
HOLD IT RIGHT THERE!
WHAT'D YOU SCARE ALL THOSE KIDS FOR? THAT WASN'T VERY NICE!
WAIT A SECOND … YOU CAN SEE ME!?

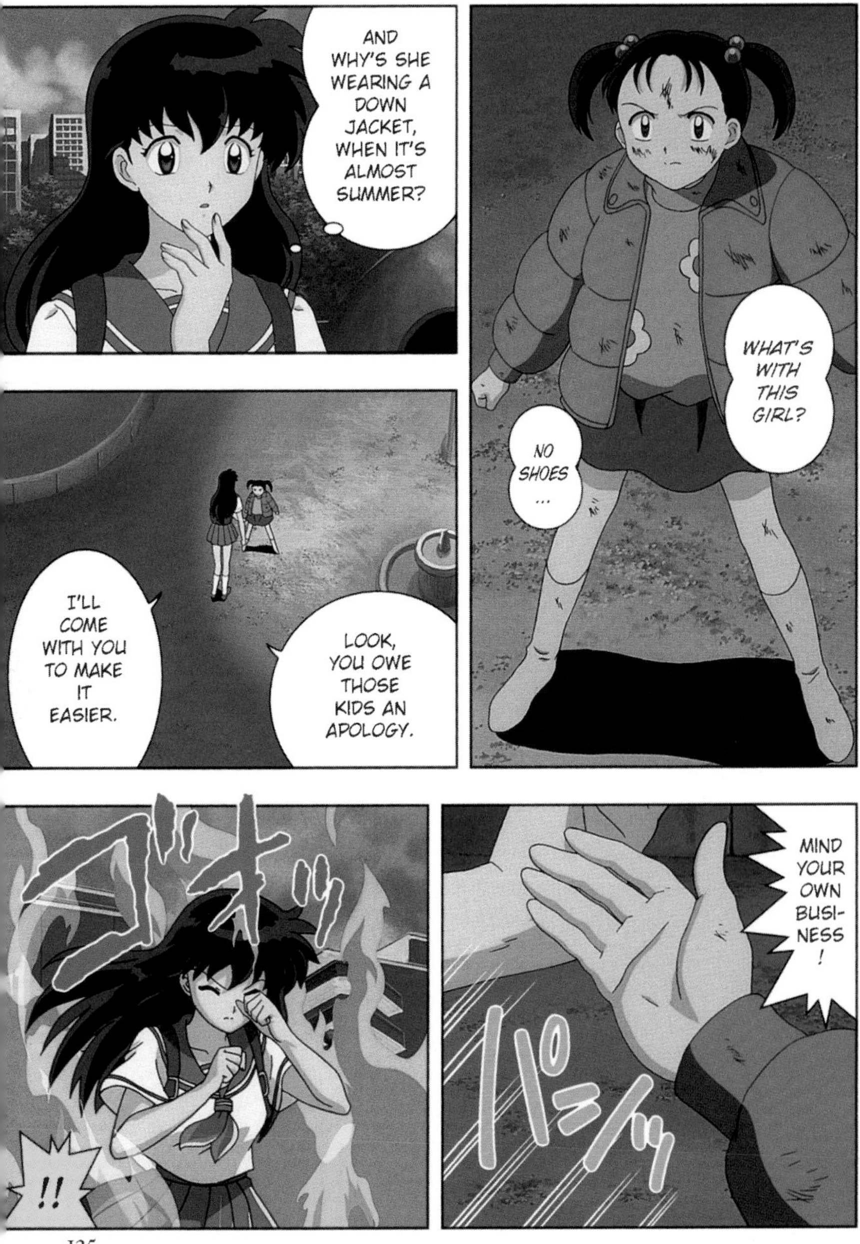
WHAT'S WITH THIS GIRL?
NO SHOES ...
AND WHY'S SHE WEARING A DOWN JACKET, WHEN IT'S ALMOST SUMMER?
LOOK, YOU OWE THOSE KIDS AN APOLOGY.
I'LL COME WITH YOU TO MAKE IT EASIER.
MIND YOUR OWN BUSI-NESS!
パシッ
ゴォッ
!!

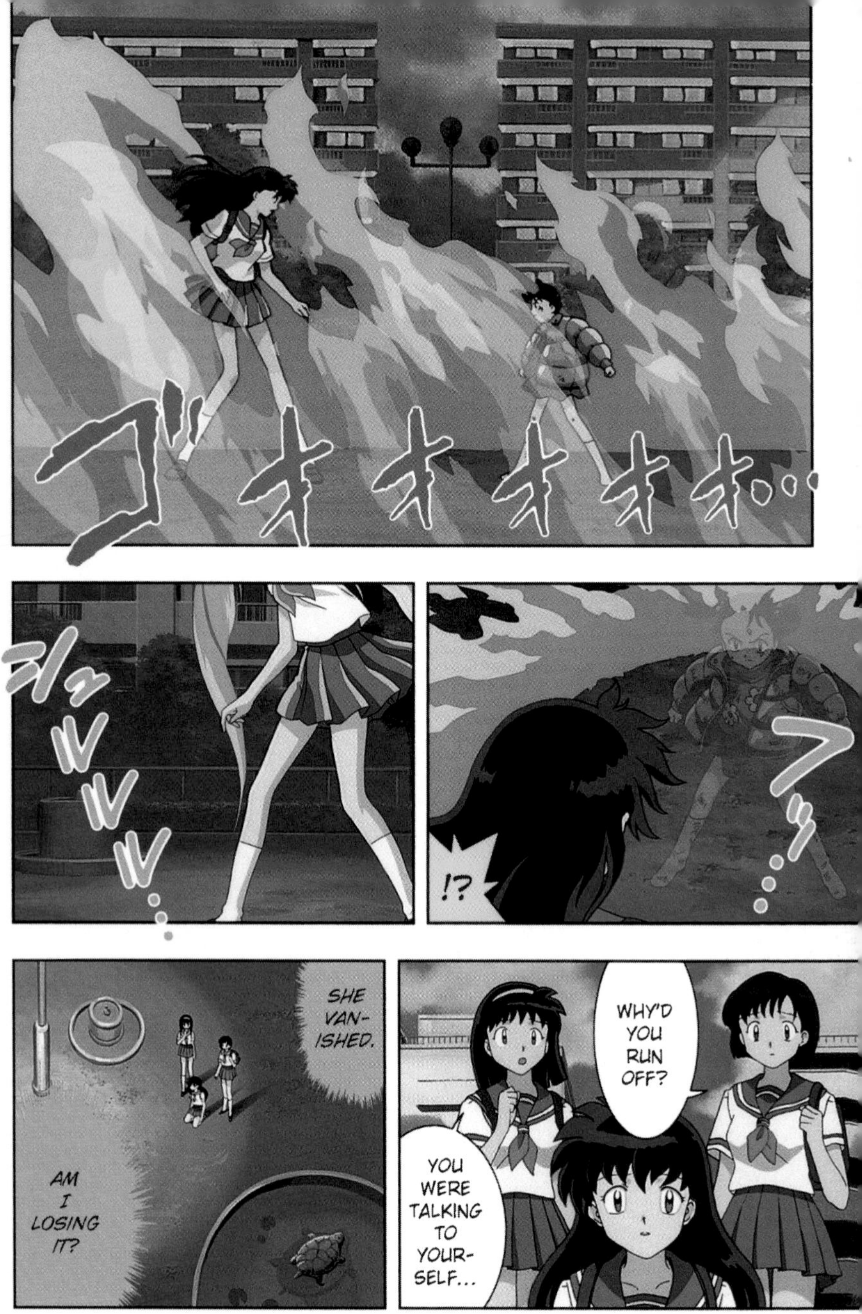

ゴオオオオ…
!?
フッ…
シュルルル…
WHY'D YOU RUN OFF?
YOU WERE TALKING TO YOUR-SELF…
SHE VAN-ISHED.
AM I LOSING IT?

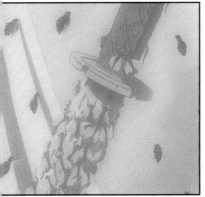

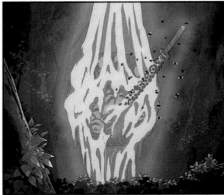

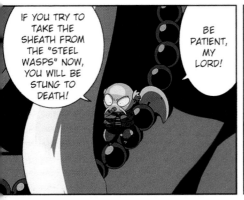

HOW MUCH LONGER IS THIS GONNA TAKE!?
BE PATIENT, MY LORD!
IF YOU TRY TO TAKE THE SHEATH FROM THE "STEEL WASPS" NOW, YOU WILL BE STUNG TO DEATH!
THE SHEATH WAS BADLY CRACKED DURING YOUR BATTLE...

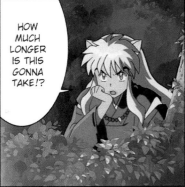

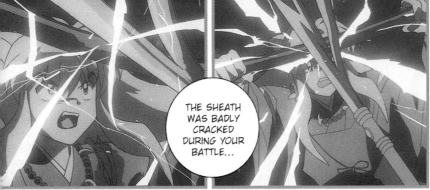

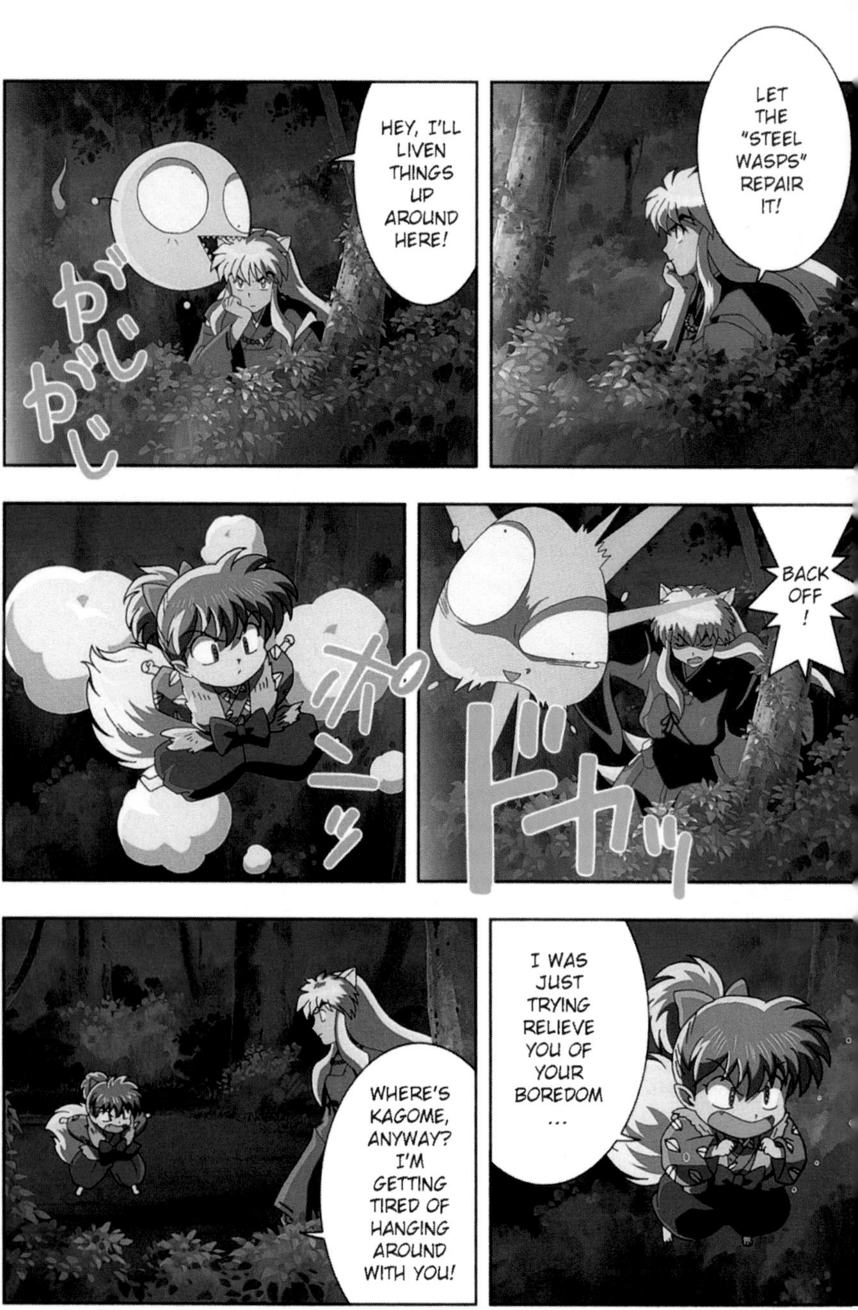
LET THE "STEEL WASPS" REPAIR IT!
HEY, I'LL LIVEN THINGS UP AROUND HERE!
BACK OFF!
ドカッ
ポンッ
I WAS JUST TRYING RELIEVE YOU OF YOUR BOREDOM ...
WHERE'S KAGOME, ANYWAY? I'M GETTING TIRED OF HANGING AROUND WITH YOU!

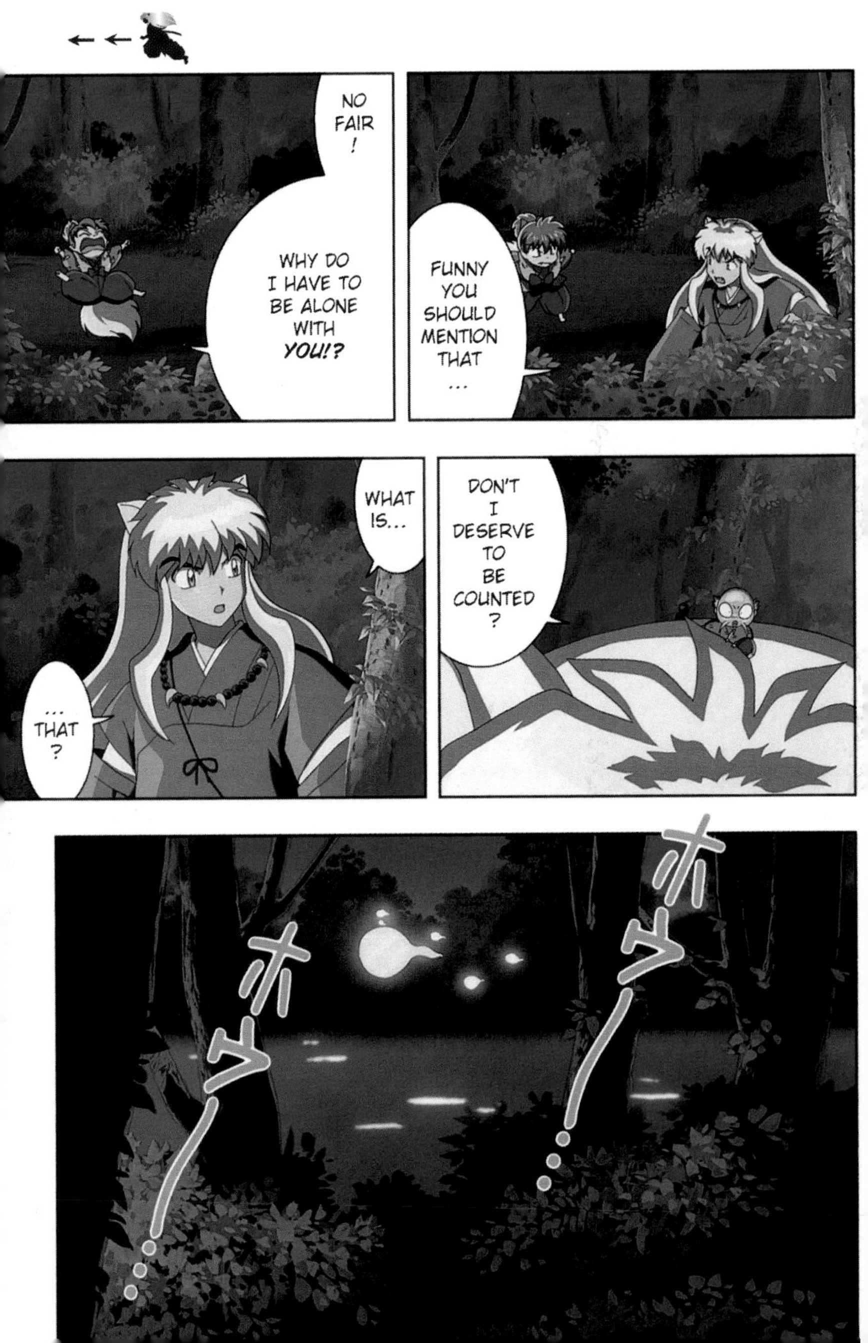
FUNNY YOU SHOULD MENTION THAT...
NO FAIR!
WHY DO I HAVE TO BE ALONE WITH *YOU!?*
DON'T I DESERVE TO BE COUNTED?
WHAT IS...
...THAT?
ホワー…
ホワー…

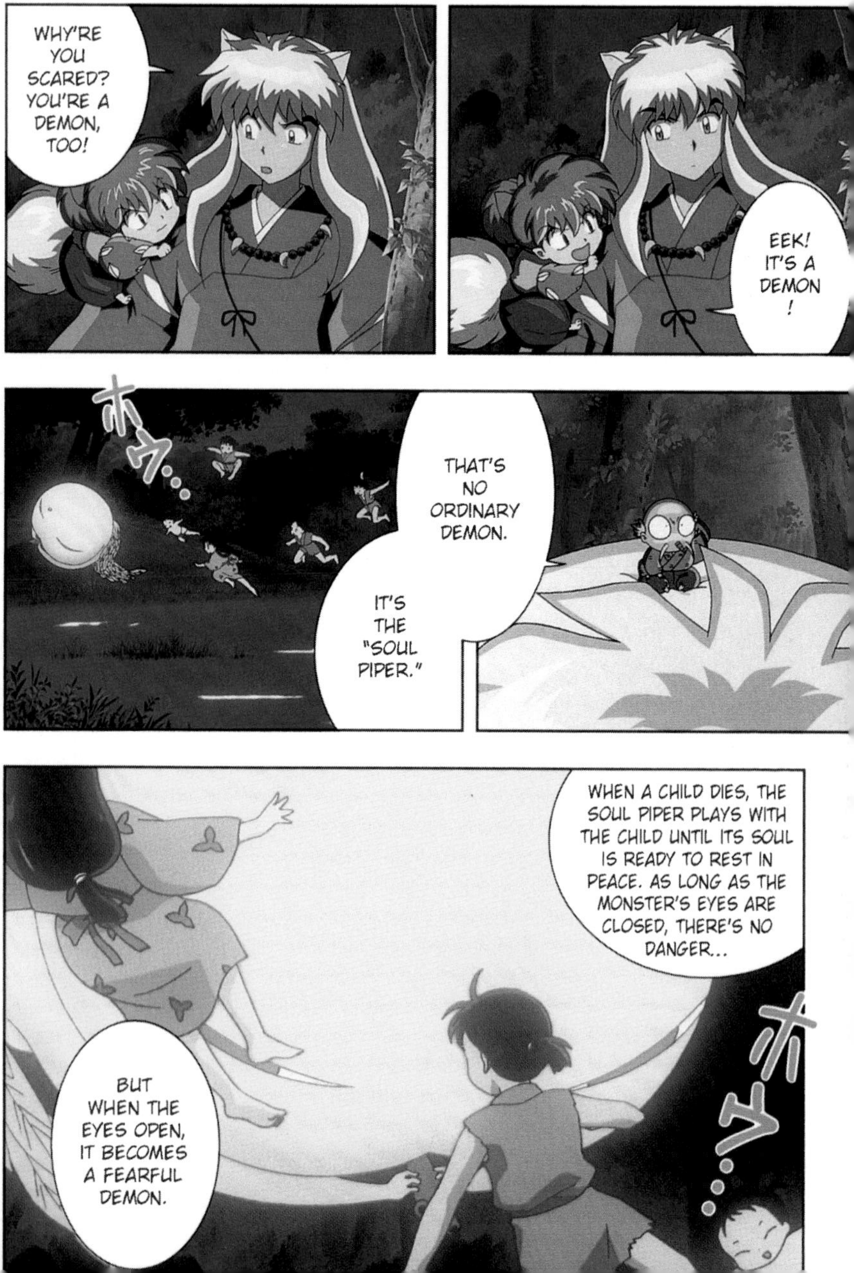
EEK! IT'S A DEMON!
WHY'RE YOU SCARED? YOU'RE A DEMON, TOO!
THAT'S NO ORDINARY DEMON.
IT'S THE "SOUL PIPER."
ホウ…
WHEN A CHILD DIES, THE SOUL PIPER PLAYS WITH THE CHILD UNTIL ITS SOUL IS READY TO REST IN PEACE. AS LONG AS THE MONSTER'S EYES ARE CLOSED, THERE'S NO DANGER...
ホウ…
BUT WHEN THE EYES OPEN, IT BECOMES A FEARFUL DEMON.

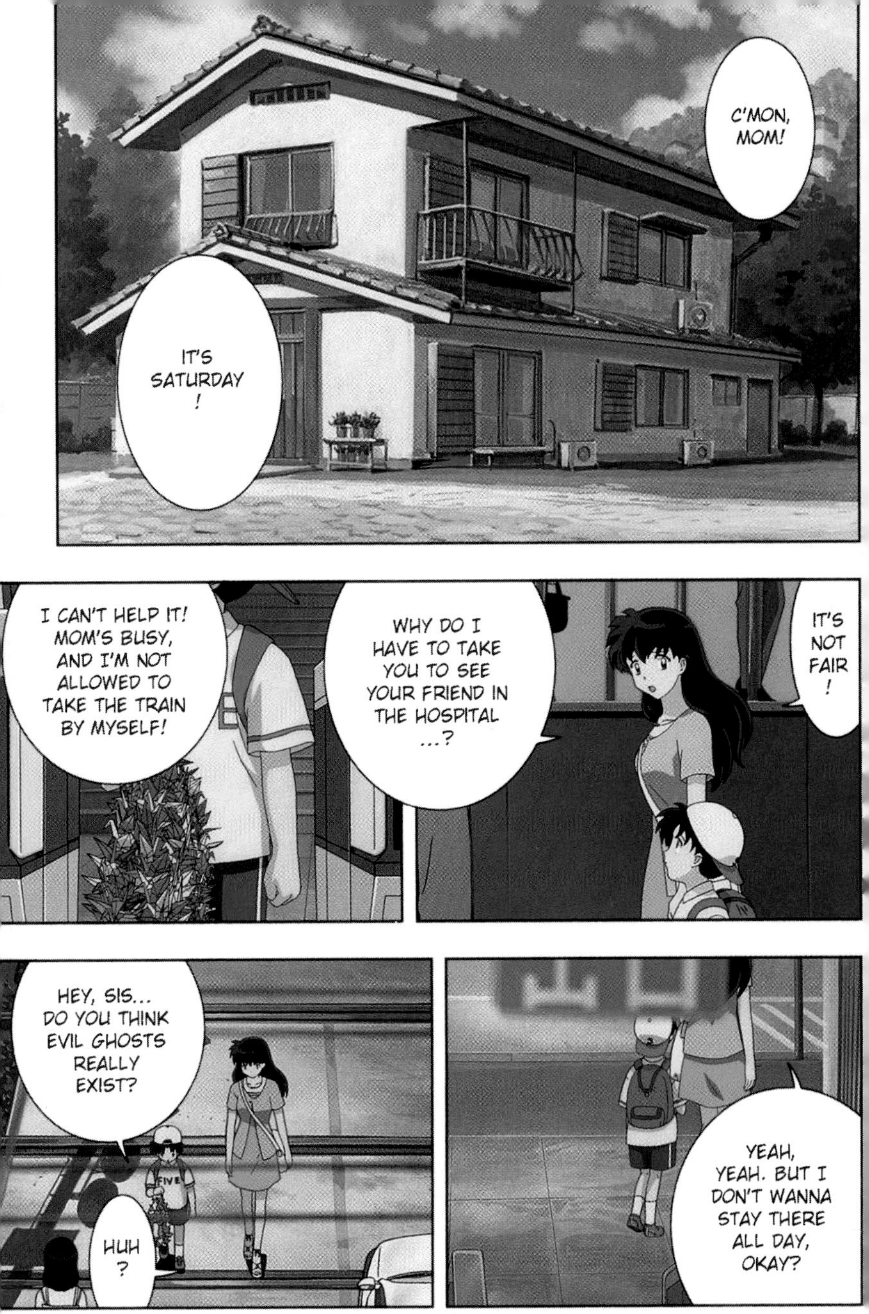
C'MON, MOM!
IT'S SATURDAY!
IT'S NOT FAIR!
WHY DO I HAVE TO TAKE YOU TO SEE YOUR FRIEND IN THE HOSPITAL...?
I CAN'T HELP IT! MOM'S BUSY, AND I'M NOT ALLOWED TO TAKE THE TRAIN BY MYSELF!
YEAH, YEAH. BUT I DON'T WANNA STAY THERE ALL DAY, OKAY?
HEY, SIS... DO YOU THINK EVIL GHOSTS REALLY EXIST?
HUH?
FIVE

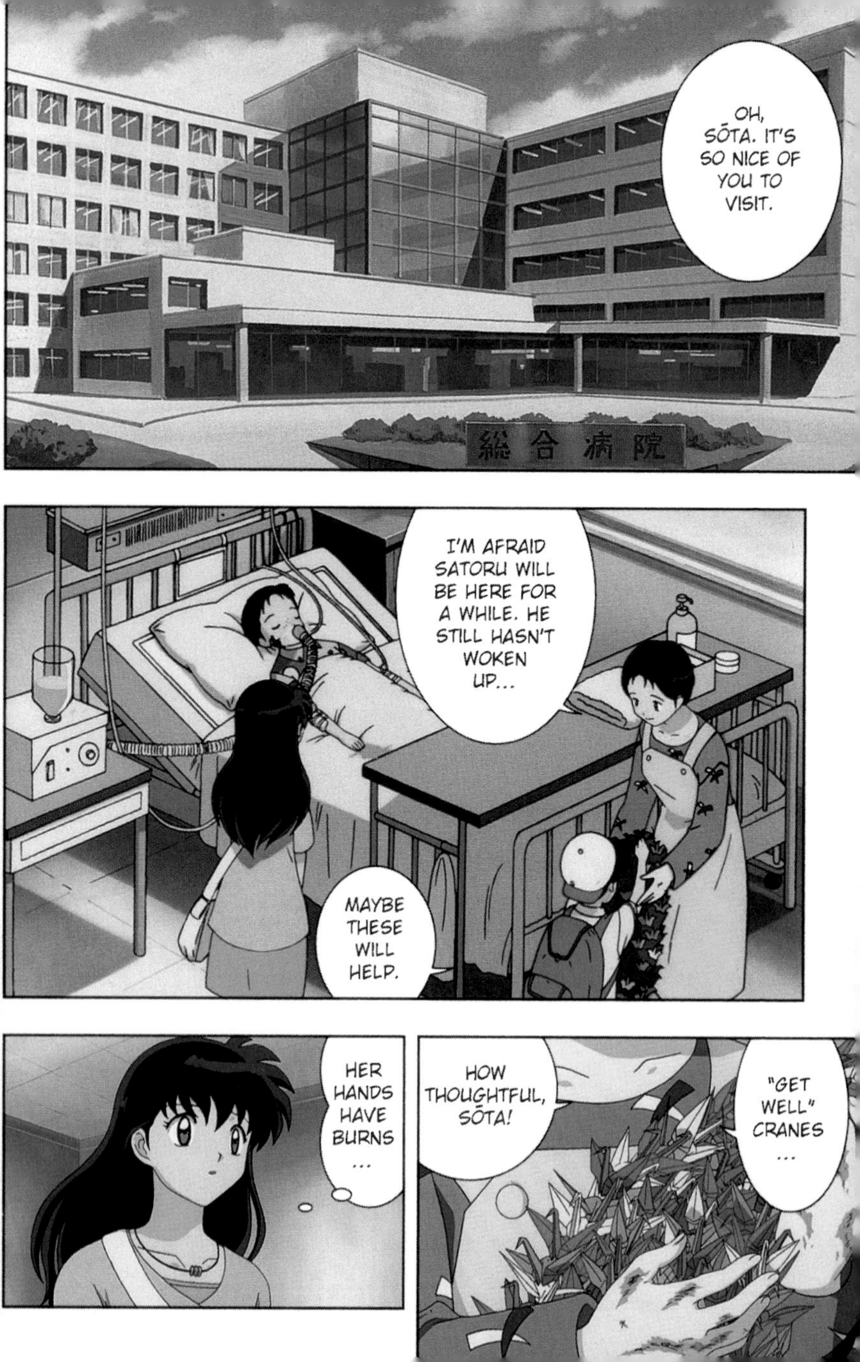
OH, SŌTA. IT'S SO NICE OF YOU TO VISIT.
総合病院
I'M AFRAID SATORU WILL BE HERE FOR A WHILE. HE STILL HASN'T WOKEN UP...
MAYBE THESE WILL HELP.
"GET WELL" CRANES ...
HOW THOUGHTFUL, SŌTA!
HER HANDS HAVE BURNS ...

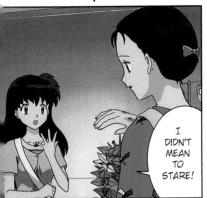

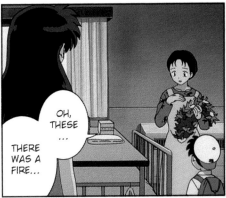

OH, THESE...
THERE WAS A FIRE...
I DIDN'T MEAN TO STARE!
LUCKILY *HE* WASN'T BURNED...
スッ...

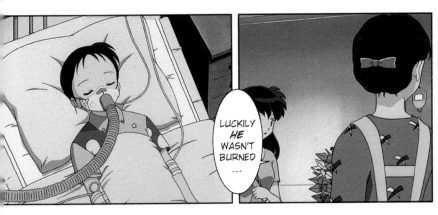

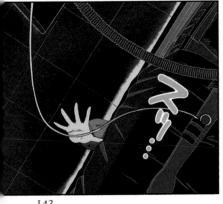

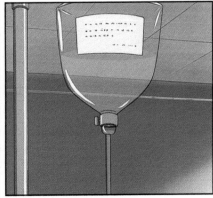

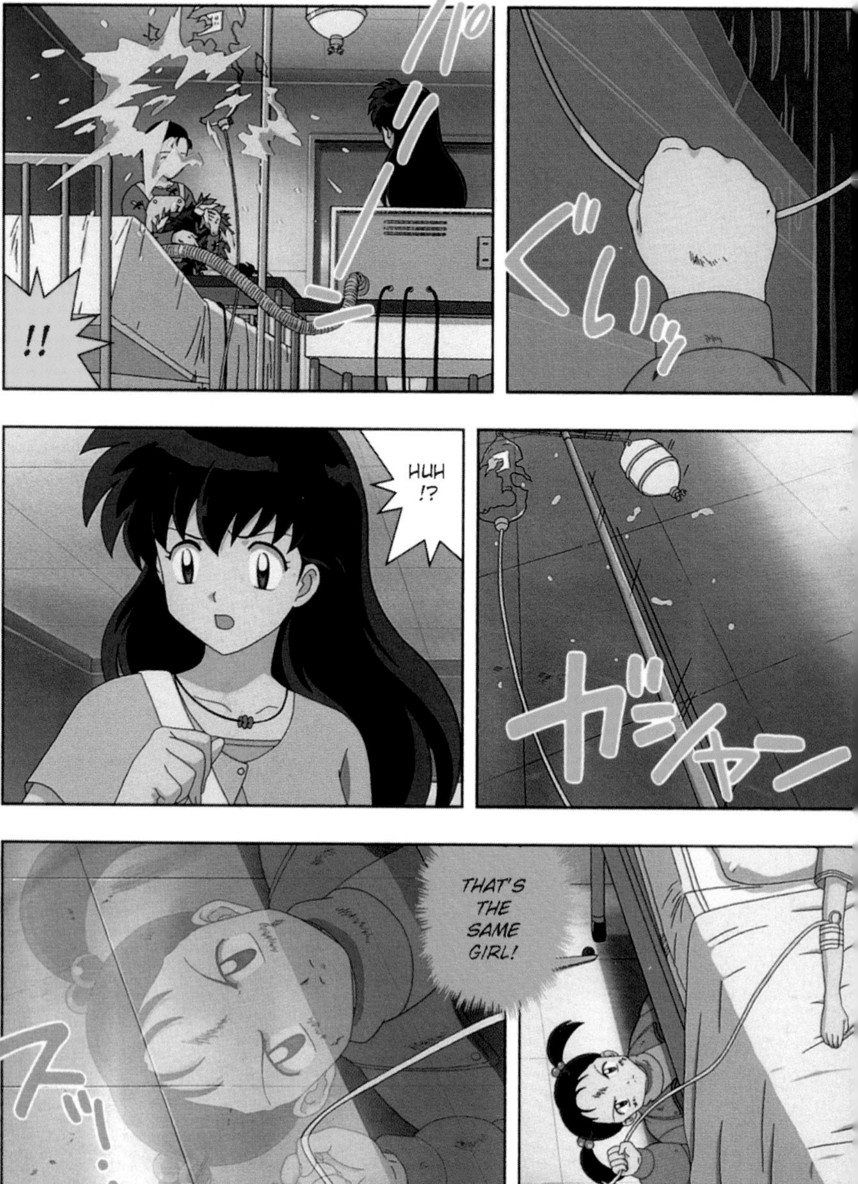
ぐいっ
パリーン
!!
ガシャーン
HUH !?
THAT'S THE SAME GIRL!
スッ…

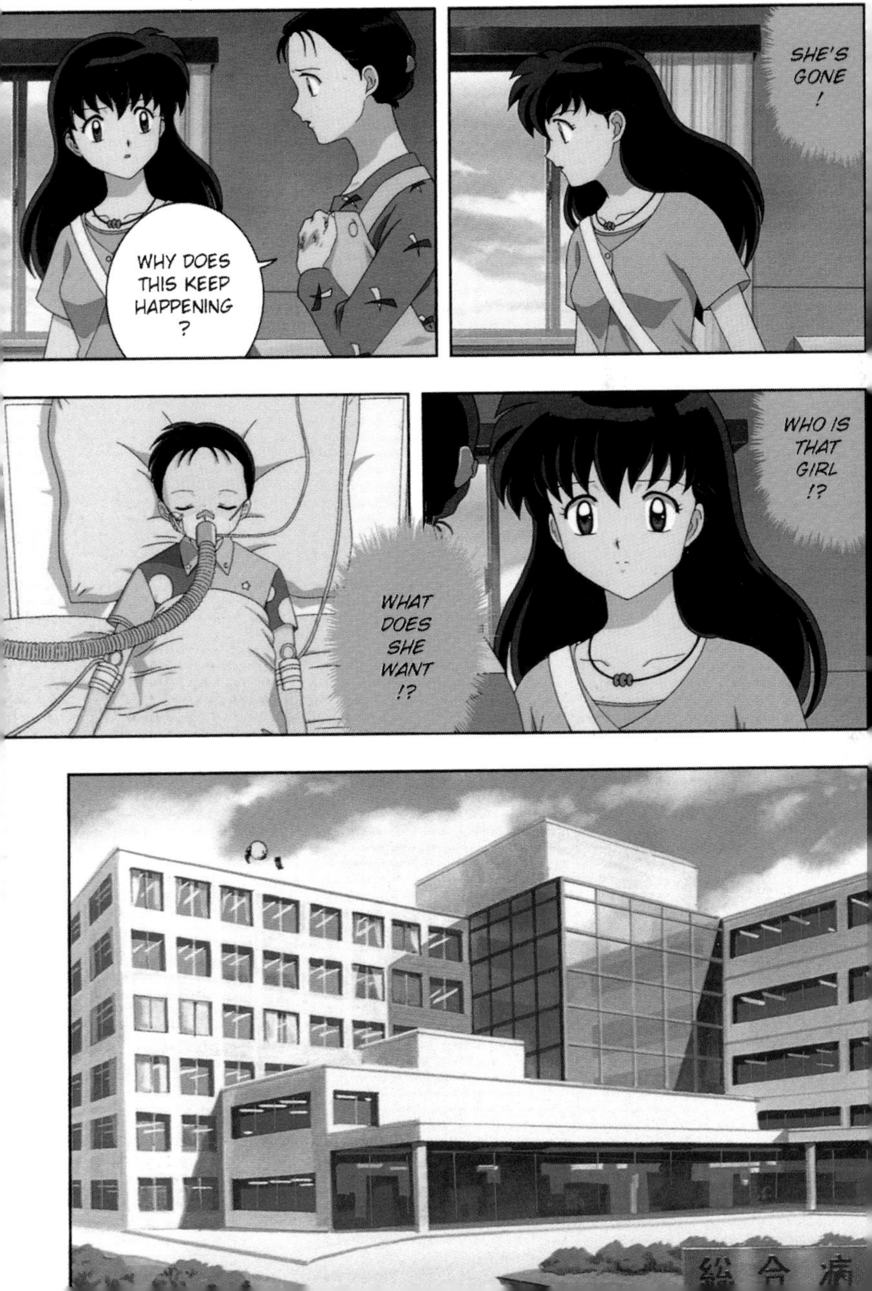
SHE'S GONE !
WHY DOES THIS KEEP HAPPENING ?
WHO IS THAT GIRL !?
WHAT DOES SHE WANT !?
総合病

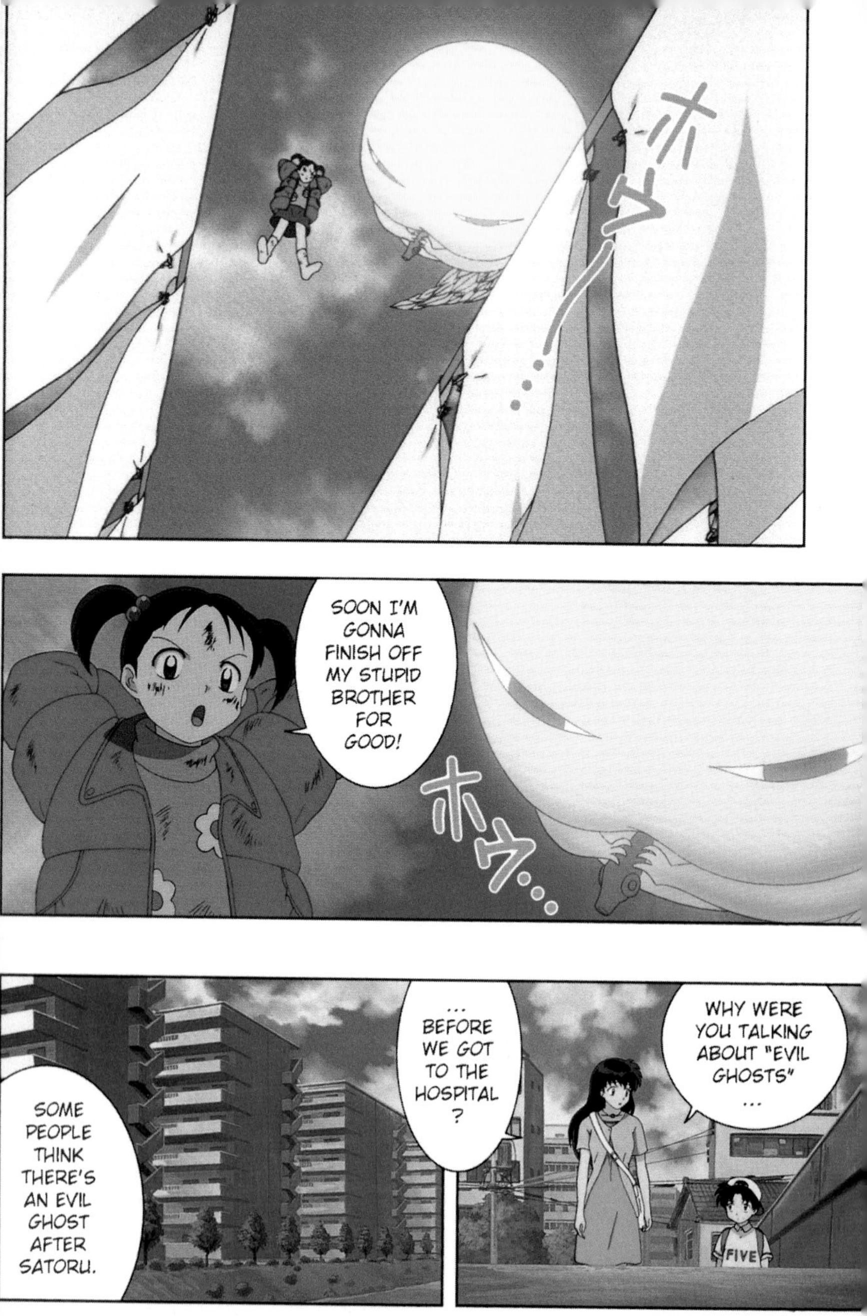
ホウー…
SOON I'M GONNA FINISH OFF MY STUPID BROTHER FOR GOOD!
ホウ…
WHY WERE YOU TALKING ABOUT "EVIL GHOSTS" …
… BEFORE WE GOT TO THE HOSPITAL ?
FIVE
SOME PEOPLE THINK THERE'S AN EVIL GHOST AFTER SATORU.

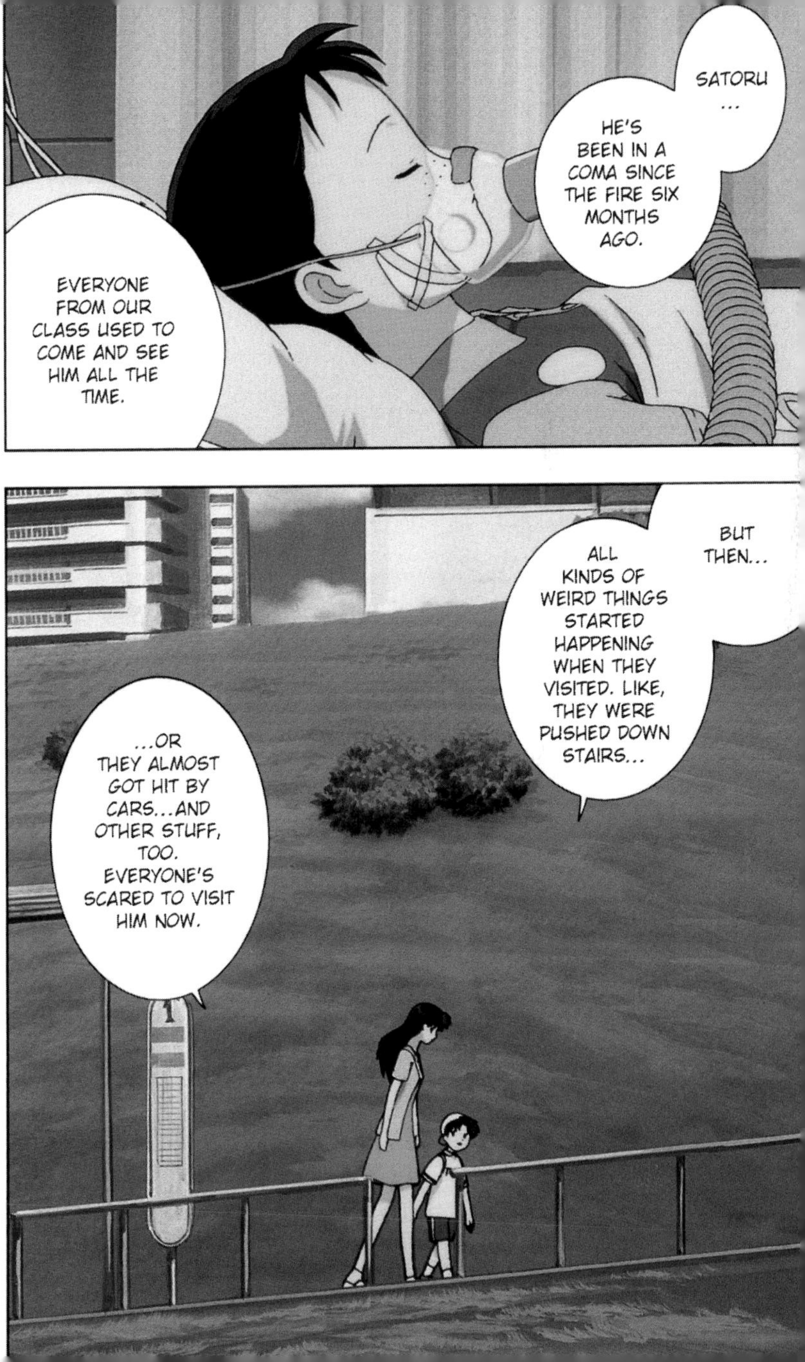
SATORU ...
HE'S BEEN IN A COMA SINCE THE FIRE SIX MONTHS AGO.
EVERYONE FROM OUR CLASS USED TO COME AND SEE HIM ALL THE TIME.
BUT THEN...
ALL KINDS OF WEIRD THINGS STARTED HAPPENING WHEN THEY VISITED. LIKE, THEY WERE PUSHED DOWN STAIRS...
...OR THEY ALMOST GOT HIT BY CARS...AND OTHER STUFF, TOO. EVERYONE'S SCARED TO VISIT HIM NOW.
1

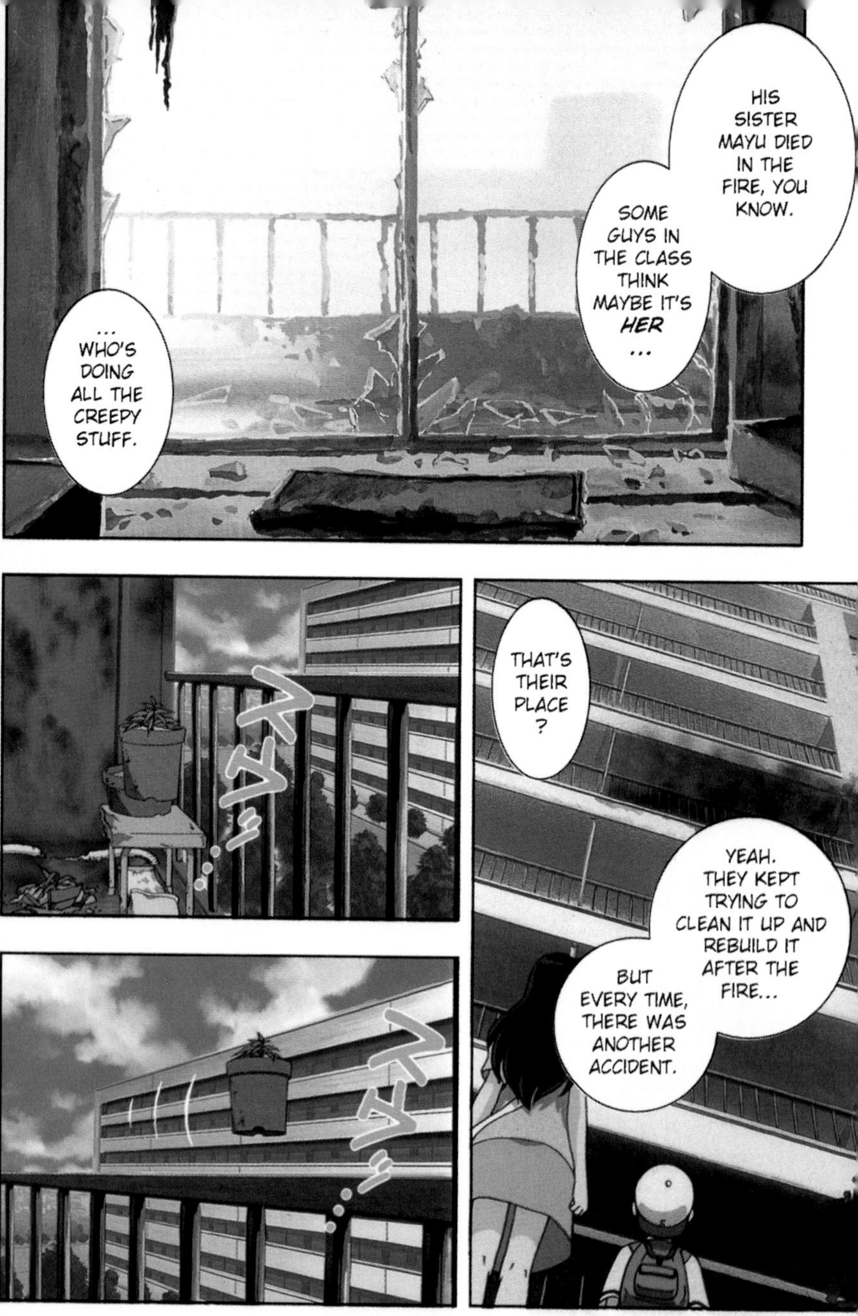
HIS SISTER MAYU DIED IN THE FIRE, YOU KNOW.
SOME GUYS IN THE CLASS THINK MAYBE IT'S ***HER*** ...
... WHO'S DOING ALL THE CREEPY STUFF.
THAT'S THEIR PLACE ?
YEAH. THEY KEPT TRYING TO CLEAN IT UP AND REBUILD IT AFTER THE FIRE...
BUT EVERY TIME, THERE WAS ANOTHER ACCIDENT.

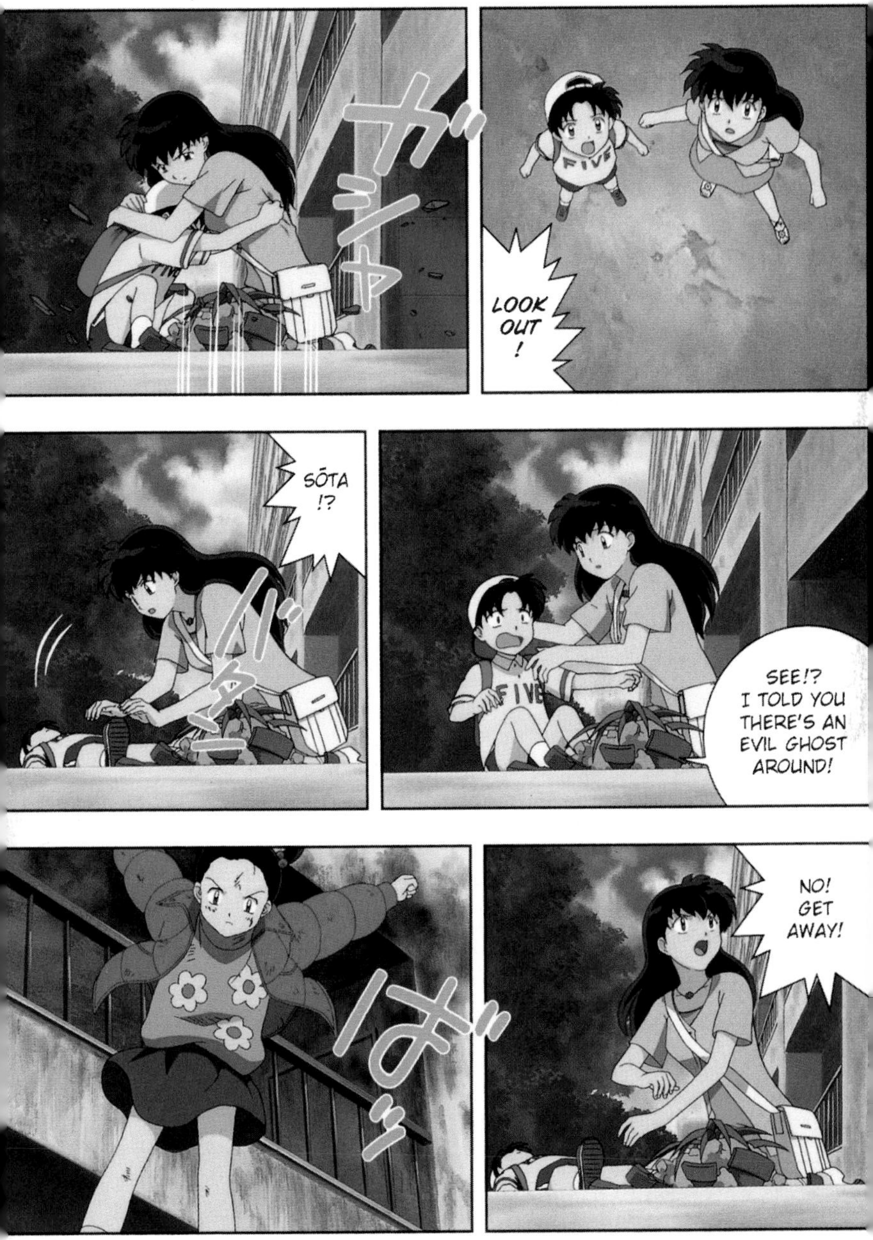
LOOK OUT!
ガシャ
SEE!? I TOLD YOU THERE'S AN EVIL GHOST AROUND!
SŌTA !?
バタ
NO! GET AWAY!
ばっ

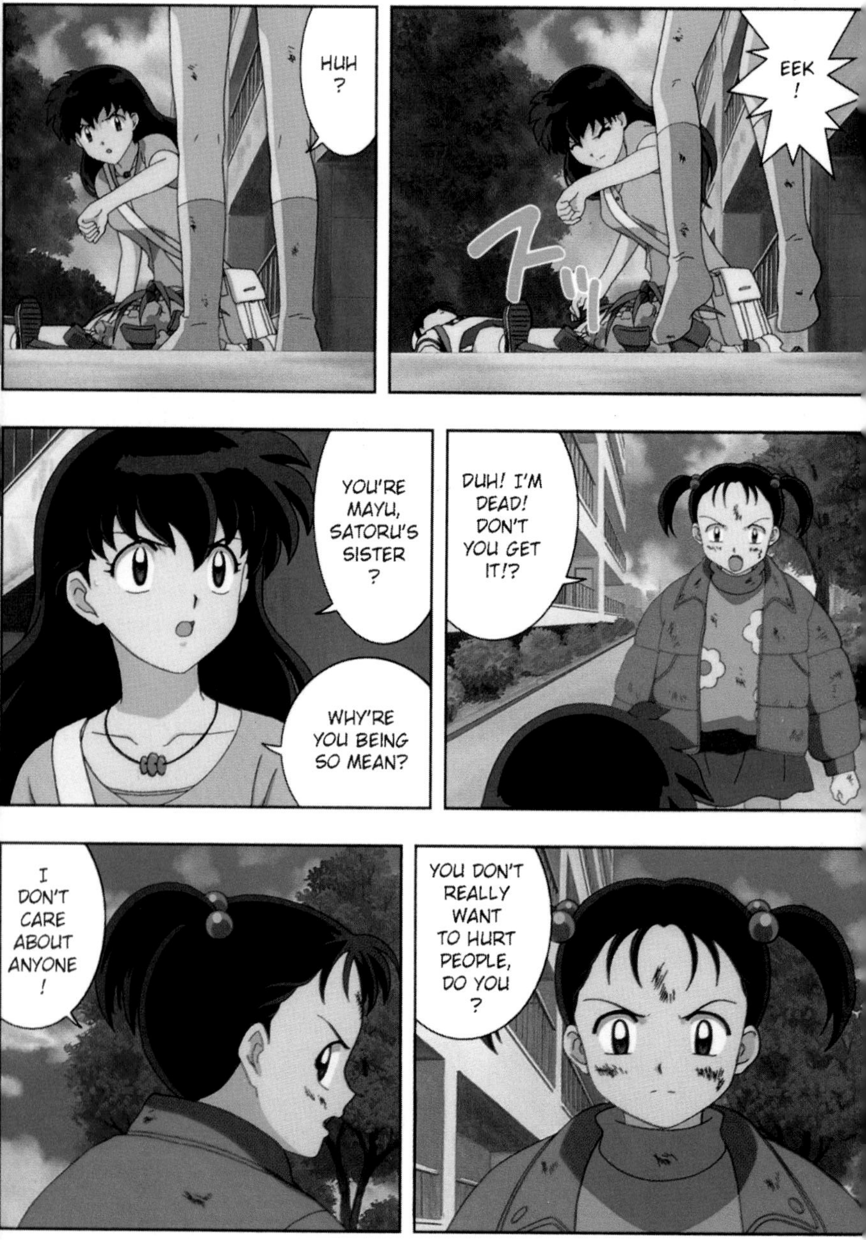

EEK!
ズッ
HUH?
DUH! I'M DEAD! DON'T YOU GET IT!?
YOU'RE MAYU, SATORU'S SISTER?
WHY'RE YOU BEING SO MEAN?
YOU DON'T REALLY WANT TO HURT PEOPLE, DO YOU?
I DON'T CARE ABOUT ANYONE!

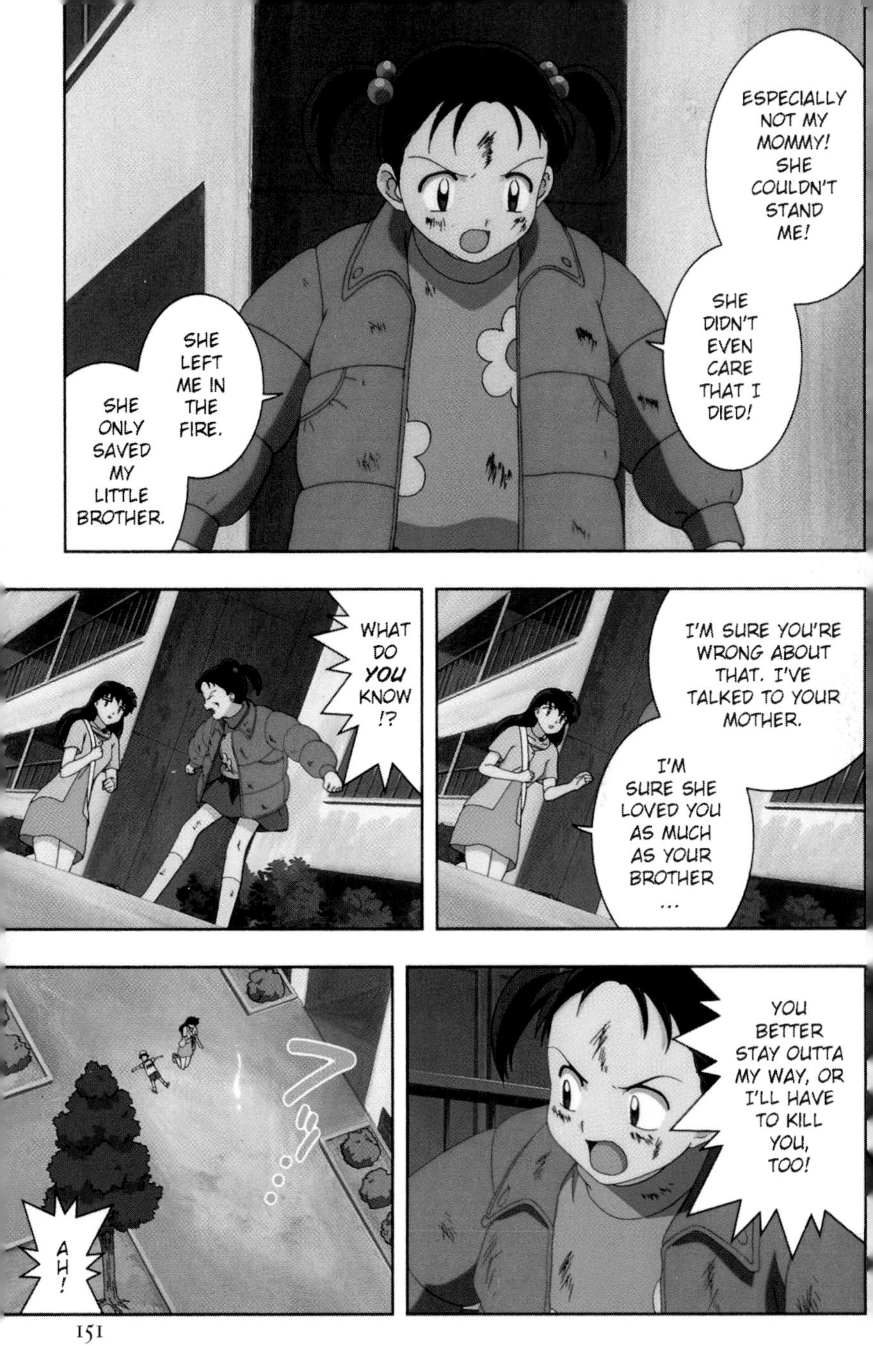
ESPECIALLY NOT MY MOMMY! SHE COULDN'T STAND ME!
SHE DIDN'T EVEN CARE THAT I DIED!
SHE LEFT ME IN THE FIRE.
SHE ONLY SAVED MY LITTLE BROTHER.
I'M SURE YOU'RE WRONG ABOUT THAT. I'VE TALKED TO YOUR MOTHER.
I'M SURE SHE LOVED YOU AS MUCH AS YOUR BROTHER...
WHAT DO *YOU* KNOW!?
YOU BETTER STAY OUTTA MY WAY, OR I'LL HAVE TO KILL YOU, TOO!
AH!

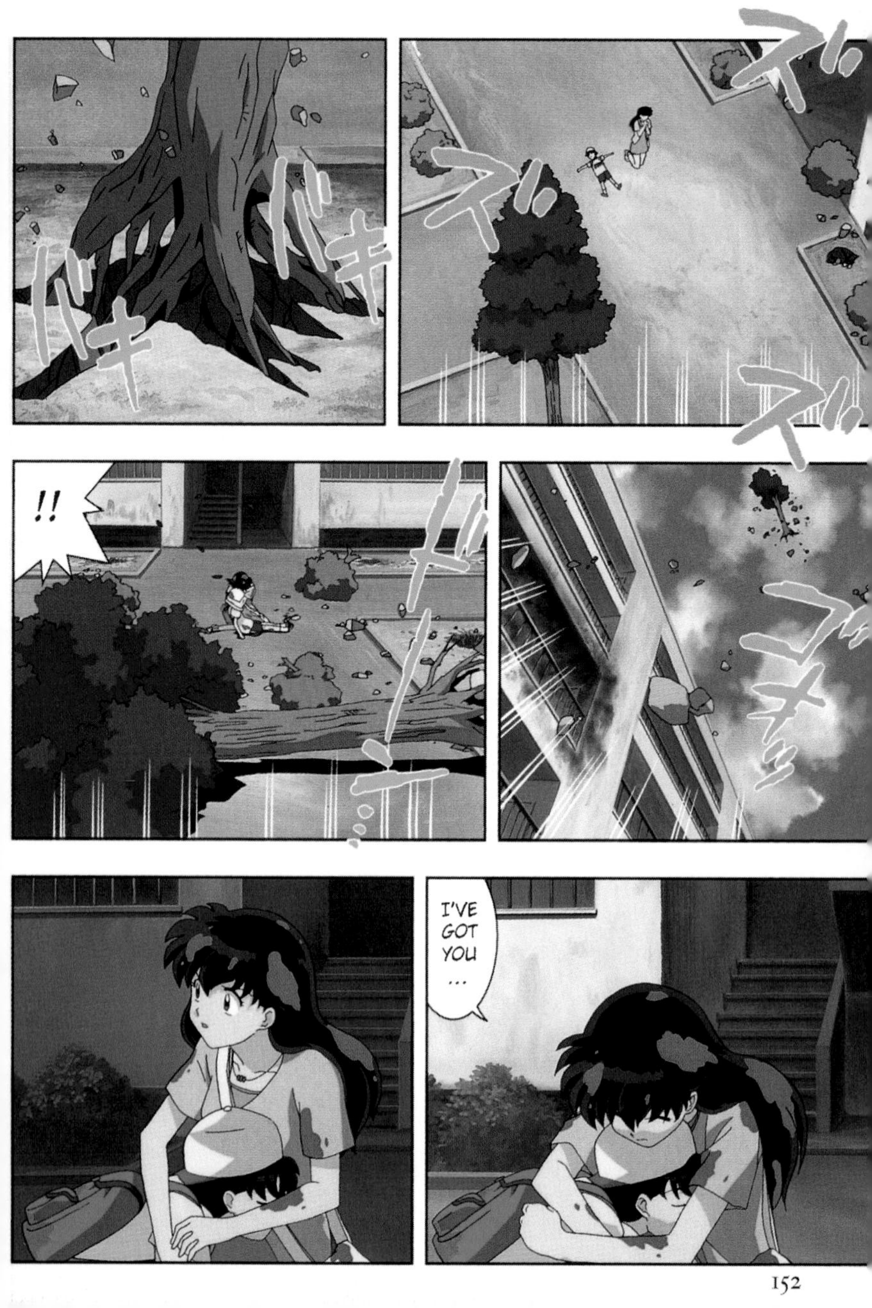
バキ
バキ
!!
I'VE GOT YOU ...

ホワ…
WHAT IS THAT !?
!!!
ホワー…
ホワ…

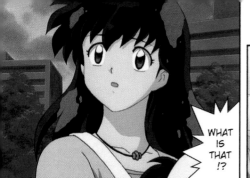

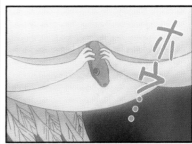

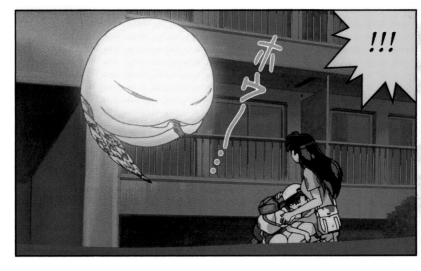

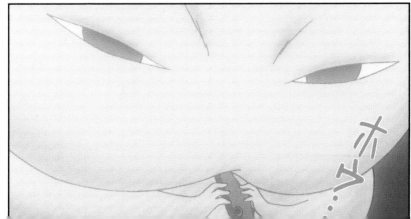

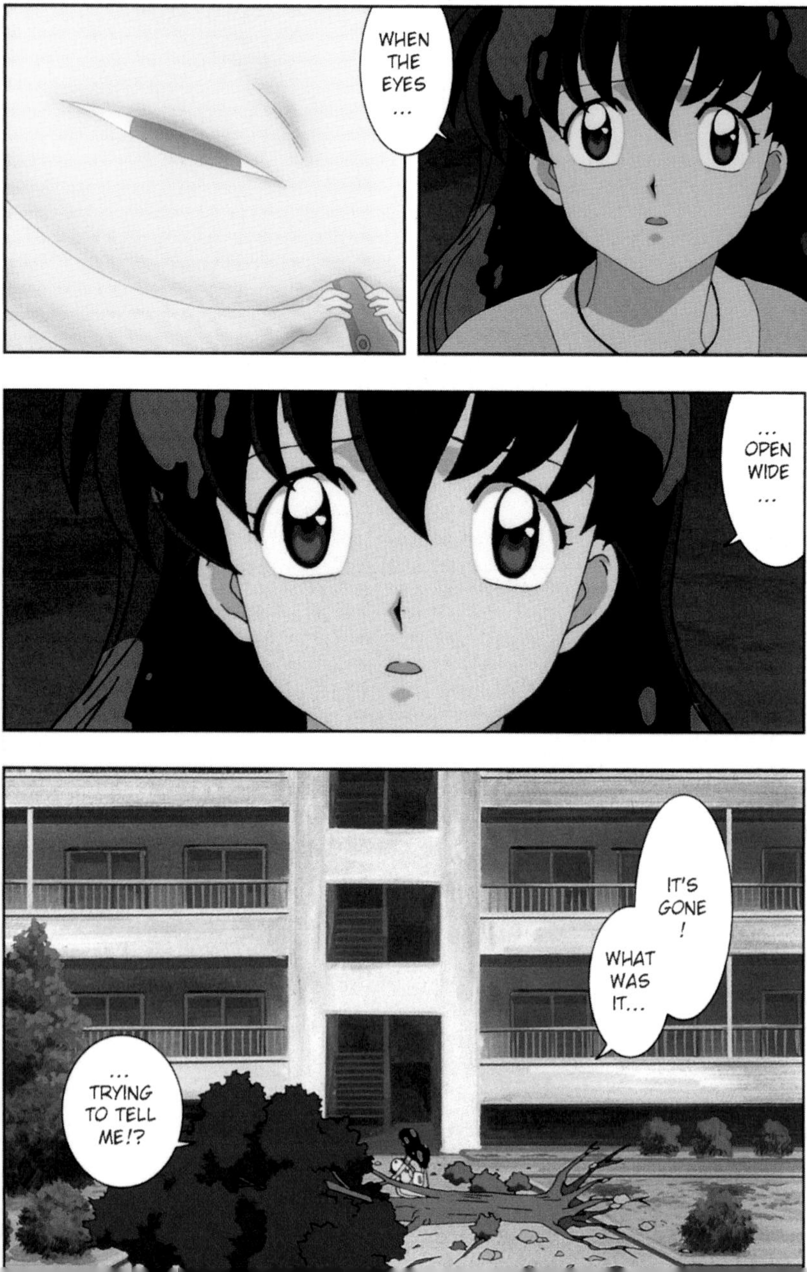
WHEN THE EYES ...
... OPEN WIDE ...
IT'S GONE!
WHAT WAS IT...
... TRYING TO TELL ME!?

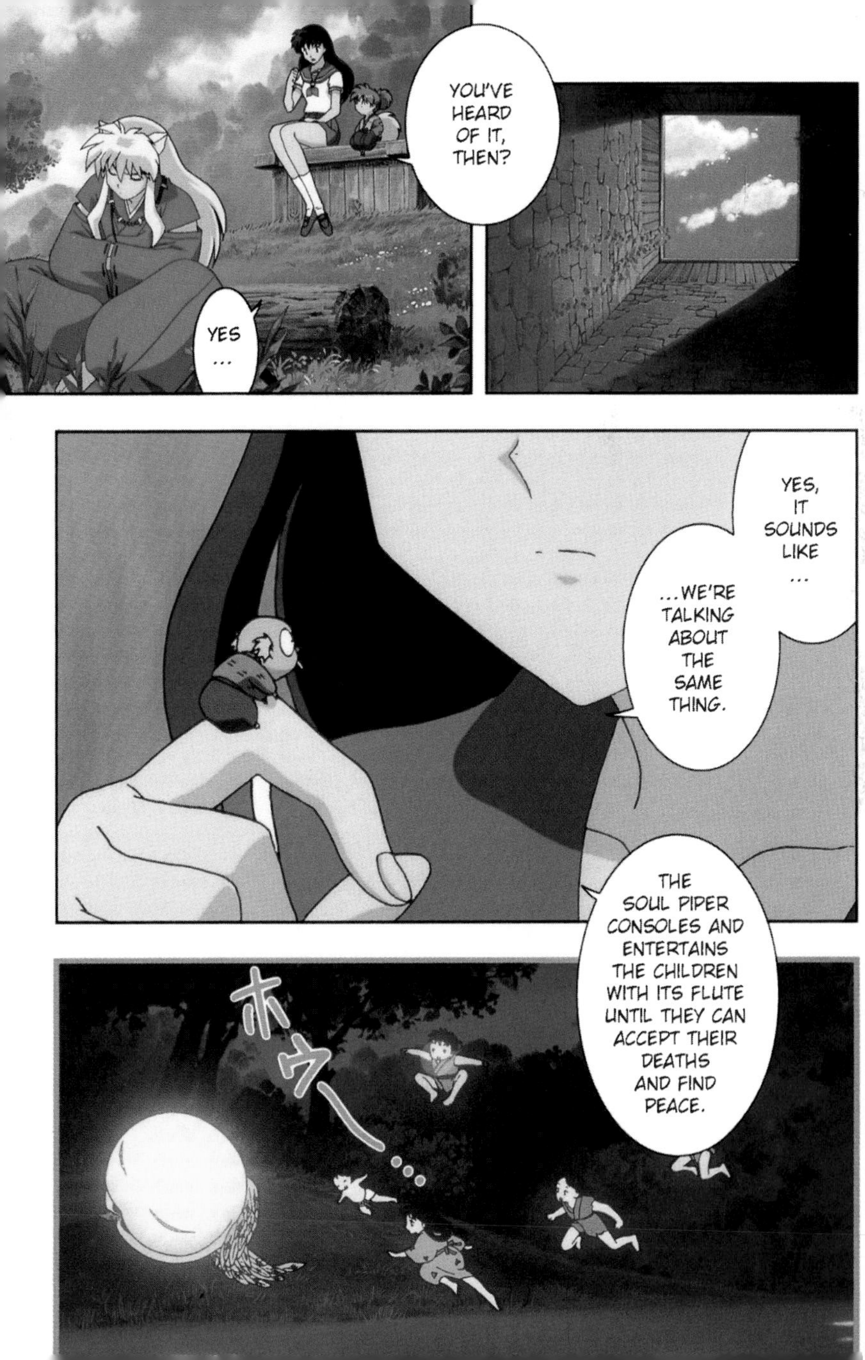
YOU'VE HEARD OF IT, THEN?
YES ...
YES, IT SOUNDS LIKE ...
...WE'RE TALKING ABOUT THE SAME THING.
THE SOUL PIPER CONSOLES AND ENTERTAINS THE CHILDREN WITH ITS FLUTE UNTIL THEY CAN ACCEPT THEIR DEATHS AND FIND PEACE.
ホウ～...

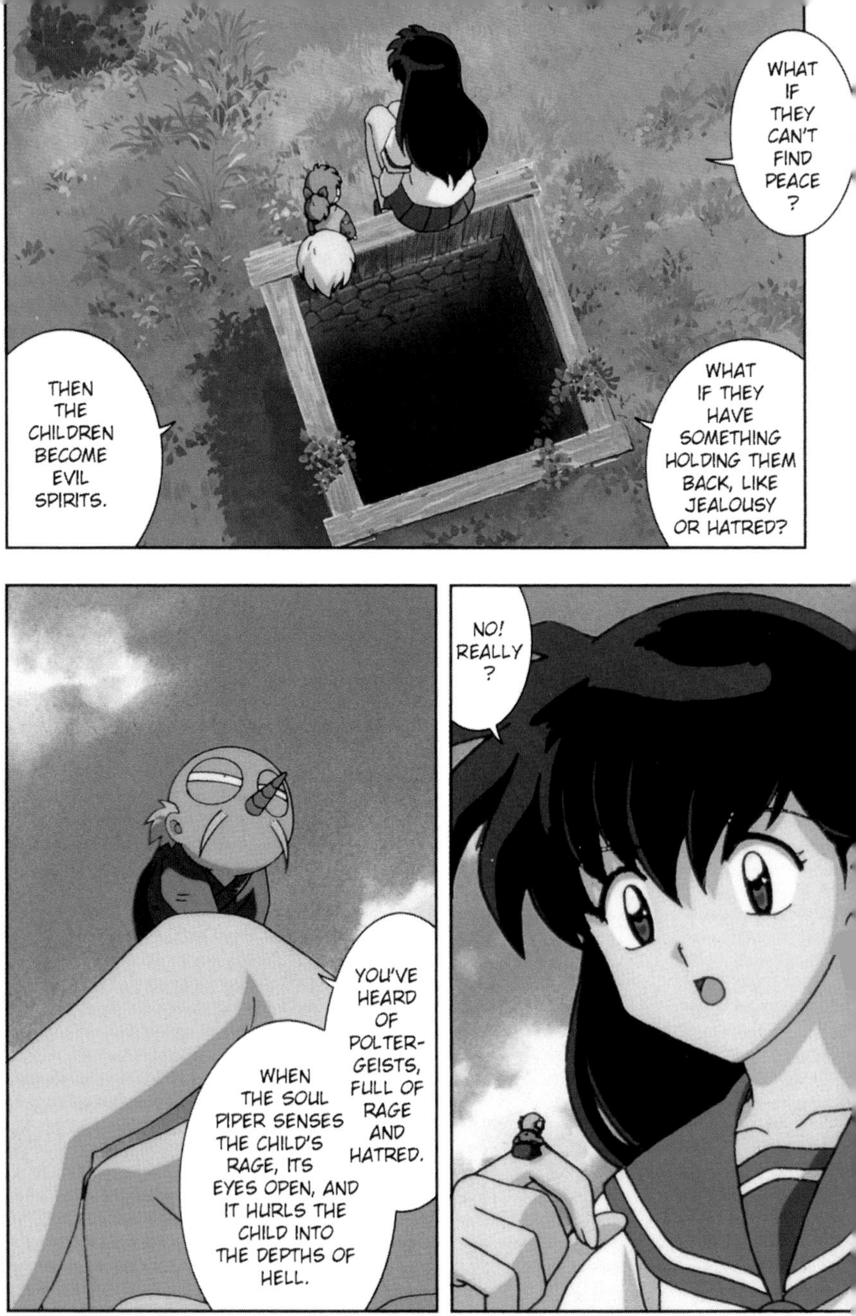
WHAT IF THEY CAN'T FIND PEACE ?
WHAT IF THEY HAVE SOMETHING HOLDING THEM BACK, LIKE JEALOUSY OR HATRED?
THEN THE CHILDREN BECOME EVIL SPIRITS.
NO! REALLY ?
YOU'VE HEARD OF POLTER-GEISTS, FULL OF RAGE AND HATRED.
WHEN THE SOUL PIPER SENSES THE CHILD'S RAGE, ITS EYES OPEN, AND IT HURLS THE CHILD INTO THE DEPTHS OF HELL.

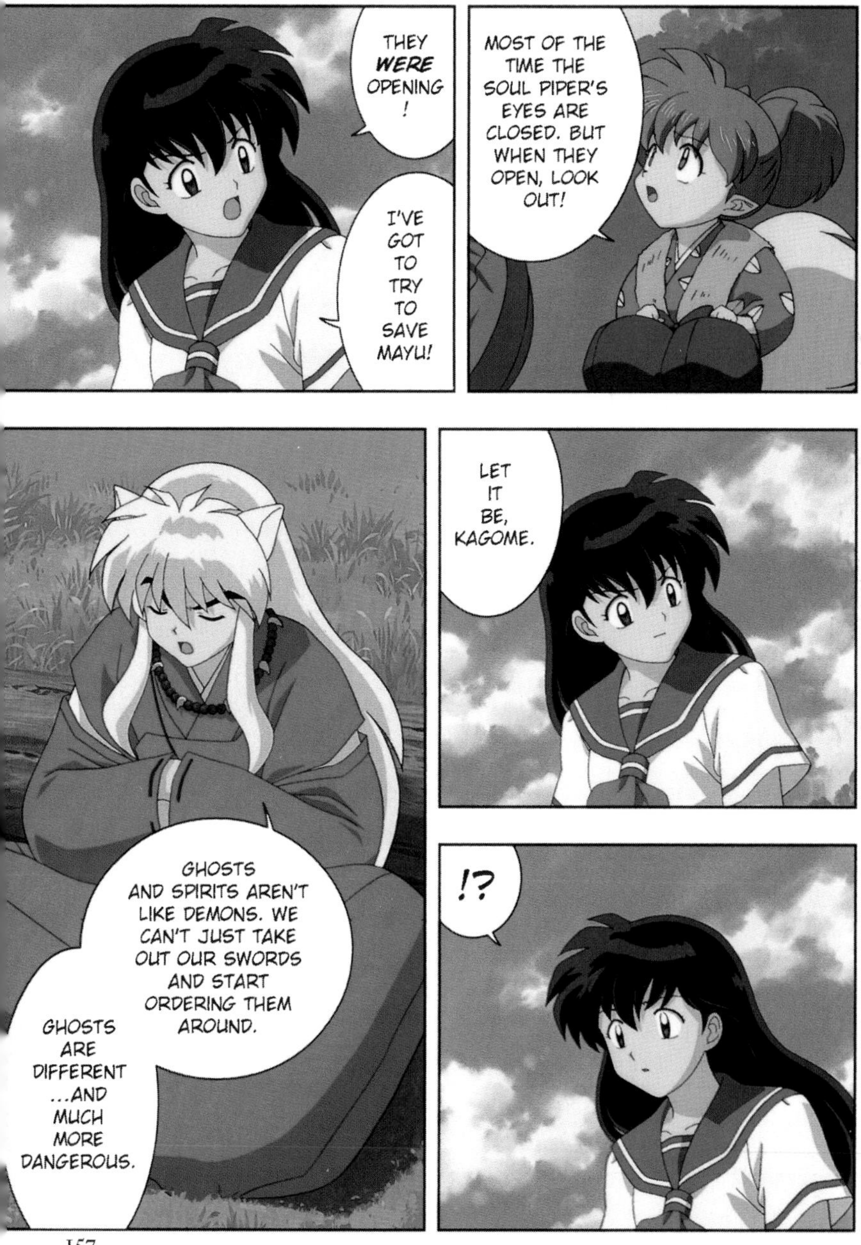
MOST OF THE TIME THE SOUL PIPER'S EYES ARE CLOSED. BUT WHEN THEY OPEN, LOOK OUT!
THEY ***WERE*** OPENING!
I'VE GOT TO TRY TO SAVE MAYU!
LET IT BE, KAGOME.
!?
GHOSTS AND SPIRITS AREN'T LIKE DEMONS. WE CAN'T JUST TAKE OUT OUR SWORDS AND START ORDERING THEM AROUND.
GHOSTS ARE DIFFERENT ...AND MUCH MORE DANGEROUS.

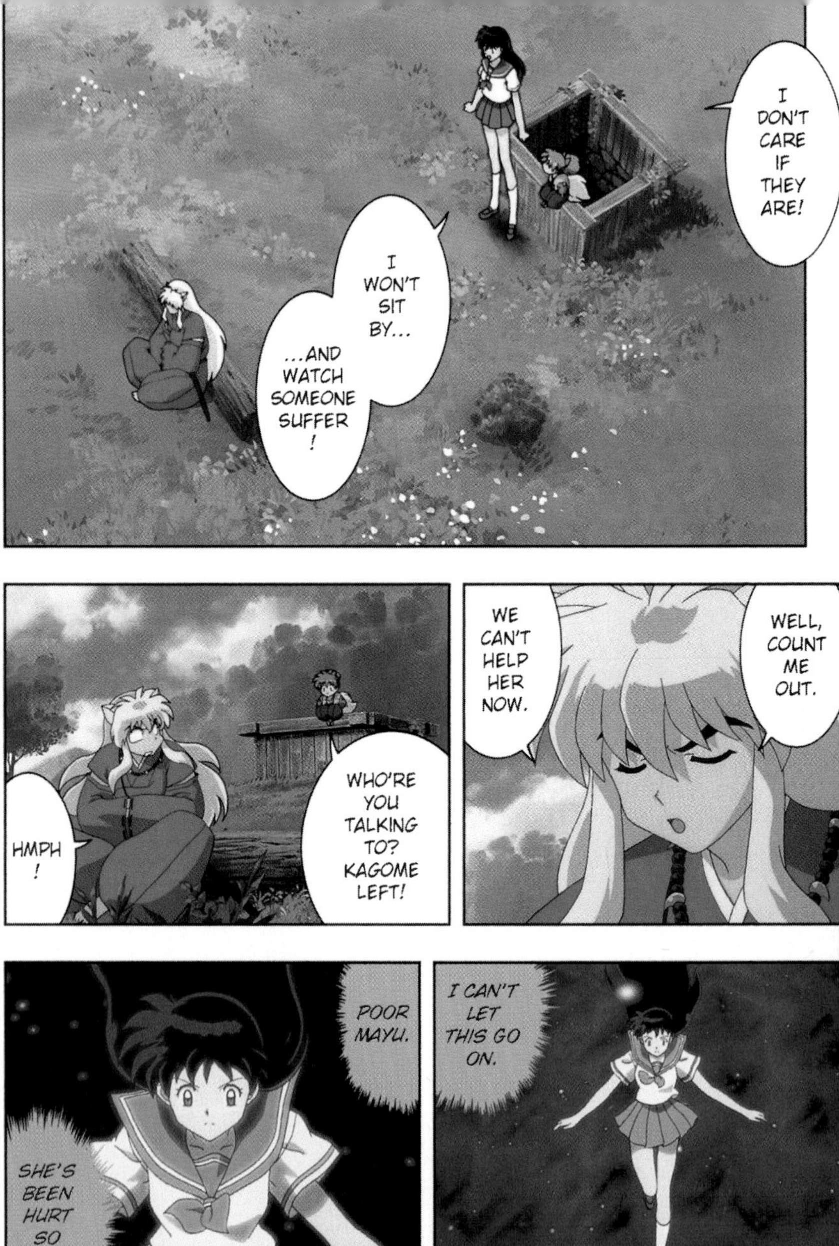
I DON'T CARE IF THEY ARE!
I WON'T SIT BY...
...AND WATCH SOMEONE SUFFER!
WELL, COUNT ME OUT.
WE CAN'T HELP HER NOW.
WHO'RE YOU TALKING TO? KAGOME LEFT!
HMPH!
I CAN'T LET THIS GO ON.
POOR MAYU.
SHE'S BEEN HURT SO MUCH...

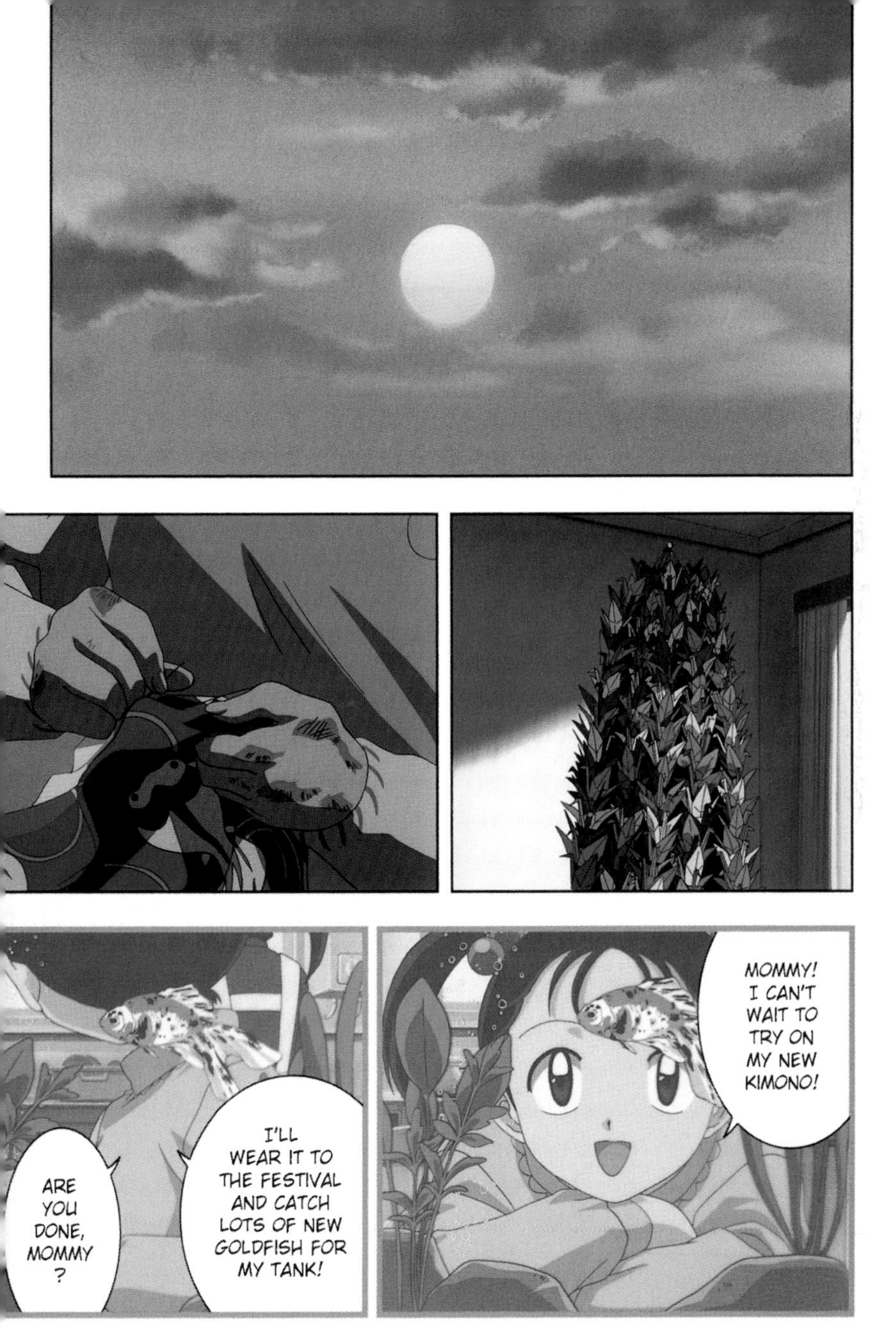
MOMMY! I CAN'T WAIT TO TRY ON MY NEW KIMONO!
I'LL WEAR IT TO THE FESTIVAL AND CATCH LOTS OF NEW GOLDFISH FOR MY TANK!
ARE YOU DONE, MOMMY?

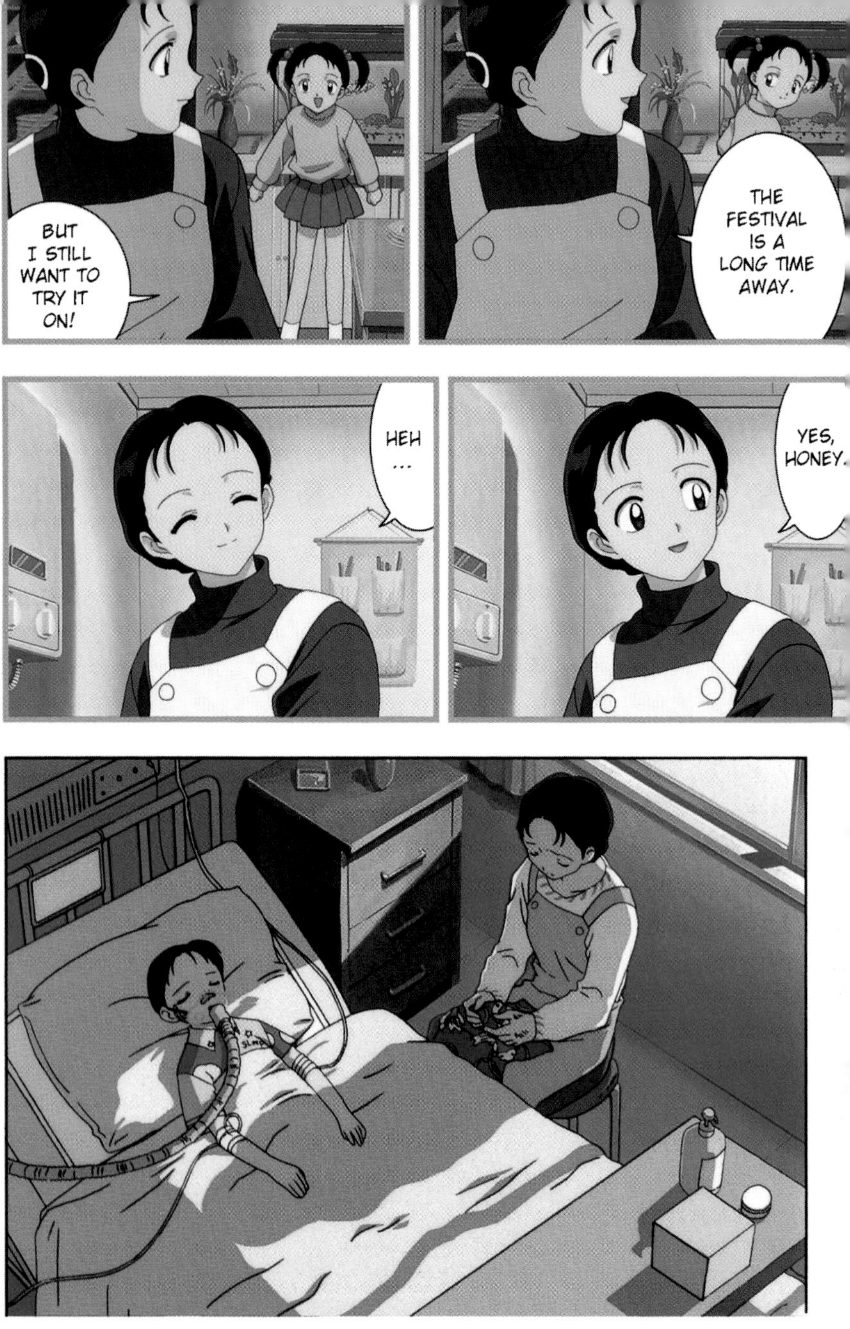
THE FESTIVAL IS A LONG TIME AWAY.
BUT I STILL WANT TO TRY IT ON!
YES, HONEY.
HEH ...

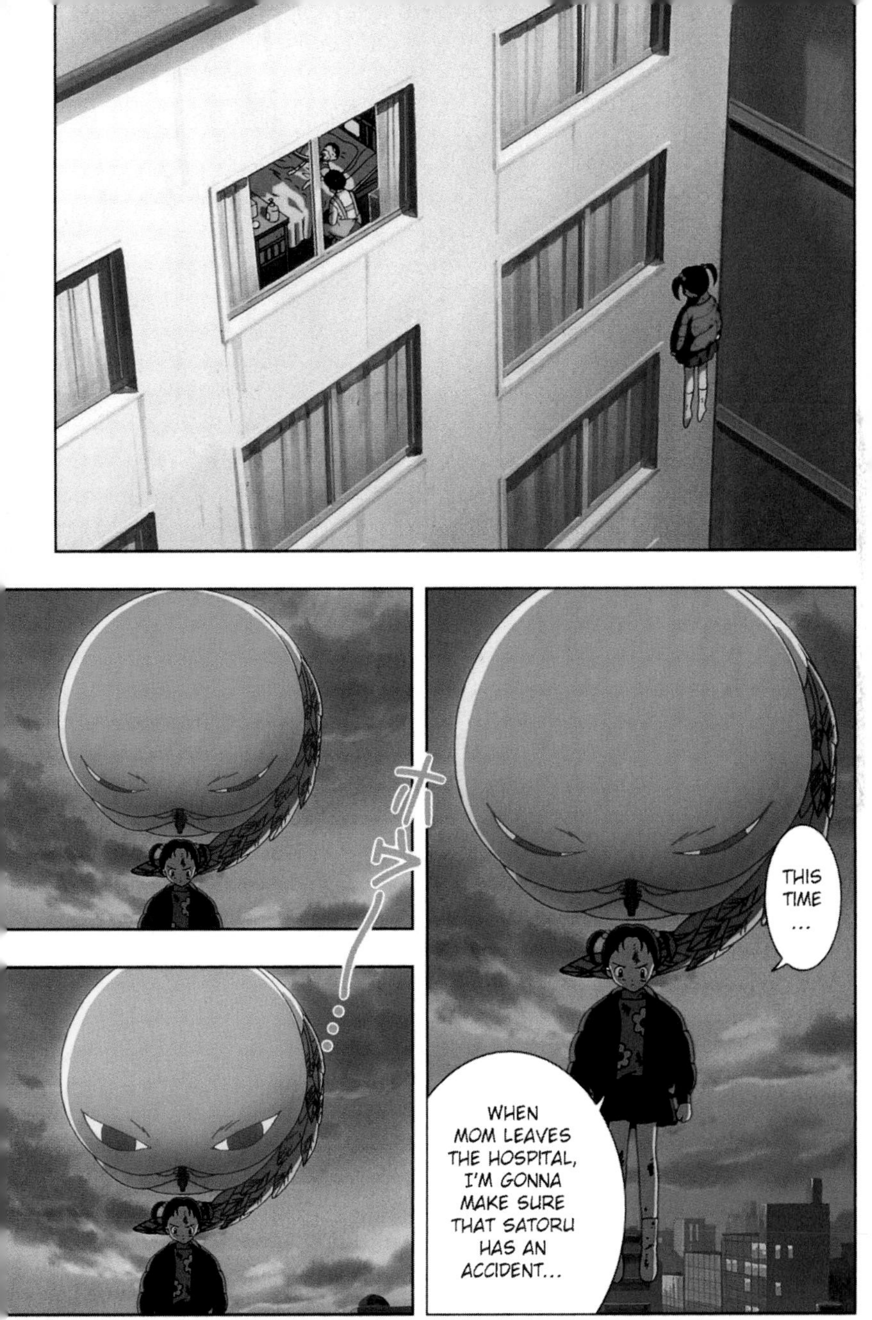

THIS TIME ...
WHEN MOM LEAVES THE HOSPITAL, I'M GONNA MAKE SURE THAT SATORU HAS AN ACCIDENT...
...

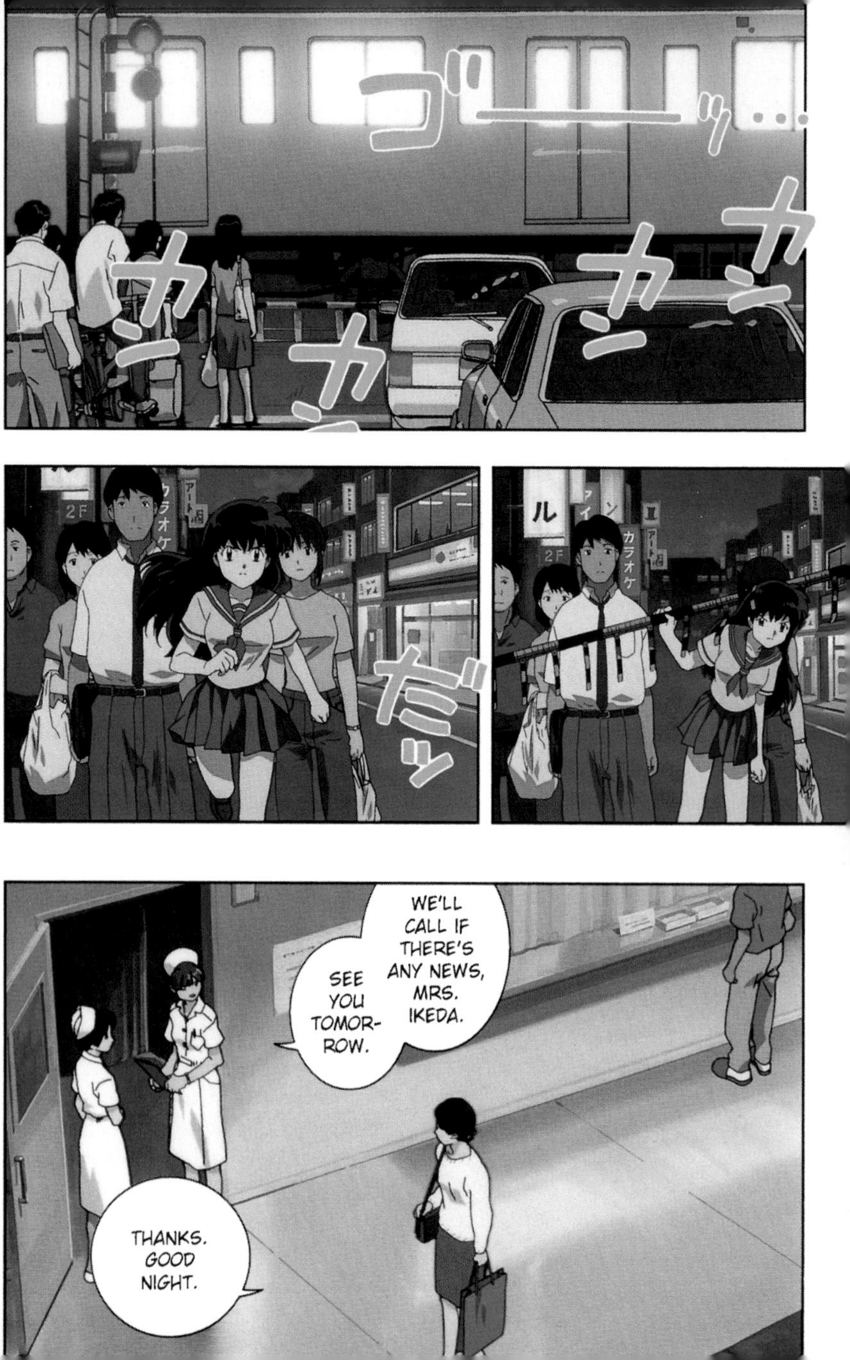
ゴーーーッ…
カンカン
カンカン
カラオケ
2F
カラオケ
2F
だッ
WE'LL CALL IF THERE'S ANY NEWS, MRS. IKEDA.
SEE YOU TOMORROW.
THANKS. GOOD NIGHT.

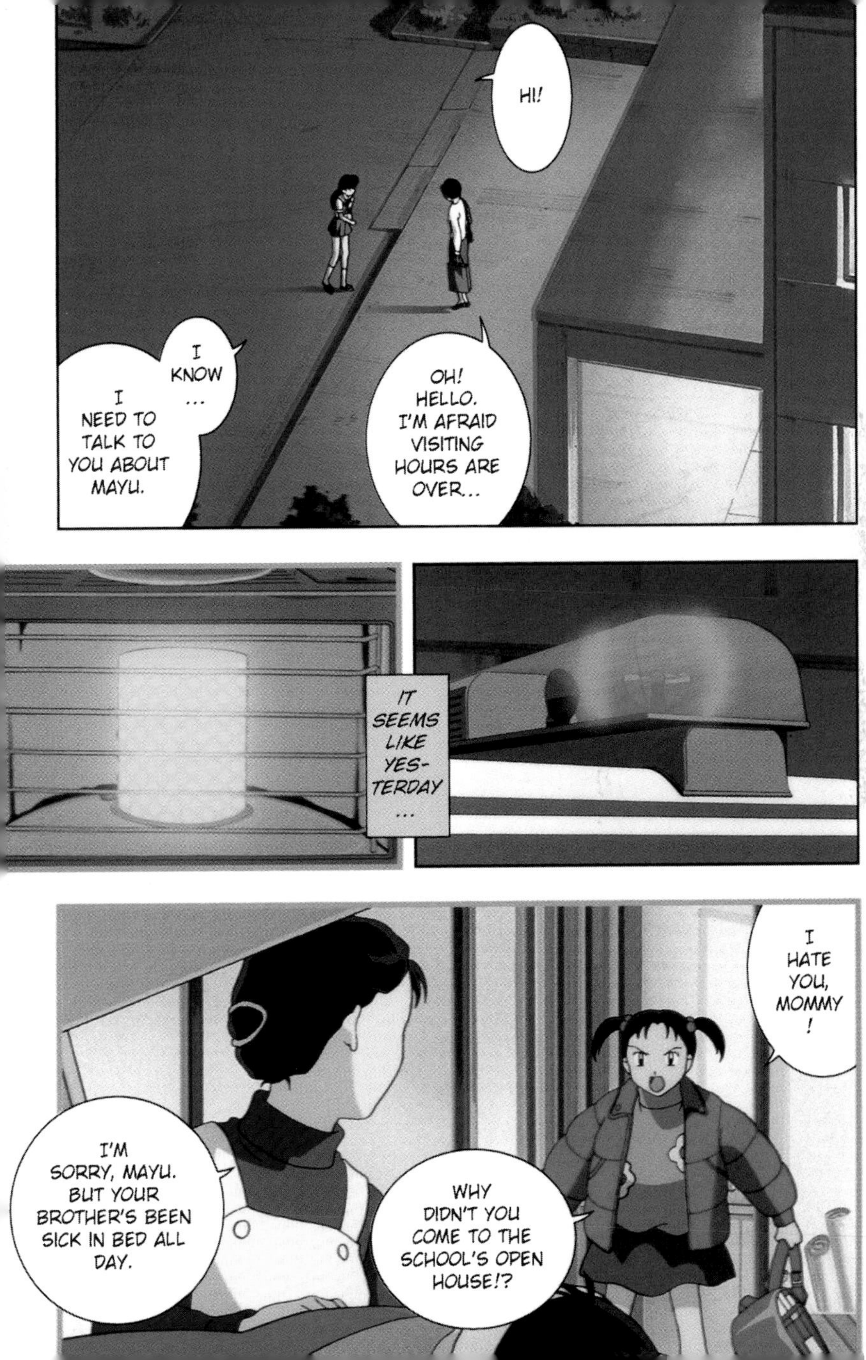
HI!
OH! HELLO. I'M AFRAID VISITING HOURS ARE OVER...
I KNOW...
I NEED TO TALK TO YOU ABOUT MAYU.
IT SEEMS LIKE YES-TERDAY...
I HATE YOU, MOMMY!
WHY DIDN'T YOU COME TO THE SCHOOL'S OPEN HOUSE!?
I'M SORRY, MAYU. BUT YOUR BROTHER'S BEEN SICK IN BED ALL DAY.

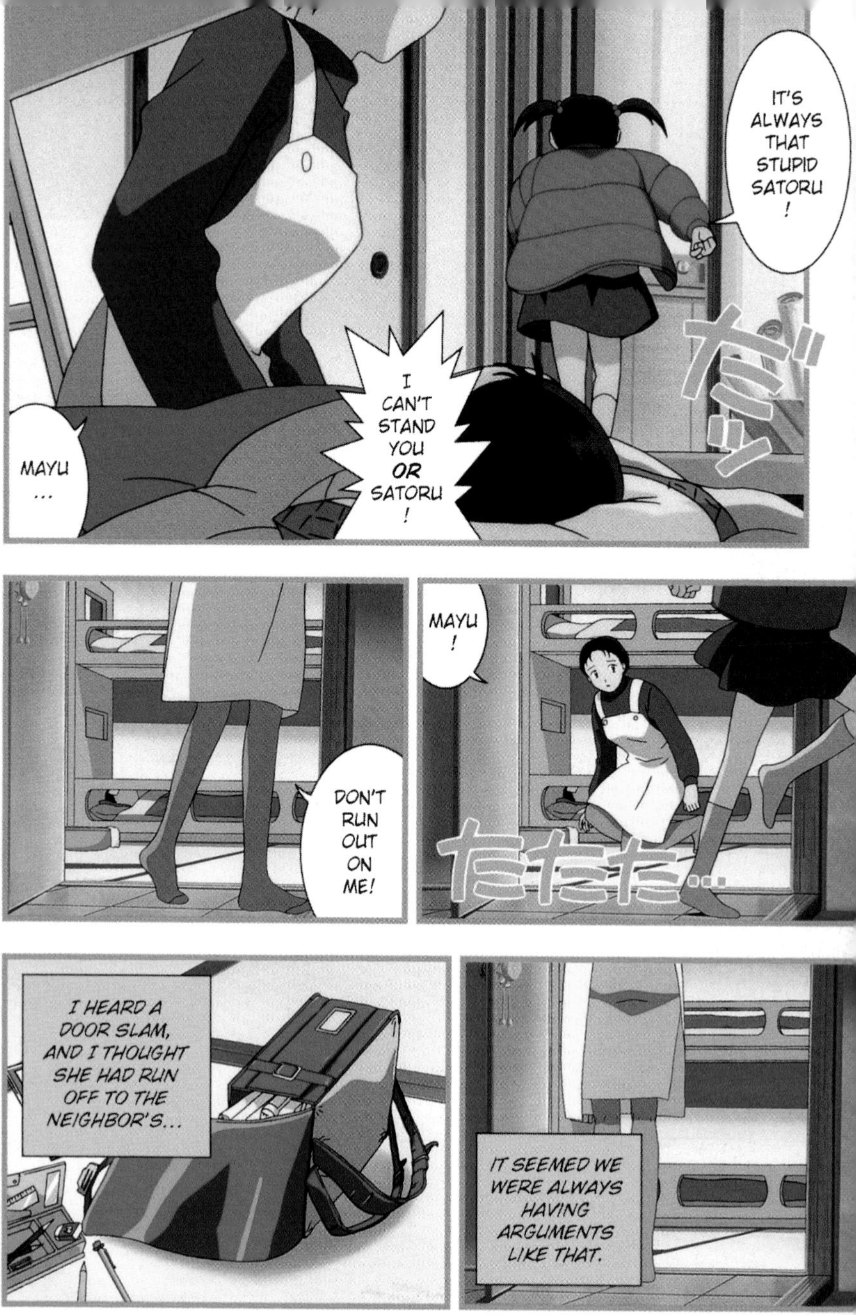
IT'S ALWAYS THAT STUPID SATORU!
ダンッ
I CAN'T STAND YOU **OR** SATORU!
MAYU...
MAYU!
たたた...
DON'T RUN OUT ON ME!
IT SEEMED WE WERE ALWAYS HAVING ARGUMENTS LIKE THAT.
I HEARD A DOOR SLAM, AND I THOUGHT SHE HAD RUN OFF TO THE NEIGHBOR'S...

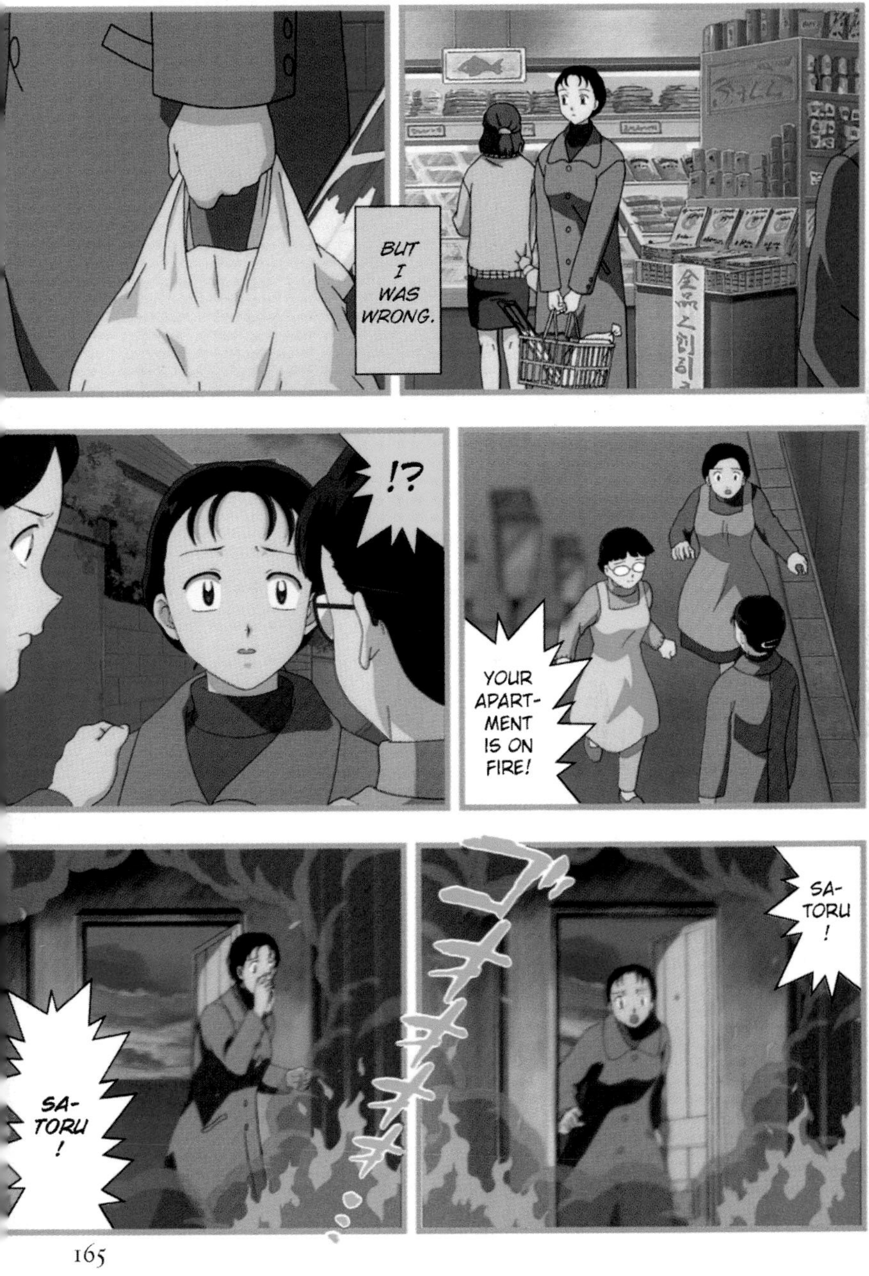
BUT I WAS WRONG.
YOUR APART-MENT IS ON FIRE!
!?
SA-TORU!
SA-TORU!

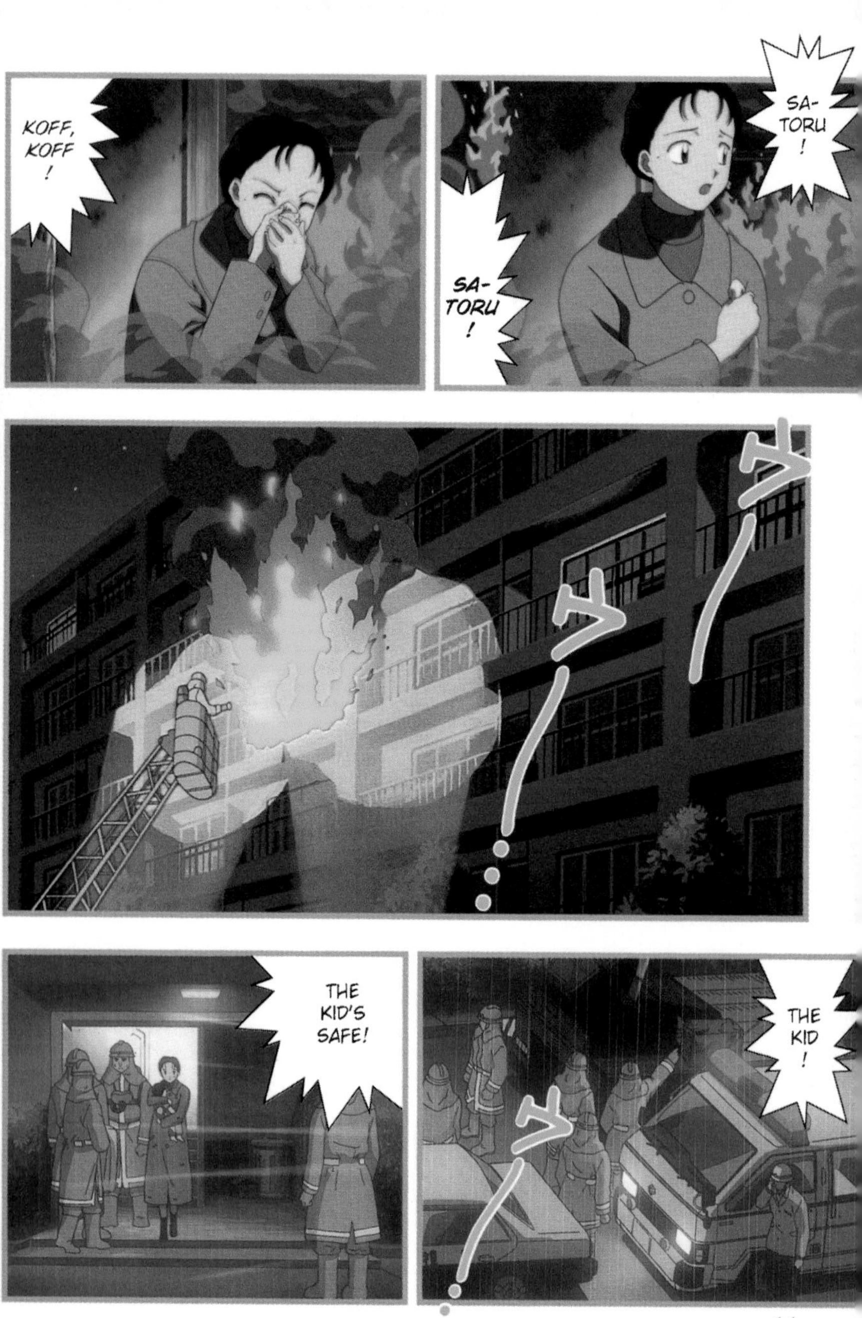

SA-TORU!
SA-TORU!
KOFF, KOFF!
THE KID!
THE KID'S SAFE!

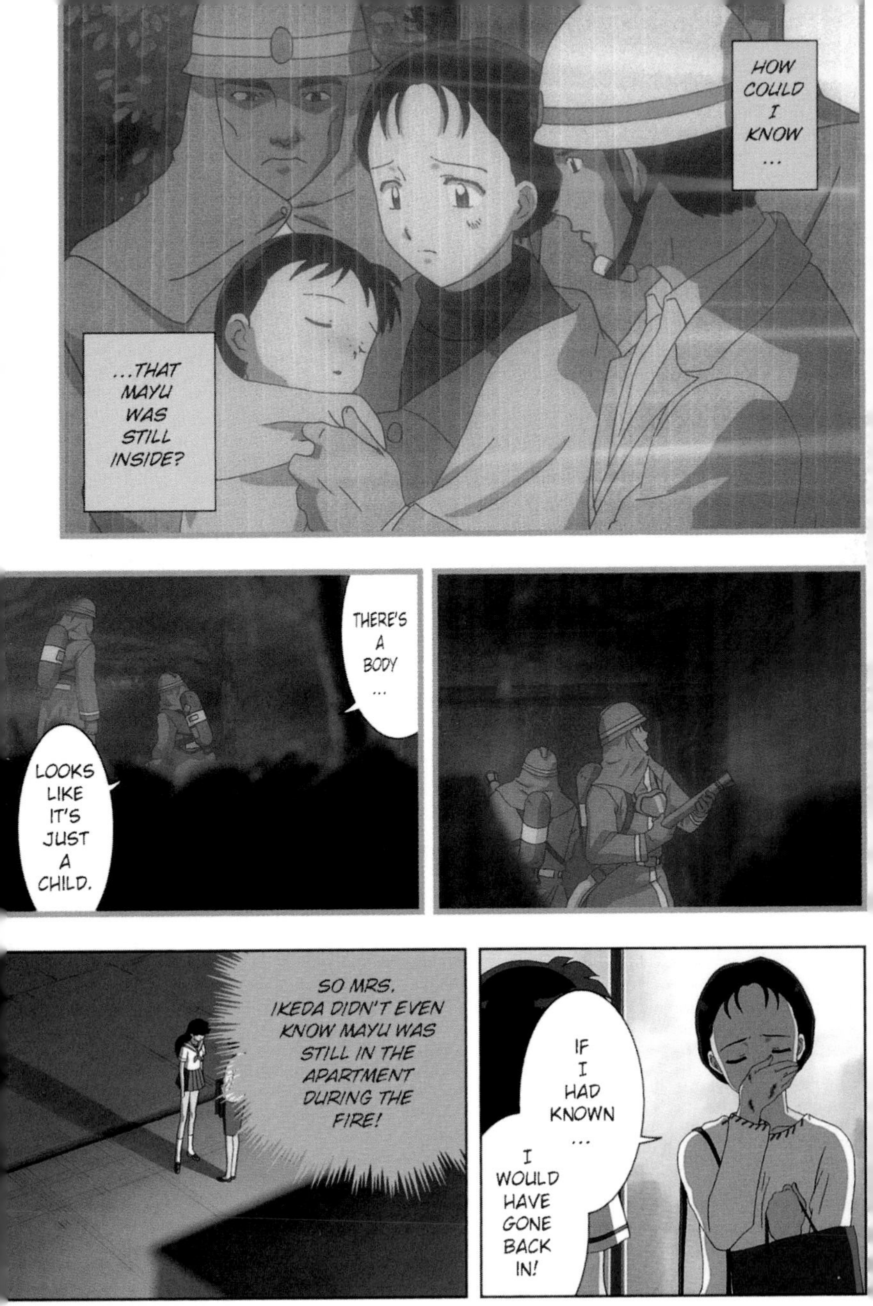
HOW COULD I KNOW ...
...THAT MAYU WAS STILL INSIDE?
THERE'S A BODY ...
LOOKS LIKE IT'S JUST A CHILD.
IF I HAD KNOWN ...
I WOULD HAVE GONE BACK IN!
SO MRS. IKEDA DIDN'T EVEN KNOW MAYU WAS STILL IN THE APARTMENT DURING THE FIRE!

THAT'S SATORU'S ROOM!

パリーン

!!

ボワン

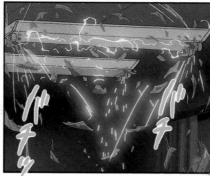

バチチ

MAYU, NO! STOP IT!

バシーッ

IT'S MAYU!

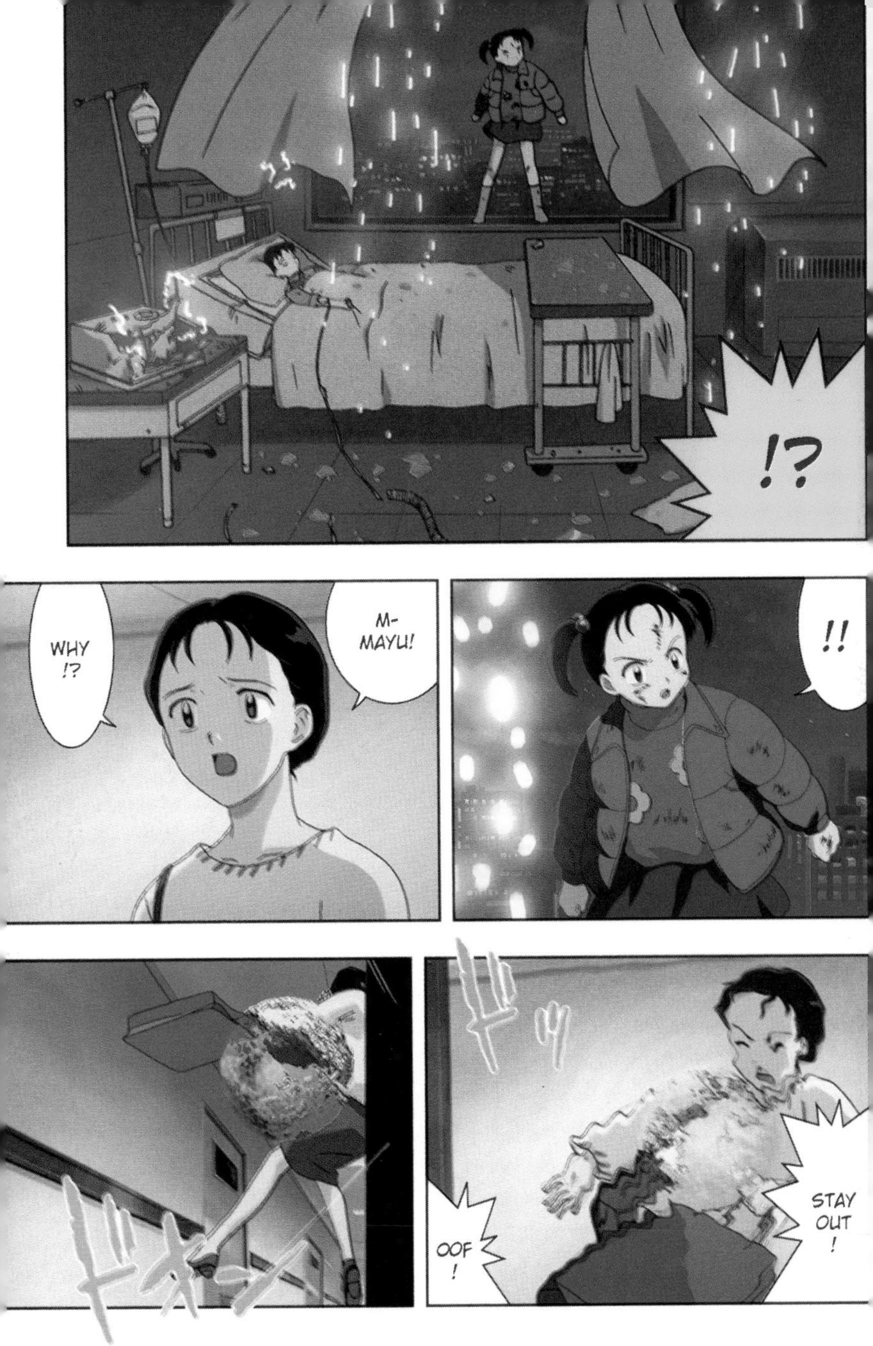
!?
!!
M-MAYU!
WHY !?
STAY OUT !
OOF !

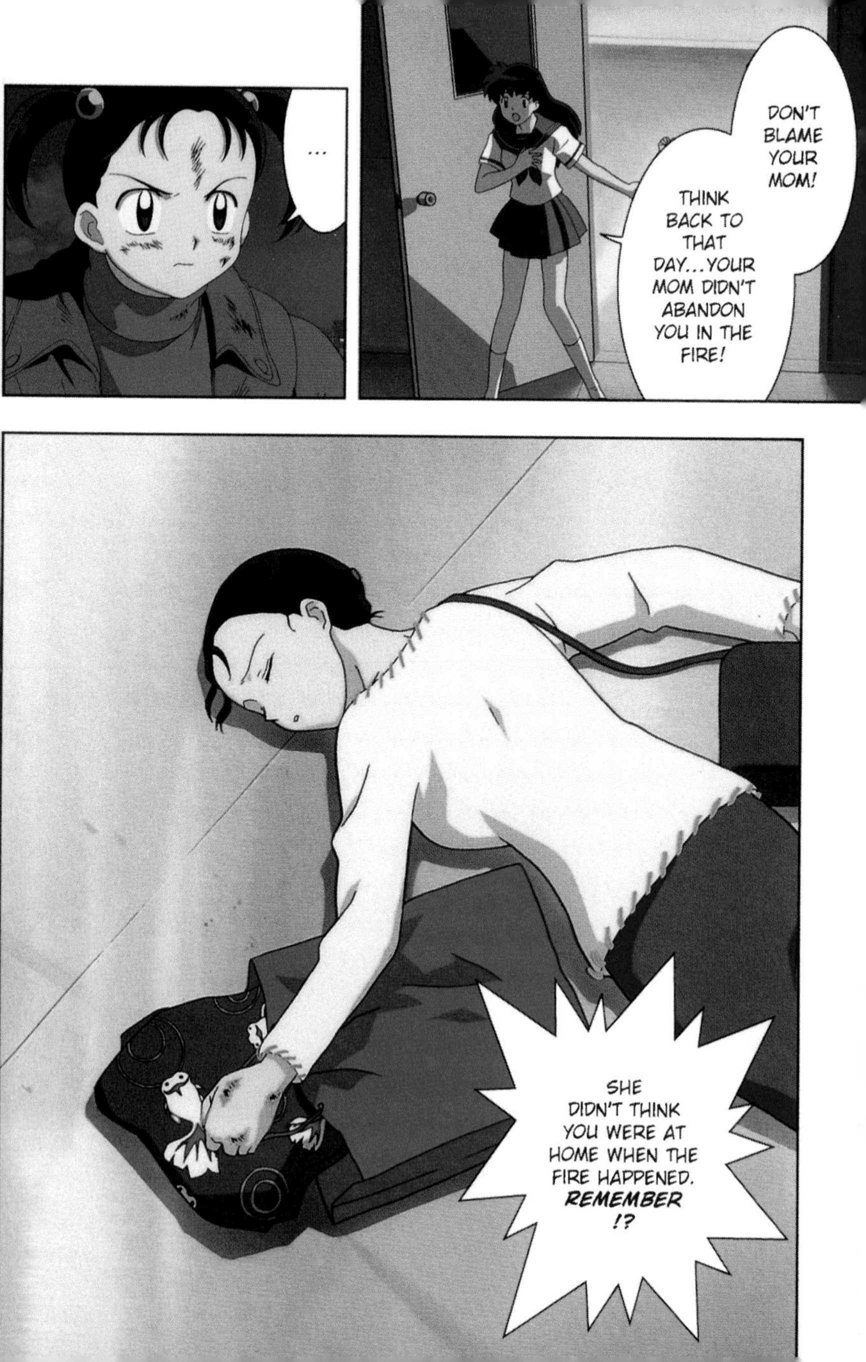
DON'T BLAME YOUR MOM!
THINK BACK TO THAT DAY...YOUR MOM DIDN'T ABANDON YOU IN THE FIRE!
...
SHE DIDN'T THINK YOU WERE AT HOME WHEN THE FIRE HAPPENED. **REMEMBER!?**

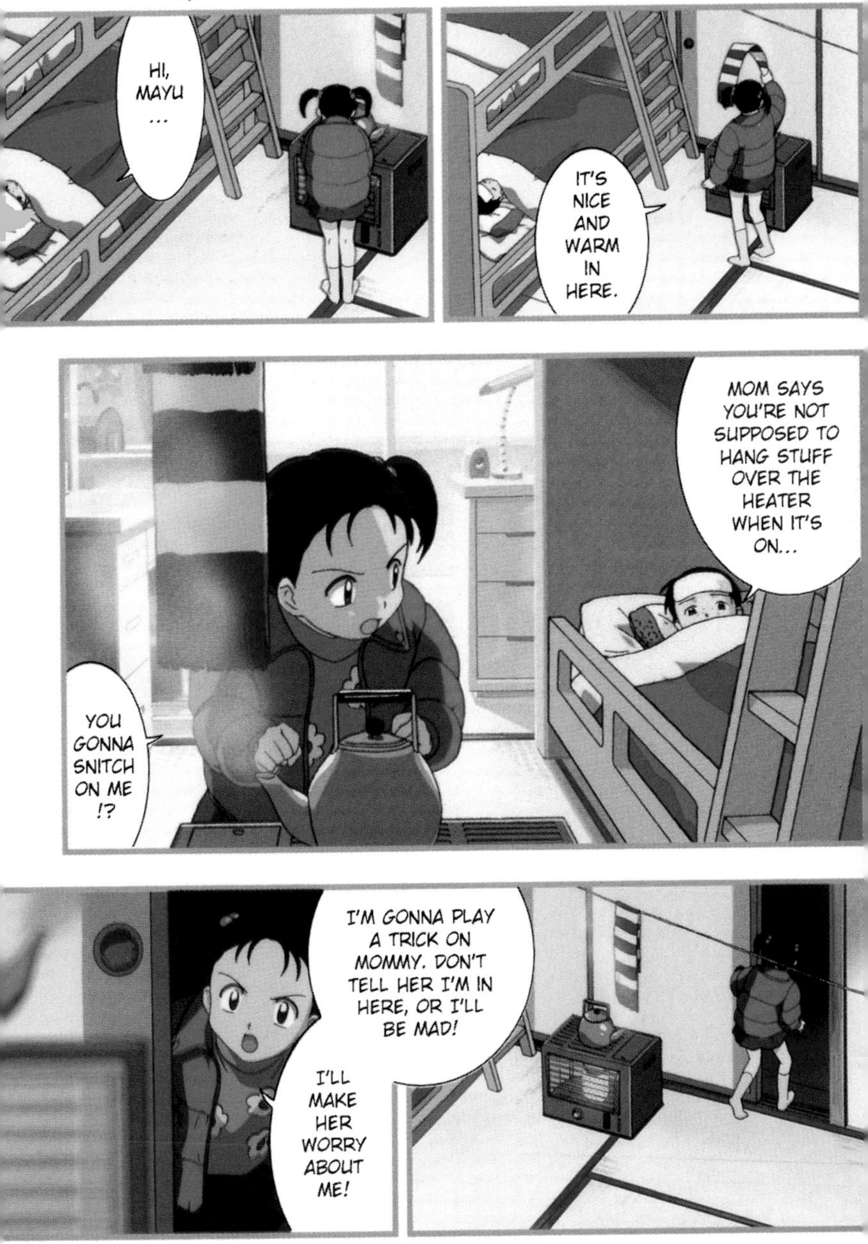

IT'S NICE AND WARM IN HERE.
HI, MAYU ...
MOM SAYS YOU'RE NOT SUPPOSED TO HANG STUFF OVER THE HEATER WHEN IT'S ON...
YOU GONNA SNITCH ON ME !?
I'M GONNA PLAY A TRICK ON MOMMY. DON'T TELL HER I'M IN HERE, OR I'LL BE MAD!
I'LL MAKE HER WORRY ABOUT ME!

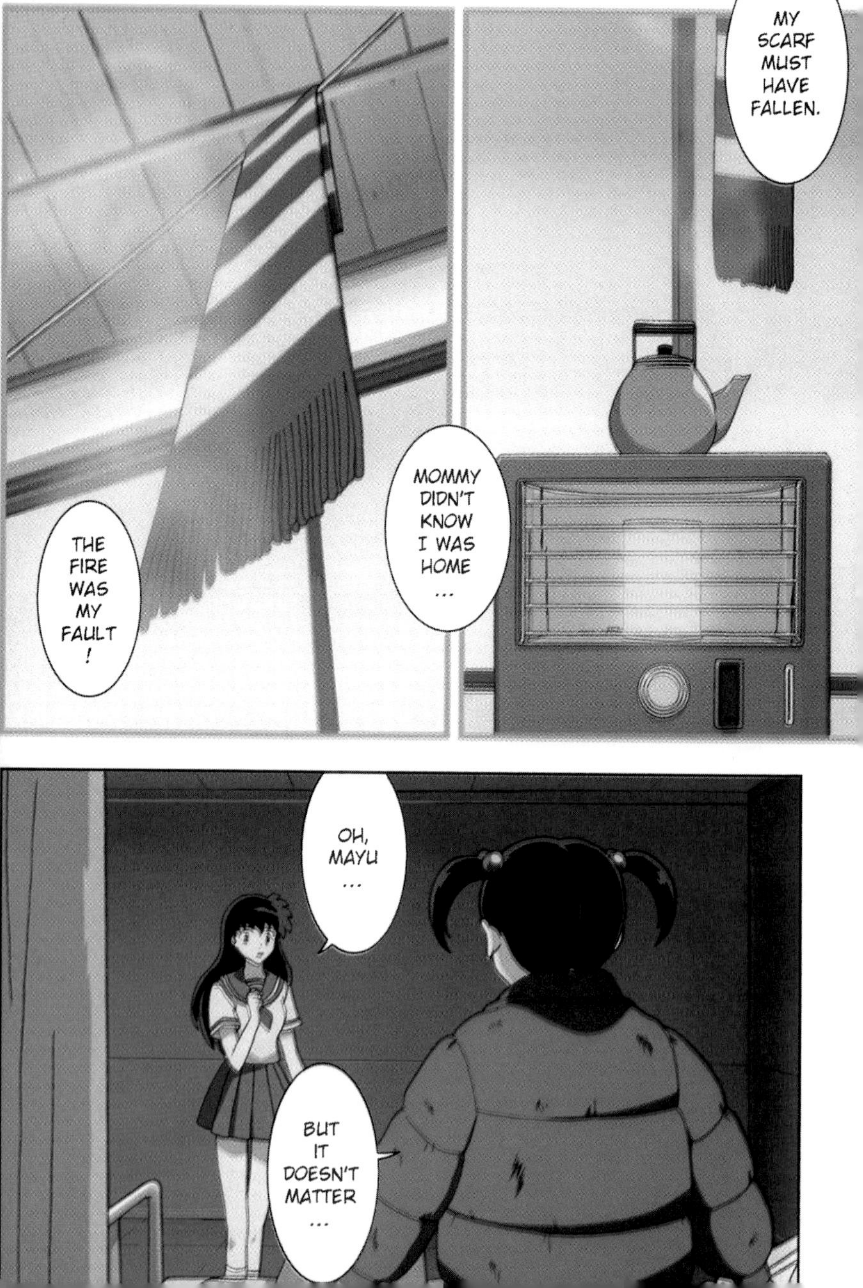
MY SCARF MUST HAVE FALLEN.
MOMMY DIDN'T KNOW I WAS HOME ...
THE FIRE WAS MY FAULT!
OH, MAYU ...
BUT IT DOESN'T MATTER ...

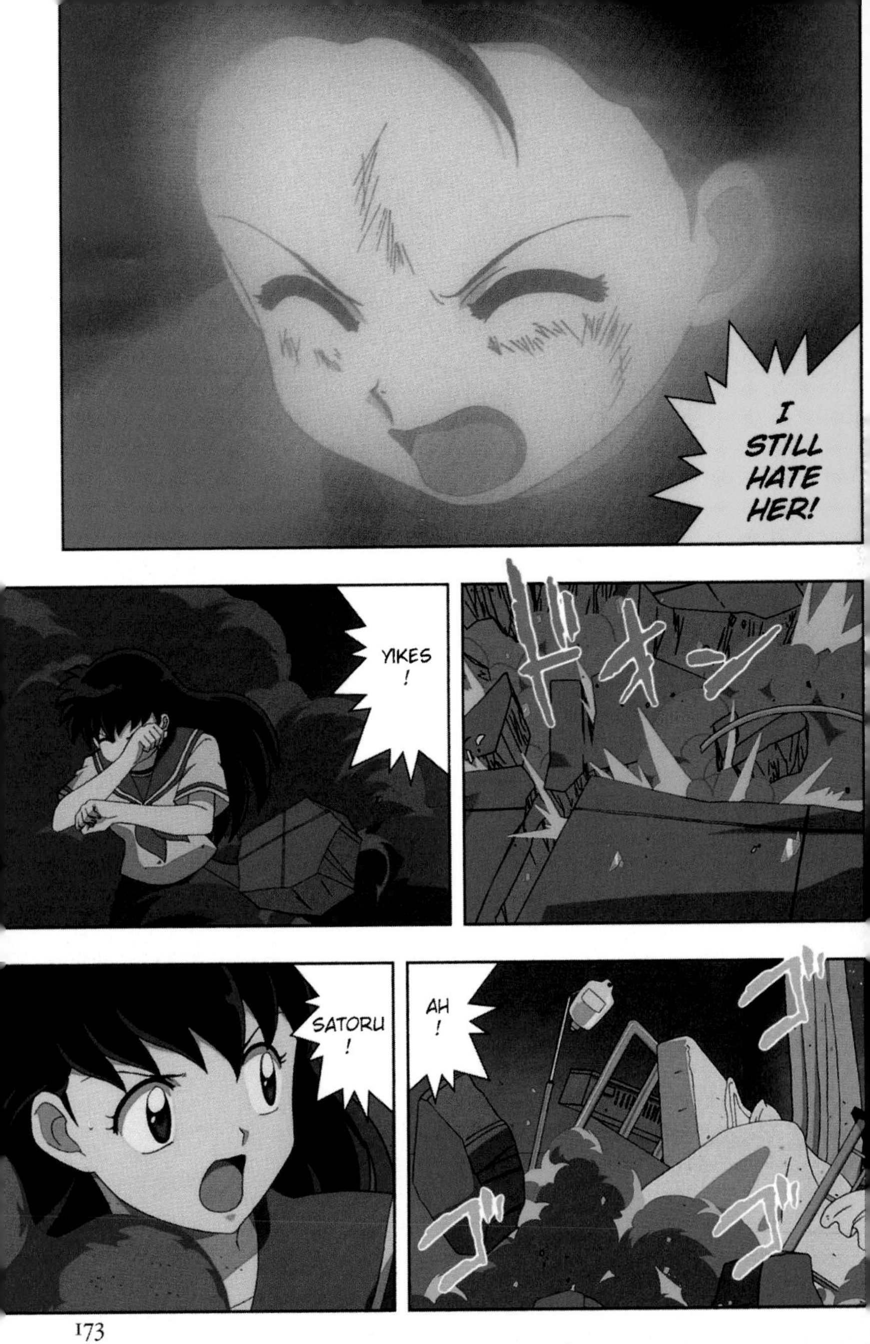
I STILL HATE HER!
ドオーン
YIKES!
AH!
SATORU!

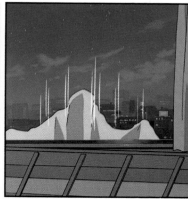

YAAH!

HE FELL ...

THAT POOR BOY!

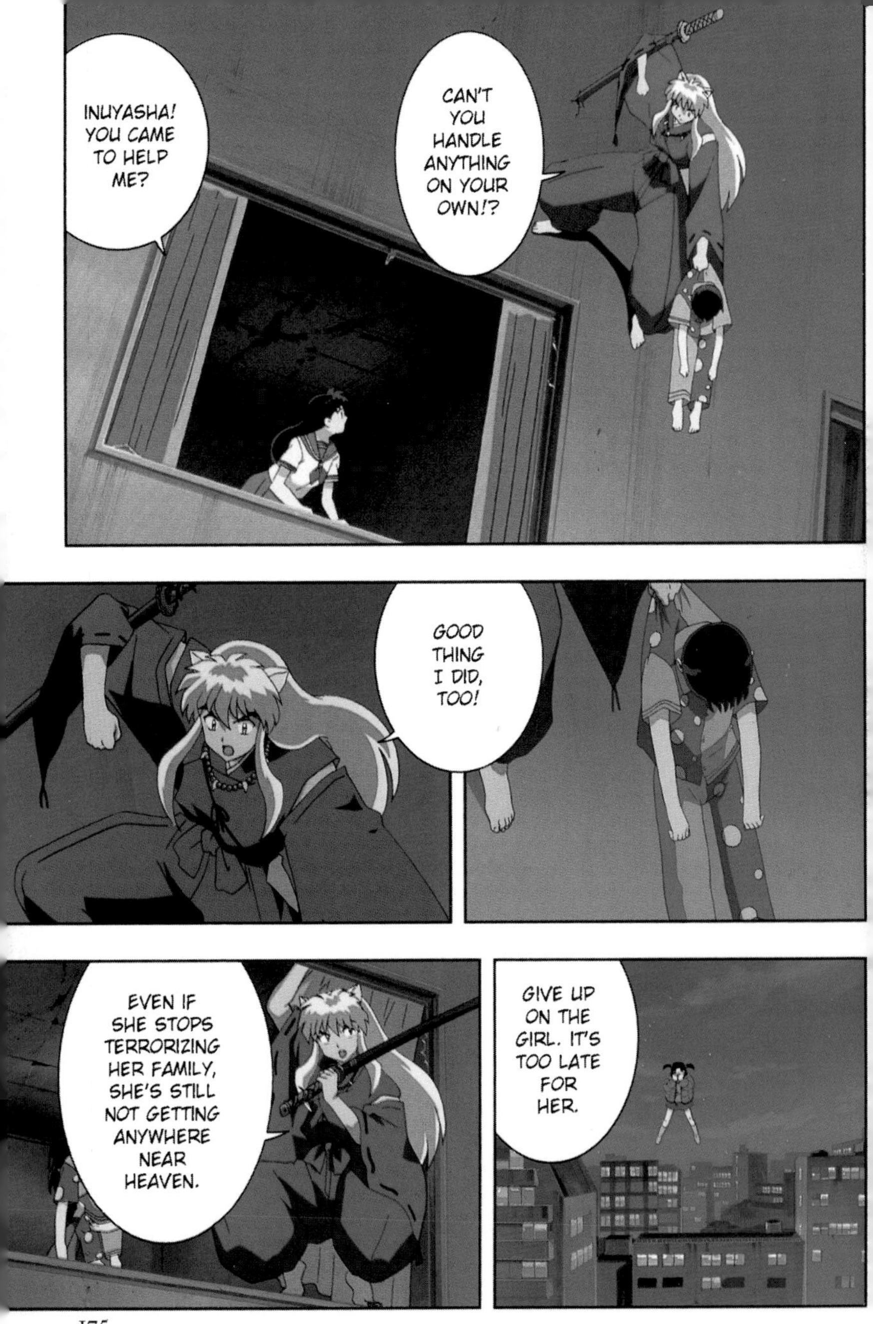
INUYASHA! YOU CAME TO HELP ME?
CAN'T YOU HANDLE ANYTHING ON YOUR OWN!?
GOOD THING I DID, TOO!
EVEN IF SHE STOPS TERRORIZING HER FAMILY, SHE'S STILL NOT GETTING ANYWHERE NEAR HEAVEN.
GIVE UP ON THE GIRL. IT'S TOO LATE FOR HER.

THE EYES !

WHAT IS THIS !?

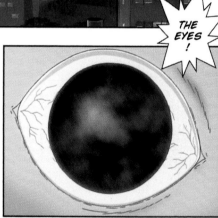

LET ME GO!

I WANNA STAY HERE !

176

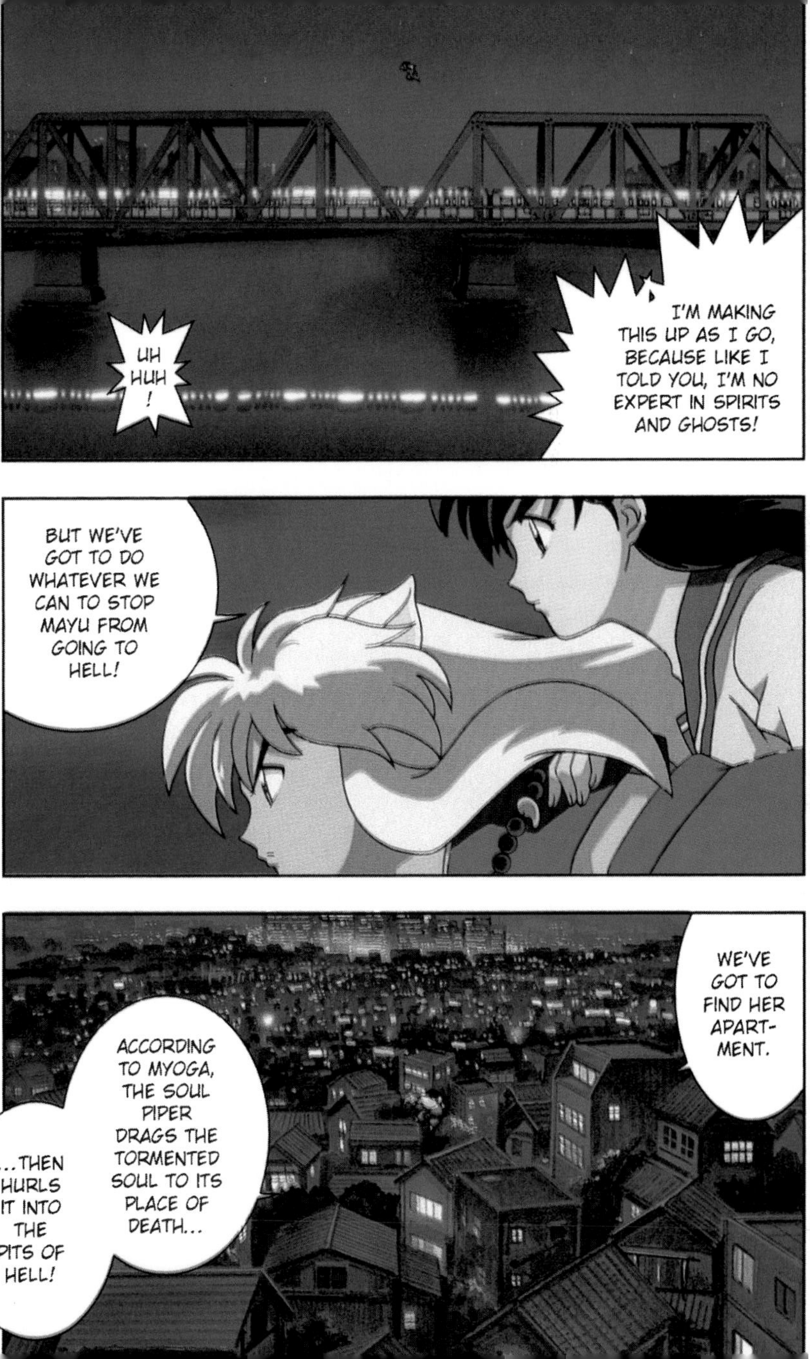
I'M MAKING THIS UP AS I GO, BECAUSE LIKE I TOLD YOU, I'M NO EXPERT IN SPIRITS AND GHOSTS!
UH HUH!
BUT WE'VE GOT TO DO WHATEVER WE CAN TO STOP MAYU FROM GOING TO HELL!
WE'VE GOT TO FIND HER APARTMENT.
ACCORDING TO MYOGA, THE SOUL PIPER DRAGS THE TORMENTED SOUL TO ITS PLACE OF DEATH...
...THEN HURLS IT INTO THE PITS OF HELL!

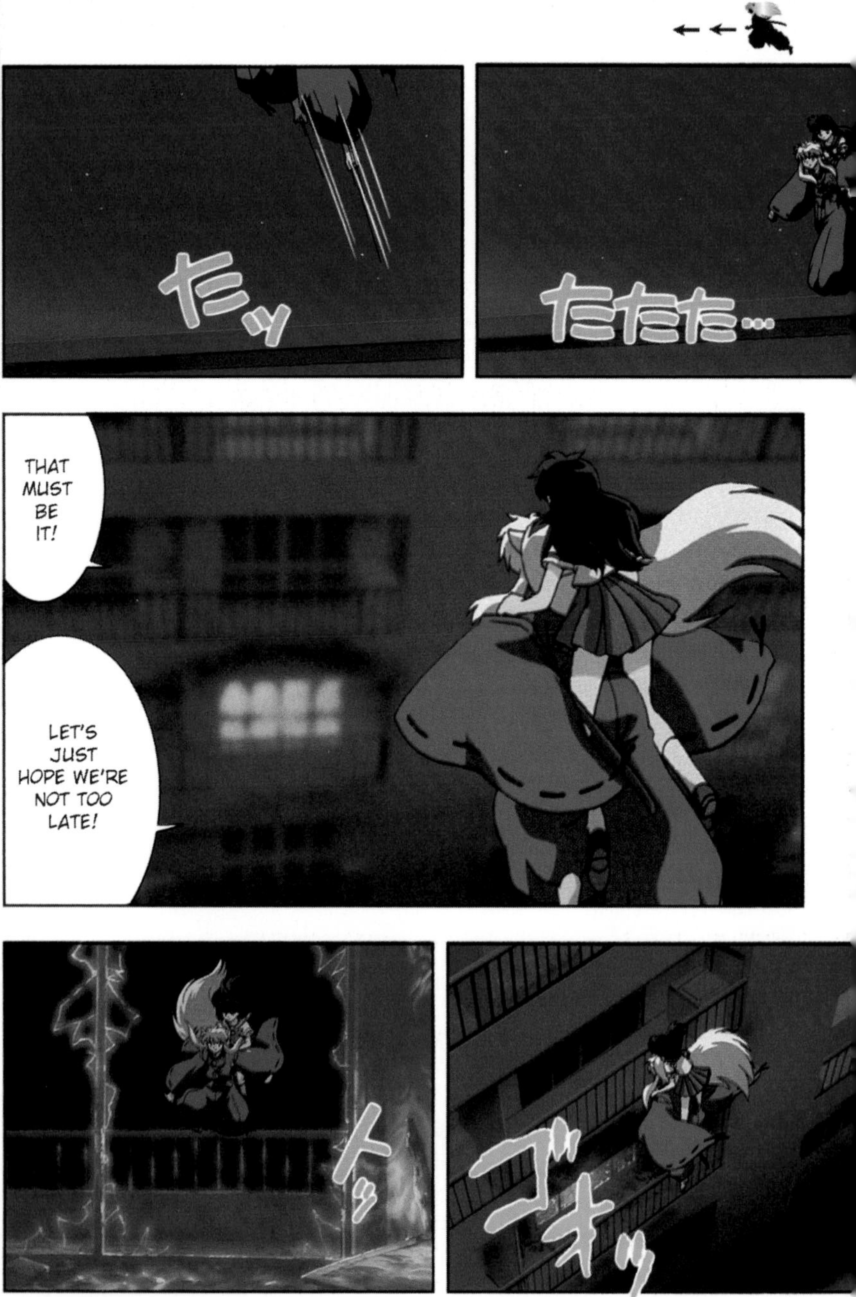
たたたた…
たッ
THAT MUST BE IT!
LET'S JUST HOPE WE'RE NOT TOO LATE!
ゴオッ
トッ

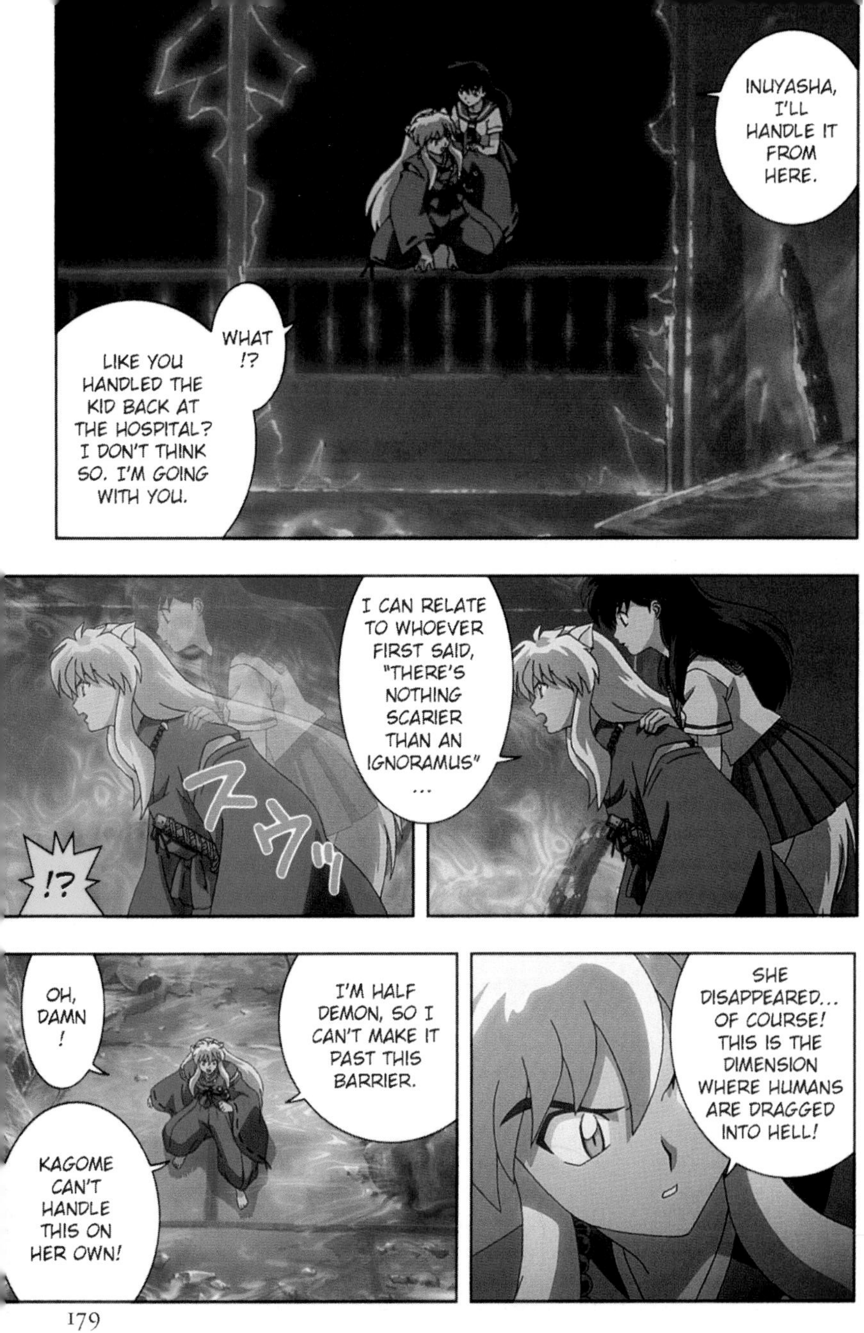
INUYASHA, I'LL HANDLE IT FROM HERE.
WHAT!?
LIKE YOU HANDLED THE KID BACK AT THE HOSPITAL? I DON'T THINK SO. I'M GOING WITH YOU.
I CAN RELATE TO WHOEVER FIRST SAID, "THERE'S NOTHING SCARIER THAN AN IGNORAMUS"...
スウッ
!?
SHE DISAPPEARED... OF COURSE! THIS IS THE DIMENSION WHERE HUMANS ARE DRAGGED INTO HELL!
I'M HALF DEMON, SO I CAN'T MAKE IT PAST THIS BARRIER.
OH, DAMN!
KAGOME CAN'T HANDLE THIS ON HER OWN!

WHERE AM I?
WHY'S IT SO DARK?
A LIGHT ?
AH !

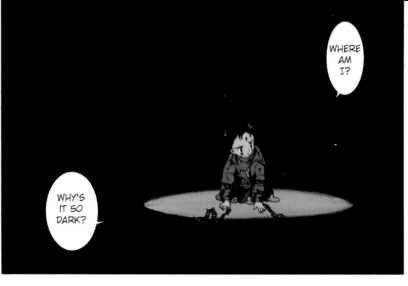

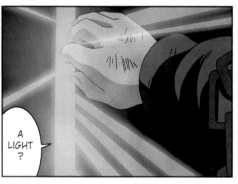

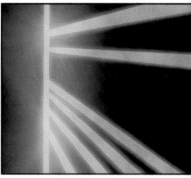

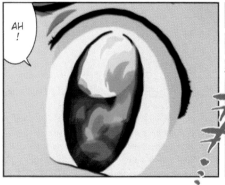

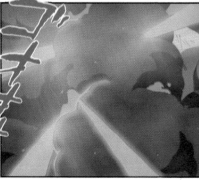

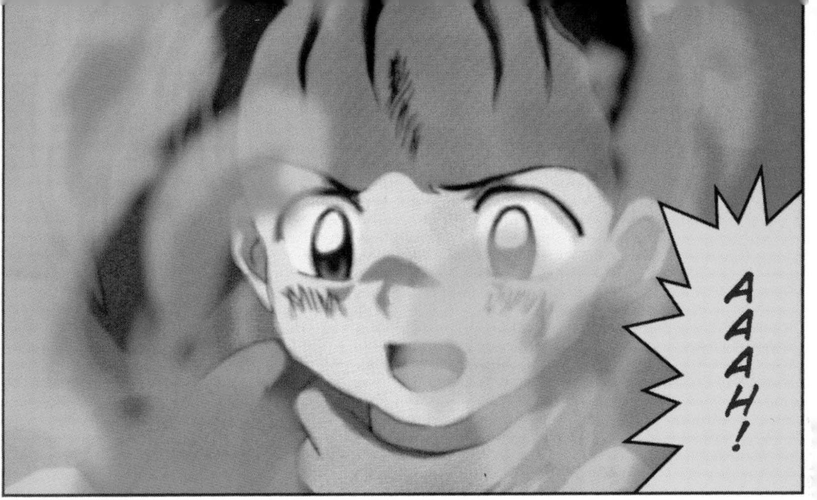
AAAH!

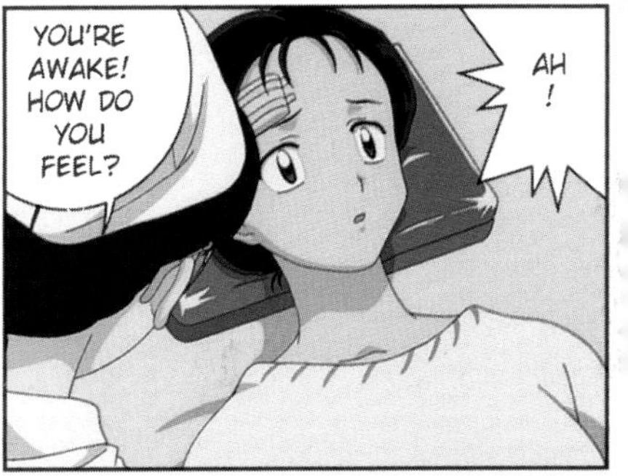
AH!
YOU'RE AWAKE! HOW DO YOU FEEL?

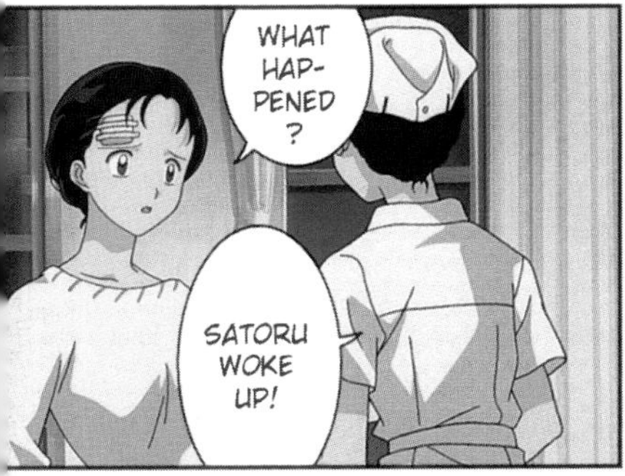
WHAT HAPPENED?
SATORU WOKE UP!

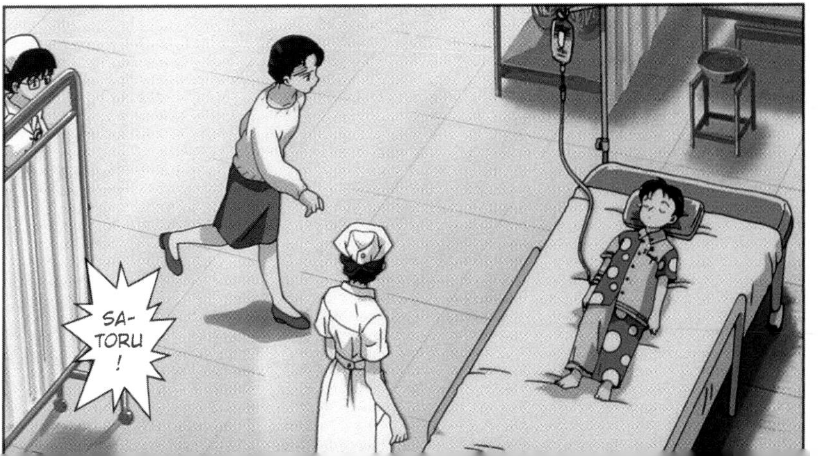
SATORU!

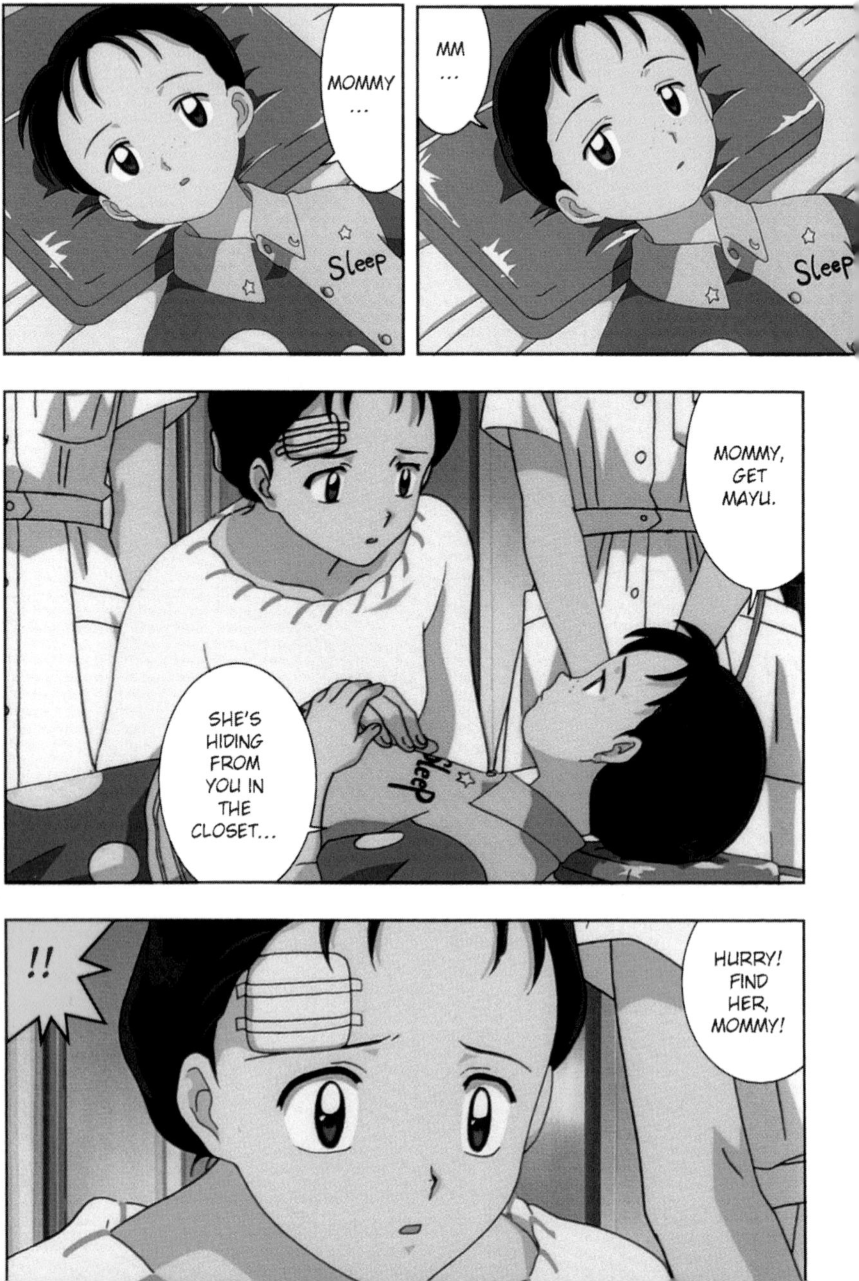

MM ...
Sleep
MOMMY ...
Sleep
MOMMY, GET MAYU.
SHE'S HIDING FROM YOU IN THE CLOSET...
Sleep
HURRY! FIND HER, MOMMY!
!!

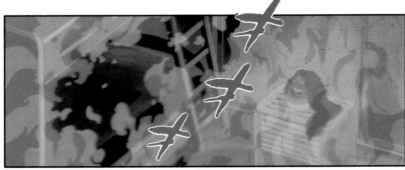

I'M AT MY HOUSE. THIS IS HOW I DIED.

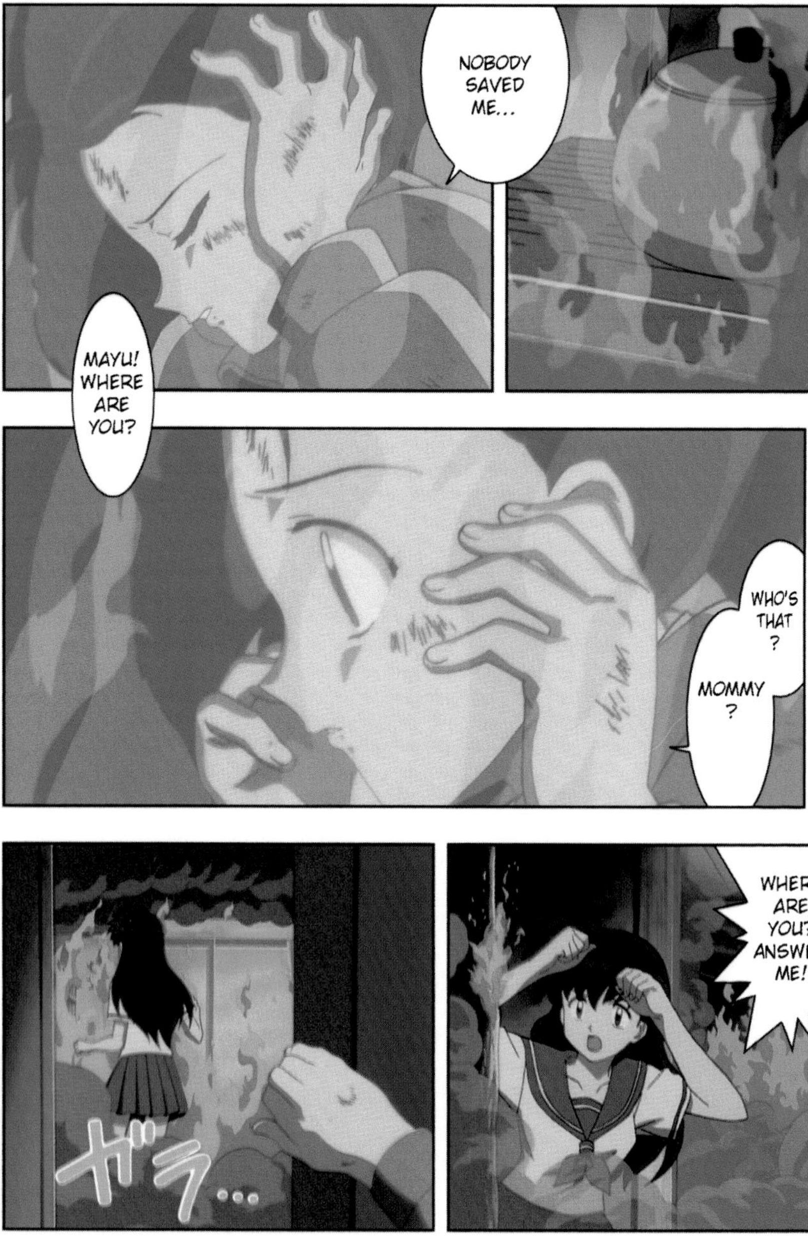
NOBODY SAVED ME...
MAYU! WHERE ARE YOU?
WHO'S THAT? MOMMY?
WHERE ARE YOU? ANSWER ME!
ガラ...

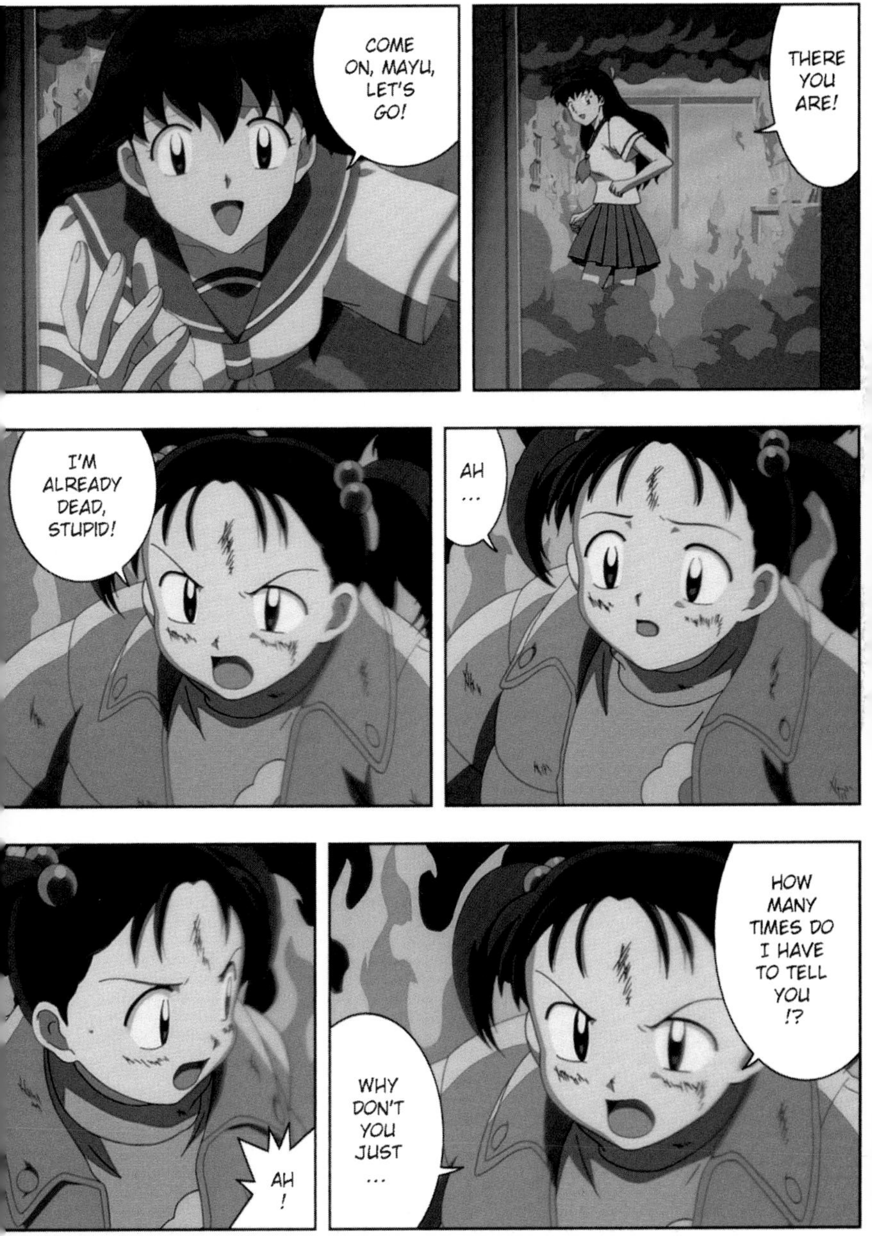
THERE YOU ARE!
COME ON, MAYU, LET'S GO!
AH ...
I'M ALREADY DEAD, STUPID!
HOW MANY TIMES DO I HAVE TO TELL YOU !?
WHY DON'T YOU JUST ...
AH !

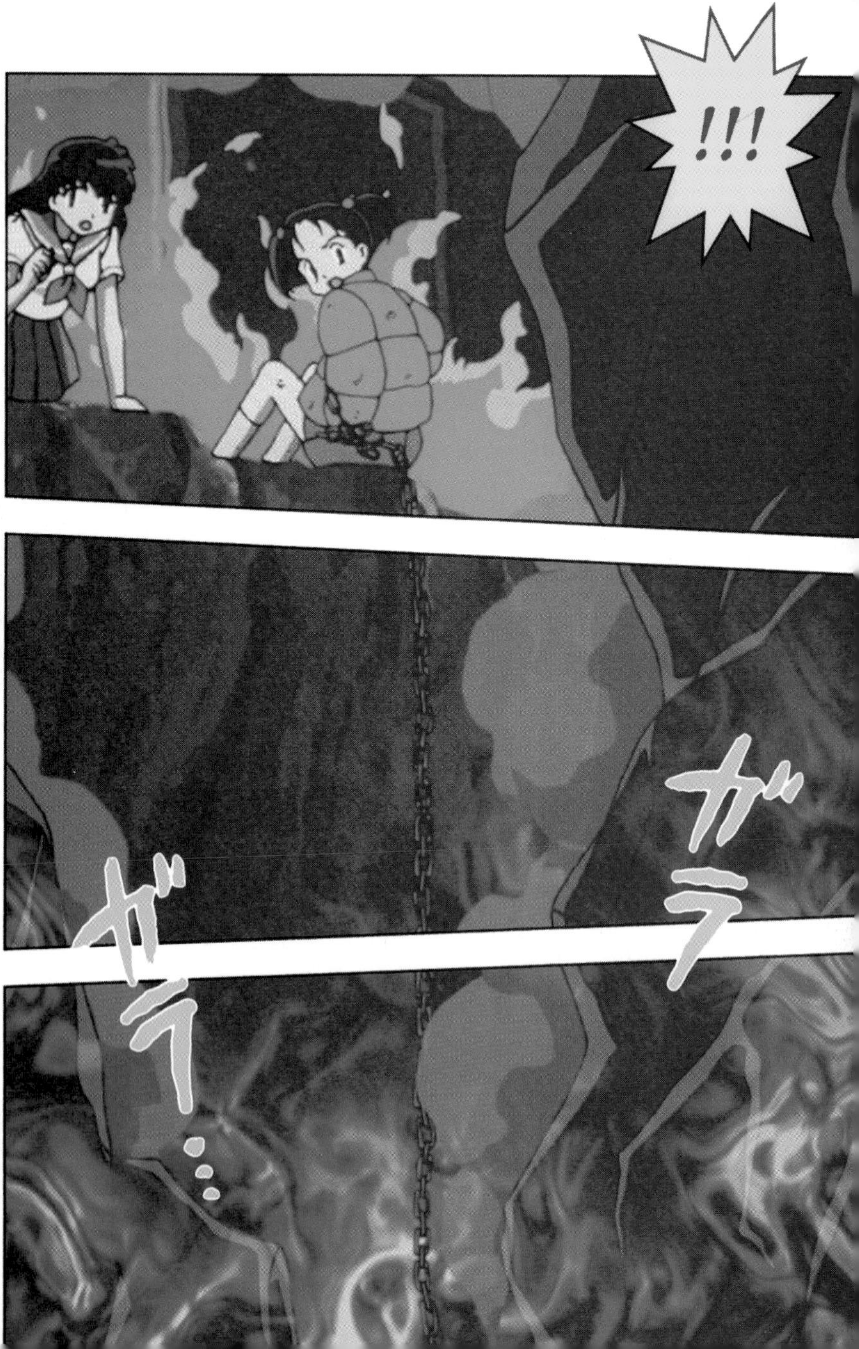
!!!
ガラ
ガラ…

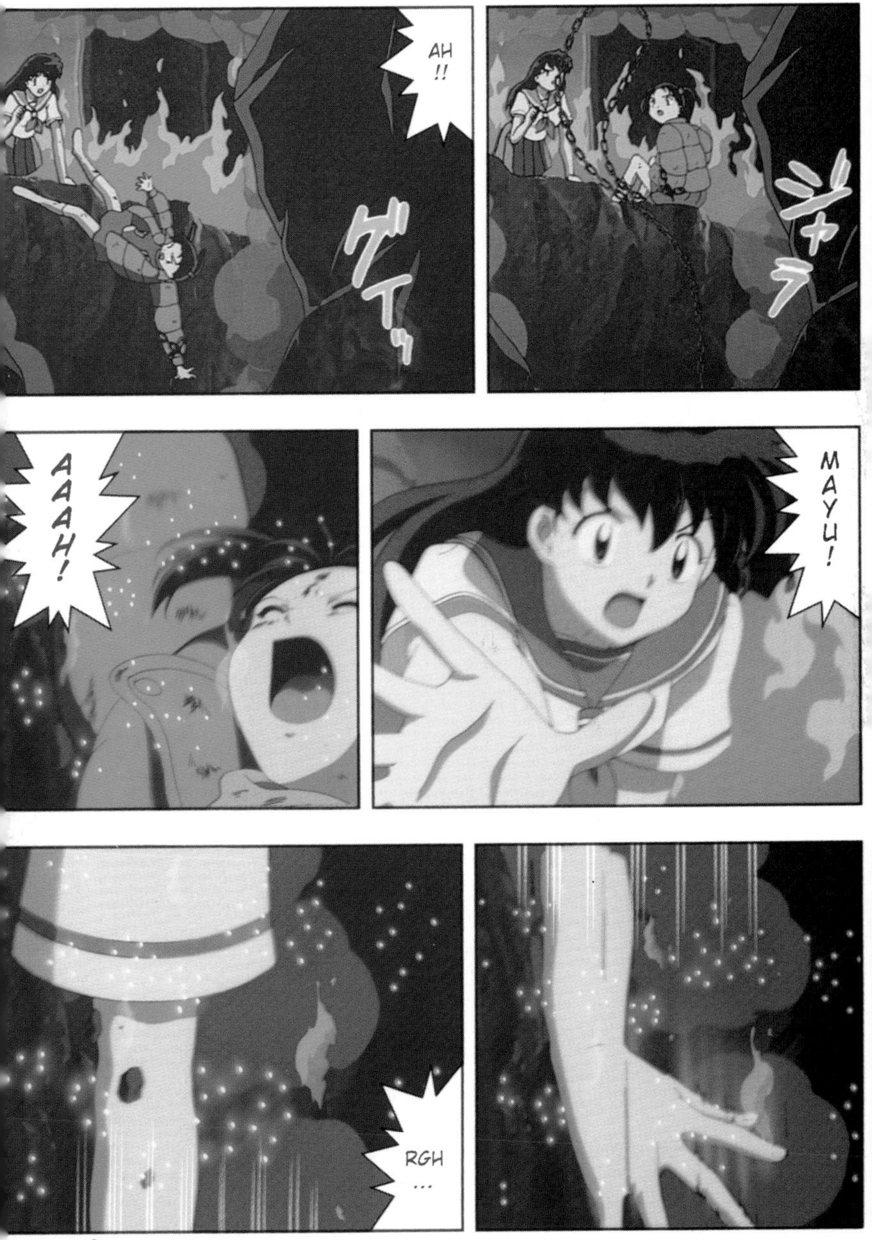
ジャラ
AH !!
グイッ
MAYU!
AAAAH!
RGH ...

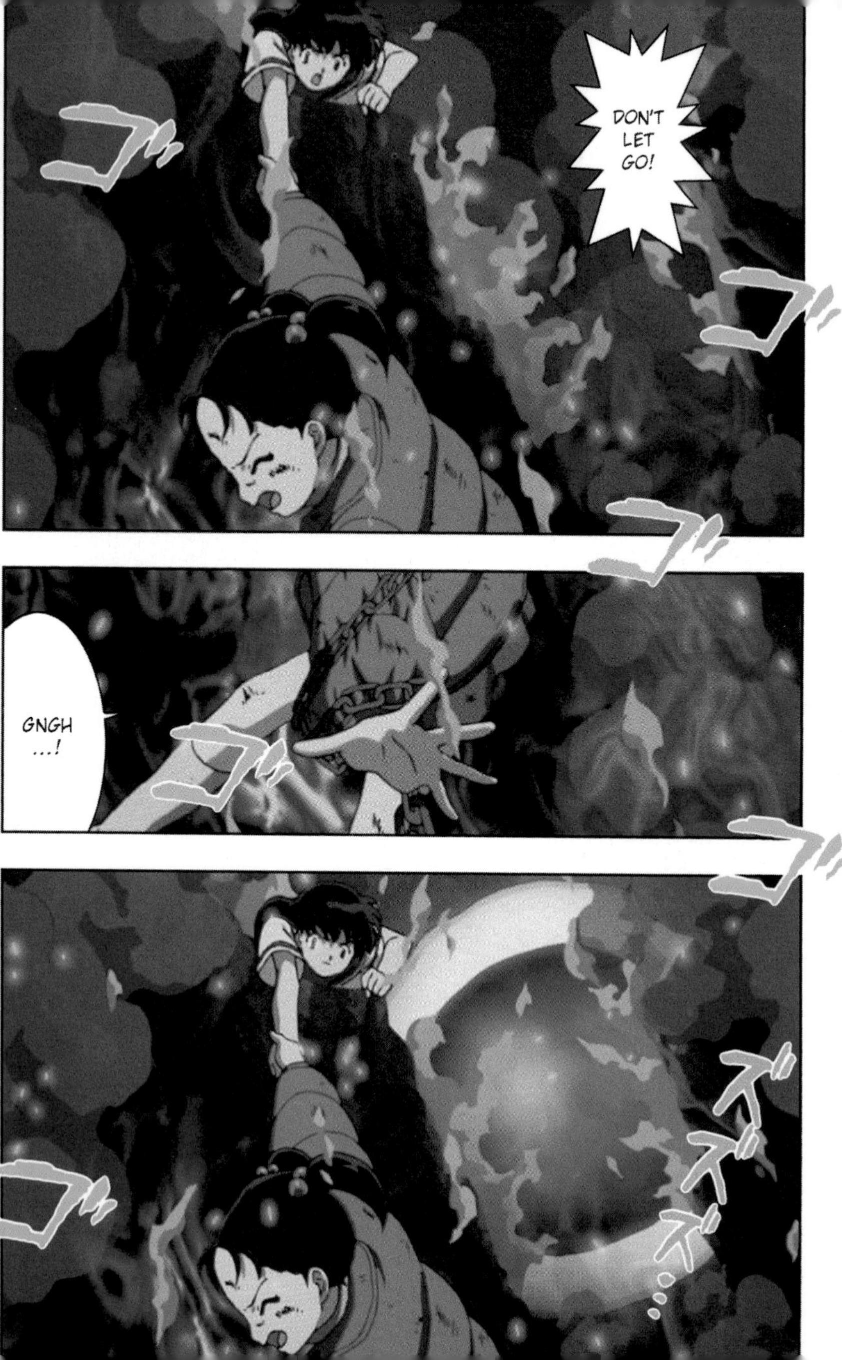
DON'T LET GO!
GNGH ...!

OOH,
UNGH
…

YOU
HAVE
TO GO
HOME!

GO
HOME AND
MAKE UP
WITH YOUR
MOTHER!

RGH
!

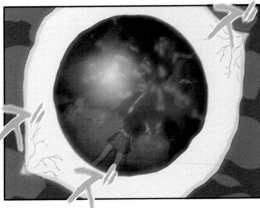

R
N
G
H
!

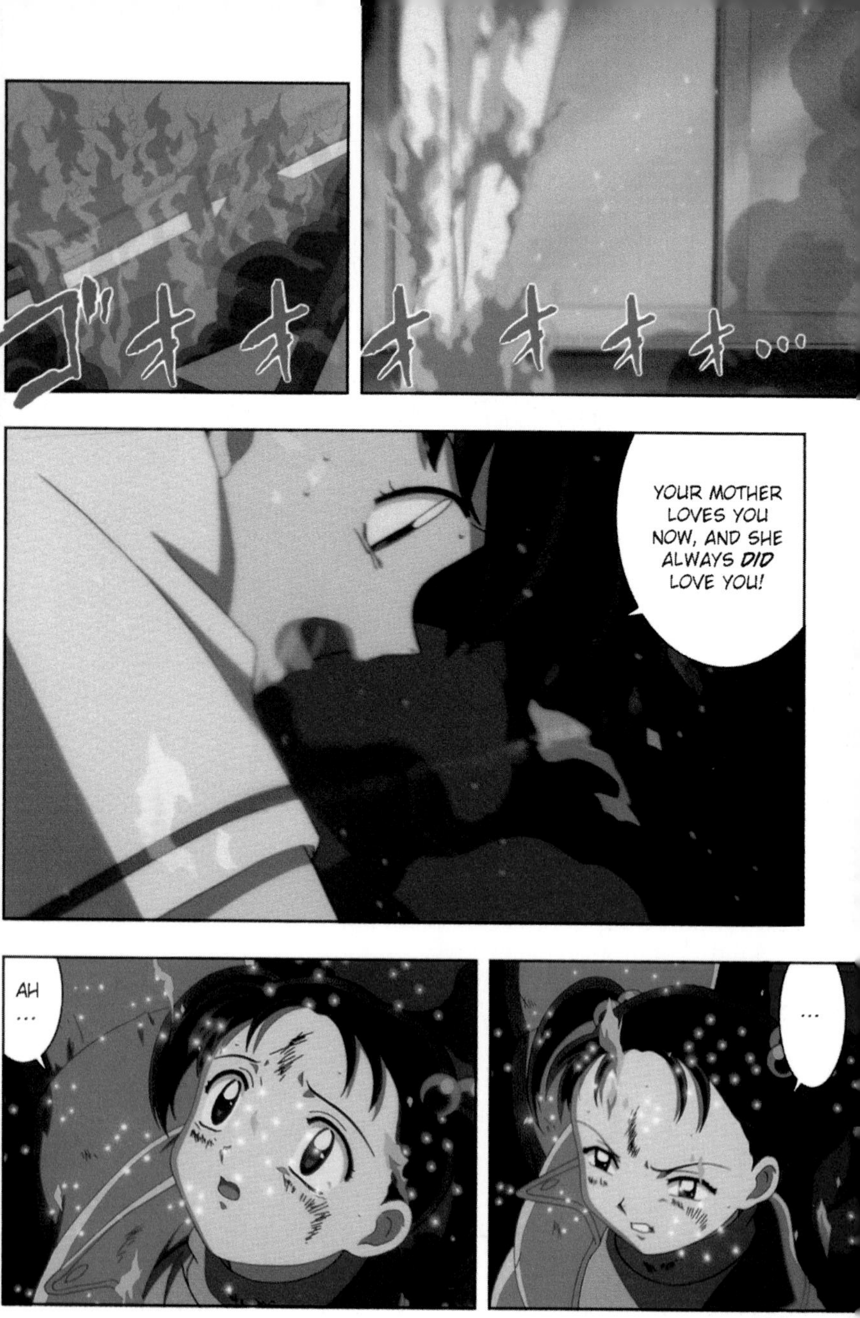
ゴオオオオオオ…
YOUR MOTHER LOVES YOU NOW, AND SHE ALWAYS ***DID*** LOVE YOU!
...
AH ...

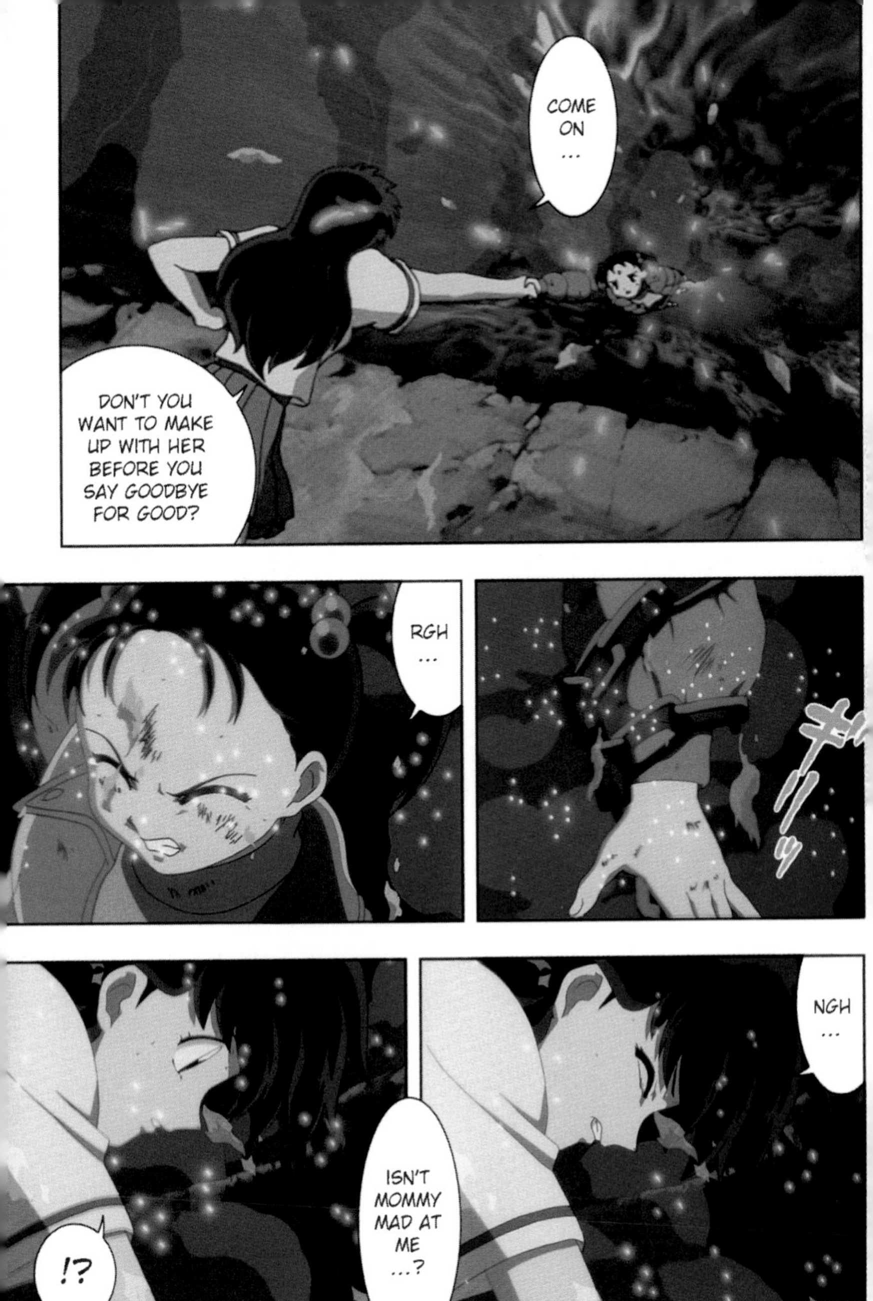
COME ON ...
DON'T YOU WANT TO MAKE UP WITH HER BEFORE YOU SAY GOODBYE FOR GOOD?
RGH ...
NGH ...
ISN'T MOMMY MAD AT ME ...?
!?

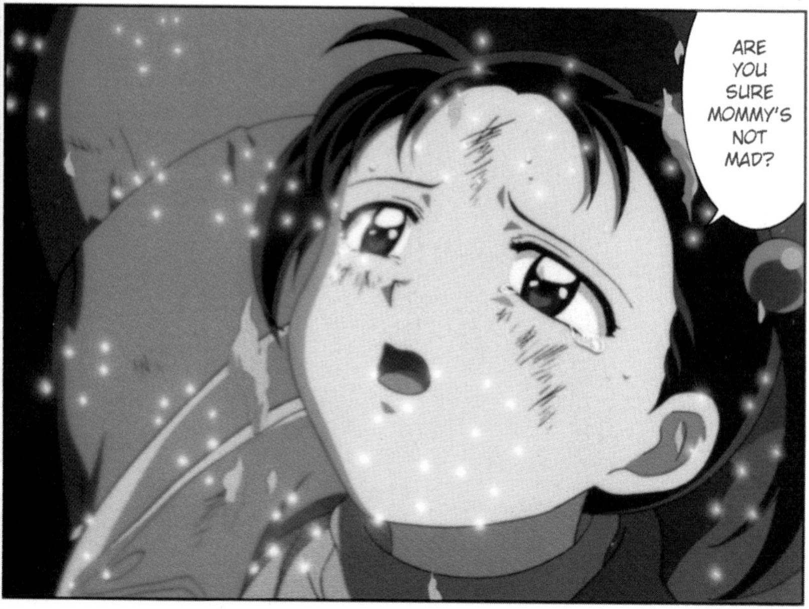
ARE YOU SURE MOMMY'S NOT MAD?

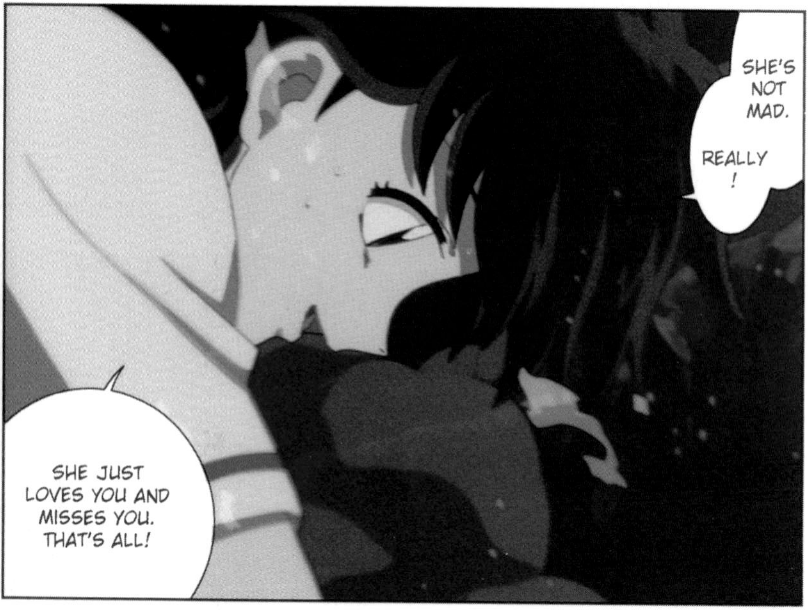
SHE'S NOT MAD.
REALLY!
SHE JUST LOVES YOU AND MISSES YOU. THAT'S ALL!

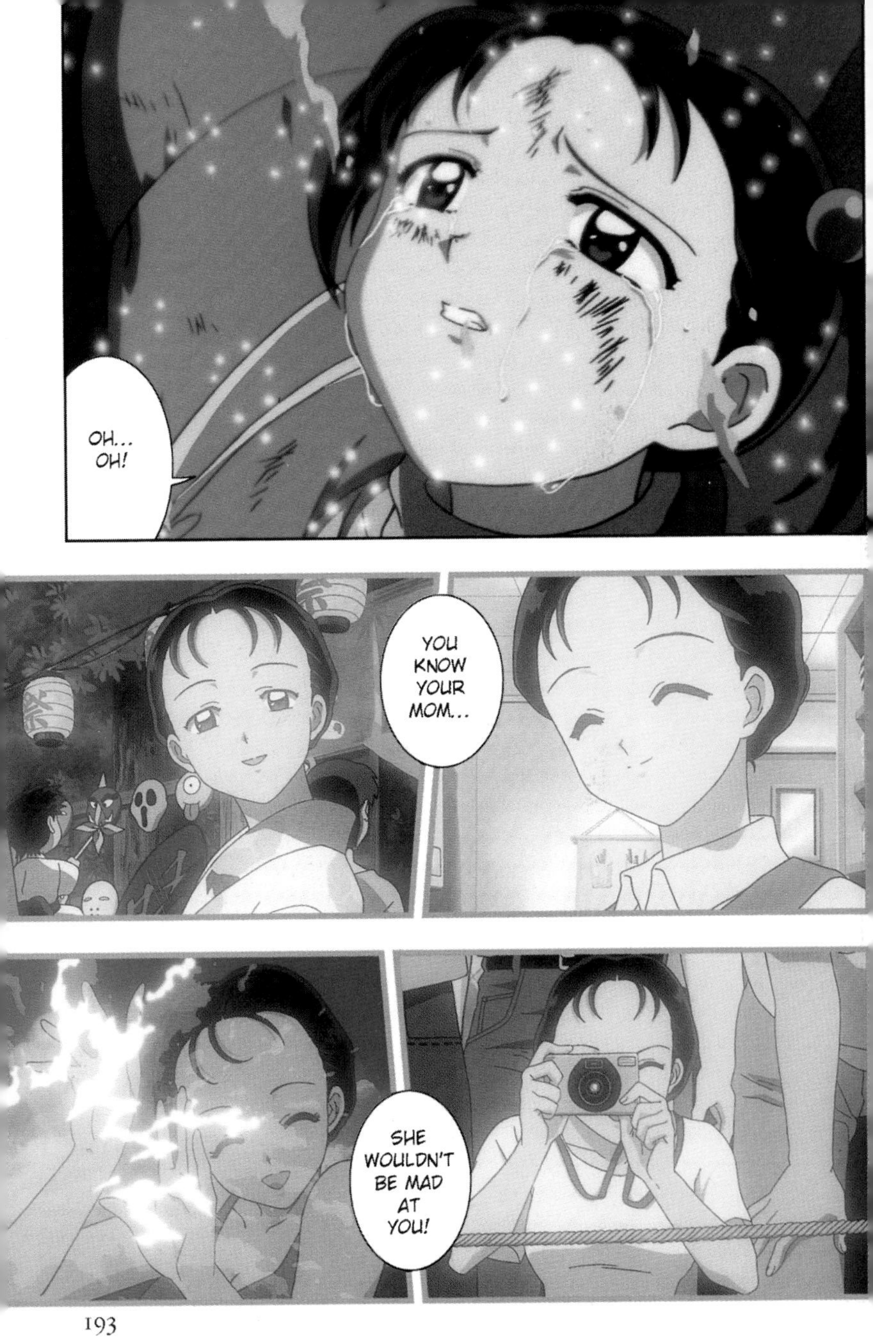
OH... OH!
YOU KNOW YOUR MOM...
SHE WOULDN'T BE MAD AT YOU!

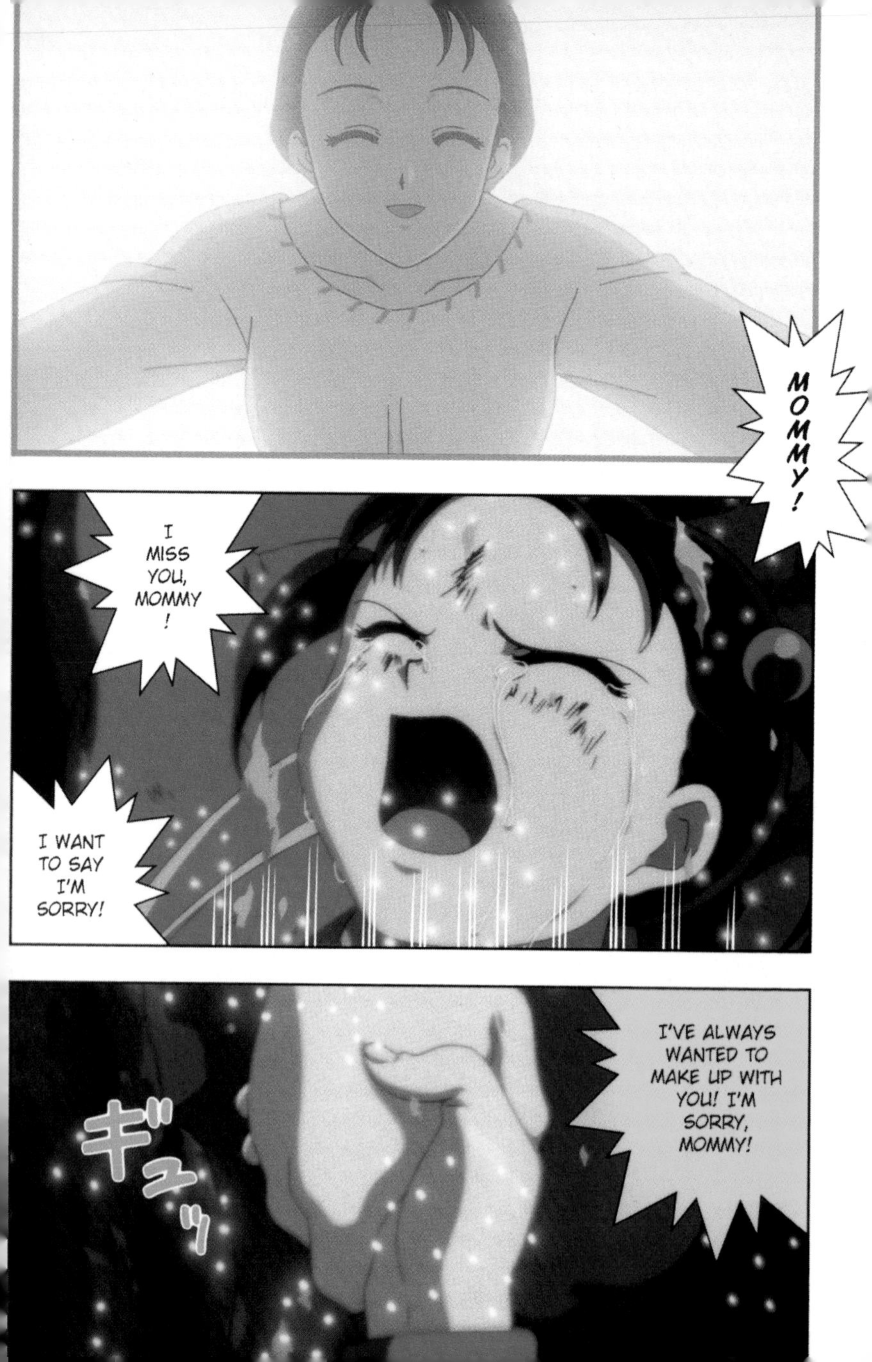
MOMMY!
I MISS YOU, MOMMY!
I WANT TO SAY I'M SORRY!
I'VE ALWAYS WANTED TO MAKE UP WITH YOU! I'M SORRY, MOMMY!
ギュッ

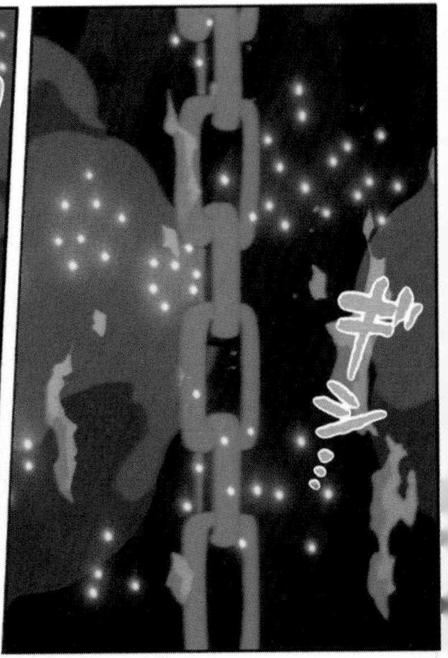
ギシ…

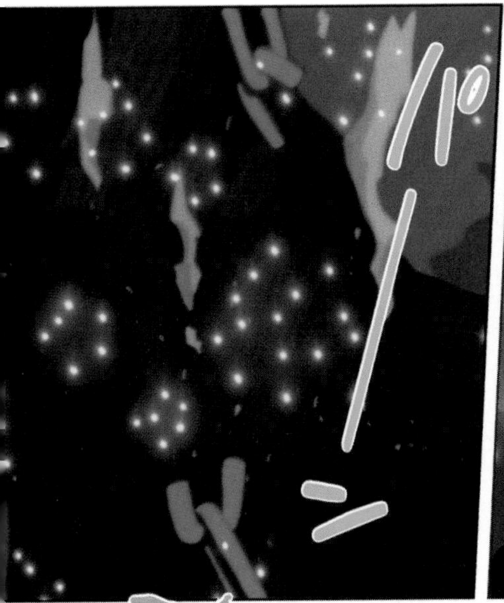
パーン

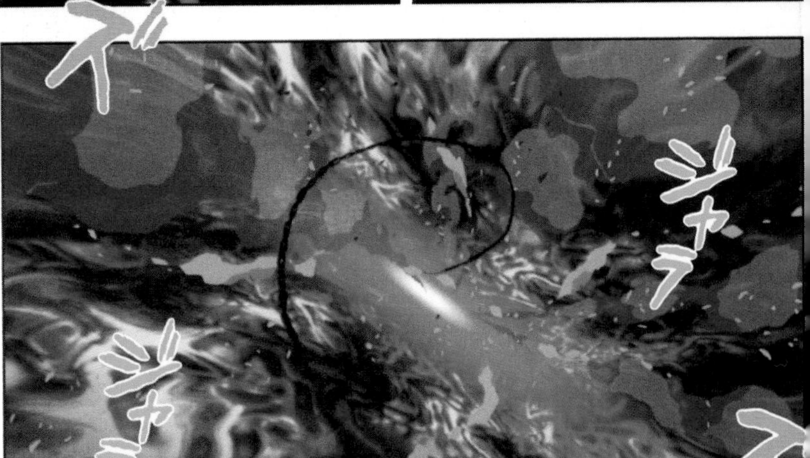
ジャラ
ズ
ス
ジャラ…
ズ

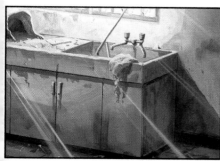

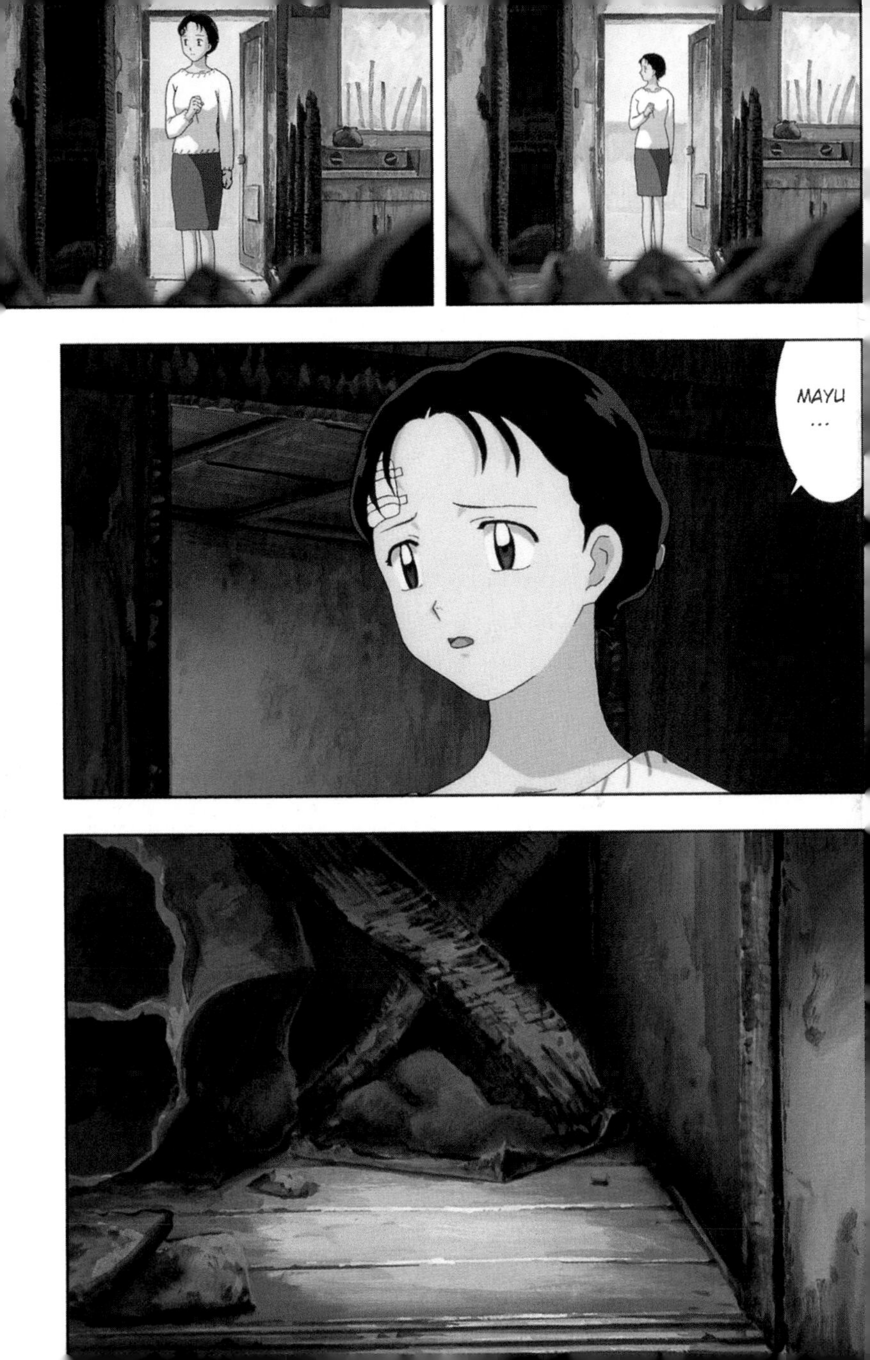
MAYU ...

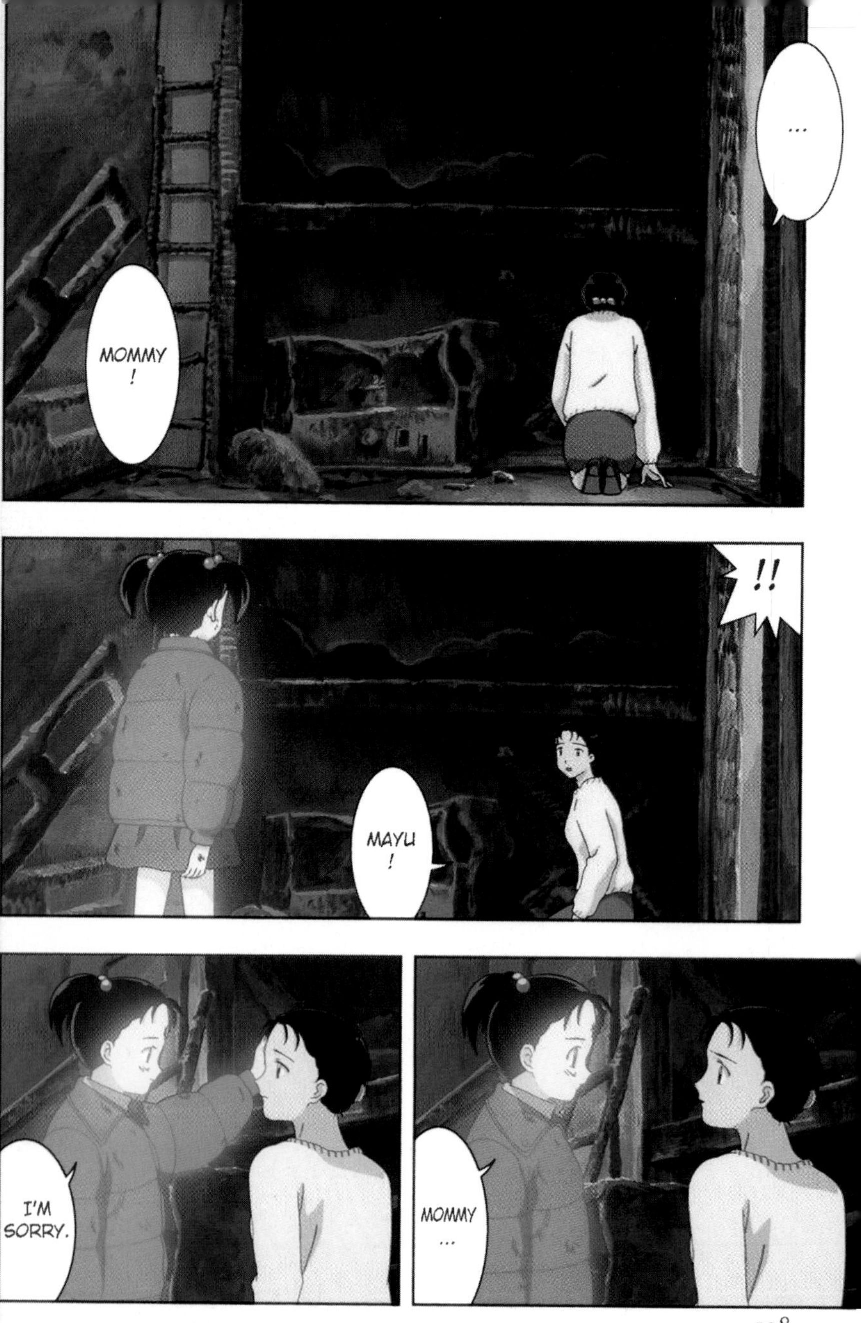
...
MOMMY !
!!
MAYU !
MOMMY ...
I'M SORRY.

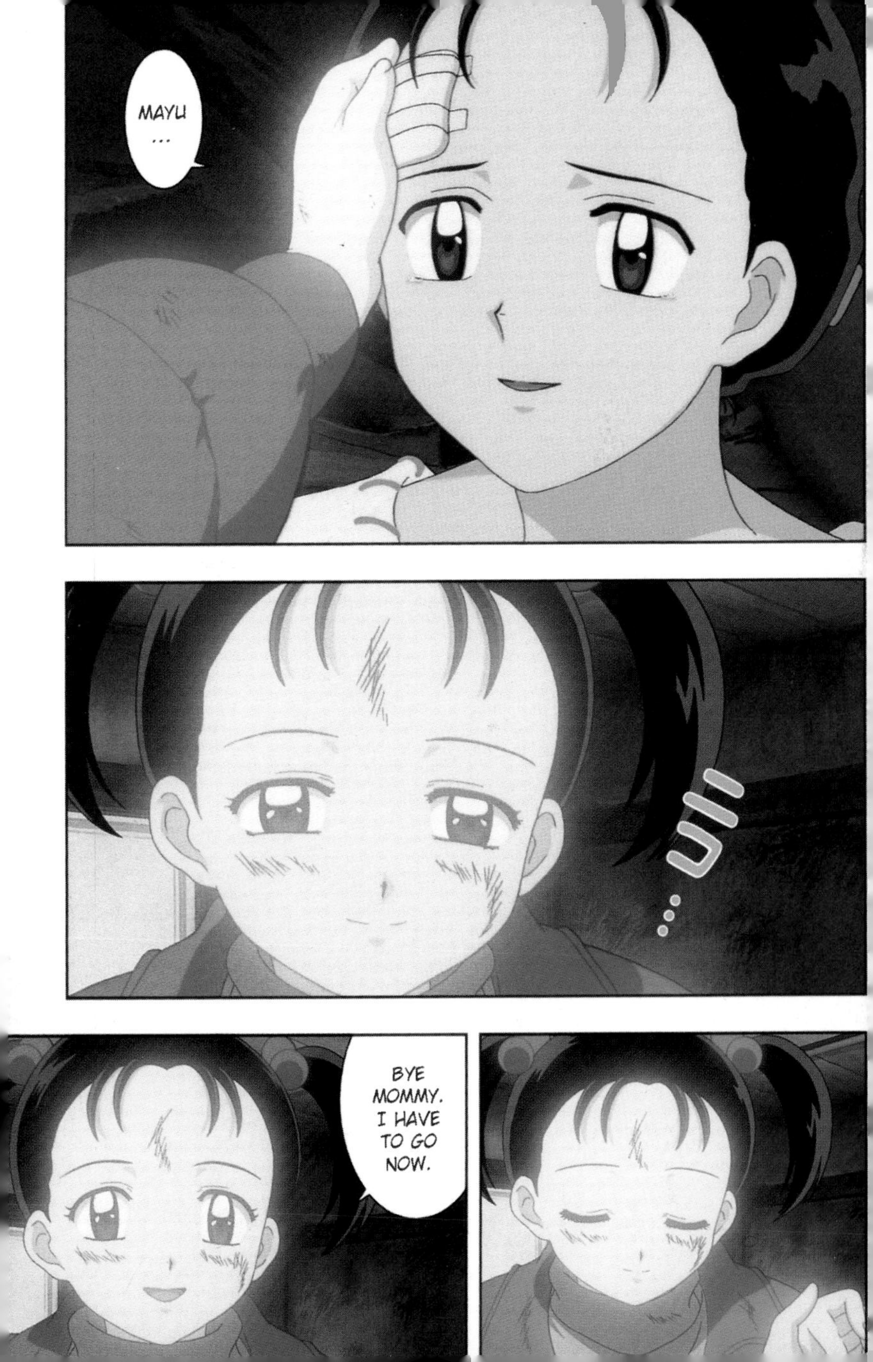
MAYU ...
BYE MOMMY. I HAVE TO GO NOW.

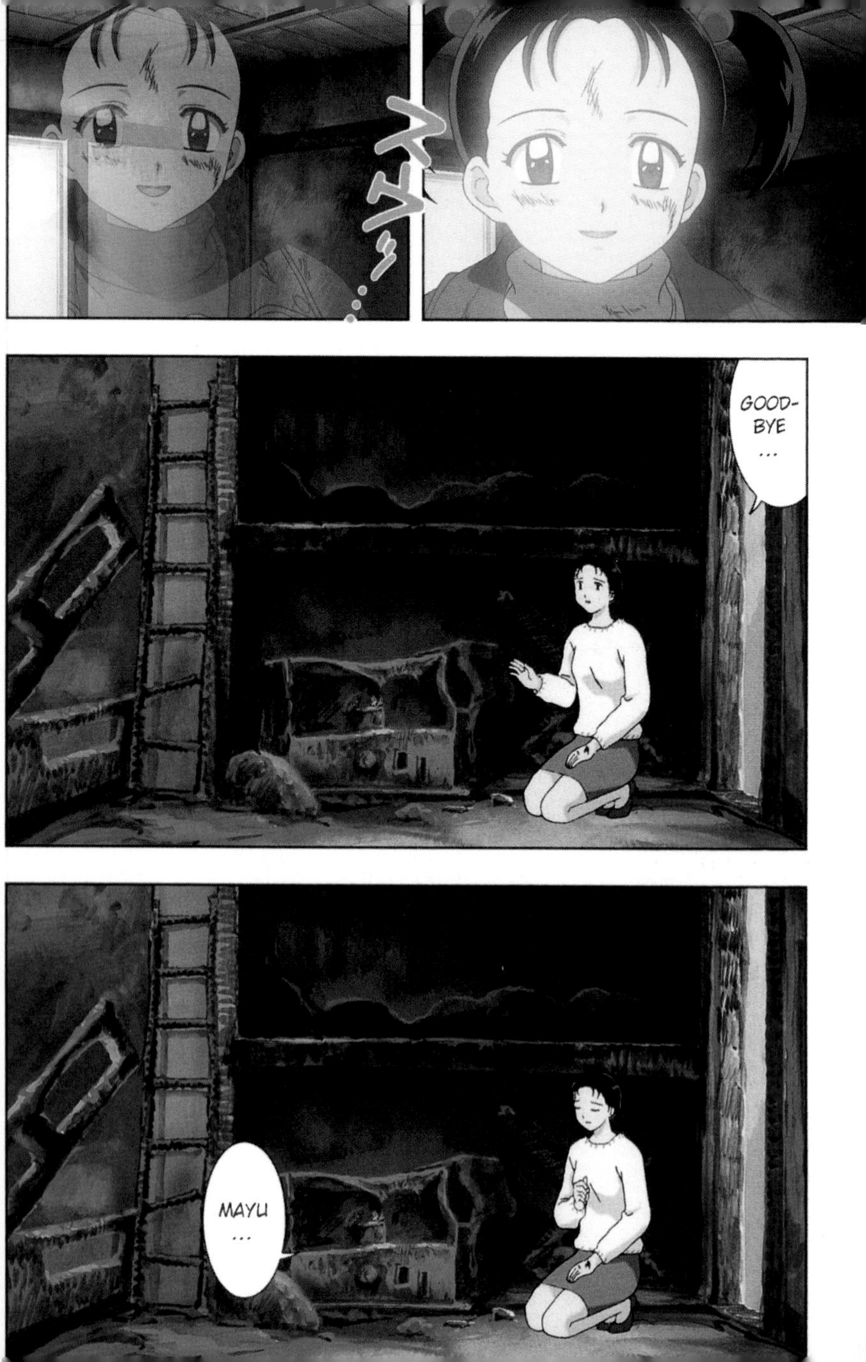

スゥッ…
GOOD-BYE ...
MAYU ...

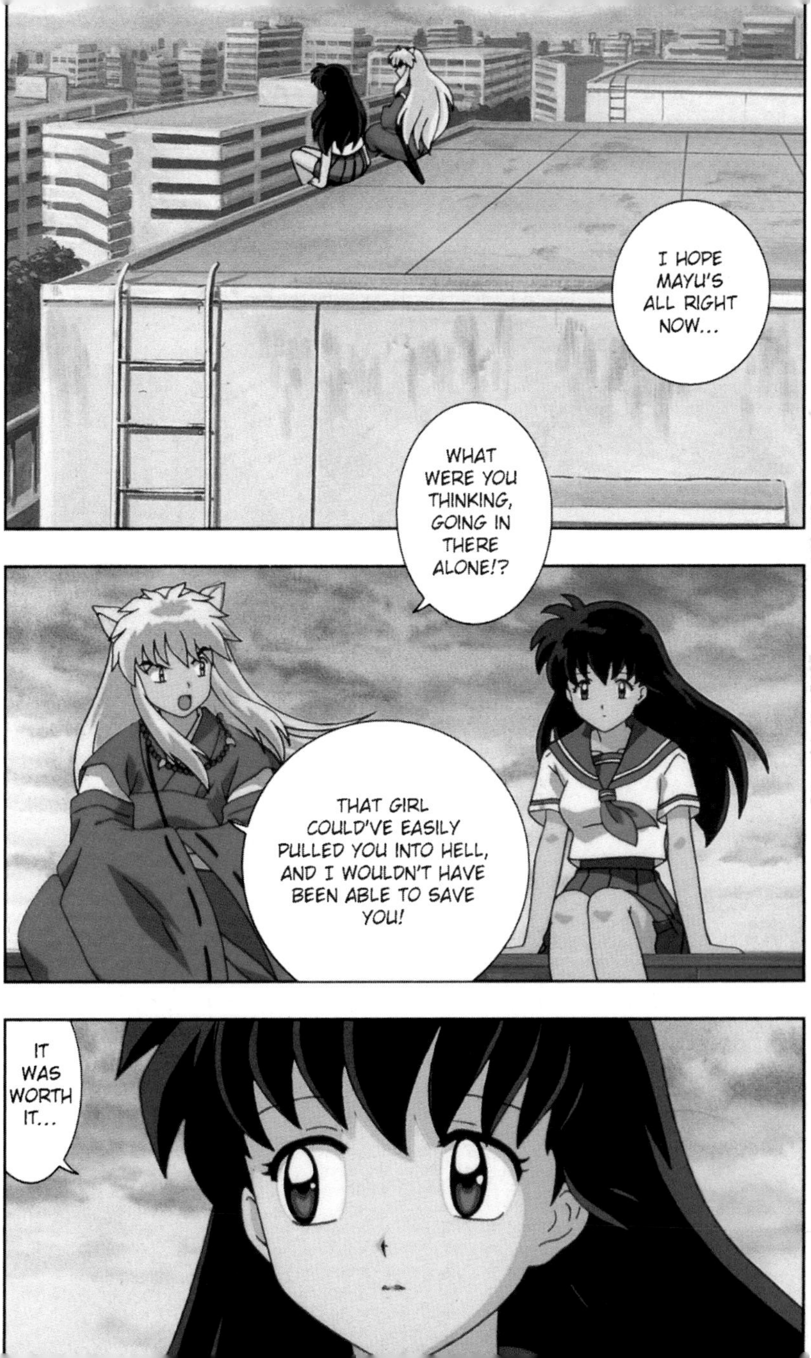
I HOPE MAYU'S ALL RIGHT NOW...
WHAT WERE YOU THINKING, GOING IN THERE ALONE!?
THAT GIRL COULD'VE EASILY PULLED YOU INTO HELL, AND I WOULDN'T HAVE BEEN ABLE TO SAVE YOU!
IT WAS WORTH IT...

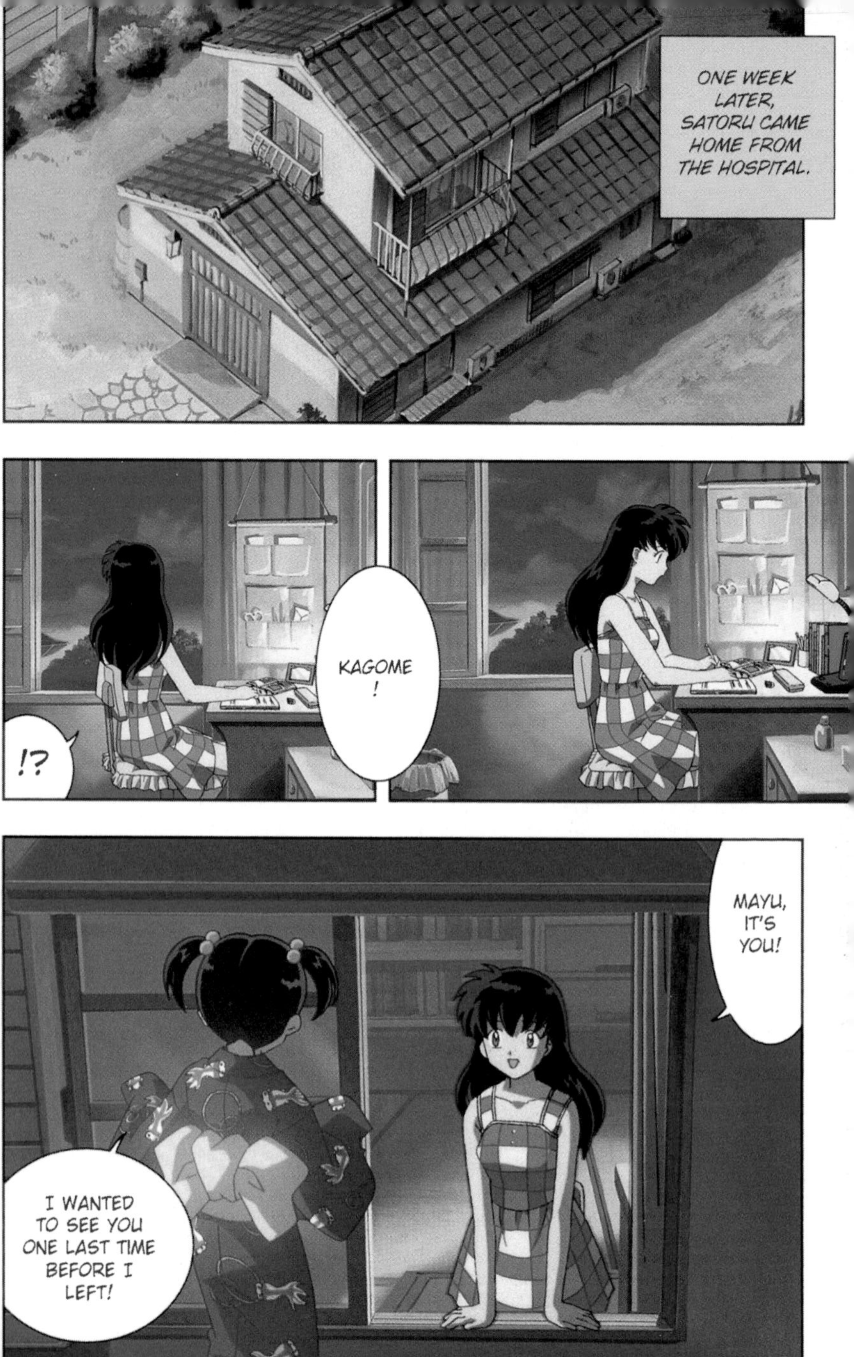
ONE WEEK LATER, SATORU CAME HOME FROM THE HOSPITAL.
KAGOME !
!?
MAYU, IT'S YOU!
I WANTED TO SEE YOU ONE LAST TIME BEFORE I LEFT!

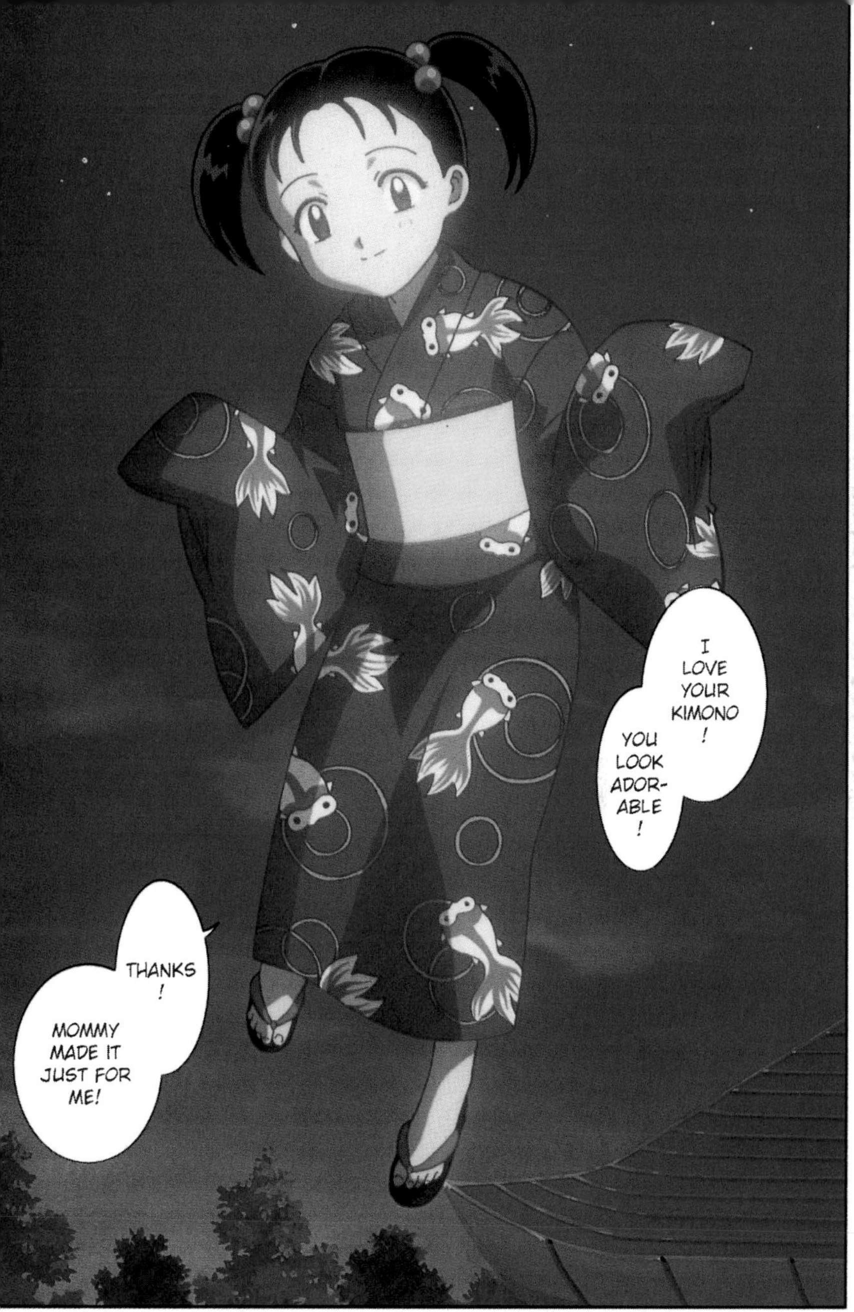
I LOVE YOUR KIMONO!
YOU LOOK ADOR-ABLE!
THANKS!
MOMMY MADE IT JUST FOR ME!

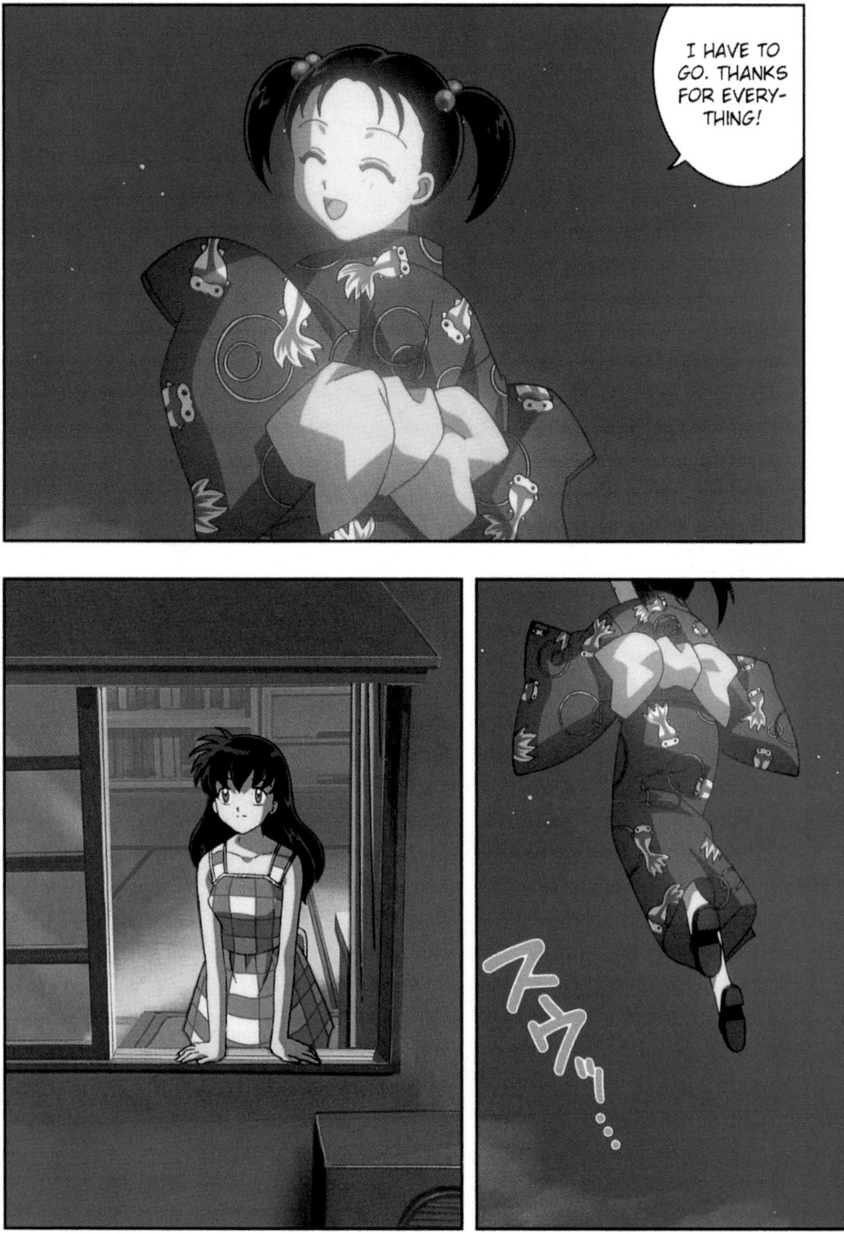
I HAVE TO GO. THANKS FOR EVERY-THING!

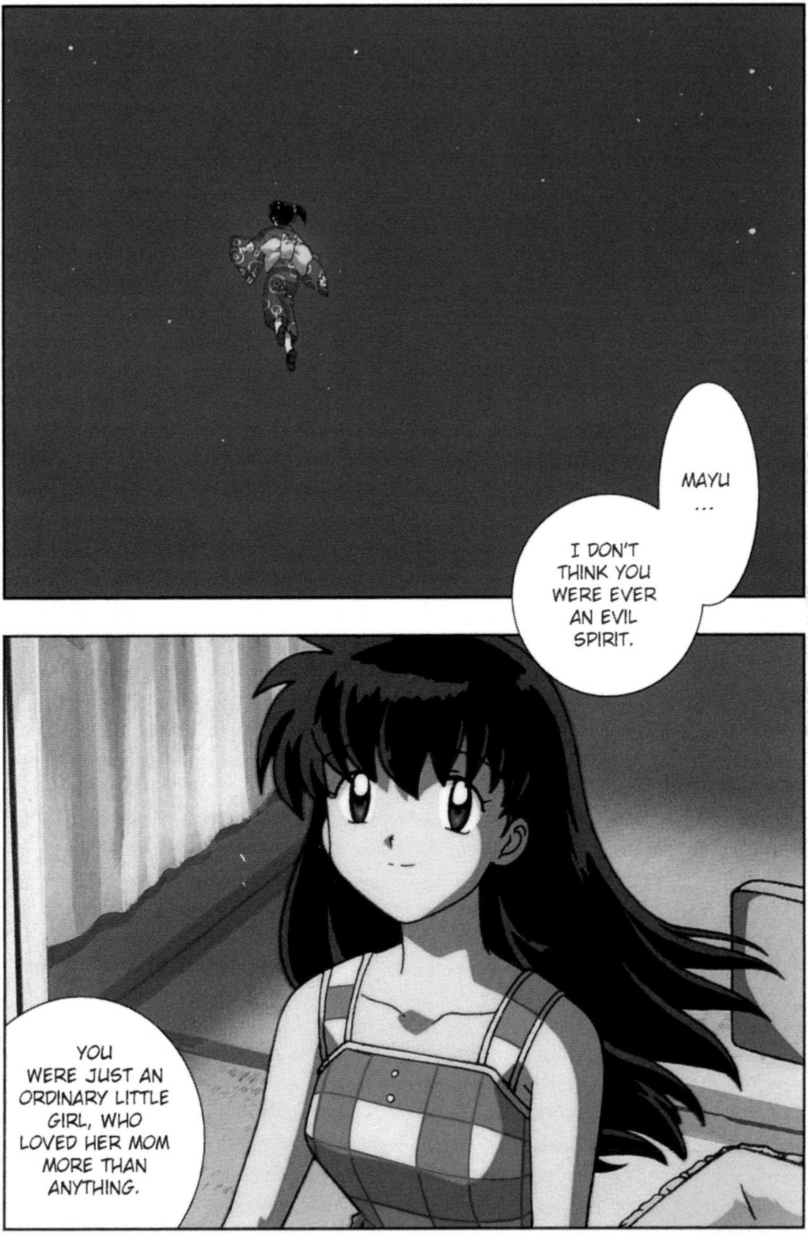
MAYU ...
I DON'T THINK YOU WERE EVER AN EVIL SPIRIT.
YOU WERE JUST AN ORDINARY LITTLE GIRL, WHO LOVED HER MOM MORE THAN ANYTHING.

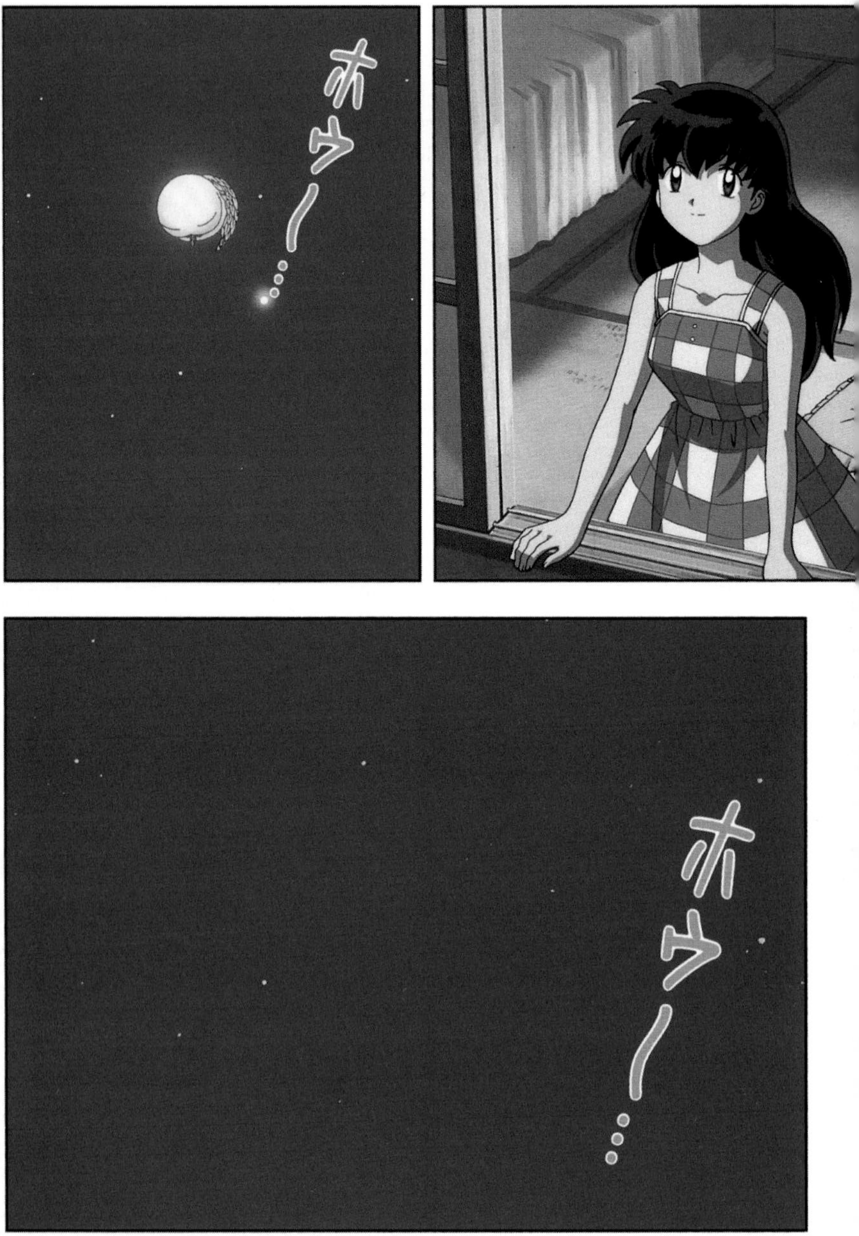
ホウー…
ホウー…

Glossary of Sound Effects

Each entry includes: the location, indicated by page number and panel number (so 3.1 means page 3, panel number 1); the phonetic romanization of the original Japanese; and our English "translation"—we offer as close an English equivalent as we can.

16.1   FX: Shururu... (spin spin)
16.2   FX: Koro... (wobble, as top comes to a stop)

17.1   FX: Goh! (flames)
17.2   FX: Dohn (flames)
17.4   FX: Dohn dohn (fire)

19.1   FX: Goh! (throws flames)
19.2   FX: Dohn (flames hit)

20.3   FX: Shurururu... (hair unspools)
20.4   FX: Ta (running footstep)
20.6   FX: Supo! (arrow pops out)

21.5   FX: Doka! (grab)

22.2   FX: Doka! (kick)
22.3   FX: Dosa! (falls and lands)

23.1   FX: Doka! (Inuyasha struck by pike)
23.2   FX: Dosa! (Inuyasha falls)

24.5   FX: Ba! (pounce)

25.1   FX: Doka! (smack)
25.2   FX: Dosa! (Shippo lands)

27.1   FX: Da! (leap)
27.2   FX: Ga! (chomp)

28.1   FX: Ga ga! (smack)
28.2   FX: Doka! (whap)

29.3   FX: Ba! (Inuyasha's blades of blood)
29.4   FX: Bachi bachi! (crackle crackle)

30.2   FX: Ba! (runs for sword)

Episode 10:
"Phantom Showdown–The Thunder Brothers vs. Tetsusaiga"

6.1   FX: Bari bari bari (crackle, crackle, crackle)
6.2   FX: Bari bari (more crackling)
6.3   FX: Bari (crackle)
6.4   FX: Gei! (clash of metal on metal)
6.5   FX: Bun! (boom)

8.3   FX: Goh! (Hiten's magic)
8.4   FX: Dohn (boom)

9.2   FX: Gin! (metal on metal smash)
9.3   FX: Bachi bachi! (pike on sword)
9.4   FX: Bachi bachi! (blades clanging)
9.5   FX: Gin! (clang)

10.5   FX: Don! (smack)

11.2   FX: Zu—n... (whump)
11.3   FX: Moh moh... (dust clearing)
11.5   FX: Pon! (pop)

12.3   FX: Gin! (metal on metal)

13.1   FX: Dosa! (Kagome lands on her butt)
13.4   FX: Da! (Kagome runs away)
13.5   FX: Ga! (Kagome trips)
13.6   FX: Za! (whump)

14.2   FX: Bun! (spinning top flies)
14.3   FX: Kyuru kyuru (whirring)
14.3   FX: Gya gya gya (top spins faster)
14.4   FX: Gya gya gya (top spinning harder)

15.1   FX: Dosa! (Manten falls down)

30.3 FX: Ga! (Inuyasha grabs sword)
30.4 FX: Bun! (sword flying through air)
30.5 FX: Goh! (sword flies, misses Hiten)

31.1 FX: Toh! (Inuyasha lands)
31.3 FX: Doka! (sword slices through)
31.4 FX: Zuun… (big thump)

33.1 FX: Dohn (sound of bolt)
33.2 FX: Za! (Kagome falls)

36.1 FX: Ta! (Inuyasha touches down)

37.2 FX: Gabu! (chomp)
37.3 FX: Gafu gafu (Manten being consumed)

38.6 FX: Kaa! (lightning ball noise)

39.1 FX: Da! (jumps)
39.2 FX: Dohn (explosion)

41.2 FX: Kaa! (flying lightning ball)
41.3 FX: Goh! (getting bigger)
41.5 FX: Go go go (getting bigger)

42.3 FX: Dohn (impact)
42.5 FX: Gohhhhh… (ball dissipates)

43.1 FX: Gohhhhh… (ball dissipates)
43.2 FX: Shu shu… (aftermath sounds)

44.5 FX: Da! (leap)

45.2 FX: Doh! (ball created)
45.3 FX: Kaa! (gets big)
45.4 FX: Bari bari (crackling)
45.6 FX: Doh! (sound of stab)

46.2 FX: Dohn (Inuyasha falls)

47.4 FX: Ga! (slash)
47.5 FX: Bari bari (crackle crackle)

48.5 FX: Goh! (lightning strike)

49.3 FX: Kuru! (Shippo transforms)

49.5 FX: Pon! (pop)

50.1 FX: Guwa! (swoosh)
50.2 FX: Bari bari! (crackle crackle)
50.3 FX: Za! (Inuyasha slams to ground)

51.3 FX: Doshu! (whoosh)
51.5 FX: Shurururu…(arrow flies through air)
51.6 FX: Ga! (smash)

52.5 FX: Bari bari bari (crackle crackle crackle)

53.4 FX: Bari bari (crackling)
53.5 FX: Bari (more crackling)
53.5 FX: Poi! (flicking Myoga away)
53.6 FX: Go! (lump pops up)

54.1 FX: Bari bari (crackling)
54.3 FX: Baki! (punch)
54.4 FX: Za! (Hiten sails through air)
54.5 FX: Dohn! (Hiten smacks into ground)

56.2 FX: Kaa! (magic building)

57.2 FX: Ba! (Inuyasha touches down)
57.3 FX: Kin! (metal on metal)
57.4 FX: Pishi! (lightning)
57.6 FX: Bari bari (crackling)

58.1 FX: Bari bari bari (crackling)

60.1 FX: Kaaa… (fire starts to burn)
60.3 FX: Goh! (flames roaring)
60.4 FX: Ka! (ball of fire forms)
60.5 FX: Dohn (mysterious magic sound)

61.5 FX: Go! (Inuyasha rushes Hiten)

63.1 FX: Gaki! (fight sound)
63.2 FX: Bari bari (crackling)
63.4 FX: Bari bari (more crackling)

64.1 FX: Goh! (blade flies through air)
64.3 FX: Pashi! (Inuyasha catches sword)

65.1 FX: Bun! (sword swing)

90.1 FX: Pi—po— (ambulance siren)
90.1/2 FX: Pi—po— (siren)
90.2 FX: Pi—po— (siren)

91.2 FX: Ta ta ta… (running)

92.4 FX: Suu… (mask appears)
92.5 FX: Zaba! (mask splashes out of water)

93.5 FX: Doga! (cars crash)

94.1 FX: Doga! (bang, smash)
94.2 FX: Goh! (engine roar)

95.1 FX: Gohhhhh… (engine roar)

98.1 FX: Gata gata (rattle rattle)

99.1 FX: Doka! (crash)
99.2 FX: Zu—n (skid)
99.3 FX: Gara gara gara (ladder being raised)
99.4 FX: Doga! (smash)
99.5 FX: Zu zu (wall crunching)
99.6 FX: Za! (Kagome and Sôta fall to floor)

100.4 FX: Koro… (bottle rolling)

101.1 FX: Ba! (Kagome dives for jewels)
101.2 FX: Pashi (she grabs them)
101.4 FX: Da! (Kagome grabs Sôta)
101.5 FX: Ta ta ta… (running)
101.6 FX: Ta ta ta… (more running)

102.4 FX: Gohn… (ladder swivels)

103.1 FX: Doh doh doh doh (splat)

104.4 FX: Ta ta ta… (running)
104.5 FX: Zu zu zu (slimy sound)

105.1 FX: Ta ta ta… (running)
105.5 FX: Ba! (Sôta falls)

106.1 FX: Becha (lands on well bottom)
106.3 FX: Za za! (Sôta pounds on ground)
106.5 FX: Kaa! (magic working)

65.5 FX: Pa—n (Hiten vaporizes)

66.1 FX: Poro! (jewel shards fall)

67.3 FX: Da! (Inuyasha runs)
67.4 FX: Gui! (grab)
67.6 FX: Shurururu… (magical mist dissipates)

69.3 FX: Ba! (yanks hand away)

Episode 11:
"Terror of the Ancient Noh Mask"

72.5 FX: Ba! (leap)
72.5 FX: Shaka shaka (Inuyasha flies)

74.4 FX: Doga! (boulder falls)

75.2 FX: Ba! (leaping into well)
75.3 FX: Kaa! (magic taking place in well)

76.3 FX: Basha (splash)
76.4 FX: Poh! (Kagome lands)
76.5 FX: Basha (splash)

80.5 FX: Kira kira (sparkling)
80.6 FX: Poh… (magic activating)

82.3 FX: Chirin chirin (bike bell)

84.3 FX: Kira kira (sparkle sparkle)

87.3 FX: Ban! (door opens)
87.4 FX: Boh! (things bursting into flame)
87.5 FX: Goto! (package falls)
87.6 FX: Pa—n (package explodes)

88.1 FX: Gohhhhh… (flames)
88.3 FX: Ga! (picks up bucket)
88.4 FX: Basha (splash)

89.2 FX: Bi! (throwing spell scrolls)
89.3 FX: Bo bo! (mask burns talismans)
89.4/5 FX: Gohhhhh… (burning)

132.4 FX: Fu… (Kagome shifts to another awareness/dimension)

133.1 FX: Shu! (setting fire to fireworks)
133.2 FX: Pa! (dropping fireworks)
133.3 FX: Shururusu… (fireworks spinning)
133.4 FX: Pan pan pan (fireworks going off)
133.5 FX: Pan! (more fireworks)

134.3 FX: Da! (Kagome dashes off)
134.4 FX: Ta ta ta… (running)

135.4 FX: Pashi! (slaps hand away)
135.5 FX: Goh! (flames)

136.1 FX: Gohhhhhh… (flames)
136.2 FX: Fu… (girl disappears)
136.3 FX: Shururuu… (fire disappears)

138.2 FX: Gaji gaji (chomp chomp)
138.3 FX: Doka! (smack)
138.4 FX: Pon! (pop)

139.5 FX: Ho—h… ho—h… (flute music)

140.3 FX: Hoh… (flute music)
140.4 FX: Hoh… (flute music)

143.6 FX: Su… (hand slips out)

144.1 FX: Gui! (grab)
144.2 FX: Pari—n (bottle explodes)
144.3 FX: Gashan (tube comes loose)
144.6 FX: Zu… (pulls)

146.1 FX: Ho—h… (flute music)
146.2 FX: Hoh…. (flute music)

148.3 FX: Suu… (flower pot levitates)
148.4 FX: Suu… (moves off balcony)

149.2 FX: Gasha (crash)
149.4 FX: Batan (Sôta faints)
149.6 FX: Ba! (jumps)

150.1 FX: Su! (Mayu lands)

107.4 FX: Goh! (Inuyasha flies)

108.1 FX: Toh! (Inuyasha touches down)
108.1 FX: Ga—! (engine rumbling)

110.1 FX: Doh doh doh (blob rising up)
110.5 FX: Zuba! (slash)

111.1 FX: Becho (splat)

114.4 FX: Ga! (Noh mask bites)

115.2 FX: Zubu zubu… (blob drawing Inuyasha in)
115.5 FX: Suu… (mask rises)
115.6 FX: Goh! (mask lunges)

116.1 FX: Pashi! (mask rushes at Kagome)
116.2 FX: Za! (mask attacks)

117.1 FX: Da! (running)
117.2 FX: Goh! (mask flies)
117.3 FX: Ga! (Sôta trips)
117.4 FX: Dosa! (Sôta falls)
117.5 FX: Koro koro… (rolling)

118.3 FX: Ta ta ta… (running)
118.5 FX: Ba! (turns around abruptly)

119.2 FX: Zuba! (Inuyasha escapes goop)
119.3 FX: Ta! (leap)
119.5 FX: Zuba! (mask is slashed)

120.1 FX: Pa—n (mask cut in two)
120.2 FX: Kaaaaa… (magic released)
120.3 FX: Shuuu… (jewel fragment drops)
120.4 FX: Koron… (jewel falls)

123.3 FX: Da! (Kagome runs off)

Episode 12:
"The Soul Piper and the Mischievous Little Soul"

126.1 FX: Dosa! (plop)

151.5 FX: Fu… (Mayu disappears)

152.1 FX: Zu zu zu (Mayu tearing stuff up)
152.2 FX: Baki baki (tree being uprooted)
152.3 FX: Goh! (tree flies)
152.4 FX: Dohn … (tree falls)

153.1 FX: Hoh… (flute music)
153.3 FX: Ho—h… (flute music)
153.4 FX: Hoh… (flute music)

155.3 FX: Ho—h… (flute music)

161.3/4 FX: Ho—h… (flute music)

162.1 FX: Go—… (train passing)
162.1 FX: Kan kan kan kan
(bell clanging at train crossing)
162.3 FX: Da! (running)

164.1 FX: Da! (Mayu runs out)
164.2 FX: Ta ta ta… (running)

165.4/5 FX: Gohhhh… (flames)

166.3 FX: Ooh— Ooh—… (sirens)
166.4 FX: Ooh—… (siren)

168.1 FX: Pari—n (glass breaks)
168.2 FX: Bachi bachi! (light bulbs exploding and shorting out)
168.3 FX: Bohn (large bang)
168.4 FX: Ban! (door slams open)

169.4 FX: Doh! (impact of Mayu running into mom)
169.5 FX: Dohn (Mayu's mom knocked back)

173.2 FX: Dohn (Mayu destroys stuff)
173.4 FX: Go go go (banging)

174.2 FX: Da! (runs to window)

176.3 FX: Jara… (chains clanking)

178.1 FX: Ta ta ta… (running)
178.2 FX: Ta! (jumps)

178.4 FX: Goh! (flying through the air)
178.5 FX: Toh! (lands)

179.3 FX: Suu! (Kagome goes to next dimension)

180.4/5 FX: Gohhhh… (fire)

183.1/2/3 FX: Gohhhhhhhhh… (flames)

184.4 FX: Gara… (door sliding open)

186.2/3 FX: Gara gara… (portal to hell opens)

187.1 FX: Jara (chains clanking)
187.2 FX: Gui! (Mayu being pulled in)

188.1/2/3 FX: Go go go go go go (flames of hell)
188.3 FX: Zu zu zu… (slipping from Kagome's grip)

189.1 FX: Giri… (chains tightening and pulling)
189.5 FX: Zu zu zu (Mayu slipping)

190.1/2 FX: Gohhhhhhh… (flames)

191.2 FX: Giri! (chains tightening)

194.3 FX: Gyu! (hands squeeze)

195.1 FX: Gishi… (chains loosen)
195.2 FX: Pa—n (chains let go)
195.3 FX: Jara jara (chains let go)
195.3 FX: Zu zu zu (portal to hell closing)

199.2 FX: Niko… (smile)

200.1/2 FX: Suu… (Mayu disappears)

204.2 FX: Suu… (Mayu floats away)

206.2 FX: Ho—h… (flute music)
206.3 FX: Ho—h… (flute music)

INUYASHA™

Rated #1 on Cartoon Network's Adult Swim!

In its original, unedited form!

maison ikkoku™

The beloved romantic comedy of errors—a fan favorite!

Ranma ½™

The zany, wacky study of martial arts at its best!

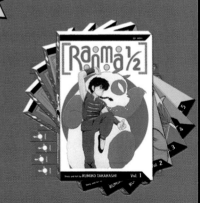

COMPLETE OUR SURVEY AND LET
US KNOW WHAT YOU THINK!

☐ Please do NOT send me information about VIZ products, news and events, special offers, or other information.

☐ Please do NOT send me information from VIZ's trusted business partners.

Name: _____

Address: _____

City: _____ **State:** _____ **Zip:** _____

E-mail: _____

☐ **Male** ☐ **Female** **Date of Birth** (mm/dd/yyyy): ___ / ___ / ___ (Under 13? Parental consent required)

What race/ethnicity do you consider yourself? (please check one)

☐ Asian/Pacific Islander ☐ Black/African American ☐ Hispanic/Latino

☐ Native American/Alaskan Native ☐ White/Caucasian ☐ Other: _____

What VIZ product did you purchase? (check all that apply and indicate title purchased)

☐ DVD/VHS _____

☐ Graphic Novel _____

☐ Magazines _____

☐ Merchandise _____

Reason for purchase: (check all that apply)

☐ Special offer ☐ Favorite title ☐ Gift

☐ Recommendation ☐ Other _____

Where did you make your purchase? (please check one)

☐ Comic store ☐ Bookstore ☐ Mass/Grocery Store

☐ Newsstand ☐ Video/Video Game Store ☐ Other: _____

☐ Online (site: _____)

What other VIZ properties have you purchased/own? _____

_____

How many anime and/or manga titles have you purchased in the last year? How many were VIZ titles? (please check one from each column)

ANIME	MANGA	VIZ
☐ None	☐ None	☐ None
☐ 1-4	☐ 1-4	☐ 1-4
☐ 5-10	☐ 5-10	☐ 5-10
☐ 11+	☐ 11+	☐ 11+

I find the pricing of VIZ products to be: (please check one)

☐ Cheap   ☐ Reasonable   ☐ Expensive

What genre of manga and anime would you like to see from VIZ? (please check two)

☐ Adventure   ☐ Comic Strip   ☐ Science Fiction   ☐ Fighting

☐ Horror   ☐ Romance   ☐ Fantasy   ☐ Sports

What do you think of VIZ's new look?

☐ Love It   ☐ It's OK   ☐ Hate It   ☐ Didn't Notice   ☐ No Opinion

Which do you prefer? (please check one)

☐ Reading right-to-left

☐ Reading left-to-right

Which do you prefer? (please check one)

☐ Sound effects in English

☐ Sound effects in Japanese with English captions

☐ Sound effects in Japanese only with a glossary at the back

THANK YOU! Please send the completed form to:

VIZ Survey
42 Catharine St.
Poughkeepsie, NY 12601

All information provided will be used for internal purposes only. We promise not to sell or otherwise divulge your information.